Jon E. Lewis is a writer and historian. His many previous books include the best-selling *The Mammoth Book of the Edge*, *The Mammoth Book of How It Happened: Everest* and *The Mammoth Book of Wild Journeys*.

D0599861

Also available

The Mammoth Book of

POLAR JOURNEYS

**42 eye-witness accounts of adventure
and tragedy in the Artic and Antartica**

Edited by JON E. LEWIS

ROBINSON
London

Constable & Robinson Ltd
3 The Lanchesters
162 Fulham Palace Road
London W6 9ER
www.constablerobinson.com

First published in the UK by Robinson,
an imprint of Constable & Robinson Ltd, 2007

Collection and editorial material copyright © J. Lewis-Stempel, 2007

All rights reserved. This book is sold subject to the condition that it
shall not, by way of trade or otherwise, be lent, re-sold, hired out or
otherwise circulated in any form of binding or cover other than that
in which it is published and without a similar condition including
this condition being imposed on the subsequent purchaser.

A copy of the British Library Cataloguing in Publication Data is
available from the British Library.

ISBN-13: 978-1-84529-430-4
ISBN-10: 1-84529-430-0

Printed and bound in the EU

1 3 5 7 9 10 8 6 4 2

"I'm just going outside and may be some time"
                    Captain Laurence Oates, c. 16 March 1912

"A few toes aren't much to give to achieve the Pole"
                    Lieutenant Robert Peary, Winter 1898–9

Contents

Timeline

KEY DATES	THE ARCTIC	THE ANTARCTIC
45 million BC		Antarctica settles into present position and cools dramatically
30,000 BC	Evidence of Siberian hunters in Russian far north	
20,000 BC	Last Ice Age at its height	
5000 BC	First migration of Inuit to North America	
982 AD	Erik the Red sails for Greenland	
1576–8	Briton Martin Frobisher makes three attempts to locate Northwest Passage	
1592		Englishman John Davis discovers Falkland Islands
1596–7	Third expedition of Dutchman Wilhelm Barents (Barentz) to Northeast Passage discovers Spitzbergen but is blocked by ice near Novaya Zemlya	
1610	English sailor Henry Hudson enters Hudson Bay; in 1611 his crew mutiny, casting Hudson and his son adrift, and return home	

KEY DATES	THE ARCTIC	THE ANTARCTIC
1616	William Baffin discovers Baffin Bay during search for NW Passage	
1733–41	Russian Great Northern Expedition, led by Dane Vitus Bering, explores Northeast Passage	
1772–5		James Cook's round-the-world RN expedition crosses Antarctic Circle twice
1819	John Barrow (GB) enters Barrow Straits	
1820		Russian navigator Fabian Bellinghausen becomes first person to sight Antarctica
1821		Sealers Nathaniel Palmer (US) and George Powell (GB) discover South Orkney Islands
1823		Englishman James Weddell sails to a record 74° South
1827	William Parry (GB) aboard *Hecla* reaches 82°45′ North, a northing record that will stand for half a century	
1840		Lt Charles Wilkes of the US Exploring Expedition sights Wilkes Land
1841		Sir James Clark Ross RN discovers Victoria Land and Ross Sea
1845	Sir John Franklin's 137-strong expedition disappears after entering Northwest Passage	

KEY DATES	THE ARCTIC	THE ANTARCTIC
1850–3	Robert McClure (GB) becomes first person to complete Northwest Passage (by boat and sledge)	
1871–3	Charles Hall reaches 82°11′ North aboard the *Polaris*	
1878–9	Baron Nils Nordenskiold of Sweden successfully traverses NorthEast Passage; the *Jeannette*, under command of De Long USN begins search for the North Pole and founders off Siberia.	
1888	Norwegian scientist Fridtjof Nansen makes first crossing of Greenland (on skis)	
1893–6	Fridtjof Nansen's purpose-built ship *Fram* is deliberately stuck in Arctic ice; when the drift fails to take the *Fram* near the North Pole, Nansen and Johansen set off with dogs and kayaks and reach within 360 km of the Pole.	
1897	Salomon Andrée's balloon *Eagle* crashes 82°93′N; Andrée and his two companions survive only to die later on walk to Spitzbergen	
1898	Robert Peary (US) makes his first bid for North Pole	De Gerlache and crew of *Belgica* first to over winter in Antarctica

KEY DATES	THE ARCTIC	THE ANTARCTIC
1900	Italian sledge party led by Captain Umberto Cagni reach 86°33′ N, a record.	
1901–4		Robert F. Scott's *Discovery* expedition to Antarctica
1904		Establishment of first whaling station at Grytviken on South Georgia
1905	Amundsen (Nor) sails through NW Passage	
1907–9		Ernest Shackleton's *Nimrod* expedition to Antarctica reaches to within 97 miles of the geographical Pole; three of the *Nimrod* expedition reach South Magnetic Pole
1908	Frederick Cook (US) reaches the North Pole, 21 April; his claim is widely disbelieved	
1909	Robert Peary reaches North Pole, 6 April; serious doubts later arise over accuracy of his records	
1911		Roald Amundsen (Nor) becomes first to South Pole (14 December)
1912		Scott's *Terra Nova* expedition reaches Pole (17 Jan); all expeditioners (Scott, Evans, Oates, Wilson, Bowers) die on return journey
1925	Amundsen and Ellsworth reach 88°N on Dornier flying boat	

KEY DATES	THE ARCTIC	THE ANTARCTIC
1926	Richard Byrd claims to fly over the North Pole (9 May); Roald Amundsen, Lincoln Ellsworth and Umberto Nobile aboard the airship *Norge* become the first to see indisputably see the North Pole (13 May)	
1928	Crash of the *Norge* in the Arctic; Amundsen lost in rescue search; George Hubert Wilkins (Aus) and Carl Ben Eielson (US) fly across the Polar Sea	
1929		Byrd, Bernt Balchen, Harold June and Ashley McKinley becomes first to fly over South Pole
1935		Caroline Mikkelsen (Nor) first woman to set foot in Antarctica; Lincoln Ellsworth (US) first to fly across Continent
1947		Operation Highjump by USN establishes Little America base and takes over 70,000 aerial photographs of Antarctica
1948	Russian expedition under Alexander Kuznetsov fly to and land on the North Pole, the first to indisputably set foot there.	
1954		First permanent scientific station set up, Antarctica

KEY DATES	THE ARCTIC	THE ANTARCTIC
1956		Conrad Shinn (USA) lands at South Pole
1955–8		British Commonwealth Trans-Antarctic Expedition crosses continent
1958	Nuclear submarine *USS Nautilus* becomes first submarine to reach North Pole	
1959		Antarctic Treaty signed
1960	USS *Seadragon* makes first undersea transit of Northwest Passage	
1968	American team led by Ralph Plaisted reach North Pole overland by snowmobile.	
1968–9	Wally Herbert becomes first man to cross the Arctic Ocean	
1977	Soviet ice-breaker *Arktika* becomes first surface vessel to reach North Pole	
1978	Naomi Uemura (Jap) becomes first person to reach North Pole in a solo trek across Arctic ice	
1979–82	Ranulph Fiennes and Charlie Burton achieve the first circumpolar navigation of the Earth	
1986	Ann Bancroft becomes first woman to travel to North Pole on foot	
2003	Ben Saunders (GB, 25) becomes youngest person to make unsupported return trip to North Pole	

PART ONE

The North Pole

"The Pole at last. The prize of three centuries. My dream and goal for twenty years. Mine at last!"

Commander Robert Peary, 6 April 1909

Introduction: the North Pole

There is more than one North Pole. There is the North Magnetic Pole (to which the compass needle points, and which is presently out in the Canadian Arctic); the North Geomagnetic Pole (about 79° 13′ N, 71° 16′ W); the Northern Pole of Inaccessibility (the point furthest from land); and then there is the North Geographical Pole. The latter is the absolute top of the world, 90 degrees North, the end of the Earth which points toward the North Star, Polaris. It is this North Pole, above all its near-named rivals, which haunts the human imagination, which has so beguiled explorers.

The North Pole, if one thinks about it, is a strange object of desire. There is nothing there, except drifting ice fifteen feet thick and the odd wandering bird, for even polar bears do not hunt 450 miles from land. The ocean at the North Pole is 13,410 feet deep. For six months of the year the North Pole has continous sunlight. For the other six months, the sun does not appear above the horizon.

The first men to head Polewards were 16th-century British and Dutch sailors seeking a new trade route to the Orient. Unhappily these first seekers of the "Northwest Passage" were under the impression that the top of the globe was ringed by an ice wall, and when this was smashed through they could tack on the breeze to the Pole itself. Hundreds of adventurers died of scurvy, famine, hypothermia before this notion was definitively disabused in the 19th century. There was only ice, ice and more ice.

The dog's share of the initial exploration of the Arctic was done by the British, particularly the Royal Navy (the first realistic bid for the North Pole was led by William Parry RN in 1827, using sledges for travel over the frozen ice) but increasingly explorers of other nations began to trespass on the "British" Pole. On his

Fram expedition of 1893, the Norwegian Nansen achieved 86° 15′ North, while the Italian Duke of Aruzzi's expedition of 1899 reached 86°34′. Above all, it was the Americans who sought the laurels of being first to 90° North. And so it was that Frederick Cook of the US claimed the North Pole in 1908 – only to have his claim deried by Robert Peary of the US, who demanded that *his* visit of 1909 was the first to the Pole. The American aviator Byrd made a claim to fly to the North Pole in 1926 – although this too was likely specious. The first men to indisputably see the North Pole were an international team of Roald Amundsen (Norway), Lincoln Ellsworth (US) and Umberto Nobile (Italy), who flew there in a dirigible, again in 1926. But at least the first proven overland visit to the North Pole was by an American, even if it did have to wait until 1968, when Ralph Plaisted went to the top of the world by skidoo.

Skidoos, feet, skis, sledges, dirigibles, aeroplanes, submarines – the North Pole has now been attained by all these means. It has even been attained by ship, if a rather more robust vessel than the wooden merchantmen that took the first trips Polewards in the 1500s. The Russian ship *Arkita*, which reached the Pole in 1977, was powered by a nuclear engine and the steel skin of the bows was 20 inches thick. The purpose of the *Arktika* expedition was scientific research, but just over a decade later the Russians began running trips to the North Pole on their icebreakers.

The North Pole had become a tourist destination.

The "Heroic" era of North Pole and Arctic exploration was definitively killed in the moment the first paying visitors arrived at 90° North. Even so, the cold desert that lies at Farthest North still remains a place of awe and inspiration, a place where the intrepid (or foolhardy) can test themselves, should they choose, against Nature's cruellest beauty.

The March to Fort Enterprise

Sir John Franklin RN

A veteran of the Trafalgar battle, John Franklin RN was an Arctic explorer by Admiralty order; he was appointed to the "Discovery Service" expedition to the North Pole in 1818 by a naval board that could find little else to do with an ageing lieutenant. The expedition barely made it north of Spitzbergen before beating a hasty retreat; the following year the Admiralty sent Franklin north again, this time for an overland reconnaissance of Canada's Arctic territory above the Great Slave Lake. Lieutenant Franklin's small party consisted of himself, surgeon Dr John Richardson, two Royal Navy midshipmen and about a dozen French and Chippewyan "voyageurs". The Arctic winter overtook Franklin on 6 September 1821, when three feet of snow fell and the thermometer showed 20 degrees Fahrenheit. The expedition had already run out of food. Franklin's subsequent survival march to Fort Enterprise is one of the most dramatic in Polar history:

25 October

In the afternoon we had a heavy fall of snow, which continued all night. A small quantity of *tripe de roche* (lichen) was gathered; and Crédit, who had been hunting, brought in the antlers and backbone of a deer which had been killed in the summer. The wolves and birds of prey had picked them clean, but there still remained a quantity of the spinal marrow which they had not been able to extract. This, although putrid, was esteemed a valuable prize, and the spine being divided into portions, was distributed equally. After eating the marrow, which was so acrid as to excoriate the lips, we rendered the bones friable by burning, and ate them also.

On the following morning the ground was covered with snow

to the depth of a foot and a half, and the weather was very stormy. These circumstances rendered the men again extremely despondent: a settled gloom hung over their countenances, and they refused to pick *tripe de roche*, choosing rather to go entirely without eating than to make any exertion. The party which went for gum returned early in the morning without having found any; but St Germain said he could still make the canoe with the willows, covered with canvas, and removed with Adam to a clump of willows for that purpose. Mr Back accompanied them to stimulate his exertion, as we feared the lowness of his spirits would cause him to be slow in his operations. Augustus went to fish at the rapid, but a large trout having carried away his bait, we had nothing to replace it . . .

The sensation of hunger was no longer felt by any of us, yet we were scarcely able to converse upon any other subject than the pleasures of eating. We were much indebted to Hepburn at this crisis. The officers were unable from weakness to gather *tripe de roche* themselves, and Samandré, who had acted as our cook on the journey from the coast, sharing in the despair of the rest of the Canadians, refused to make the slightest exertion. Hepburn, on the contrary, animated by a firm reliance on the beneficence of the Supreme Being, tempered with resignation to his will, was indefatigable in his exertions to serve us, and daily collected all the *tripe de roche* that was used in the officers' mess. Mr Hood could not partake of this miserable fare, and a partridge which had been reserved for him was, I lament to say, this day stolen by one of the men . . .

About noon Samandré coming up, informed us that Crédit and Vaillant could advance no further. Some willows being discovered in a valley near us, I proposed to halt the party there, whilst Dr Richardson went back to visit them. I hoped too, that when the sufferers received the information of a fire being kindled at so short a distance they would be cheered, and use their utmost efforts to reach it, but this proved a vain hope. The doctor found Vaillant about a mile and a half in the rear, much exhausted with cold and fatigue. Having encouraged him to advance to the fire, after repeated solicitations he made the attempt, but fell down amongst the deep snow at every step. Leaving him in this situation, the doctor went about half a mile farther back, to the spot where Crédit was said to have halted, and the track being nearly obliterated by the snow drift, it became unsafe for him to go further. Returning he passed Vaillant, who having moved only a few yards in his absence, had fallen down, was unable to rise, and could scarcely answer his questions. Being unable to afford him any effectual assistance, he hastened on to inform us of his situation. When J. B. Belanger had heard the melancholy account, he went immediately to aid Vaillant, and bring up his burden. Respecting Crédit, we were informed by Samandré, that he had stopped a short distance behind Vaillant, but that his intention was to return to the encampment of the preceding evening.

When Belanger came back with Vaillant's load, he informed us that he had found him lying on his back, benumbed with cold, and incapable of being roused. The stoutest men of the party were now earnestly entreated to bring him to the fire, but they declared themselves unequal to the task; and, on the contrary, urged me to allow them to throw down their loads, and proceed to Fort Enterprise with the utmost speed. A compliance with their desire would have caused the loss of the whole party, for the men were totally ignorant of the course to be pursued, and none of the officers, who could have directed the march, were sufficiently strong to keep up at the pace they would then walk; besides, even supposing them to have found their way, the strongest men would certainly have deserted the weak. Something, however, was absolutely necessary to be done, to relieve them as much as possible from their burdens, and the officers consulted on the subject. Mr Hood and Dr Richardson proposed to remain behind, with a single attendant, at the first place where sufficient wood and *tripe de roche* should be found for ten days' consumption; and that I should proceed as expeditiously as possible with the men to the house, and thence send them immediate relief. They strongly urged that this arrangement would contribute to the safety of the rest of the party, by relieving them from the burden of a tent, and several other articles; and that they might afford aid to Crédit, if he should unexpectedly come up. I was distressed beyond description at the thought of leaving them in such a dangerous situation, and for a long time combated their proposal; but they strenuously urged, that this step afforded the

only chance of safety for the party, and I reluctantly acceded to it.
The ammunition, of which we had a small barrel, was also to be
left with them, and it was hoped that this deposit would be a
strong inducement for the Indians to venture across the barren
grounds to their aid. We communicated this resolution to the
men, who were cheered at the slightest prospect of alleviation to
their present miseries, and promised with great appearance of
earnestness to return to those officers, upon the first supply of
food.

The party then moved on; Vaillant's blanket and other necessaries were left in the track, at the request of the Canadians,
without any hope, however, of his being able to reach them. After
marching till dusk without seeing a favourable place for encamp-
ing, night compelled us to take shelter under the lee of a hill,
amongst some willows, with which, after many attempts, we at
length made a fire. It was not sufficient, however, to warm the
whole party, much less to thaw our shoes; and the weather not
permitting the gathering of *tripe de roche*, we had nothing to cook.
The painful retrospection of the melancholy events of the day
banished sleep, and we shuddered as we contemplated the dreadful effects of this bitterly cold night on our two companions, if
still living. Some faint hopes were entertained of Crédit's surviving the storm, as he was provided with a good blanket, and had
leather to eat.

The weather was mild next morning. We left the encampment
at nine, and a little before noon came to a pretty extensive thicket
of small willows, near which there appeared a supply of *tripe de
roche* on the face of the rocks. At this place Dr Richardson and Mr
Hood determined to remain, with John Hepburn, who volunteered to stop with them. The tent was securely pitched, a few
willows collected, and the ammunition and all other articles were
deposited, except each man's clothing, one tent, a sufficiency of
ammunition for the journey, and the officers' journals. I had only
one blanket, which was carried for me, and two pair of shoes. The
offer was now made for any of the men, who felt themselves too
weak to proceed, to remain with the officers, but none of them
accepted it. Michel alone felt some inclination to do so. After we
had united in thanksgiving and prayers to Almighty God, I
separated from my companions, deeply afflicted that a train of

melancholy circumstances should have demanded of me the severe trial of parting, in such a condition, from friends who had become endeared to me by their constant kindness and co-operation, and a participation of numerous sufferings. This trial I could not have been induced to undergo, but for the reasons they had so strongly urged the day before, to which my own judgment assented, and for the sanguine hope I felt of either finding a supply of provision at Fort Enterprise, or meeting the Indians in the immediate vicinity of that place, according to my arrangements with Mr Wentzel and Akaitcho. Previously to our starting, Peltier and Benoit repeated their promises, to return to them with provision, if any should be found at the house, or to guide the Indians to them, if any were met.

Greatly as Mr Hood was exhausted, and indeed, incapable as he must have proved, of encountering the fatigue of our very next day's journey, so that I felt his resolution to be prudent, I was sensible that his determination to remain was chiefly prompted by the disinterested and generous wish to remove impediments to the progress of the rest. Dr Richardson and Hepburn, who were both in a state of strength to keep pace with the men, besides this motive which they shared with him, were influenced in their resolution to remain, the former by the desire which had distinguished his character, throughout the Expedition, of devoting himself to the succour of the weak, and the latter by the zealous attachment he had ever shown towards his officers.

We set out without waiting to take any of the *tripe de roche*, and walking at a tolerable pace, in an hour arrived at a fine group of pines, about a mile and a quarter from the tent. We sincerely regretted not having seen these before we separated from our companions, as they would have been better supplied with fuel here, and there appeared to be more *tripe de roche* than where we had left them.

Descending afterwards into a more level country, we found the snow very deep, and the labour of wading through it so fatigued the whole party, that we were compelled to encamp, after a march of four miles and a half. Belanger and Michel were left far behind, and when they arrived at the encampment appeared quite exhausted. The former, bursting into tears, declared his inability to proceed, and begged me to let him go back next morning to the tent, and shortly afterwards Michel made the same request. I was in hopes they might recover a little strength by the night's rest, and therefore deferred giving any permission *until* morning. The sudden failure in the strength of these men cast a gloom over the rest, which I tried in vain to remove, by repeated assurances that the distance to Fort Enterprise was short, and that we should, in all probability, reach it in four days. Not being able to find any *tripe de roche*, we drank an infusion of the Labrador tea plant (*ledum palustre*), and ate a few morsels of burnt leather for supper. We were unable to raise the tent, and found its weight too great to carry it on, we, therefore, cut it up, and took a part of the canvass for a cover. The night was bitterly cold, and though we lay as close to each other as possible, having no shelter, we could not keep ourselves sufficiently warm to sleep. A strong gale came on after midnight, which increased the severity of the weather. In the morning Belanger and Michel renewed their request to be permitted to go back to the tent, assuring me they were still weaker than on the preceding evening, and less capable of going forward; and they urged, that the stopping at a place where there was a supply of *tripe de roche* was their only chance of preserving life; under these circumstances, I could not do otherwise than yield to their desire. I wrote a note to Dr Richardson and Mr Hood, informing them of the pines we had passed, and recommending their removing thither. Having found that Michel was carrying a considerable quantity of ammunition, I desired him to divide it among my party, leaving him only ten balls and a little shot, to kill any animals he might meet on his way to the tent. This man was very particular in his inquiries respecting the direction of the house, and the course we meant to pursue; he also said, that if he should be able, he would go and search for Vaillant and Crédit; and he requested my permission to take Vaillant's blanket, if he should find it, to which I agreed, and mentioned it in my notes to the officers.

Scarcely were these arrangements finished, before Perrault and Fontano were seized with a fit of dizziness, and betrayed other symptoms of extreme debility. Some tea was quickly prepared for them, and after drinking it, and eating a few morsels of burnt leather, they recovered, and expressed their desire to go forward; but the other men, alarmed at what they had just witnessed, became doubtful of their own strength, and, giving way to absolute dejection, declared their inability to move. I now earnestly pressed upon them the necessity of continuing our journey, as the only means of saving their own lives, as well as those of our friends at the tent; and, after much entreaty, got them to set out at ten a.m.: Belanger and Michel were left at the encampment, and proposed to start shortly afterwards. By the time we had gone about two hundred yards, Perrault became again dizzy, and desired us to halt, which we did, until he, recovering, offered to march on. Ten minutes more had hardly elapsed before he again desired us to stop, and, bursting into tears, declared he was totally exhausted, and unable to accompany us further. As the encampment was not more than a quarter of a mile distant, we recommended that he should return to it, and rejoin Belanger and Michel, whom we knew to be still there, from perceiving the smoke of a fresh fire; and because they had not made any preparation for starting when we quitted them. He readily acquiesced in the proposition, and having taken a friendly leave of each of us, and enjoined us to make all the haste we could in sending relief, he turned back, keeping his gun and ammunition. We watched him until he was nearly at the fire, and then proceeded. During these detentions, Augustus becoming impatient of the delay had walked on, and we lost sight of him. The labour we experienced in wading through the deep snow induced us to cross a moderate-sized lake, which lay in our track, but we found this operation far more harassing. As the surface of the ice was perfectly smooth, we slipped at almost every step, and were frequently blown down by the wind, with such force as to shake our whole frames.

Poor Fontano was completely exhausted by the labour of this traverse, and we made a halt until his strength was recruited, by which time the party was benumbed with cold. Proceeding again, he got on tolerably well for a little time; but being again seized with faintness and dizziness, he fell often, and at length exclaimed that he could go no further. We immediately stopped, and endeavoured to encourage him to persevere, until we should find some willows to encamp; he insisted, however, that he could not march any longer through this deep snow; and said, that if he should even reach our encampment this evening, he must be left there, provided *tripe de roche* could not be procured to recruit his strength. The poor man was overwhelmed with grief, and seemed desirous to remain at that spot. We were about two miles from the place where the other men had been left, and as the track to it was beaten, we proposed to him to return thither, as we thought it probable he would find the men still there; at any rate, he would be able to get fuel to keep him warm during the night; and, on the next day, he could follow their track to the officer's tent; and, should the path be covered by the snow, the pines we had passed yesterday would guide him, as they were yet in view.

I cannot describe my anguish on the occasion of separating from another companion under circumstances so distressing. There was, however, no alternative. The extreme debility of the rest of the party put the carrying him quite out of the question, as he himself admitted; and it was evident that the frequent delays he must occasion if he accompanied us, and did not gain strength, would endanger the lives of the whole. By returning he had the prospect of getting to the tent where *tripe de roche* could be obtained, which agreed with him better than with any other of the party, and which he was always very assiduous in gathering. After some hesitation, he determined on going back, and set out, having bid each of us farewell in the tenderest manner. We watched him with inexpressible anxiety for some time, and were rejoiced to find, though he got on slowly, that he kept on his legs better than before. Antonio Fontano was an Italian, and had served many years in De Meuron's regiment. He had spoken to me that very morning, and after his first attack of dizziness, about his father; and had begged, that should he survive, I would take him with me to England, and put him in the way of reaching home.

The party was now reduced to five persons, Adam, Peltier, Benoit, Samandré, and myself. Continuing the journey, we came, after an hour's walk, to some willows, and encamped under the shelter of a rock, having walked in the whole four miles and a half. We made an attempt to gather some *tripe de roche*, but could not, owing to the severity of the weather. Our supper, therefore, consisted of tea and a few morsels of leather.

Augustus did not make his appearance, but we felt no alarm at his absence, supposing he would go to the tent if he missed our track. Having fire, we procured a little sleep. Next morning the breeze was light and the weather mild, which enabled us to collect some *tripe de roche*, and to enjoy the only meal we had had for four days. We derived great benefit from it, and walked with considerably more ease than yesterday. Without the strength it supplied, we should certainly have been unable to oppose the strong breeze we met in the afternoon. After walking about five miles, we came upon the borders of Marten Lake, and were rejoiced to find it frozen, so that we could continue our course straight for Fort Enterprise. We encamped at the first rapid in Winter River amidst willows and alders; but these were so frozen, and the snow fell so thick, that the men had great difficulty in making a fire. This proving insufficient to warm us, or even thaw our shoes, and having no food to prepare, we crept under our blankets. The arrival in a well-known part raised the spirits of the men to a high pitch, and we kept up a cheerful conversation until sleep overpowered us. The night was very stormy, and the morning scarcely less so; but, being desirous to reach the house this day, we commenced our journey very early. We were gratified by the sight of a large herd of rein-deer on the side of the hill near the track, but our only hunter, Adam, was too feeble to pursue them. Our shoes and garments were stiffened by the frost, and we walked in great pain until we arrived at some stunted pines, at which we halted, made a good fire, and procured the refreshment of tea. The weather becoming fine in the afternoon, we continued our journey, passed the Dog-rib Rock, and encamped among a clump of pines of considerable growth, about a mile further on. Here we enjoyed the comfort of a large fire, for the first time since our departure from the sea-coast; but this gratification was purchased at the expense of many severe falls in crossing a stony valley, to get at these trees. These was no *tripe de roche*, and we drank tea and ate some of our shoes for supper. Next morning, after taking the usual repast of tea, we proceeded to the house. Musing on what we were likely to find there, our minds were agitated between hope and fear, and, contrary to the custom we had kept up, of supporting our spirits by conversation, we went silently forward.

At length we reached Fort Enterprise, and to our infinite disappointment and grief found it a perfectly desolate habitation.

There was no deposit of provision, no trace of the Indians, no letter from Mr Wentzel to point out where the Indians might be found. It would be impossible to describe our sensations after entering this miserable abode, and discovering how we had been neglected: the whole party shed tears, not so much for our own fate, as for that of our friends in the rear, whose lives depended entirely on our sending immediate relief from this place.

I found a note, however, from Mr Back, stating that he had reached the house two days before, and was going in search of the Indians, at a part where St Germain deemed it probable they might be found. If he was unsuccessful, he purposed walking to Fort Providence, and sending succour from thence; but he doubted whether either he or his party could perform the journey to that place in their present debilitated state. It was evident that any supply that could be sent from Fort Providence would be long in reaching us, neither could it be sufficient to enable us to afford any assistance to our companions behind, and that the only relief for them must be procured from the Indians. I resolved, therefore, on going also in search of them; but my companions were absolutely incapable of proceeding, and I thought by halting two or three days they might gather a little strength, whilst the delay would afford us the chance of learning whether Mr Back had seen the Indians.

We now looked round for the means of subsistence, and were gratified to find several deer skins, which had been thrown away during our former residence. The bones were gathered from the heap of ashes; these with the skins, and the addition of *tripe de roche*, we considered would support us tolerably well for a time. As to the house, the parchment being torn from the windows, the apartment we selected for our abode was exposed to all the rigour of the season. We endeavoured to exclude the wind as much as possible, by placing loose boards against the apertures. The temperature was now between 15° and 20° below zero. We procured fuel by pulling up the flooring of the other rooms, and water for cooking, by melting the snow. Whilst we were seated round the fire, singeing the deer-skin for supper, we were rejoiced by the unexpected entrance of Augustus. He had followed quite a different course from ours, and the circumstance of his having found his way through a part of the country he had never been in before, must be considered a remarkable proof of sagacity. The unusual earliness of this winter became manifest to us from the state of things at this spot. Last year at the same season, and still later, there had been very little snow on the ground, and we were surrounded by vast herds of reindeer; now there were but few recent tracks of these animals, and the snow was upwards of two feet deep. Winter River was then open, now it was frozen two feet thick.

When I arose the following morning, my body and limbs were so swollen that I was unable to walk more than a few yards. Adam was in a still worse condition, being absolutely incapable of rising without assistance. My other companions happily experienced this inconvenience in a less degree, and went to collect bones, and some *tripe de roche*, which supplied us with two meals. The bones were quite acrid, and the soup extracted from them excoriated the mouth if taken alone, but it was somewhat milder when boiled with *tripe de roche*, and we even thought the mixture palatable, with the addition of salt, of which a cask had been fortunately left here in the spring. Augustus to-day set two fishing lines below the rapid. On his way thither he saw two deer, but had not strength to follow them.

On the 13th the wind blew violently from south-east, and the snow drifted so much that the party were confined to the house. In the afternoon of the following day Belanger arrived with a note from Mr Back, stating that he had seen no trace of the Indians, and desiring further instructions as to the course he should pursue. Belanger's situation, however, required our first care, as he came in almost speechless, and covered with ice, having fallen into a rapid, and, for the third time since we left the coast, narrowly escaped drowning. He did not recover sufficiently to answer our questions, until we had rubbed him for some time, changed his dress, and given him some warm soup. My companions nursed him with the greatest kindness, and the desire of restoring him to health, seemed to absorb all regard for their own situation. I witnessed with peculiar pleasure this conduct so different from that which they had recently pursued, when every tender feeling was suspended by the desire of self-preservation. They now no longer betrayed impatience or despondency, but were composed and cheerful, and had entirely given up the practice of swearing, to which the Canadian voyagers are so addicted.

I undertook the office of cooking, and insisted they should eat twice a day whenever food could be procured; but as I was too weak to pound the bones, Peltier agreed to do that in addition to his more fatiguing task of getting wood. We had a violent snow storm all the next day, and this gloomy weather increased the depression of spirits under which Adam and Samandré were labouring. Neither of them would quit their beds; and they scarcely ceased from shedding tears all day; in vain did Peltier and myself endeavour to cheer them. We had even to use much entreaty before they would take the meals we had prepared for them. Our situation was indeed distressing, but in comparison with that of our friends in the rear, we thought it happy. Their condition gave us unceasing solicitude, and was the principal subject of our conversation.

Though the weather was stormy on the 26th, Samandré assisted me to gather *tripe de roche*. Adam, who was very ill, and could not now be prevailed upon to eat this weed, subsisted principally on bones, though he also partook of the soup. The *tripe de roche* had hitherto afforded us our chief support, and we naturally felt great uneasiness at the prospect of being deprived of it, by its being so frozen as to render it impossible for us to gather it.

We perceived our strength decline every day, and every exertion began to be irksome; when we were once seated the greatest effort was necessary in order to rise, and we had frequently to lift each other from our seats; but even in this pitiable condition we conversed cheerfully, being sanguine as to the speedy arrival of the Indians. We calculated indeed that if they should be near the situation where they had remained last winter, our men would have reached them by this day. Having expended all the wood which we could procure from our present dwelling, without danger of its fall, Peltier began this day to pull down the partitions of the adjoining houses. Though these were only distant-about twenty yards, yet the increase of labour in carrying the wood fatigued him so much, that by the evening he was exhausted. On the next day his weakness was such, especially in the arms, of which he chiefly complained, that he with difficulty lifted the hatcher; still he perserved, while Samandré and I assisted him in bringing in the wood, but our united strength could only collect sufficient to replenish the fire four times in the course of the day. As the insides of our mouths had become sore from eating the bone-soup, we relinquished the use of it, and now boiled the skin, which mode of dressing we found more palatable than frying it, as we had hitherto done.

On the 29th, Peltier felt his pains more severe, and could only cut a few pieces of wood. Samandré, who was still almost as weak, relieved him a little time, and I aided them in carrying in the wood. We endeavoured to pick some *tripe de roche*, but in vain, as it was entirely frozen. In turning up the snow, in searching for bones, I found several pieces of bark, which proved a valuable acquisition, as we were almost destitute of dry wood proper for kindling the fire. We saw a herd of reindeer sporting on the river, about half a mile from the house; they remained there a long time, but none of the party felt themselves strong enough to go after them, nor was there one of us who could have fired a gun without resting it.

Whilst we were seated round the fire this evening, discoursing about the anticipated relief, the conversation was suddenly interrupted by Peltier's exclaiming with joy, "*Ah! le monde!*" imagining that he heard the Indians in the other room; immediately afterwards, to his bitter disappointment, Dr Richardson and Hepburn entered, each carrying his bundle. Peltier, however, soon recovered himself enough to express his delight at their safe arrival, and his regret that their companions were not with them. When I saw them alone my own mind was instantly filled with apprehensions respecting my friend Hood, and our other companions, which were immediately confirmed by the doctor's melancholy communication, that Mr Hood and Michel were dead. Perrault and Fontano had neither reached the tent, nor been heard of by them. This intelligence produced a melancholy despondency in the minds of my party, and on that account the particulars were deferred until another opportunity. We were all shocked at beholding the emaciated countenances of the doctor and Hepburn, as they strongly evidenced their extremely debilitated state. The alteration in our appearance was equally distressing to them, for since the swellings had subsided we were little more than skin and bone. The doctor particularly remarked the sepulchral tone of our voices, which he requested us to make more cheerful if possible, unconscious that his own partook of the same key.

Hepburn having shot a partridge, which was brought to the house, the doctor tore out the feathers, and having held it to the fire a few minutes divided it into six portions. I and my three companions ravenously devoured our shares, as it was the first morsel of flesh any of us had tasted for thirty-one days, unless, indeed, the small grizzly particles which we found occasionally adhering to the pounded bones may be termed flesh. Our spirits were revived by this small supply, and the doctor endeavoured to raise them still higher by the prospect of Hepburn's being able to kill a deer next day, as they had seen, and even fired at, several near the house. He endeavoured, too, to rouse us into some attention to the comfort of our apartment, and particularly to roll up, in the day, our blankets, which (expressly for the convenience of Adam and Samandré) we had been in the habit of leaving by the fire where we lay on them. The doctor having brought his prayer book and testament, some prayers and psalms, and portions of scripture, appropriate to our situation, were read, and we retired to bed.

Next morning the doctor and Hepburn went out early in search of deer; but though they saw several herds and fired some shots, they were not so fortunate as to kill any, being too weak to hold their guns steadily. The cold compelled the former to return soon, but Hepburn persisted until late in the evening.

My occupation was to search for skins under the snow, it being now our object immediately to get all that we could, but I had not strength to drag in more than two of those which were within twenty yards of the house, until the doctor came and assisted me. We made up our stock to twenty-six, but several of them were putrid, and scarcely eatable, even by men suffering the extremity of famine. Peltier and Samandré continued very weak and dispirited, and they were unable to cut fire-wood. Hepburn had in consequence that laborious task to perform after he came back. The doctor having scarified the swelled parts of Adam's body, a large quantity of water flowed out, and he obtained some ease, but still kept his bed . . .

I may here remark that, owing to our loss of flesh, the hardness of the floor, from which we were only protected by a blanket, produced soreness over the body, and especially those parts on which the weight rested in lying, yet to turn ourselves for relief was a matter of toil and difficulty. However, during this period, and indeed all along, after the acute pains of hunger, which lasted but three or four days, had subsided, we generally enjoyed the comfort of a few hours' sleep. The dreams which for the most part, but not always, accompanied it, were usually (though not invariably) of a pleasant character, being very often about the enjoyments of feasting. In the day-time we fell into the practice of conversing on common and light subjects, although we sometimes discussed with seriousness and earnestness topics connected with religion. We generally avoided speaking directly of our present sufferings, or even of the prospect of relief. I observed, that in proportion as our strength decayed, our minds exhibited symptoms of weakness, evinced by a kind of unreasonable pettishness with each other. Each of us thought the other weaker in intellect than himself, and more in need of advice and assistance. So trifling a circumstance as a change of place, recommended by one as being warmer and more comfortable, and refused by the other from a dread of motion, frequently called forth fretful expressions which were no sooner uttered than atoned for, to be repeated perhaps in the course of a few minutes. The same thing often occurred when we endeavoured to assist each other in carrying wood to the fire; none of us were willing to receive assistance, although the task was disproportioned to our strength. On one of these occasions, Hepburn was so convinced of this waywardness that he exclaimed, "Dear me, if we are spared to return to England, I wonder if we shall recover our understandings."

7 November

Adam had passed a restless night, being disquieted by gloomy apprehensions of approaching death, which we tried in vain to dispel. He was so low in the morning as to be scarcely able to speak. I remained in bed by his side, to cheer him as much as possible. The doctor and Hepburn went to cut wood. They had hardly begun their labour when they were amazed at hearing the report of a musket. They could scarcely believe that there was really anyone near, until they heard a shout, and immediately espied three Indians close to the house. Adam and I heard the latter noise, and I was fearful that a part of the house had fallen upon one of my companions, a disaster which had in fact been thought not unlikely. My alarm was only momentary; Dr Richardson came in to communicate the joyful intelligence that relief had arrived.

Franklin returned to England to find himself a celebrity, an intrepid explorer of "frozen regions".

Promoted to captain, Franklin was returned to the Arctic in 1825, this time to chart 1600 miles of Arctic coastline. Although Franklin's mission was successful enough for him to be granted a knighthood it was not successful enough to persuade the Royal Navy to sponsor more Arctic exploration. To make a gentleman's ends meet Franklin took on the governorship of Van Diemen's Land (Tasmania), a penal colony.

Twenty years later, balding and gone to fat, the 59-year-old Sir John Franklin was given one last chance at Arctic glory. Piecing together the results of its own and other Arctic explorations, the Royal Navy realized that the solution to the puzzle that was the Northwest Passage must be near in time. It was only right that England, which had spent 300 years on the quest, took the glory. So it was that Franklin – the Admiralty's third choice – was given command of the best ever equipped expedition to find the Northwest Passage: two steam-powered, iron plated ships, 24 officers and 110 men. The expedition left England in May 1845. Two months later Franklin's ships were spotted in Baffin Bay. And then disappeared.

Extensive searches failed to find any trace of Franklin or his men, until John Rae's Arctic coastal survey of 1854 encountered "Eskimaux" who had salvaged articles from dead Franklin expeditionaries. Three years later, Lady Franklin sent out Francis McClintock to find her husband's remains and McClintock was able to confirm the fate of the missing men:

7 May 1859

To avoid snow-blindness, we commenced night marching. Crossing over from Matty Island towards the shore of King William's Island, we continued our march southward until midnight, when we had the good fortune to arrive at an inhabited snow village. We found ten or twelve huts and thirty or forty natives of King William's Island; I do not think any of them had ever seen white people alive before, but they evidently regarded us as friends. We halted at a little distance, and pitched our tent, the better to secure small articles from being stolen whilst we bartered with them.

I purchased from them six pieces of silver plate, bearing the crests or initials of Franklin, Crozier, Fairholme, and McDonald; they also sold us bows and arrows of English woods, uniform and other buttons, and offered us a heavy sledge made of two short stout pieces of curved wood, which no mere boat could have furnished them with, but this of course we could not take away; the silver spoons and forks were readily sold for four needles each.

They were most obliging and peaceably disposed but could not resist the temptation to steal, and were importunate to barter everything they possessed. There was not a trace of fear, every countenance was lighted up with joy; even the children were not shy, nor backward either, in crowding about us, and poking in everywhere. One man got hold of our saw, and tried to retain it, holding it behind his back, and presenting his knife in exchange; we might have had some trouble in getting it from him, had not one of my men mistaken his object in presenting the knife towards me, and run out of the tent with a gun in his hand; the saw was instantly returned, and these poor people seemed to think they never could do enough to convince us of their friendliness; they repeatedly tapped me gently on the breast, repeating the words "Kammik toomee" (We are friends).

Having obtained all the relics they possessed, I purchased some seal's flesh, blubber, frozen venison, dried and frozen salmon, and sold some of my puppies. They told us it was five days' journey to the wreck – one day up the inlet still in sight, and four days overland; this would bring them to the western coast of King

William's Island; they added that but little now remained accessible of the wreck, their countrymen having carried almost everything away. In answer to an enquiry, they said she was without masts; the question gave rise to some laughter amongst them, and they spoke to each other about *fire*, from which Petersen thought they had burnt the masts through close to the deck in order to get them down.

There had been *many books*, they said, but all have long ago been destroyed by the weather; the ship was forced on there in the fall of the year by the ice. She had not been visited during this past winter, and an old woman and a boy were shown to us who were the last to visit the wreck; they said they had been at it during the preceding winter.

Petersen questioned the woman closely, and she seemed anxious to give all the information in her power. She said many of the white men dropped by the way as they went to the Great River; that some were buried and some were not . . .

Farthest North

William Edward Parry

Sir William Parry was one of the countless Royal Navy officers dispatched Northwards on exploration duties by a service which, having defeated the French in the Napoleonic Wars, needed justification for its existence. Parry's first Arctic voyage came in 1818, and four more followed, the crowning glory of them being his attempt on the Pole in 1827 – the first realistic tilt at the target in all history. Parry's principal method of travel was the "sledge-boat" which, as its name suggested, was a flat-bottomed boat (20 feet long) with two runners mounted underneath – ideal, it was supposed, for use on both ice and open water. The sledges were to be pulled by Royal Navy seamen, establishing a tradition of "man-hauling" that reached its apogee in the Antarctic journeys of Scott. Setting out from Spitzbergen on 21 June, Parry's party included Lieutenant James Clark Ross, himself to become famous as a polar explorer:

. . . I left the ship at five p.m. with our two boats, which we named the *Enterprise* and *Endeavour*, Mr Beverly being attached to my own, and Lieutenant Ross, accompanied by Mr Bird, in the other. Besides these, I took Lieutenant Crozier in one of the ship's cutters, for the purpose of carrying some of our weight as far as Walden Island, and also a third store of provisions to be deposited on Low Island, as an intermediate station between Walden Island and the ship. As it was still necessary not to delay our return beyond the end of August, the time originally intended, I took, with me only seventy-one days provisions; which, including the boats and every other article, made up a weight of 268 lbs per man; and as it appeared highly improbable, from what we had seen of the very rugged nature of the ice we should first have to encounter, that either the reindeer, the snow-shoes, or the wheels would prove of any service for some time to come, I gave up the idea of taking them. We, however, constructed out of the snow-shoes four excellent sledges for dragging a part of our baggage over the ice; and these proved of invaluable service to us, while the rest of the things just mentioned would only have been an encumbrance.

Having received the usual salutation of three cheers from those we left behind, we paddled through a quantity of loose ice at the entrance of the bay, and then steered, in a perfectly open sea, and with calm and beautiful weather, for the western part of Low Island, which we reached at half past two on the morning of the 22d.

Having deposited the provisions, we set off at four a.m., paddling watch and watch, to give the people a little rest. It was still quite calm; but there being much ice about the island, and a thick fog coming on, we were several hours groping our way clear of it. The walruses were here very numerous, lying in herds upon the ice, and plunging into the water to follow us as we passed. The sound they utter is something between bellowing and very loud snorting, which, together with their grim, bearded countenances and long tusks, makes them appear, as indeed they are, rather formidable enemies to contend with. Under our present circumstances, we were very well satisfied not to molest them, for they would soon have destroyed our boats if one had been wounded; but I believe they are never the first to make the attack. We landed upon the ice still attached to Walden Island at 3.30 a.m. on the 23d. Our flat-bottomed boats rowed heavily with their loads, but proved perfectly safe, and very comfortable. The men being much fatigued, we rested here some hours, and, after making our final arrangements with Lieutenant Crozier, parted with him at three in the afternoon, and set off for Little Table Island. Finding there was likely to be so much open water in this neighbourhood in the autumn, I sent directions to Lieutenant Foster to have a spare boat deposited at Walden Island in time for our return, in case of any accident happening to ours.

The land-ice, which still adhered to the Seven Islands, was very little more broken off than when the *Hecla* had been here a week before; and we rowed along its margin a part of the way to Little Table Island, where we arrived at ten p.m. We here examined and re-secured the provisions left on shore, having found our depot at Walden Island disturbed by the bears. The prospect to the northward at this time was very favourable, there being only a small quantity of loose ice in sight; and the weather still continuing calm and clear, with the sea as smooth as a mirror, we set off without delay, at half past ten, taking our final leave of the Spitzbergen shores, as we hoped, for at least two months. Steering due north, we made good progress, our latitude by the sun's meridian altitude at midnight being 80 deg. 51' 13". A beautifully coloured rainbow appeared for some time, without any appearance of rain falling. We observed that a considerable current was setting us to the eastward just after leaving the land, so that we had made a N.N.E. course, distance about ten miles, when we met with some ice, which soon becoming too close for farther progress, we landed upon a high hummock to obtain a better view. We here perceived that the ice was close to the northward, but to the westward we discovered some open water, which we reached after two or three hours' paddling, and found it a wide expanse, in which we sailed to the northward without obstruction, a fresh breeze having sprung up from the S.W. The weather soon after became very thick, with continued snow, requiring great care in looking out for the ice, which made its appearance after two hours' run, and gradually became closer, till at length we were stopped by it at noon, and obliged to haul the boats upon a small floe-piece, our latitude by observation being 81 deg. 12' 51".

Our plan of travelling being nearly the same throughout this excursion, after we first entered upon the ice, I may at once give some account of our usual mode of proceeding. It was my intention to travel wholly at night, and to rest by day, there being, of course, constant daylight in these regions during the summer season. The advantages of this plan, which was occasionally deranged by circumstances, consisted, first, in our avoiding the intense and oppressive glare from the snow during the time of the sun's greatest altitude, so as to prevent, in some degree, the painful inflammation in the eyes called "snow blindness", which is common in all snowy countries. We also thus enjoyed greater warmth during the hours of rest, and had a better chance of drying our clothes; besides which, no small advantage was derived from the snow being harder at night for travelling. The only disadvantage of this plan was, that the fogs were somewhat more thick by night than by day, though even in this respect there was less difference than might have been supposed, the temperature during the twenty-four hours undergoing but little variation. This travelling by night and sleeping by day so completely inverted the natural order of things, that it was difficult to persuade ourselves of the reality. Even the officers and myself, who were all furnished with pocket chronometers, could not always bear in mind at what part of the twenty-four hours we had arrived; and there were several of the men who declared, and I believe truly, that they never knew night from day during the whole excursion.

When we rose in the evening, we commenced our day by prayers, after which we took off our fur sleeping-dresses and put on those for travelling; the former being made of camlet, lined with racoon-skin, and the latter of strong blue box-cloth. We made a point of always putting on the same stockings and boots for travelling in, whether they dried during the day or not; and I believe it was only in five or six instances, at the most, that they were not either wet or hard-frozen. This, indeed, was of no consequence, beyond the discomforture of first putting them on in this state, as they were sure to be thoroughly wet in a quarter of an hour after commencing our journey; while, on the other hand, it was of vital importance to keep dry things for sleeping in. Being "rigged" for travelling, we breakfasted upon warm cocoa and biscuit, and, after stowing the things in the boats and on the sledges, so as to secure them as much as possible from wet, we set off on our day's journey, and usually travelled from five to five and a half hours, then stopped an hour to dine, and again travelled four, five, or even six hours, according to circumstances. After this we halted for the night, as we called it, though it was usually early in the morning, selecting the largest surface of ice we happened to be near for hauling the boats on, in order to avoid the danger of its breaking up by coming in contact with other masses, and also to prevent drift as much as possible. The boats were placed close alongside each other, with their sterns to the wind, the snow or wet cleared out of them, and the sails, supported by the bamboo masts and three paddles, placed over them as awnings, an entrance being left at the bow. Every man then immediately put on dry stockings and fur boots, after which we set about the necessary repairs of boats, sledges, or clothes; and, after serving the provisions for the succeeding day, we went to supper. Most of the officers and men then smoked their pipes, which served to dry the boats and awnings very much, and usually raised the temperature of our lodgings 10 deg. or 15 deg. This part of the twenty-four hours was often a time, and the only one, of real enjoyment to us; the men told their stories and "fought all their battles o'er again," and the labours of the day, unsuccessful as they too often were, were forgotten. A regular watch was set during our resting-time, to look out for bears or for the ice breaking up round us, as well as to attend to the drying of the clothes, each man alternately, taking this duty for one hour. We then concluded our day with prayers, and, having put on our fur-dresses, lay down to sleep with a degree of comfort, which perhaps few persons would imagine possible under such circumstances; our chief inconvenience being that we were somewhat pinched for room, and therefore obliged to stow rather closer than was quite agreeable. The temperature, while we slept, was usually from 36 deg. to 45 deg., according to the state of the external atmosphere; but on one or two occasions in calm and warm weather, it rose as high as 60 deg. to 66 deg., obliging us to throw off a part of our fur-dress. After we had slept seven hours, the man appointed to boil the cocoa roused us when it was ready by the sound of a bugle, when we commenced our day in the manner before described.

Our allowance of provisions for each man per day was as follows:

Biscuit	10 ounces.
Pemmican	9 ounces.
Sweetened Cocoa Powder	1 ounce, to make one pint.
Rum	1 gill.
Tobacco	3 ounces per week.

Our fuel consisted entirely of spirits of wine, of which two pints formed our daily allowance, the cocoa being cooked in an iron boiler over a shallow iron lamp, with seven wicks; a simple apparatus, which answered our purpose remarkably well. We usually found one pint of the spirits of wine sufficient for preparing our breakfast, that is, for heating twenty-eight pints of water, though it always commenced from the temperature of 32 deg. If the weather was calm and fair, this quantity of fuel brought it to the boiling point in about an hour and a quarter; but more generally the wicks began to go out before it had reached 200 deg. This, however, made a very comfortable meal to persons situated as we were. Such, with very little variation, was our regular routine during the whole of this excursion.

We set off on our first journey over the ice at ten p.m. on the 24th, Table Island bearing S.S.W., and a fresh breeze blowing from W.S.W., with thick fog, which afterward changed to rain. The bags of pemmican were placed upon the sledges, and the bread in the boats, with the intention of securing the latter from wet; but this plan we were soon obliged to relinquish. We now commenced upon very slow and laborious travelling, the pieces of ice being of small extent and very rugged, obliging us to make three journeys, and sometimes four, with the boats and baggage, and to launch several times across narrow pools of water. We stopped to dine at five a.m. on the 25th, having made, by our log (which we kept very carefully, marking the courses by compass, and estimating the distances), about two miles and a half of northing; and, again setting forward, proceeded till eleven a.m., when we halted to rest; our latitude, by observation at noon, being 81 deg. 15′ 13″.

Setting out again at half past nine in the evening, we found our way to lie over nothing but small, loose, rugged masses of ice, separated by little pools of water, obliging us constantly to launch and haul up the boats, each of which operations required them to be unloaded, and occupied nearly a quarter of an hour. It came on to rain very hard on the morning of the 26th; and, finding we were making very little progress (having advanced not more than half a mile in four hours), and that our clothes would be soon wet through, we halted at half past one, and took shelter under the awnings. The weather improving at six o'clock, we again moved forward, and travelled till a quarter past eleven, when we hauled the boats upon the only tolerably large floe-piece in sight. The rain had very much increased the quantity of water lying upon the ice, of which nearly half the surface was now covered with numberless little ponds of various shapes and extent. It is a remarkable fact, that we had already experienced, in the course of this summer, more rain than during the whole of seven previous summers taken together, though passed in latitudes from 7 deg. to 15 deg. lower than this. A great deal of the ice over which we passed to-day presented a very curious appearance and structure, being composed, on its upper surface, of number-less irregular, needle-like crystals, placed vertically, and nearly close together; their length varying, in different pieces of ice, from five to ten inches, and their breadth in the middle about half an inch, but pointed at both ends. The upper surface of ice having this structure sometimes looks like greenish velvet; a vertical section of it, which frequently occurs at the margin of floes, resembles, while it remains compact, the most beautiful satin-spar, and asbestos when falling to pieces. At this early part of the season, this kind of ice afforded pretty firm footing; but, as the summer advanced, the needles became more loose and moveable, rendering it extremely fatiguing to walk over them, besides cutting our boots and feet, on which account the men called them "penknives".

We pursued our journey at half past nine p.m., with the wind at N.E., and thick weather, the ice being so much in motion as to make it very dangerous to cross in loaded boats, the masses being all very small. On this account we halted at midnight, having waded three quarters of a mile through water from two to five inches deep upon the ice. The thermometer was at 33 deg.

At seven a.m. on the 28th, we came to a floe covered with high and rugged hummocks, which opposed a formidable obstacle to our progress, occurring in two or three successive tiers, so that we had no sooner crossed one than another presented itself. Over one of these we hauled the boats with extreme difficulty by a "stand-ing pull", and the weather being then so thick that we could see no pass across the next tier, we were obliged to stop at nine a.m. While performing this laborious work, which required the boats to be got up and down places almost perpendicular, James Parker, my coxswain, received a severe contusion in his back, by the boat falling upon him from a hummock, and the boats were constantly subject to very heavy blows, but sustained no damage.

The weather continued very foggy during the day, but a small
lane of water opening out at no great distance from the margin of
the floe, we launched the boats at eight in the evening among
loose drift-ice, and, after some time, landed on a small floe to the
eastward, the only one in sight, with the hope of its leading to the
northward. It proved so rugged that we were obliged to make
three, and sometimes four journeys with the boats and provisions, and this by a very circuitous route; so that the road, by
which we made a mile of northing, was full a mile and a half in
length, and over this we had to travel at least five, and sometimes
seven times. Thus, when we halted to dine at two a.m., after six
hours' severe toil, and much risk to the men and boats, we had
only accomplished about a mile and a quarter in a N.N.E.
direction. After dining we proceeded again till half past six,
and then halted, very much fatigued with our day's work, and
having made two miles and a half of northing. We were here in
latitude, by account, 81 deg. 23″, and in longitude, by the
chronometers, 21 deg. 32′ 34″ E., in which situation the variation
of the magnetic needle was observed to be 15 deg. 31′ westerly.
We now enjoyed the first sunshine since our entering the ice, and
a great enjoyment it was, after so much thick and wet weather.
We rose at half past four p.m., in the hopes of pursuing our
journey; but, after hauling the boats to the edge of the floe, found
such a quantity of loose, rugged ice to the northward of us, that
there was no possibility, for the present, of getting across or
through it. Observing a small opening at 10.30 p.m., we launched
the boats, and hauled them across several pieces of ice, some of
them being very light and much decayed. Our latitude, by the
sun's meridian altitude at midnight, was 81 deg. 23′; so that we
had made only eight miles of northing since our last observation
at noon on the 25th.

The 30th commenced with snowy and inclement weather,
which soon rendered the atmosphere so thick that we could no
longer see our way, obliging us to halt till two p.m., when we
crossed several small pools with great labour and loss of time. We
had generally very light ice this day, with some heavy, rugged
pieces intermixed; and, when hauling across these, we had sometimes to cut with axes a passage for the boats among the hummocks. We also dragged them through a great many pools of fresh

water, to avoid the necessity of going round them. The wind freshening up from the S.S.W., we afterward found the ice gradually more and more open, so that, in the course of the day, we made by rowing, though by a very winding channel, five miles of northing; but were again stopped by the ice soon after midnight, and obliged to haul up on the first mass that we could gain, the ice having so much motion that we narrowly escaped being "nipped". We set out at 11.30 a.m. on the 1st July, the wind still fresh from the S.W., and some snow falling: but it was more than an hour before we could get away from the small pieces of ice on which we slept, the masses beyond being so broken up and so much in motion, that we could not, at first, venture to launch the boats. Our latitude, observed at noon, was 81 deg. 30′ 41″. After crossing several pieces, we at length got into a good "lead" of water, four or five miles in length; two or three of which, as on the preceding day, occurred under the lee of a floe, being the second we had yet seen that deserved that name. We then passed over four or five small floes, and across the pools of water that lay between them. The ice was now less broken up, and sometimes tolerably level; but from six to eighteen inches of soft snow lay upon it in every part, making the travelling very fatiguing, and obliging us to make at least two, and sometimes three, journeys with our loads. We now found it absolutely necessary to lighten the boat as much as possible, by putting the bread-bags on the sledges, on account of the "runners" of the boats sinking so much deeper into the snow; but our bread ran a great risk of being wetted by this plan.

We halted at eleven p.m. on the 1st, having traversed from ten to eleven miles, and made good, by our account, seven and half in a N.b.W. direction. We again set forward at ten a.m. on the 2d, the weather being calm, and the sun oppressively warm, though with a thick fog. The temperature in the shade was 35 deg. at noon, and only 47 deg. in the sun; but this, together with the glare from the snow, produced so painful a sensation in most of our eyes, as to make it necessary to halt at one p.m., to avoid being blinded. We therefore took advantage of this warm weather to let the men wash themselves, and mend and dry their clothes, and then set out again at half past three. The snow was, however, so soft as to take us up to our knees at almost every other step, and frequently still deeper; so that we were sometimes five minutes together in moving a single empty boat, with all our united strength. It being impossible to proceed under these circumstances, I determined to fall into our night-travelling again, from which we had of late insensibly deviated. We therefore halted at half past five, the weather being now very clear and warm, and many of the people's eyes beginning to fail. We did not set out again till after midnight, with the intention of giving the snow time to harden after so warm a day; but we found it still so soft as to make the travelling very fatiguing. Our way lay at first across a number of loose pieces, most of which were from five to twenty yards apart, or just sufficiently separated to give us all the labour of launching and hauling up the boats, without the advantage of making any progress by water; while we crossed, in other instances, from mass to mass, by laying the boats over as bridges, by which the men and the baggage passed. By these means, we at length reached a floe about a mile in length, in a northern direction; but it would be difficult to convey an adequate idea of the labour required to traverse it. The average depth of snow upon the level parts was about five inches, under which lay water four or five inches deep; but, the moment we approached a hummock, the depth to which we sank increased to three feet or more, rendering it difficult at times to obtain sufficient footing for one leg to enable us to extricate the other. The pools of fresh water had now also become very large, some of them being a quarter of a mile in length, and their depth above our knees. Through these we were prevented taking the sledges, for fear of wetting all our provisions; but we preferred transporting the boats across them, notwithstanding the severe cold of the snow-water, the bottom being harder for the "runners" to slide upon. On this kind of road we were, in one instance, above two hours in proceeding a distance of one hundred yards.

We halted at half past six a.m. to dine; and to empty our boots and wring our stockings, which, to our feelings, was almost like putting on dry ones; and again set out in an hour, getting at length into a "lane" of water a mile and a quarter long, in a N.N.E. direction. We halted for the night at half an hour before midnight, the people being almost exhausted with a laborious day's work, and our distance made good to the northward not exceeding two miles and a quarter. We allowed ourselves this night a hot supper, consisting of a pint of soup per man, made of an ounce of pemmican each, and eight or ten birds, which we had killed in the course of the last week; and this was a luxury which persons thus situated could perhaps alone duly appreciate.

We rose and breakfasted at nine p.m.; but the weather had gradually become so inclement and thick, with snow, sleet, and a fresh breeze from the eastward, that we could neither have seen our way, nor have avoided getting wet through had we moved. We therefore remained under cover; and it was as well that we did so, for the snow soon after changed to heavy rain, and the wind increased to a fresh gale, which unavoidably detained us till 7.30 p.m. on the 4th. The rain had produced even a greater effect than the sun in softening the snow. Lieutenant Ross and myself, in performing our pioneering duty, were frequently so beset in it, that sometimes, after trying in vain to extricate our legs, we were obliged to sit quietly down for a short time to rest ourselves and then make another attempt; and the men, in dragging the sledges, were often under the necessity of crawling upon all-fours to make any progress at all. Nor would any kind of snow-shoes have been of the least service, but rather an encumbrance to us, for the surface was so irregular, that they would have thrown us down at every other step. We had hitherto made use of the Lapland shoes, or *kamoogas*, for walking in, which are excellent for dry snow; but there being now so much water upon the ice, we substituted the Esquimaux boots, which had been made in Greenland expressly for our use, and which are far superior to any others for this kind of travelling. Just before halting, at six a.m. on the 5th, the ice at the margin of the floe broke while the men were handing the provisions out of the boats; and we narrowly escaped the loss of a bag of cocoa, which fell overboard, but fortunately rested on a "tongue". The bag being made of Mackintosh's waterproof canvas, the cocoa did not suffer the slightest injury.

We rose at five p.m., the weather being clear and fine, with a moderate breeze from the south; no land was in sight from the highest hummocks, nor could we perceive anything but broken loose ice in any direction. We hauled across several pieces which were scarcely fit to bear the weight of the boats, and in such cases used the precaution of dividing our baggage, so that, in case of the ice breaking or turning over, we should not lose all at once. The farther we proceeded, the more the ice was broken; indeed, it was much more so here than we had found it since first entering the "pack". After stopping at midnight to dine and to obtain the meridian altitude, we passed over a floe full of hummocks, a mile and a half in length; but any kind of floe was relief to us after the constant difficulty we had experienced in passing over loose ice.

After several hours of very beautiful weather, a thick fog came on early on the morning of the 6th July, and at five a.m. we halted, having got to the end of the flow, and only made good two miles and a half to the northward. The fog continued very thick all day; but, being unwilling to stop on this account, we set out again at half past six in the evening, and passed over several small flat pieces with no great difficulty, but with much loss of time in launching and hauling up the boats. Towards the end of our day's journey, we landed on the only really level floe we had yet met with. It was, however, only three quarters of a mile in length, but, being almost clear of snow, afforded such good travelling, that, although much fatigued at the time, we hauled the boats and all the baggage across it at one journey, at the rate of about two miles an hour, and halted at the northern margin at five a.m. on the 7th. The prospect beyond was still very unfavourable, and at eight in the evening, when we again launched the boats, there was not a piece of large or level ice to be seen in a northern direction.

We halted at six a.m. on the 8th, in time to avoid a great deal of rain which fell during the day, and again proceeded on our journey at eight in the evening, the wind being fresh from the E.S.E., with thick, wet weather. We now met with detached ice of a still lighter kind than before, the only floe in sight being much to the eastward of our course. This we reached after considerable labour, in the hope of its leading to the northward, which it did for about one mile, and we then came to the same kind of loose ice as before. On the morning of 9 July, we enjoyed the indescribable comfort of two or three hours' clear, dry weather, but had scarcely hung up our wet clothes, after halting at five a.m., when it again came on to rain; but, as everything was as wet as it could be, we left them out to take their chance. The rain continued most of the day, but we set out at half past seven p.m., crossing loose ice, as usual, and much of the surface consisting of detached vertical needles. After an hour, the rain became so heavy that we halted to save our shirts, which were the only dry clothes belonging to us. Soon after midnight, the rain being succeeded by one of the thickest fogs I ever saw, we again proceeded, groping our way almost yard by yard from one small piece of ice to another, and were very fortunate in hitting upon some with level surfaces, and also a few tolerable-sized holes of water. At half past two we reached a floe which appeared at first a level and large one; but, on landing, we were much mortified to find it so covered with immense ponds, or, rather, small lakes of fresh water, that, to accomplish two miles in a north direction, we were under the necessity of walking from three to four, the water being too deep for wading, and from two hundred yards to one third of a mile in length. We halted at six a.m., having made only one mile and three quarters in a N.N.W. direction, the wind still blowing fresh from the eastward, with a thick fog. We were in latitude 82 deg. 3′ 19″, and longitude, by chronometers, 23 deg. 17′ E., and we found the variation of the magnetic needle to be 13 deg. 41′ westerly. We moved again at seven p.m., with the weather nearly as foggy as before, our road lying across a very hummocky floe, on which we had considerable difficulty in getting the boats, the ice being extremely unfavourable both for launching and hauling them up. After stopping an hour at midnight to dine, we were again annoyed by a heavy fall of rain, a phenomenon almost as new to us in these regions until this summer, as it was harassing and unhealthy. Being anxious, however, to take advantage of a lane of water that seemed to lead northerly, we launched the boats, and by the time that we had crossed it, which gave us only half a mile of northing, the rain had become much harder, and our outer clothes, bread bags, and boats were thoroughly wet. After this we had better travelling on the ice, and also crossed one or two larger holes of water than we had met with for a long time, and halted for our night's rest at half past seven a.m., after nearly twelve hours' hard, but not altogether unsuccessful labour, having traversed about twelve miles, and made good by our account, seven and a half, in a N.W.b.N. direction. The rain ceased soon after we had halted, but was succeeded, by a thick, wet fog, which obliged us, when we continued our journey, to put on our travelling clothes in the same dripping state as when we took them off. The wind continued fresh from the southeastward, and at nine p.m. the weather suddenly cleared up, and gave us once more the inconceivably cheering, I had almost said the blessed, sight of a blue sky, with hard, well-defined white clouds floating across it. We halted at six a.m., after making, by our day's exertions, only three miles and a half of northing, our latitude at this time being 82 deg. 14' 28", and our longitude, by chronometers, 22 deg. 4' E. The thermometer was from 35 deg. to 36 deg. in the shade during most of the day, and this, with a clear sky overhead, was now absolute luxury to us. Setting out again at seven p.m., we crossed a small lane of water to another floe; but this was so intersected by ponds, and by streams running into the sea, that we had to make a very circuitous route, some of the ponds being half-a mile in length. Notwithstanding the immense quantity of water still upon the ice, and which always afforded us a pure and abundant supply of this indispensable article, we now observed a mark round the banks of all the ponds, showing that the water was less deep in them, by several inches, than it had been somewhat earlier in the summer; and, indeed, from about this time, some small diminution in its quantity began to be perceptible to ourselves. We halted for our resting-time at six a.m. on the 13th, having gained only two miles and a half of northing, over a road of about four, and this accomplished by ten hours of fatiguing exertion. We were here in latitude, by the noon observation, 82 deg. 17' 10", and could find no bottom with four hundred fathoms of line. We launched the boats at seven in the evening, the wind being moderate from the E.S.E., with fine, clear weather, and were still mortified in finding that no improvement took place in the road over which we had to travel; for the ice now before us was, if possible, more broken up and more difficult to pass over than ever. Much of it was also so thin as to be extremely dangerous for the provisions; and it was often a nervous thing to see our whole means of existence lying on a decayed sheet, having holes quite through it in many parts, and which the smallest motion among the surrounding masses might have instantly broken into pieces. There was, however, no choice, except between this road and the more rugged though safer hummocks, which cost ten times the labour to pass over. Mounting one of the highest of these at nine p.m., we could discover nothing to the northward but the same broken and irregular surface; and we now began to doubt whether we should at all meet with the solid fields of unbroken ice which every account had led us to expect in a much lower latitude than this. A very strong, yellow ice-blink overspread the whole northern horizon.

We stopped to dine at half an hour past midnight, after more than five hours unceasing labour, in the course of which time we had only accomplished a mile and a half due north, though we had traversed from three to four, and walked at least ten, having made three journeys a great part of the way. We had launched and hauled up the boats four times, and dragged them over twenty-five separate pieces of ice. After dinner we continued the same kind of travelling, which was, beyond all description, harassing to the officers and men. In crossing from mass to mass, several of which were separated about half the length of our sledges, the officers were stationed at the most difficult places to see that no precaution, was omitted which could ensure the safety of the provisions. Only one individual was allowed to jump over at a time, or to stand near either margin, for fear of the weight being too great for it; and when three or four men had separately crossed, the sledge was cautiously drawn up to the edge, and the word being given, the men suddenly ran away with the ropes, so as to allow no time for its falling in if the ice should break. Having at length succeeded in reaching a small floe, we halted at half past six a.m., much wearied by nearly eleven hours' exertion, by which we had only advanced three miles and a half in a N.N.W. direction. We rose at six p.m., and prepared to set out, but it rained so hard and so incessantly that it would have been impossible to move without a complete drenching. It held up a little at five, and at six we set out; but the rain soon recommenced, though less heavily than before. At eight the rain again became heavier, and we got under shelter of our awnings for a quarter of an hour, to keep our shirts and other flannel clothes dry; these being the only things we now had on which were not thoroughly wet. At nine we did the same, but before ten were obliged to halt altogether, the rain coming down in torrents, and the men being much exhausted by continued wet and cold, though the thermometer was at 36 deg., which was somewhat above our usual temperature. At half past seven p.m. we again pursued our journey, and, after much laborious travelling, we were fortunate, considering the fog, in hitting upon a floe which proved the longest we had yet crossed, being three miles from south to north, though alternately rugged and flat. From this we launched into a lane of water half a mile long from east to west, but which only gave us a hundred and fifty yards of northing.

The floe on which we stopped to dine, at one a.m. on the 16th, was not more than four feet thick, and its extent half a mile square; and on this we had the rare advantage of carrying all our loads at one journey. At half past six the fog cleared away, and gave us beautiful weather for drying our clothes, and once more the cheerful sight of the blue sky. We halted at half past seven, after being twelve hours on the road, having made a N.b.W. course, distance only six miles and a quarter, though we had traversed nine miles. We saw, during this last journey, a mallemucke and a second Ross gull: and a couple of small flies (to us an event of ridiculous importance) were found upon the ice.

We again pursued our way at seven in the evening, having the unusual comfort of putting on dry stockings, and the no less rare luxury of delightfully pleasant weather, the wind being moderate from the S.S.E. It was so warm in the sun, though the temperature in the shade was only 35 deg., that the tar was running out of the seams of the boats; and a blackened bulb held against the paint-work raised the thermometer to 72 deg. The floes were larger today, and the ice, upon the whole, of heavier dimensions than any we had yet met with. The general thickness of the floes, however, did not exceed nine or ten feet, which is not more than the usual thickness of those in Baffin's Bay and Hudson's Strait.

The 17 July being one of the days on which the Royal Society of Edinburgh have proposed to institute a series of simultaneous meteorological observations, we commenced an hourly register of every phenomenon which came under our notice, and which our instruments and other circumstances would permit, and continued most of them throughout the day. Our latitude, observed at noon, was 82 deg. 32′ 10″, being more than a mile to the southward of the reckoning, though the wind had been constantly from that quarter during the twenty-four hours.

After midnight the road became, if possible, worse, and the prospect to the northward more discouraging than before; nothing but loose and very small pieces of ice being in sight, over which the boats were dragged almost entirely by a "standing-pull". The men were so exhausted with their day's work, that it was absolutely necessary to give them something hot for supper, and we again served a little cocoa for that purpose. They were also put into good spirits by our having killed a small seal, which, the following night, gave us an excellent supper. The meat of these young animals is tender, and free from oiliness; but it certainly has a smell and a look which would not have been agreeable to any but very hungry people like ourselves. We also considered it a great prize on account of its blubber, which gave us fuel sufficient for cooking six hot messes for our whole party, though the animal only weighed thirty pounds in the whole.

Setting out at half past seven in the evening, we found the sun more distressing to the eyes than we had ever yet had it, bidding defiance to our crape veils and wire-gauze eye-shades; but a more effectual screen was afforded by the sun becoming clouded about nine p.m. At half past nine we came to a very difficult crossing among the loose ice, which, however, we were encouraged to attempt by seeing a floe of some magnitude beyond it. We had to convey the sledges and provisions one way, and to haul the boats over by another. One of the masses over which the boats came began to roll about while one of them was upon it, giving us reason to apprehend its upsetting, which must have been attended with some very serious consequence: fortunately, however, it retained its equilibrium long enough to allow us to get the boat past it in safety, not without several of the men falling overboard, in consequence of the long jumps we had to make, and the edges breaking with their weight.

On the morning of the 20th we came to a good deal of ice, which formed a striking contrast with the other, being composed of flat bay-floes, not three feet thick, which would have afforded us good travelling had they not recently been broken into small pieces, obliging us to launch frequently from one to another. These floes had been the product of the last winter only, having probably been formed in some of the interstices left between the larger bodies; and, from what we saw of them, there could be little doubt of their being all dissolved before the next autumnal frost. We halted at seven a.m., having, by our reckoning, accomplished six miles and a half in a N.N.W. direction, the distance traversed being ten miles and a half. It may therefore be imagined how great was our mortification in finding that our latitude, by observation at noon, was only 82 deg. 36′ 52″, being less than *five* miles to the northward of our place at noon on the 17th, since which time we had certainly travelled *twelve* in that direction.

At five a.m. on the 21st, having gone ahead, as usual, upon a bay-floe, to search for the best road, I heard a more than ordinary noise and bustle among the people who were bringing up the boats behind. On returning to them, I found that we had narrowly, and most providentially, escaped a serious calamity; the floe having broken under the weight of the boats and sledges, and the latter having nearly been lost through the ice. Some of the men went completely through, and one of them was only held up by his drag-belt being attached to a sledge which happened to be on firmer ice. Fortunately the bread had, by way of security, been kept in the boats, or this additional weight would undoubtedly have sunk the sledges, and probably some of the men with them. As it was, we happily escaped, though we hardly knew how, with a good deal of wetting; and, cautiously approaching the boats, drew them to a stronger part of the ice, after which we continued our journey till half past six a.m., when we halted to rest, having travelled about seven miles N.N.W., our longitude by chronometers being 19 deg. 52′ east, and the latitude 82 deg. 39′ 10″, being only two miles and a quarter to the northward of the preceding day's observation, or four miles and a half to the southward of our reckoning.

Our sportsmen had the good fortune to kill another seal today, rather larger than the first, which again proved a most welcome addition to our provisions and fuel. Indeed, after this supply of the latter, we were enabled to allow ourselves every night a pint of warm water for supper, each man making his own soup from such a portion of his bread and pemmican as he could save from dinner. Setting out again at seven in the evening, we were not sorry to find the weather quite calm, which sailors account "half a fair wind"; for it was now evident that nothing but a southerly breeze could enable us to make any tolerable progress, or to regain what we had lately lost.

Our travelling tonight was the very best we had during this

excursion; for though we had to launch and haul up the boats frequently, an operation which, under the most favourable circumstances, necessarily occupies much time, yet the floes being large and tolerably level, and some good lanes of water occurring, we made, according to the most moderate calculation, between ten and eleven miles in a N.N.E. direction, and traversed a distance of about seventeen. We halted at a quarter past eight a.m. after more than twelve hours' actual travelling, by which the people were extremely fatigued; but, while our work seemed to be repaid by anything like progress, the men laboured with great cheerfulness to the utmost of their strength. The ice over which we had travelled was by far the largest and heaviest we met with during our whole journey; this, indeed, was the only occasion on which we saw anything answering in the slightest degree to the descriptions given of the main ice. The largest floe was from two and a half to three miles square, and in some places the thickness of the ice was from 15 to 20 feet. However, it was a satisfaction to observe that the ice had certainly improved; and we now ventured to hope that, for the short time that we could still pursue our outward journey, our progress would be more commensurate with our exertions than it had hitherto proved. In proportion, then, to the hopes we had begun to entertain, was our disappointment in finding, at noon, that we were in latitude 82 deg. 43' 5", or not quite four miles to the northward of yesterday's observation, instead of the ten or eleven which we had travelled! We halted at seven a.m. on the 23d, after a laborious day's work, and, I must confess, a disheartening one to those who knew to how little effect we were struggling; which, however, the men did not, though they often laughingly remarked that "we were a long time getting to this 83 deg.!" Being anxious to make up, in some measure, for the drift which the present northerly wind was in all probability occasioning, we rose earlier than usual, and set off at half past four in the evening. At half past five p.m. we saw a very beautiful natural phenomenon. A broad white fog-bow first appeared opposite the sun, as was very commonly the case; presently it became strongly tinged with, the prismatic colours, and soon afterward no less than five other complete arches were formed within the main bow, the interior ones being gradually narrower than those without, but the whole of them beautifully coloured.

The larger bow, and the one next within it, had the red on the outer or upper part of the circle, the others on the inner side.

We halted at a quarter past three on the morning of the 24th, having made four miles and a half N.N.E., over a road of about seven and a half, most of which we traversed, as usual, three times. We moved again at four p.m. over a difficult road, composed of small and rugged ice. So small was the ice now around us, that we were obliged to halt for the night at two a.m. on the 25th, being upon the only piece in sight, in any direction, on which we could venture to trust the boats while we rested. Such was the ice in the latitude of 82¾ deg.

The wind had now got round to the W.N.W., with raw, foggy weather, and continued to blow fresh all day. Snow came on soon after our halting, and about two inches had fallen when we moved again at half past four p.m. We continued our journey in this inclement weather for three hours, hauling from piece to piece, and not making more than three quarters of a mile progress, till our clothes and bread-bags had become very wet, and the snow fell so thick that we could no longer see our way. It was therefore necessary to halt, which we did at half past seven, putting the awnings over the boats, changing our wet clothes, and giving the men employment for the mere sake of occupying their minds. The weather improving towards noon on the 26th, we obtained the meridian altitude of the sun, by which we found ourselves in latitude 82 deg. 40′ 23″; so that, since our last observation (at midnight on the 22d), we had lost by drift no less than thirteen miles and a half; for we were now more than three miles to the *southward* of that observation, though we had certainly travelled between ten and eleven due north in this interval! Again, we were but one mile to the north of our place at noon on the 21st, though we had estimated our distance made good at twenty-three miles. Thus it appeared that for the last five days we had been struggling against a southerly drift exceeding four miles per day.

It had, for some time past, been too evident that the nature of the ice with which we had to contend was such, and its drift to the southward, especially with a northerly wind, so great, as to put beyond our reach anything but a very moderate share of success in travelling to the northward. Still, however, we had been anxious to reach the highest latitude which our means would allow, and with this view, although our whole object had long become unattainable, had pushed on to the northward for thirty-five days, or until half our resources were expended, and the middle of our season arrived. For the last few days the eighty-third parallel was the limit to which we had ventured to extend our hopes; but even this expectation had become considerably weakened since the setting in of the last northerly wind, which continued to drive us to the southward, during the necessary hours of rest, nearly as much as we could gain by eleven or twelve hours of daily labour. Had our success been at all proportionate to our exertions, it was my full intention to proceed a few days beyond the middle of the period for which we were provided, trusting to the resources we expected to find at Table Island. But I could not but consider it as incurring useless fatigue to the officers and men, and unnecessary wear and tear for the boats, to persevere any longer in the attempt. I determined, therefore, on giving the people one entire day's rest, which they very much needed, and time to wash and mend their clothes, while the officers were occupied in making all the observations which might be interesting in this latitude; and then to set out on our return on the following day. Having communicated my intentions to the people, who were all much disappointed at finding how little their labours had effected, we set about our respective occupations, and were much favoured by a remarkably fine day.

The highest latitude we reached was probably at seven a.m. on the 23d, when, after the midnight observation, we travelled, by our account, something more than a mile and a half, which would carry us a little beyond 82 deg. 45'. Some observations for the magnetic intensity were obtained at this station. We here found no bottom with five hundred fathoms of line. At the extreme point of our journey, our distance from the Hecla was only 172 miles in a S. 8 deg. W. direction. To accomplish this distance, we had traversed, by our reckoning, 292 miles, of which about 100 were performed by water, previous to our entering the ice. As we travelled by far the greater part of our distance on the ice three, and not unfrequently five, times over, we may safely multiply the length of the road by two and a half; so that our whole distance, on a very moderate calculation, amounted to 580 geographical or 668 statute miles, being nearly sufficient to have reached the Pole in a direct line.

It had been an heroic effort. Parry's party had reached a record furthest North and brought back a mass of valuable scientific information.

Escape from the Ice

George E. Tyson

A member of Charles Hall's Polaris *expedition to set a "farthest north" record, Captain Tyson was unloading cargo when he became separated from the ship by cracking ice on the night of 15 October 1872. Trapped with Tyson on the floe were 18 crew and Inuit helpers. For days they hoped* the Polaris *would return to collect them but it never did, leaving them to drift south for six months in one of the epics of Arctic survival.*

Adrift, Oct. 1872

Blowing a strong gale from the north-west. I think it must have been about 6 p.m., on the night of the 15th, when we were nipped with the ice. The pressure was very great. The vessel did not lift to it much; she was not broad enough – was not built flaring, as the whalers call it; had she been built so she would have risen to the ice, and the pressure would not have affected her so much; but, considering all, she bore it nobly. I was surprised at her great strength.

In the commencement of the nip, I came out of my room, which was on the starboard side of the ship, and looked over the rail, and saw that the ice was pressing heavily. I then walked over to the port side. Most of the crew were at this time gathered in the waist, looking over at the floe to which we were fastened. I saw that the ship rose somewhat to the pressure, and then immediately came down again on the ice, breaking it, and riding it under her. The ice was very heavy, and the vessel groaned and creaked in every timber.

At this time the engineer, Schuman, came running from below, among the startled crew, saying that "the vessel had started a leak aft, and that the water was gaining on the pumps." The vessel had been leaking before this, and they were already pumping – Peter and Hans, I think, with the small pump in the starboard alleyway.

I then walked over toward my room on the starboard side. Behind the galley I saw Sailing-master Buddington, and told him what the engineer said. He threw up his arms, and yelled out to "throw every thing on the ice!" Instantly everything was confusion, the men seizing every thing indiscriminately, and throwing it overboard. These things had previously been placed upon the deck in anticipation of such a catastrophe; but as the vessel, by its rising and falling motion, was constantly breaking the ice, and as no care was taken how or where the things were thrown, I got overboard, calling some of the men to help me, and tried to move what I could away from the ship, so it should not be crushed and lost; and also called out to the men on board to stop throwing things till we could get the things already endangered out of the way; but still much ran under the ship.

It was a dark night, and I could scarcely see the stuff – whether it was on the ice or in the water. But we worked away three or four hours, when the ice on the starboard side let the ship loose again. We had been tied to the floe of ice by ice-anchors and hawsers, but when the piece on the starboard drifted off she righted from her beam-ends and broke away. I had been on board just before she broke loose, and asked Buddington "how much water the vessel was making?" and he told me, "no more than usual."

I found that the engineer's statement was a false alarm. The vessel was strong, and no additional leak had been made; but as the ice lifted her up, the little water in the hold was thrown over, and it made a rush, and he thought that a new leak had been sprung. When I found she was making no more water, I went on the ice again to try and save the provisions, if possible. While so engaged, the ice commenced cracking; I told Buddington of it, he meantime calling out to "get everything back as far as possible on the ice." Very shortly after, the ice exploded under our feet, and broke in many places, and *the ship broke away in the darkness, and we lost sight of her in a moment.*

     Gone!
     But an ice-bound horror
     Seemed to cling to air.

It was snowing at the time also; it was a terrible night. On the 15th of October it may be said that the Arctic night commences; but in addition to this the wind was blowing strong from the south-east; it was snowing and drifting, and was fearfully dark; the wind was exceedingly heavy, and so bad was the snow and sleet that one could not even look to the windward. We did not know who was on the ice or who was on the ship; but I knew some of the children were on the ice, because almost the last thing I had pulled away from the crushing heel of the ship were some musk-ox skins; they were lying across a wide crack in the ice, and as I pulled them toward me to save them, I saw that there were *two or three of Hans's children rolled up in one of the skins;* a slight motion of the ice, and in a moment more they would either have been in the water and drowned in the darkness, or crushed between the ice.

It was nearly ten o'clock when the ship broke away, and we had been at work since six; the time seemed long, for we were working all the time. Hannah was working, but I did not see Joe or Hans. We worked till we could scarcely stand. They were throwing things constantly over to us till the vessel parted.

Some of the men were on small pieces of ice. I took the "little donkey" – a small scow – and went for them; but the scrow was almost instantly swamped; then I shoved off one of the whale-boats, and took off what men I could see, and some of the men took the other boat and helped their companions, so that we were all on firm ice at last.

We did not dare to move about much after that, for we could not see the size of the ice we were on, on account of the storm and darkness. All the rest but myself – the men, women, and children – sought what shelter they could from the storm by wrapping themselves in the musk-ox skins, and so laid down to rest. I alone walk the floe all night.

Morning came at last; I could then see what had caused the immense pressure on the ship, though I knew she must go adrift when I heard the ice cracking. The floe to which the ship was fastened had been crushed and pressed upon by heavy icebergs, which was the immediate cause of its breaking up. This I could not see last night, but I saw all in the morning.

Fortunately, we had the two boats on our piece of the floe. This was a nearly circular piece, about four miles in circumference. It was not level, but was full of hillocks, and also ponds, or small lakes, which had been formed by the melting of the ice during the short summer. The ice was of various thicknesses. Some of the mounds, or hills, were probably thirty feet thick, and the flat parts not more than ten or fifteen. It was very rough; the hillocks were covered with snow; indeed, the surface was all snow from the last storm. Some of the men whom I now found on the ice were those whom I had picked off of the smaller pieces last night in the darkness. I could now see who they were. These men were thirty or forty yards from the main floe, and I pushed off the boat and went for them. Some of the men, too, had taken their shipmates off of small pieces. I do not think any body was lost last night. I think all that are not here are on the ship. I should think they would soon be coming to look for us.

Those who laid down on the ice were all snowed under – but that helped to keep them warm. Perhaps I should have lain down too, if I had had any thing to lie on; but the others had taken all the skins, and I would not disturb them to ask for one.

Oct. 16

Why does not the *Polaris* come to our rescue? This is the thought that now fills every heart, and has mine ever since the first dawn of light this morning. I scanned the horizon, but could see nothing of the vessel; but I saw a lead of water which led to the land. The gale had abated; it was almost calm. I looked around upon the company with me upon the ice, and then upon the provisions which we had with us. Besides myself there were eighteen persons, namely: Frederick Meyers, meterologist; John Herron, steward; William Jackson, cook. – *Seamen:* J. W. C. Kruger (called Robert); Fred. Jamka; William Lindermann; Fred. Anthing; Gus. Lindquist; Peter Johnson. – *Esquimaux:* Joe; Hannah, Joe's wife; Puney, child; Hans; Merkut or Christiana, Hans's wife; Augustina, Tobias, Succi – children; Charlie Polaris, baby of Hans's.

Now, to feed all these, I saw that we had but fourteen cans of pemmican, eleven and a half bags of bread, one can of dried apples, and fourteen hams; and if the ship did not come for us, we might have to support ourselves all winter, or die of starvation. Fortunately, we had the boats. They were across the crack where I had hauled away the musk-ox skins and found the children; we had hauled both the boats on the ice to save them. I had shortly before asked Captain Buddington if he would haul the boats on board; but he had only answered by ordering every thing to be pulled as far back on the ice as possible.

As soon as I could see to do so, I walked across the floe to see where was the best lead, so that we could get to shore; and in the mean time I ordered the men to get the boats ready, for I was determined to make a start, and try and get to the land, from which I thought we might find the ship, or at least, if we did not find her, that we might meet with Esquimaux to assist us. I thought that perhaps the *Polaris* had been lost in the night, as I could see nothing of her.

I had called to the crew to rouse up and see to the boats, and at last succeeded in getting them out of the snow, and fairly awake. I told them we must reach the shore; they thought so too, but they seemed very inert, and in no hurry; they were "tired" and "hungry" and "wet" (though I think they could not have been more tired than I, who had been walking the floe all night while they slept); they had had nothing to eat since three o'clock the day before; and so they concluded they must get something to eat first. Nothing could induce them to hurry; while I, all impatience to try and get the boats off, had to wait their leisure. I might have got off myself, but I knew in that case, if the *Polaris* did not come and pick them up, they would all perish in a few days; so I waited and waited. Not satisfied to eat what was at hand, they must even set about cooking. They made a fire out of some wood which they found upon the ice. They had nothing to cook in but some flat tin pans, in which they tried to cook some of the canned meat, and also tried to make some coffee or chocolate. Then some of them insisted on changing their clothing; for several of them had secured their bags of clothing. But everything has an end, and at last I got started about 9 a.m.; but, as I feared, it was now too late; the leads were closing, and I feared a change of wind which would make it impossible to reach the shore.

The piece of ice we were on was fast, between heavy icebergs which had grounded, and was therefore stationary. The wind had now hauled to the north-east. I had no means of taking the true bearings, but it was down quartering across the land, and it was bringing the loose ice down fast. But though I feared it was too late, I determined to try. And at last we got the boats off, carrying every thing we could, and intending to come back for what was left; but when we got half-way to the shore, the loose ice which I had seen coming, crowded on our bows so that we could not get through, and we had to haul up on the ice; and soon after I saw the *Polaris!* I was rejoiced indeed, for I thought assistance was at hand.

She came around a point above us, eight or ten miles distant. We could see water over the ice that had drifted down, and we could see water inshore. I wondered why the *Polaris* did not come and look for us. Thinking, perhaps, that she did not know in which direction to look – though the set of the ice must have told which way it would drift – and though the small ice had stopped us, it was not enough to stop a ship, I did not know what to make of it. But, determined to attract her attention, if possible, I set up the colors which I had with me and a piece of India rubber cloth, and then with my spy-glass watched the vessel. She was under both steam and sail, so I went to work securing every thing, hoping that she would come for us and take us aboard. I could not see any body on deck; they, if there, were not in sight. She kept along down by the land, and then, instead of steering toward us, dropped away behind the land – Littleton Island, I suppose it is. Our signal was dark, and would surely be seen that distance on a white icefloe. I do not know what to make of this.

I wanted some poles to help build a house or tent, and I sent some of the men to the other side of the floe to get some; I knew there must be some there belonging to a house I had built of poles in which to store provisions. In going to this portion of the floe they saw the vessel behind the island, and so came back and reported; they said she was "tied up". I did not know what to think of it; but I took my spy-glass, and running to a point where they said I could see her, sure enough there she was, *tied up* – at least, all her sails were furled, and there was no smoke from her stack, and she was lying head to the wind. I suppose she was tied up to the bay-ice, which I could see with the glass.

And now our piece of ice, which had been stationary, commenced drifting; and I did not feel right about the vessel not coming for us. I began to think she did not mean to. I could not think she was disabled, because we had so recently seen her steaming; so I told the men we *must* get to the other side of the floe, and try and reach the land, perhaps lower down than the vessel was, but so that we might eventually reach her. I told them to prepare the boats. I threw away everything to make them light, except a little provision – enough to last perhaps two or three days.

I told the men, while they were getting the boats ready, I would run across the ice and see if there was an opportunity to take the water, or where was the best place, so that they would not have to haul the boats uselessly. I ran across as quick as I could. I was very tired, for I had had nothing but some biscuit and a drink of the blood-soup to eat; but I saw there was an opportunity to get through, and that seemed to renew my strength. The small ice did not now appear to be getting in fast enough to prevent our getting across. But in these gales it is astonishing how quickly the ice closes together, and I knew we were liable to be frozen up at any moment; so I hurried back to the boats and told them "we must start immediately".

There was a great deal of murmuring – the men did not seem to realize the crisis at all. They seemed to think more of saving their clothes than their lives. But I seemed to see the whole winter before me. Either, I thought, the *Polaris* is disabled and can not come for us, or else, God knows why, Captain Buddington don't mean to help us; and then there flashed through my mind the remembrance of a scene and a fearful experience which had happened to me before, in which his indifference had nearly cost me my life and those of all my crew. But I believed he thought too much of Puney and the cook to leave us to our fate without an effort. Then the thought came to me, what shall I do with all these people, if God means we are to shift for ourselves, without ship, or shelter, or sufficient food, through the long, cold, dark winter? I knew that sometime the ice would break up; that at least it would break up into small pieces – too small to live upon. From the disposition which some of the men had shown, I knew it would be very difficult to make them do what was needful for their own safety. And then there were all those children and the two women!

It appeared to me then that if we did not manage to get back to the ship, that it was scarcely possible but that many, if not all of us, would perish before the winter was over; and yet, while all these visions were going through my brain, these men, whose lives I was trying to save, stood muttering and grumbling because I did not want the boats overloaded to get through the pack-ice. They insisted on carrying every thing. They were under no discipline – they had been under none since Captain Hall's death. They loaded one boat full with all sorts of things, much of which was really trash, but which they would carry. We were going to drag the boat across the floe to where we could take the water. I went on, and told the Esquimaux to follow me across the floe. I had not gone more than two hundred yards before a hurricane burst upon me. I nevertheless persevered and got across the ice, and when I got to the lead of water saw that the natives had not followed me! Whether they thought too much of their property, or whether they were afraid of the storm, I do not know; but the cook had followed me, and when he saw they had not come he ran back for them.

The men still murmured about getting into the boat which they had dragged over so overloaded, but I would have shoved off as long as I had the strength to do it; but when I looked for the oars, there were but three, and there was *no rudder!* I had told them to prepare the boat while I was gone to look for a lead, and this was the way they had done it. I had told them to see that all was right, including sails; but they did not wish to go, and that probably accounts for it. I am afraid we shall all have to suffer much from their obstinacy.

Perhaps if we had started we could not have reached either land or ship, but it was certainly worth trying. Why they prefer to stay on this floe I can not imagine; but to start with only three oars and no rudder, the wind blowing furiously, and no good, earnest help, was useless. I tried it, but the men were unwilling; and in the crippled condition of the boat it was no wonder that we were blown back like a feather. I was, therefore, compelled to haul the boat back on the ice. The men by this time were really exhausted, and I could not blame them so much for not working with more energy.

Night was now coming on; our day was lost, and our opportunity with it. We must prepare for another night on the ice.

"We had to leave the boat where she was; we were all too tired to attempt to drag her back. We also left in her the clothing and other things the men had been so anxious to save in the morning.

I went back toward the centre of the floe, and put up a little canvas tent, and then, eating a little frozen meat and a little ship-bread, I was glad enough to creep in, pull a musk-ox skin over me and get a little rest, drifting in the darkness I knew not whither; for I had had no rest since the night of the 14th – the night before we parted with the ship. All of the afternoon of the 15th I was at work, and all of that night I walked the floe. All the next day I was going and coming across the ice, and laboring with the men and boats, trying to work through the pack; and when night came the ice-floe proved a refreshing bed, where I slept soundly till morning, when I was suddenly awakened by hearing a loud cry from the natives, which made me quickly crawl out from between my wet ox-skins.

It had snowed during the night; but that was nothing. *The ice had broken!* separating us from the boat which we had left, being unable to haul it the night before. The old house, made of poles, in which there was also six bags of bread, remained on the old floe, and we were left on a very small piece of ice. The Esquimaux, Mr Meyers, and myself had made our extemporized lodgings on the thickest part of the floe, and when the ice parted we were all on this portion. As soon as I saw the position of affairs, I called the men out, desiring them to go for the boat and bread. It could have been done with safety, for there was no sea running between the broken floe, and they had not separated much at that time; but I could not move them – they were afraid. At least they did not go.

So we drifted, having one boat on our piece of ice, while one of our boats, part of the provisions, and the house of poles, remained on the main part of the original floe. And so we drift, apparently to the south-west, for I have neither compass nor chronometer with me; my compass is in that other boat, and even my watch is on board of the *Polaris*. *Our* piece of ice is perhaps one hundred and fifty yards across each way.

Oct. 17

Quite a heavy sea is running; piece after piece is broken from our floe. God grant we may have enough left to stand upon! The vessel could now come to us in clear water, if she is in condition either to steam or sail. I told the natives who are with me they must try and catch some seal. Hans was engaged as hunter, servant, and dog-driver; and Joe is one of the best hunters to be found, if there is anything to catch. If we can only get seal enough, we can live; but without seal we can have no warm food, for we shall have to cook with the blubber-oil, as the natives do. The natives have caught three seals, and could have caught more, but for the thoughtlessness of the men who gathered around and frightened them off; then the weather set in so bad they could do no more; it was thick and heavy. Weather continued bad, but the gale moderated toward the morning of the 18th. When it cleared, I could see the land – about six miles away. I thought it might be the east shore; but, having no compass and no chart, could hardly be sure where we were. "Young ice", or new ice, had formed between us and the land; but it was not strong enough to walk upon. I was in hopes it would get firmer, and then we might perhaps get to land.

One morning – the 21st, I think – Joe was spying around, and saw the end of our abandoned boat on the same floe where we had left it. He called to me, and as soon as I saw it I started off with him to try and recover it. It was about twelve o'clock in the day, and we had not yet had our breakfast. But I was afraid we should not have so good a chance again to get it, and would not wait for any thing, for we could now get across to the old floe from our own piece of ice. Joe and I started, and got it back, with all the things, and also loaded in what bread I could carry. I fortunately had five or six dogs with me. We harnessed them to the boat, they dragging and we pushing over the bad places. We at last got it back safely to the piece of ice we were encamped upon. We saved all. We have now both boats, the natives' kyacks, and are together again.

Oct. 23

We have now given up all hopes of the *Polaris* coming to look for us. All we can do is to wait for the ice to get strong enough for us to get on shore. The worst of it is, we have no sledges; and hauling the loaded boats over the rough ice is likely to injure them, so that they would be unfit for use, should we need to take to them; but it is the only way we can do to get them over to the large floe, which now lies half-way between us and the shore. There is, too, but little time to see to work; all the light we have now is about six hours a day, and not very clear then. On cloudy and stormy days it is dark all the time. But this piece of ice will not do to winter on. So today, the ice appearing strong enough, I got the boats loaded, harnessed on the dogs, and started to regain the large floe; succeeded with the first, and then went back for the second. It is fortunate, indeed, that we have the boats. Humanly speaking, they are our salvation, for on an emergency we can use them either for the water or as sledges. Got the second one over safe, and am rejoiced at that; and they do not appear to have received any injury except what can be readily repaired. There are still two kyacks on the small floe. A native will stick to his kyack like a white man to his skin, and Joe and Hans got theirs out of the ship when Captain Buddington ordered them off.

We had now got all our principal things on the large floe, except a little stuff and these kyacks. I wanted the crew to try and help save them, but could not get them to do any thing toward it. At last Joe started alone, and then two of the men ventured over: one was the negro cook, and the other William Lindermann. One of the kyacks was saved, but the other was lost. These little boats are invaluable to the Esquimaux, who are accustomed to manage them; but no one else can do any thing with them. One might almost as well launch out on an ostrich feather and think to keep afloat, as in these unballasted little seal-skin shells. But I'm glad enough they have got one of them.

The weather has come on very bad; but, fortunately, we have got our snow-houses built. We have quite an encampment – one hut, or rather a sort of half-hut, for Mr Meyers and myself; Joe's hut for himself, Hannah, and their adopted daughter, Puney; a hut for the men, a store-hut for our provisions, and a cook-house, all united by arched alleyways built of snow; one main entrance, and smaller ones branching off to the several apartments, or huts. Hans has built his hut separately, but near by.

Joe did most of the work of building these huts – he knew best how to do it; but we all assisted. They are made in the regular Esquimau style, and the natives call them *igloos*. The way they go about it is this: the ground is first leveled off, and then one-half of the floor toward the end farthest from the entrance is slightly raised above the other or front half. The raised part is parlor and bedroom, and the front part is workshop and kitchen. The walls and arched roof are composed of square blocks of hard snow, packed hard by the force of the wind. A square of about eighteen inches of thin, compressed snow or ice, or sometimes a piece of animal membrane, is fixed in for a window. The entrance is very low, and is reached through the alleyway, so that one has to almost crawl in. At night, or whenever it storms or is very cold, the entrance is closed up, after the inmates are all in, by a block of snow.

There is hardly room to turn round in these huts, and an ordinary-sized white man can only just stand up straight in them; it is as much as an Esquimau can do in some of them; but from their form they stand the weather well. A hut is often snowed under, so that it can not be distinguished from a natural hillock; but it can not be blown over; and when there is a sufficiency of oil to burn in the lamps, these kind of huts can be kept warm enough. But from their arched form, and the material of which they are constructed, it can easily be seen that they can not be made spacious enough to properly accommodate a large party of men. The centre of the dome only admits of the upright position being maintained, as from that point the walls slope gradually, until they meet the ground. In the men's hut, for instance, the dais, or raised platform, on which they sleep, just accommodates them, lying like herrings in a box, with no superfluous room in which to turn; and only two or three of them can stand up at a time.

These huts are only used by the natives in winter. The summer sun is as fatal to them as rain would be if it fell there; but when they begin to thaw and melt, the Esquimaux take to their seal-skin tents for shelter.

The ordinary lamp in use among the natives is made out of a

soft kind of stone, indigenous to the country; it is hollowed out, like a shallow dish, with an inverted edge, on which they place a little moss for wicking, which, when lighted, sucks up the oil from the blubber; and this is all the fire they have in this cold country, either for heating their huts or for cooking. To dry their clothing, they put them in nets suspended over the lamp.

We, however, did not have even a proper lamp; but we soon contrived one out of an old pemmican can, and having no moss, we cut up a piece of canvas for wicking, and it answered very well for us; but somehow the men could not seem to understand how to use it; they either got the blubber all in a blaze, or else they got it smoking so badly that they were driven out of their hut; and so I am sorry to say that they have begun to break up one of the boats for fuel. This is bad business, but I can not stop them, situated as I am, without any other authority than such as they choose to concede to me. It will not do to thwart them too much, even for their own benefit.

These boats are not designed to carry more than six or eight men, and yet I foresee that all this company may have yet to get into the one boat to save our lives, for the ice is very treacherous. But they will do as they like.

I have been taking account of stock. By our successive expeditions, in which we gathered nearly all together which was on the ice when we were first drifted off, I find that we have our two boats (but one is being destroyed) and one kyack, and, thank God, plenty of ammunition and shot.

Of provisions we have eleven and a half bags of bread, fourteen cans of pemmican, fourteen hams, ten dozen cans of meats and soups, one can of dried apples, and about twenty pounds of chocolate and sugar mixed. The pemmican cans are large, each weighing forty-five pounds; the meats and soups are only one and two pound cans; and the hams are small ones; the dried-apple can is a twenty-two-pounder. Divide that into portions for nineteen people, with a certainty of not getting any thing more for six months (unless we reach the land, or can catch seals to live on), and it is plain we could not exist. And if we have to keep to the floe, it will be April or May before we shall drift to the whaling-grounds.

We must try once more to get on shore. Tomorrow, if the

weather permits, I will try and get the house and the lumber where we can have the use of it.

Have had a talk with Mr Meyers about the locality of our separation from the *Polaris;* he thinks we were close to North-umberland Island, but I believe it was Littleton Island; he says "he ought to know, for that he took observations only a day or two before," and of course he *ought* to be right; but still my impression is that Northumberland Island is larger than the one the *Polaris* steamed behind. I wish I had a chart, or some means of knowing for certain.

Oct. 24, Morning

Blowing strong from the north-east, and the snow is drifting; quite cold. Robert and Bill have started for the old house to get two planks to make a sledge to haul the rest of the house over on, and for general use. If it is a good day to-morrow, I hope to get all the lumber and the remains of the canvas from the old place.

Afternoon

The men came back with the planks; they were very hungry – so hungry I was compelled to break the rules, and give them some bread and pemmican to eat.

We only allow ourselves two meals a day, and Mr Meyers has made a pair of scales, with which to weigh out each one's portion, so that there should be no jealousy. We use shot for weights. Our allowance is very small – just enough to keep body and soul together; but we must economize, or our little stock will soon give out altogether.

One bad symptom has appeared: we have only had chocolate prepared for the party four times, and it is *nearly all gone!* Some one has made free with the store-house. It is too cold to set a watch; but it is plain enough to be seen that things have been meddled with.

The wind is mostly from the E.N.E. Have succeeded in getting a sledge made, and the men have brought in a load of lumber and poles from the old house; no doubt we shall be able to get it all. But our blubber is almost out, and we see no seals; if we do not get some soon we shall be in darkness, and have to eat our frozen food without thawing it – to say nothing of cooking it. We need it, too, very much to melt the fresh-water ice for drink. Fortunately there is enough of this ice in the ponds on this floe, if we can only get the means of melting it.

Our present daily allowance is eleven ounces for each adult, and half-rations for the children. I was obliged to establish a regular rate, and insist upon its observance, or we should soon have had nothing. There appears to be a good deal of discontent in some quarters, but I fear they will get less before any of us get more. Before this rule was established, some got a great deal more than others. It was hard for some of them to come down to it in consequence; and in fact it has weakened them down; but it is absolutely necessary to be careful of what we have. I am so weak myself that I stagger from sheer want of strength; and, after all, the men bear it as well as could be expected – considering, too, that they do not realize, as I do, the absolute necessity of it.

Hans has just taken two of the dogs, killed and skinned them, and will eat them. I give each of the natives the same amount of bread, and whatever else we have, as I deal out to myself. But the Esquimaux are, like all semi-civilized people, naturally improvident; while they have, they will eat, and let tomorrow take care of itself. I do not suppose an Esquimau ever voluntarily left off eating before his hunger was fully satisfied, though he knew that the next day, or for many days, he would have nothing. Sailors have some kind of an idea that a ship's company must, under some circumstances, be put on "short allowance"; but that is an idea you can never beat into the head of a native, and yet of all people they are the most subject to fluctuations of luck – sometimes having abundance, and then reduced to famine; but there is no thrift in them. They will sometimes store away provisions, and build *caches* on their traveling routes; but this is always done when they have more than they can possibly consume at the time – as when they have been fortunate enough to kill a whale or a walrus, and by no possibility can eat it all.

Oct. 26

We lost sight of the sun's disk three days ago –

> Miserable we,
> Who here entangled in the gathering ice,
> Take our last look of the descending sun;
> While full of death, and fierce with tenfold frost,
> The long, long night, incumbent o'er our heads,
> Falls horrible.

May the great and good God have mercy on us, and send us seals, or I fear we must perish. We are all very weak from having to live on such small allowance, and the entire loss of the sun makes all more or less despondent. But still we do not give up; the men have got another sled-load of poles in to-day; but the ice is very rough, and the light so dim that they can fetch but little at a time. There seems now no chance of reaching the land – we have drifted so far to the west. We are about eight or ten miles off shore. Northumberland Island bears about east from us – should think forty or fifty miles off. Should judge the latitude to be about 77° 30'. Have not drifted any the last three days. The sled has come in with two additional dogs – "Bear" and "Spike": these dogs were on the large floe, where the most of our provisions were. I suppose, since we brought the food away, they thought best to follow it. A portion of the sun just showed for a little while today – his upper limb about 7' above the horizon.

Jan. 28

Fair; light wind from the south-west. Joe and Hans off again this morning hunting for meat to feed the hungry. Very cold still; -40°.

I do not see my way clear yet. Can see no land either to the east or west, so we must be far from both shores, and are probably near the middle of the strait, with a slight set to the west. We can not be near the east coast, that is certain, for they have not so low a temperature there in this latitude. They catch whales off the coast there in February, ordinarily at Holsteinborg, and sometimes even at Disco. Yet the "German Count", as the men begin to call Mr Meyers in jest, makes his countrymen believe that we are near to the east shore.

What convinces me that we are a long way from Disco, which I know so well, is, that Disco is a very high rocky island, which, if we were near it, could certainly be seen. I have been there many times, and know all the coast south of it well. Disco can easily be seen on a clear day eighty miles distant, and I have seen it when one hundred miles off, raised by refraction – not an uncommon phenomenon on the Greenland coast.

If Meyers had been left on board the *Polaris*, these foreigners would probably have behaved better, for then they would not have had any one to mislead them about our position. His influence is naturally considerable over them, because they think he is educated, and ought to know; and being also their country-man, they probably fancy he takes more interest in their welfare; just as if it was not as much my interest to get to dry land as theirs! But I have sailed these seas too often to be much deceived about our course.

I know not whether I can keep these men quiet until the temperature rises. Perhaps it may moderate in March, and then they may yet be saved; but, should they start for the shore in February, they are lost. The sun has not yet much influence. They will find no water to drink, have but little to eat, must sleep unprotected except by their wet ox-skins, if they have the strength even to drag them along; in fact, they must perish. But if they can be induced to hold on until the season is further advanced, many cracks will be found in the ice, and some of them may lead us near the coast, or at least to open water; and in these cracks we shall find plenty of seals, and on them we can live till it is a suitable time to attempt reaching the land. At our present rate of drift, we may even be picked up by some whaler.

I have relieved parties on the ice. They had not drifted so long, to be sure, nor come so far, nor so many of them; they were all men, too – not a boat-load of women and children – but they were far away from their ships, hungry and destitute. There were some runaways from the *Ansel Gibbs*, and also another party – I forget the circumstances now – from the brig *Alert*. I have also relieved

Captain Hall two or three times on his former voyages; so I hope Providence may send *us* a rescue before it is too late.

It is now, past 3 p.m., quite light. The mercury is frozen again. It is extremely cold. Joe and Hans have not returned yet. The men are cooking, or, rather, trying to warm, some seal-*skin*, which serves us all today for lunch. We eat it *hair on*, as there is not sufficient heat to scald it off. Boiling water will take it off, but we can't get that. It is very tough. My jaws and head too ache with the exertion made to masticate it. The dogs have the advantage of us there; they will bolt down long strips of it, if they are so well off as to get it, without apparently any chewing at all. They will eat any thing but stone or metal, and make very short work of their harness, or any thing of that kind, which is left in their way.

6 p.m. The natives have returned; have had no success, and we have now lost our only dog. Joe had him with him today. On returning, the poor animal was taken sick and died. I fed him last night on what I was eating myself, seal-skin and pretty well-picked bones; it may be that the bones caused his death, as they swallow such large pieces, or it may be something has happened to him that I do not know of. Well, it is the first and only natural death that has occurred, and that, surely is wonderful; but it is astonishing what men can endure. It must be that the *hope* keeps us alive, and the poor beasts have not that to sustain them. They feel all their present misery, and can not anticipate relief. It will be a very difficult matter to capture a bear now, without a single dog.

Jan. 29

Foggy, with light east wind. The Esquimaux off, as usual, on the hunt. They do not stop for fog, cold, or wind. They understand the situation they are in, and consequently they are the only ones here I can in any measure rely on. Were it not for "little Joe", Esquimau though he be, many, if not all, of this party must have perished before now. He has built our snow-huts, and hunted constantly for us; and the seals he has captured have furnished us not only with the fresh meat so essential to our position, but without the oil from the blubber we could neither have warmed our food nor had any means of melting ice for drink. We survive through God's mercy and Joe's ability as a hunter.

We are all well but one – Hans's child, Tobias. I can doctor a sailor, but I don't understand what is the matter with this poor little fellow. His stomach is disordered and very much swollen; he has been sick now for some time. He can not eat the pemmican; so he has to live on dry bread, as we have nothing else to give him. The wonder is not that one is sick, but that any are well.

The mercury is still frozen. The men are seldom outside of their hut now. From the nature of the food we live on, and the small quantity of it, there is no imperative necessity which calls them outside – perhaps not more than once in fourteen days. Oh, it is depressing in the extreme to sit crouched up all day, with nothing to do but try and keep from freezing! Sitting long at a time in a chair is irksome enough, but it is far more wearisome when there is no proper place to sit. No books either, no Bible, no Prayer-book, no magazines or newspapers – not even a *Harper's Weekly* – was saved by any one, though there are almost always more or less of these to be found in a ship's company where there are any reading men. Newspapers I have learned to do without to a great extent, having been at sea so much of my life, where it is impossible to get them; but some sort of reading I always had before. *It is now one hundred and seven days since I have seen printed words!* What a treat a bundle of old papers would be! All the world over, I suppose some people are wasting and destroying what would make others feel rich indeed.

As it is, the thought of something good to eat is apt to occupy the mind to an extent one would be ashamed of on shipboard or ashore. We even dream of it in our sleep; and no matter what I begin to think about, before long I find, quite involuntarily, as it were, my mind has reverted to the old subject. Some of the ancients, I believe, located the soul in the stomach. I think they must have had some such experience as ours to give them the idea. I miss my coffee and soft bread-and-butter most. Give me domestic bread-and-butter and coffee, and I should feel content until we could better our condition.

Joe has returned (at 1 p.m.); the weather too thick and cold for him to accomplish anything. He was, of course, very hungry; so

was I. We had two or three yards of frozen seal's entrails left from
the last seal, and on that we lunched, eating a little blubber with
it. Poor Captain Hall used to say he really liked blubber. I like it a
good deal better than *nothing!* To men as hungry as we, almost
any thing is sweet; this that we ate was frozen as hard as the ice we
are on.

Jan. 30

The change of the moon has not benefited us. There is no
opening in the ice; the weather is too calm and cold, −34°. Could
we get a heavy southerly gale, it would rapidly break up the ice;
but we have not had a strong gale from the south all winter.

It is as well to look the future fairly in the face, and none of us can
tell who will survive to see this business out. Death is liable to
come to all men; and especially may one in my situation prepare
himself for it at any moment; and therefore, considering the
possibility, I wish here to set down a few facts, as well as my own
opinion, which, whether I live or die, I sincerely hope will come
to light.

I make the above statement not knowing whether I shall get
through this affair with life. I have told Joe and Hannah, should
any thing happen to me, to save these books [this, with other
notes, was written on small pocket blank-books – *Ed.*] and carry
them home. It is very badly written with pencil, in a dark hut, and
with very cold fingers; but, so help me God, it is all true.

My present life is perilous enough; but I can truly say that I
have felt more secure sleeping on this floe, notwithstanding the
disaffection of some of the men, than I did the last eleven months
on board the *Polaris*.

Jan. 31

Fair; light east wind; the natives off hunting very early. They
found water yesterday, but got no seals. The weather is much

warmer – only 22° below zero this morning. We are evidently drifting westward. I hope to see the land soon; but both east and west there is a heavy mist, which the sun has not power enough to disperse.

Afternoon

It has now come on thick; wind north-east. I have just lunched on seal-skin. This time we have been enabled to cook it, and I discover that it is all the better – quite tender. We not only ate the skin, but drank the greasy water it was boiled in. The time occupied in heating five quarts of water over the lamp is from two to three hours.

Hannah is now pounding the bread, preparing our pemmican tea. We pound the bread fine, then take brackish ice, or saltwater ice, and melt it in a tin pemmican can over the lamp; then put in the pounded bread and pemmican, and, when all is warm, call it "tea", and drink it. It reminds me very much of greasy dish-water; but in this climate a man can eat many things which in a warmer latitude the stomach would revolt at. The offal of better days is not despised by us now. As to dirt, we are permeated with it; and the less I think about it the better I feel, for I know not how it is to be remedied. We can scarcely get water enough melted to serve for drink.

The temperature this evening is 34° below zero – 6 p.m. The Esquimaux have returned again without game. They have been a long distance to the eastward in the direction where they discovered water yesterday, but to-day it was all frozen over. They started at seven this morning, and have but just returned; and they do all this traveling on a few ounces of food daily. It is indeed a hard struggle for life, and the result doubtful.

We have just had our pemmican tea, and have each taken a few scraps of refuse from the dirty lamp. It all helps to fill up, and keep the blood circulating. Poor little Tobias is very low – nothing but a skeleton; he can eat seal-meat, but steadily rejects pemmican. I wish I knew what to do for him.

Feb. 1

It is blowing very heavy from the north-west; too much wind for any hunting today. We keep closely housed in our dens. Should an accident happen to our floe serious enough to turn us out of our burrows, leaving us shelterless in such a storm of wind, with our blood so thin, we should none of us live long.

We are poorly off indeed today; not even a bit of skin or entrails to appease the biting hunger. For the last six or eight days we have had *something* to lunch on – either skin or frozen entrails; today we have neither; and now we realize the value of those unsavory morsels, and feel the want of them more and more every hour. So do the most unappreciated "blessings brighten as they take their flight".

March 28

We have got a bear at last! Shortly after dark last evening, we heard a noise outside of our hut. I had just taken off my boots, preparing for rest. Joe, too, was about retiring, but on hearing the noise thought it was the ice breaking up, and that he would go out and see what the situation was. He was not gone more than ten seconds before he came back, pale and frightened, exclaiming, "There is a bear close to my kyack!" The kyack was within ten feet of the entrance to the hut. Joe's rifle, and also mine, were outside – mine lying close to the kyack – Joe's was inside of it; but Joe had his pistol in the hut. Putting on my boots, we crept cautiously out, and, getting to the outer entrance, could hear the bear distinctly eating. There were several seal-skins and a good deal of blubber lying around in all directions. Some of the skins we were drying for clothing, and some were yet green. Getting outside, we could plainly see his bearship. He had now hauled some of the skins and blubber about thirty feet from the kyack, and was eating away, having a good feast. Joe crept into the sailors' hut to alarm them. While he was gone, I crept stealthily to my rifle, but in taking it I knocked down a shot-gun standing by. The bear heard it, but my rifle was already on him; he growled, I pulled the trigger, but the gun did not go; pulled the second and third time – it did not go; but I did, for the bear now came for me. Getting in the hut, I put another cartridge in, and put two reserves in my vest-pocket, and crept out again, getting a position where I could see the animal, although it was what might be called quite dark. He saw me, too, and again faced me; but this time, to my joy and his sorrow, the rifle-ball went straight to its mark – the heart I aimed for. Joe now came out of the men's hut, and cracked both a rifle and pistol at him. The bear ran about two rods, and fell dead. On skinning him in the morning, I found that the ball had entered the left-shoulder, passed through the heart, and out at the other side – a lucky shot in the dark!

This bear will at least give us a change of diet, if it is still meat. He is a fine large animal, and every part good but the liver. The meat tastes more like pork than any thing we have had to eat for a long time.

It may be thought strange by those who have never lived in this climate in an igloo, that we should leave our guns outside of the hut, instead of keeping them by us; but if brought in they would soon be spoiled, because the exhalations from the lungs condense in this atmosphere, and form moisture, which settles on every thing, and would spoil fire-arms, unless carefully cased, and we have no casings.

This bear was what is called by the whalers the "sea bear" (*Ursus maritimus*), and it is almost amphibious, as it swims quite as well as it walks, only I suppose it could not live entirely in the water; and it might live exclusively on land if it could get sufficient food. It is a modification of the common Arctic bear, and necessity makes it seek its food, which is principally seals, either upon the ice or in the water, as opportunity offers.

March 30

Night before last the wind sprung up strong from the north-west. Yesterday it increased to a gale. Huge bergs – and I do not in the least exaggerate when I say hundreds in number – were plowing their way through the ice: there was quite a heavy swell under the ice, and the broad bases of these bergs are sunk many fathoms deep in the water. The floe-ice had refrozen mostly together again, after the break-up in the middle of March, and was now once more in fragments. The gale continued heavy through the night of the 29th, keeping us on the lookout for the safety of our piece. It is still blowing heavy, with considerable swell. In the night I felt a great thump, as if a hammer a mile wide had hit us, and getting out to see what was the cause, found we had drifted foul of a large berg, and the collision had produced the sensation I have described. Well, we thumped a while on the berg, and I did not know but we should go to pieces and founder; but after finally we cleared it, and sailed on, apparently without serious injury to our brittle craft.

This morning it is snowing again, with heavy drift. We can see but a short distance before us. We are somewhere off the mouth of Hudson Strait, but how far from shore I have no means of ascertaining. Our little ice-craft is plowing its way through the sea without other guide than the Great Being above.

6 p.m. Still blowing strongly, but little snow drifting. This afternoon saw two "bladder-noses" floating on the ice; got the boat launched, and went for them. The male escaped to the water; but we got the female and her little young one. Hans, later in the day, shot another young one. When the young of the seal can be secured without shooting, it is customary to press them to death by putting the foot down heavily upon them, as by this means not only all the blood is saved, but the milk in the stomach; and among the Esquimaux this milk is highly relished. The men put some of the milk in their blood-soup. These bladder-noses, when attacked, often show considerable fight, if approached with spears or clubs. But they can do nothing against bullets but get out of the way.

Our piece of ice is gradually wearing away; last night there was a heavy sea, water all round us, and scarcely any ice to be seen; but it may close again. Latitude at noon reported 59° 41′ N.

April 1

We have been the "fools of fortune" now for five months and a half. Our piece of ice is now entirely detached from the main pack, which is to the west of us, and which would be safer than this little bit we are on, and so we have determined to take to the boat and try and regain it. To do this we must abandon all our store of meat, and we have sufficient now to last us for a month, and many other things. Among the most valuable, much of the ammunition will have to be left, on account of its weight – all the powder being put up in metallic cartridges, for preservation against damp and other accidents.

We got launched, and made some twenty miles west, but were very nearly swamped, for, notwithstanding all we had abandoned, we were still excessively overloaded, what with nineteen persons and the heavy sleeping-gear. When it is considered that the boat was only intended for six or eight men, and that we had to carry twelve men, two women, and five children, with our tent, and with absolutely necessary wrapping of skins for protection from the weather, it is not surprising that we did not make much headway. We were so crowded that I could scarcely move my arms sufficiently to handle the yoke-ropes without knocking over some child – and these children frightened and crying about all the time. Having got about twenty miles, we were compelled to hold up on the first piece of good ice we could find. It was with much difficulty that through these changes I preserved Captain Hall's writing-desk from destruction; some of the men were bound to have Joe throw it overboard, but I positively forbade it, as it was all we had belonging to our late commander.

On this ice we spread what few skins we had, set up our tent, and ate our little ration of dry bread and pemmican. Hans and his family had the boat for sleeping-quarters.

On the morning of the 2d we started again, still pushing to the west; but the wind, with snow-squalls, was against us, being from the quarter to which we were steering, and we made but little progress; what we made was S.S.W. Hauled up on another piece of ice, and encamped.

April 3

Spent part of the day repairing the boat, and fitting her up with wash-boards of canvas, to keep the water from dashing over the sides. Seals are so plenty around us now that I do not hear any more croaking about the want of meat. We can get all we want as long as our ammunition holds out. After rigging our boat up, started again, heading to the west.

April 4

After a desperate struggle, we have at last regained the "pack," and are now encamped. The sun showed itself at noon, but we are again blessed with a heavy wind from the north and snow-squalls. Our tent is not as good a protection from the wind as the snow-huts. Joe, with a little help, can build a hut in an hour, if the right kind of snow-blocks can be procured. If we were on land we could find stones to help make them of. Mr Meyers has saved his instruments, and gives us the latitude of our new home as 56° 47′ N.

We are now on a heavy piece of ice, and I hope out of immediate danger: it looks compact to the westward, but there is no ice to be trusted at this time of the year. We have had a hard battle to reach it, however, and we are all pretty well tired out.

I did not make any conversation with either Meyers or the men about abandoning the small floe; for the time had come when it was absolutely necessary to do so. I told them in the evening that if the wind abated through the night we must leave in the morning. Some objected to go back into the pack-ice, but wanted to take to the water in the boat. Had I consented to that, most would probably have been lost in the first gale; for we should have had to throw overboard every thing, sleeping-gear, even guns and ammunition; and some of the men, by their expressions, seemed to intimate that they would not have hesitated to throw over the women and children to save their own lives. Then, also, we should have had no water to drink, nor any opportunity to catch game, and, getting once thoroughly wet, our clothes would have frozen on us in the night, and we probably have frozen too, as it is still very cold.

When we finally got into the boat to try and reach the pack-ice, some again insisted, instead of sailing west, on getting out to seaward, by trying to work south in the boat, which was laden very heavy, and was, of course, low in the water, with nineteen souls aboard, ammunition, guns, skins, and several hundred pounds of seal-meat; and, consequently, the sea began to break over us, and the men became frightened, and some of them exclaimed that "the boat was sinking". Of course, I wished to reach the pack without losing any thing more than was absolutely necessary, for we really had nothing to spare; but the boat took water so badly that I saw we must sacrifice everything, and so the seal-meat was thrown over (the loss of which nearly caused our ruin), with many other things we sadly needed; but the boat had to be lightened, and so I set the example of throwing away some things I prized most highly, that the men might be induced to rid themselves of "dead-weights"; and after all was done, the boat was still overloaded fearfully; but, turning to the west, by careful management we reached the pack as I have narrated, through great peril and much loss, but with all our company saved.

April 5

Blowing a gale from the north-east, and a fearful sea running. Two pieces broke from our floe at five o'clock this morning. We had to haul all our things farther back toward the centre. Soon after another piece broke off, carrying Joe's hut with it. Fortunately, the snapping and cracking of the ice gave some warning, so that they had time to escape, and able to throw out and save some few things. No telling where it will split next. It has been a dreadful day – the more so that we can do nothing to help ourselves. If there was anything to be done, it would relieve the mind of much anxious watching. If the ice breaks up much more, we must break up with it. We shall set a watch to-night. Joe has rebuilt his hut, or rather built another. This sort of real estate is getting to be "very uncertain property".

April 6

Blowing a gale, very severe, from the north-west. We are still on the same piece of ice, for the reason that we can not get off – the sea is too rough. We are at the mercy of the elements. Joe lost another hut to-day. The ice, with a great roar, split across the floe, cutting Joe's hut right in two.

We have such a small foothold left that we can not lie down tonight. We have put our things in the boat, and are standing by for a jump.

April 7

Wind still blowing a gale, with a fearful sea running. At six o'clock this morning, while we were getting a morsel of food, the ice split right under our tent! We were just able to scramble out, but our breakfast went down into the sea. We very nearly lost our boat – and that would be equivalent to losing ourselves.

Of course, while this storm and commotion has been raging around us we could not shoot any seals, and so are obliged to starve again for a time, hoping and praying that it may not be for long. The worst of our present dearth of seals is that we have no blubber to feed the lamp, so that we can not even melt a piece of ice for water. We have, therefore, no water to drink. Every thing looks very gloomy again. All we can do is to set a watch, and be prepared for any emergency. We have set the tent up again, as we held on to that and saved it. Half of the men have got in under it to get a little rest, while the others walk around it outside. This is a very exciting period. If one attempts to rest the body, there is no rest for the mind. One and another will spring up from their sleep, and make a wild dash forward, as if avoiding some sudden danger. What little sleep I get is disturbed and unrefreshing. I wonder how long we can fight through this sort of thing.

April 8

Worse and worse! Last night at twelve, midnight, the ice worked again right between the tent and the boat, which were close together – so close that a man could not walk between them. Just there the ice split, separating the boat and tent, and with the boat was the kyack and Mr Meyers, who was on the ice beyond the boat. We stood helpless, looking at each other.

The weather as usual, blowing, snowing, and very cold, with a heavy sea running, the ice breaking, crushing, and overlapping. A sight grand indeed, but most fearful in our position – the helpless victims of this elemental rage.

Meyers can manage neither the boat nor the kyack – the boat is too heavy, the kyack of no use to any one unaccustomed to its management. Should he get in it, he would be capsized in an instant. So he cast the kyack adrift, hoping it would come to us, and that Joe or Hans could get it and come for him, and bring him a line, or assist him some way. Unfortunately, the kyack drifted to the leeward. However, Joe and Hans took their paddles and ice-spear and went for it, springing from one piece of ice to another, and so they worked over. It looks like dangerous business. We may never see them again. But all the rest of us will be lost without the boat, so they are as well off as we. They are lost unless God returns them. After an hour's struggle through what little light there is, we can just make out that they have reached the boat, which is now half a mile off. There they appear to be helpless.

It is getting too dark to see the end; it is colder, and the ice is closing around us. We can do nothing more to-night. It is calmer, and I must venture to lie down somewhere and get a little rest, to prepare for the next battle with ice and storm.

Daylight at last! Wee see them now with the boat, but they can do nothing with her. The kyack is about the same distance away in another direction. They have not strength to manage the big boat. We must venture off and try to get to them. We may as well be crushed in the ice as remain here without a boat. So I determine to try and get to them. Taking a stick in my hand, to help balance and support myself on the shifting ice-cakes, I make a start, and Kruger follows me. We jump or step, as the case may be, from one slippery wave-washed piece of ice to another – a few steps level, and then a piece higher or lower, so that we have to spring up or down. Sometimes the pieces are almost close together; then we have a good jump to reach the next, and so we go, leaping along like so many goats. On arriving where the boat was, we found our combined strength – Mr Meyers, well, he was too used up to have any – Joe, Hans, Kruger, and myself – could not stir it. I called over to the other men, and two others got over in the way we had, and still our strength was insufficient. At last all came over but two, who were afraid to venture, and after a long struggle we got her safe back to camp again, bringing Mr Meyers with us. Both he and Frederick Jamka fell in the water, but were pulled out again. Luckily for them, there were two or three dry suits among the men, so that they could change. We are all more or less wet, and Mr Meyers badly frozen.

We have taken our tent down once more, and pitched it nearer to the centre of our little piece of ice, and the boat is alongside, so that we feel comparatively safe once more. Joe has built another hut alongside the tent, and we have breakfasted on a few morsels of pemmican and bread. We have also set a watch to observe the movements of the ice, and the remainder of the men are lying down to get some sleep, of which we are all much in need. Where we are the wind is west-north-west, but outside of the "pack" there is no wind.

April 9

Things have remained quiet the last twelve hours. During the night the wind was north-west; now blowing a north-east gale outside of the "pack". The sun shone for a few minutes – about long enough to take an observation: lat. 55° 51′, approximates to that. The sea is running very high again, and threatening to wash us off every moment. The ice is much slacker, and the water, like a hungry beast, creeps nearer. Things look very bad. We are in the hands of God; he alone knows how this night will end.

Evening

The sea washed us out of our tent and the natives from their hut, and we got every thing into the boat once more, ready for a start; but I fear she can never live in such a sea. The sun set clear in a golden light, which has cheered us up with the hope of better weather. The women and children now stay in the boat for safety. The ice may split so suddenly that there would not be time to get them in if they were scattered about. The baby is kept in its mother's hood, but the rest have to be picked up and handled every time there is a change of position on the ice; but we have got thus far without losing any of them.

The sea keeps washing over, so that there is not a dry place to stand upon, nor a piece of fresh-water ice to eat. We have suffered badly with thirst. The sea has swept over all, and filled all the little depressions where we could sometimes find freshwater ice with sea-water.

10 p.m. The ice closing around us fast. The wind and sea going down.

12 *o'clock, Midnight*. Things look so quiet, and the ice is so well closed, that we have risked setting up the tent once more, and intend to try and get some sleep, for we are quite worn out.

April 10

Last night it was quite calm. Today it is cloudy and very warm. The ice is closed around, and we are prisoners still.

The other morning Mr Meyers found that his toes were frozen – no doubt from his exposure on the ice without shelter the day he was separated from us. He is not very strong at the best, and his fall in the water has not improved his condition.

April 11

Calm and cloudy. We can not, I think, be far from shore. We have seen a fox, some ravens, and other land birds. The ice is still closed around us – nothing but ice to be seen. We have two large bergs almost on top of us; but, fortunately, there is no movement of the ice, or a portion of these overhanging bergs might fall upon and crush us. It is at present calm and still.

April 12

Light wind from the south-east; nearly calm at times. Have seen some seals, but can not get them. Are very hungry, and are likely to remain so. The sun is shining for the first time in a good many days, and the weather is very pleasant. Got an observation today: lat. 55° 35′ N.

April 20

This morning while resting in our tents we were alarmed by an outcry from the watch and almost at the same moment a heavy sea swept across our floe, carrying away everything that was loose. This was but a foretaste of what was to follow. We began shipping sea after sea. Finally a tremendous wave carried away our tent, skins, most of our bed clothing, and left us destitute. Only a few things were saved which we had managed to get into the boat. The women and children were already in the boat, or the little ones would have been swept into a watery grave. All we could do under this flood of disaster was try to save the boat. All hands were called to man it in a new fashion – namely to hold on to it with might and main to prevent it being washed away. Fortunately we had a boat warp and another strong line made out of strips of *oogjook* skin and with these we secured the boat as well as we were able to projecting points of ice; but having no ice anchors these fastenings were frequently unloosed and broken, and the boat could not for one moment be trusted to their hold. All our strength was needed and we had to brace ourselves and hold on.

As soon as possible I got the boat to the edge of the ice where the seas first struck, for I knew if she remained toward the farther edge the momentum of the waves would more than master us and the boat would go. As it was we were nearly carried off, boat and all, many times during this dreadful night.

We stood from nine at night till seven in the morning enduring what I should say few, if any, have ever gone through and lived. Every little while one of the tremendous seas would lift the boat up bodily and us with it and carry it and us forward almost to the extreme opposite edge of our piece of ice. Several times the boat got partly over the edge and was hauled back by superhuman strength, which the knowledge of our desperate condition gave us. Had the water been clear it would have been hard enough. But it was full of loose ice rolling about in blocks of all shapes and sizes, and with almost every sea would come an avalanche of these, striking us on our legs and bodies and bowling us off our feet like so many pins in a bowling alley. We were all black and blue with bruises for many a day after.

So we stood, hour after hour, the sea as strong as ever, but we weakening from fatigue so that before morning we had to make Hannah and Hans's wife get out and help hold on too. This was the greatest fight for life we had yet had. Had it not been for the strength imparted to us by that last providential gift of seal meat it does not seem possible that we would have lasted the night. For twelve hours there was scarcely a sound uttered save and except the crying of the children and my orders to "hold on", "bear down", "put on all your weight", and the responsive "Aye, aye, sir," which for once came readily enough.

When daylight came I perceived a piece of ice riding quite easy near to us, and made up my mind we must reach it. The sea was fearfully rough and the men hesitated, thinking the boat would not live in such a sea. But I knew that the piece of ice we were on was still more unsafe and told them they must risk it and launch away. And away she went, the women and children being all snugly stowed in first and the rest all succeeding in getting in safely but the cook, who went overboard, but managed to cling to the gunwale of the boat and was dragged in and saved. We succeeded in reaching the other piece of ice without other accident, and having eaten a morsel of food, lay down on our new bit of floe in our wet clothes to rest. And we are all today well and sound except the bruises we received from the blows and falls.

April 28 4.30

A joyful sight – *a steamer* right ahead and bearing north of us! We hoisted our colors, and pulled toward her. She is a sealer, going south-west, and apparently working through the ice. For a few moments what joy thrilled our breasts – the sight of relief so near! But we have lost it! She did not see us, and we could not get to her; evening came down on us, and she was lost to sight.

We boarded, instead of the hoped-for steamer, a small piece of ice, and once more hauled up our boat and made our camp. The night is calm and clear. A new moon, and the stars shining brightly – the first we have seen for a week. The sea is quiet too, and we can rest in peace; for, though one steamer has passed us, we feel now that we may soon see another – that help can not be far off. We take the blubber of the seals, and build fires on the floe, so that if a steamer or any vessel approaches us in the night she will see us.

We are divided into two watches, of four hours each. We had a good pull this afternoon, and made some westing. The hope of relief keeps us even more wakeful than does the fear of danger. To see the prospect of rescue so near, though it was quickly withdrawn, has set every nerve thrilling with hope.

April 29

Morning fine and calm; the water quiet. All on the look-out for steamers, except those who had "turned in", as we still call it. Sighted a steamer about eight miles off. Called the watch, launched the boat, and made for her. After an hour's pull, gained on her a good deal; but they did not see us. Another hour, and we are beset in the ice, and can get no farther.

Landed on a small piece of ice, and hoisted our colors; then, getting on the highest part of the ice, we mustered our rifles and pistols, and all fired together, hoping by this means to attract their attention. The combined effort made a considerable report. We fired three rounds, and heard a response of three shots; at the same time the steamer headed toward us. Now we feel sure that the time of our deliverance has come.

We shout, involuntarily almost, but they are too far off yet to hear voices. Presently the steamer changes her course, and heads south, then north again, then west; we do not know what to make of it. We watch, but she does not get materially nearer. So she keeps on all day, as though she was trying to work through the ice, and could not force her way.

Strange! I should think any sailing ship, much more a steamer, could get through with ease. We repeated our experiment of firing – fired several rounds, but she came no nearer, being then four or five miles off. All day we watched, making every effort within our means to attract attention. Whether they saw us or not we do not know, but late in the afternoon she steamed away, going to the south-west; and reluctantly we abandoned the hope which had upheld us through the day. For a while she was lost to sight, but in the evening we saw her again, but farther off.

While looking at her, though no longer with the hope that she had seen us or would reach us, another steamer hove in sight; so we have two sealers near – one on each side of us. And though as yet neither have made any sign (except the firing in the morning, the cause of which now appears doubtful), yet we are beginning to count the hours which we can not help hoping will bring us help. Some of these sealers will surely come by us, or we may be able to work down to them. What if we had abandoned our boat, as the men proposed in February!

Sunset. Sighted land this evening in the south-west, about thirty-five miles distant. Mr Meyers thinks we are in lat. 49°. We are not so far south as that.

Hans caught a baby seal today, the smallest I have seen this season. Our latitude, approximate at noon to-day, 53° 0′ 5″N.

April 30

The last day of April, and the last, I hope, of our long trial.

Evening. At 5 a.m., as I was lying in the boat, it being my watch below, but which had just expired, the watch on the lookout espied a steamer coming through the fog, and the first I heard was a loud cry, "There's a steamer! there's a steamer!" On hearing the outcry, I sprang up as if endued with new life, ordered all the guns to be fired, and set up a loud, simultaneous shout; also ordered the colors set on the boat's mast, and held them erect, fearing that, like the others, she might not see or hear us, though much nearer than the others had been.

I also started Hans off with his kyack, which he had himself proposed to do, to intercept her, if possible, as it was very foggy, and I feared every moment that we should lose sight of her; but, to my great joy and relief, the steamer's head was soon turned toward us. But Hans kept on, and paddled up to the vessel, singing out, in his broken English, the unmeaning words, "American steamer", meaning to tell them that an American steamer had been lost, and he tried to tell them where we came from; but they did not understand him. We were not more than a quarter of a mile off when we first sighted her. In a few minutes she was alongside of our piece of ice.

On her approach, and as they slowed down, I took off my old Russian cap, which I had worn all winter, and, waving it over my head, gave them three cheers, in which all the men most heartily joined. It was instantly returned by a hundred men, who covered her top-gallant-mast, forecastle, and fore-rigging. We then gave three more and a "tiger", which was appropriate, surely, as she proved to be the sealer *Tigress* – a barentine of Conception Bay, Newfoundland.

Two or three of their small seal-boats were instantly lowered. We, however, now that relief was certain, threw everything from our own boat, and in a minute's time she was in the water, while the boats of the *Tigress* came on, and the crews got on our bit of ice and peeped curiously into the dirty pans we had used over the oil-fires. We had been making soup out of the blood and entrails of the last little seal which Hans had shot. They soon saw enough to convince them that we were in sore need. No words were required to make *that* plain.

Taking the women and children in their boats, we tumbled into our own, and were soon alongside of the *Tigress*. We left all we had behind, and our all was simply a few battered smoky tin pans and the *débris* of our last seal. It had already become offal in our eyes, though we had often been glad enough to get such fare.

On stepping on board, I was at once surrounded by a curious lot of people – I mean men filled with curiosity to know our story, and all asking questions of me and the men. I told them who I was, and where we were from. But when they asked me, "How long have you been on the ice?" and I answered, "Since the 15th of last October," they were so astonished that they fairly looked blank with wonder.

The Last Days

Lieutenant-Commander George W. De Long USN

Ever since Richard Chancellor in 1553 had discovered a backdoor to Muscovy, navigators had sought to prise their way through the Northeast Passage. In 1879, George De Long made the attempt from the Bering Straits end, only to have his ship, the Jeannette, *first trapped and then sunk by the ice. The only hope of survival for De Long and his crew was to reach the Lena River delta. Taking to three boats, De Long's men were almost at their destination when, on 12 September 1881, a new disaster hit. De Long recorded in his journal: "Fresh E wind; temperature 31 . . . At nine p.m. lost sight of whaleboat ahead; at ten pm lost sight of second cutter astern; wind freshening to a gale". The three crews experienced differing fates. The boat commanded by Lieutenant Charles Chipp was never seen again. The second boat, commanded by George Melville, the chief engineer, reached the eastern Lena and all 11 men were saved by local hunters. De Long's boat, meanwhile, landed in the uninhabited northern Lena region. Their only hope at salvation was a hundred mile walk up the river to Bulun. This extract fron De Long's diary speaks for itself:*

1 October, Saturday

One hundred and eleventh day, and a new month. Called all hands as soon as the cook announced boiling water, and at 6.45 had our breakfast; one half pound of deer meat and tea. Sent Nindemann and Alexey to examine main river, other men to collect wood. The doctor resumed the cutting away of poor Ericksen's toes this morning. No doubt it will have to continue until half his feet are gone, unless death ensues, or we get to some settlement. Only one toe left now. Temperature 18°.

At 7.30 Nindemann and Alexey were seen to have crossed, and I immediately sent men to carry one load over.

Left the following record:

Saturday, 1 October 1881.

Fourteen of the officers and men of the U.S. Arctic Steamer *Jeannette* reached this hut on Wednesday, 28 September, and having been forced to wait for the river to freeze over, are proceeding to cross to the west side this a.m. on their journey to reach some settlement on the Lena River. We have two days' provisions, but having been fortunate enough thus far to get game in our pressing needs, we have no fear for the future.

Our party are all well, except one man, Ericksen, whose toes have been amputated in consequence of frost-bite. Other records will be found in several huts on the east side of this river, along which we have come from the northward.

George W. de Long,
Lieutenant U.S. Navy, Commanding Expedition.

At 8.30 we made the final trip, and got our sick man over in safety. From there we proceeded until 11.20, dragging our man on the sled. Halted for dinner; one half pound meat and tea each. At one went ahead again until 5.05.

Actually under way: 8.30 to 9.15, 9.30 to 10.20, 10.30 to 11.20, 1.00 to 1.40, 1.50 to 2.10, 2.20 to 2.40, 3.00 to 3.25, 3.35 to 4.00, 4.15 to 4.35, 4.45 to 5.05. Total, 5 h. 15 m. At least two miles an hour. Distance made good ten to twelve miles.

And where are we? I think at the beginning of the Lena River at last. "Sagastyr" has been to us a myth. We saw two old huts at a distance, and that was all, but they were out of our reach, and the day not half gone. Kept on ice all the way, and therefore I think we were over water, but the stream was so narrow and so crooked that it never could have been a navigable water. My chart is simply useless. I must go on plodding to the southward, trusting in God to guide me to a settlement, for I have long since realized that we are powerless to help ourselves.

A bright, calm, beautiful day. Bright sunshine to cheer us up, an icy road, and one day's rations yet. Boots frozen, of course, and balled up. No hut in sight, and we halt on a bluff to spend a cold and comfortless night. Supper one half pound of meat and tea. Made a rousing fire, built a log bed, set a watch (two hours each) to keep the fire going, and at eight p.m. crawled into our blankets

2 October, Sunday

I think we all slept fairly well until midnight; but from that time it was so cold and uncomfortable that sleep was out of the question. At 4.30 we were all out and in front of the fire, daylight just appearing. Ericksen kept talking in his sleep all night, and effectually kept those awake who were not already awakened by the cold.

Breakfast five a.m. One half pound meat and tea. Bright, cloudless morning. Light N. airs. At seven went ahead, following frozen water wherever we could find it, and at 9.20 I feel quite sure we have gone some distance on the main river. I think our gait was at least two miles an hour, and our time under way two hours four minutes. I call our forenoon work at least six miles: 7.00 to 7.35, 7.45 to 8.05, 8.15 to 8.30, 8.40 to 8.50, 9.20 to 9.40, 9.50 to 10.12, 10.22 to 10.40, 10.55 to 11.15. Dinner camp. 1.00 to 1.30, 1.40 to 2.00, 2.15 to 2.35, 2.45 to 3.00, 3.20 to 3.40, 3.50 to 4.05, 4.15 to 4.20.

Divine service before dinner. Dinner one half pound meat and tea. Started ahead at one p.m., and by 4.15 had completed two marching hours and made four miles. I was much bewildered by the frequent narrowing of the river to a small vein of ice, and the irregular rambling way in which it ran. Frequently it led us into a sand bank or deep snow, and our floundering around was both exhaustive of energy and consumptive of time. There is no use denying it, we are pretty weak. Our food is not enough to keep up our strength, and when we lose a night's sleep we feel it keenly. I had several bad falls on the ice this afternoon which shook me up pretty badly. A freshening N.E. wind had blown the efflorescence off the ice, and left smooth, clear spots as clear as glass. Frozen boots are but poor foot gear, and besides cramping the feet, are like boots of iron in walking. Slip, slide, and down you are on your back.

At 4.05 p.m. I saw more wood than we had sighted since our dinner camp, and but little ahead. I therefore called a halt and 'camped', i.e., sat down, made a fire and got supper. Then we stood by for a second cold and wretched night. There was so much wind that we had to put our tent halves up for a screen, and sit shivering in our half blankets.

3 October, Monday

One hundred and thirteenth day. At midnight it was so fearfully cold and wretched that I served out tea to all hands, and on that we managed to struggle along until five a.m., when we ate our last deer meat and had more tea. Our remaining food now consists of four fourteenths pounds pemmican each, and a half-starved dog. May God again incline unto our aid. How much farther we have to go before reaching a shelter or a settlement, He alone knows.

Brisk wind. Ericksen seems failing. He is weak and tremulous, and the moment he closes his eyes talks incessantly in Danish, German and English. No one could sleep even if our other surroundings permitted.

For some cause my watch stopped at 10.45 last night while one of the men on watch had it. I set it as near as I could come to the time by guessing, and we must run by that until I can do better. Sun rose yesterday morning at 6.40 by the watch when running all right: 7.05 to 7.40 (35 m.), 7.50 to 8.20 (30 m.), 8.30 to 9.00 (30 m.), 9.15 to 9.35 (20 m.), 9.50 to 10.10 (20 m.), 10.25 to 10.40 (15 m.), 11.00 to 11.20, 11.30 to 11.50, 11.50 dinner – 1 h. 55 m. – 2 h. 35 m., say five miles.

Our forenoon's walk I put as above at five miles. Some time and distance was lost by crossing the river upon seeing numerous fox-traps. A man's track was also seen in the snow, bound south, and we followed it until it crossed the river to the west bank again. Here we were obliged to go back in our tracks, for the river was open in places, and we could not follow the man's track direct. Another of the dozen shoals which infest the river swung us off to the eastward, too, and I hastened to get on the west bank again, reaching there at 11.50 for dinner. Our last four fourteenths pound pemmican.

At 1.40 got under way again and made a long fleet until 2.20. While at the other side of the river Alexey said he saw a hut, and during our dinner camp he again saw it. Under our circumstances my desire was to get to it as speedily as possible. As Alexey pointed out it was on the left bank of the river of which we were now on the right side looking south. But a sand bank gave us excellent walking for a mile, until we took to the river ice and got across it diagonally. Here, at 2.20, I called a rest, and Alexey mounted the bluff to take a look again. He now announced that he saw a second but about one and a quarter miles back from the coast, the first hut being about the same distance south and on the edge of the bluff. The heavy dragging across country of a sick man on a sled made me incline to the hut on the shore, since, as the distance was about the same, we could get over the ice in one third of the time. Nindemann, who climbed the bluff, while he saw that the object inland was a hut, was not so confident about the one on the shore. Alexey, however, was quite positive, and not seeing very well myself I unfortunately took his eyes as best and ordered an advance along the river to the southward.

Away we went, Nindemann and Alexey leading, and had progressed about a mile when, splash! in I went through the ice up to my shoulders before my knapsack brought me up. While I was crawling out, in went Gortz to his neck about fifty yards behind me, and behind him in went Mr Collins to his waist. Here was a time. The moment we came out of the water we were one sheet of ice, and danger of frost-bite was imminent. Along we hobbled, however, until we came, at 3.45, abreast the point on which the hut was seen. Here Nindemann climbed the bluff, followed by the doctor. At first the cry was, "All right, come ahead," but no sooner were we all up than Nindemann shouted, "There is no hut here."

To my dismay and alarm nothing but a large mound of earth was to be seen, which, from its regular shape and singular position would seem to have been built artificially for a beacon; so sure was Nindemann that it was a hut that he went all around it looking for a door, and then climbed on top to look for a hole in the roof. But of no avail. I ordered a camp to be made in a hole in the bluff face, and soon before a roaring fire we were drying (and burning) our clothes, while the cold wind ate into our backs.

And now for supper! Nothing remained but the dog. I therefore ordered him killed and dressed by Iversen, and soon after a kind of stew was made of such parts as could not be carried, of which everybody except the doctor and myself eagerly partook. To us it was a nauseating mess and – but why go on with such a disagreeable subject. I had the remainder weighed, and I am quite sure we had twenty-seven pounds. The animal was fat and – as he had been fed on pemmican – presumably clean, but –

Immediately upon halting I had sent off Alexey with his gun toward the hut island, to determine whether that was a myth like our present one. He returned about dark, certain that it was a large hut, for he had been inside of it, and had found some deer meat, scraps and bones. For a moment I was tempted to start everybody for it, but Alexey was by no means sure he could find it in the dark, and if we lost our way we should be worse off than before. We accordingly prepared to make the best of it where we were.

We three wet people were burning and steaming before the fire. Collins and Gortz had taken some alcohol, but I could not get it down. Cold, wet, with a raw N.W. wind impossible to avoid or screen, our future was a wretched, dreary night. Ericksen soon became delirious, and his talking was a horrible accompaniment to the wretchedness of our surroundings. Warm we could not get, and getting dry seemed out of the question. Nearly everybody seemed dazed and stupefied, and I feared that some of us would perish during the night. How cold it was I do not know, for my last thermometer was broken in my many falls on the ice, but I think it must have been below zero. A watch was set to keep the fire going and we huddled around it, and thus our third night without sleep was passed. If Alexey had not wrapped his sealskin around me and sat down alongside of me to keep me warm by the heat of his body, I think I should have frozen to death. As it was I steamed, and shivered, and shook. Ericksen's groans and rambling talk rang out on the night air, and such a dreary, wretched night I hope I shall never see again.

4 October, Tuesday

One hundred and fourteenth day. At the first approach of daylight we all began to move around, and the cook was set to work making tea. The doctor now made the unpleasant discovery that during the night Ericksen had got his gloves off and that now his hands were frozen. Men were at once set to work rubbing them, and by six a.m. we had so far restored circulation as to risk moving the man. Each one had hastily swallowed a cup of tea, and got his load in readiness. Ericksen was quite unconscious, and we lashed him on the sled. A S.W. gale was blowing, and the sensation of cold was intense; but at six a.m. we started, made a forced fleet of it, and at eight a.m. had got the man and ourselves, thank God, under the cover of a hut large enough to hold us. Here we at once made a fire, and for the first time since Saturday morning last got warm.

The doctor at once examined Ericksen and found him very low indeed. His pulse was very feeble, he was quite unconscious, and under the shock of the exposure of the past night he was sinking very fast. Fears were entertained that he might not last many hours, and I therefore called upon every one to join with me in reading the prayers for a sick person before we sought any rest for ourselves. This was done in a quiet and reverent manner, though I fear my broken utterances made but little of the service audible. Then setting a watch we all, except Alexey, laid down to sleep at ten a.m. Alexey went off to hunt, but returned at noon wet, having broken through the ice and fallen in the river.

At six p.m. all roused up, and I considered it necessary to think of some food for my party. Half a pound of dog was fried for each one and a cup of tea given, and that constituted our day's food. But we were so grateful that we were not exposed to the merciless S.W. gale that tore around us that we did not mind short rations.

5 October, Wednesday

One hundred and fifteenth day. The cook commenced at 7.30 to get tea, made from yesterday's tea leaves. Nothing can be served out to eat until evening. One half pound dog per day is our food until some relief is afforded us. Alexey went off hunting again at nine, and I set the men to work collecting light sticks enough to make a flooring for the house, for the frozen ground thawing under everybody has kept them damp and wet and robbed them of much sleep.

S.W. gale continues. Mortification has set in in Ericksen's leg and he is sinking. Amputation would be of no use, for he would probably die under the operation. He is partially conscious. At twelve Alexey came back, having seen nothing. He crossed the river this time, but unable longer to face the cold gale was obliged to return.

I am of the opinion that we are on Tit Ary Island, on its eastern side, and about twenty-five miles from Ku Mark Surka, which I take to be a settlement. This is a last hope, for our Sagastyr has long since faded away. The hut in which we are is quite new, and clearly not the astronomical station marked on my chart. In fact this hut is not finished, having no door and no porch. It may be intended for a summer hut, though the numerous set fox-traps would lead me to suppose that it would occasionally be visited at other times. Upon this last chance and one other seem to rest all our hopes of escape, for I can see nothing more to be done. As soon as this gale abates I shall send Nindemann and one other man to make a forced march to Ku Mark Sarka for relief. At six p.m. served out one half pound of dog meat and second-hand tea, and then went to sleep.

6 October, Thursday

One hundred and sixteenth day. Called all hands at 7.30. Had a cup of third-hand tea with one half ounce of alcohol in it. Everybody very weak. Gale moderating somewhat. Sent Alexey out to hunt. Shall start Nindemann and Noros at noon to make the forced march to Ku Mark Surka. At 8.45 a.m. our messmate Ericksen departed this life. Addressed a few words of cheer and comfort to the men. Alexey came back empty-handed. Too much drifting snow. What in God's name is going to become of us – fourteen pounds dog meat left, and twenty-five miles to a possible settlement? As to burying Ericksen, I cannot dig a grave, for the ground is frozen and we have nothing to dig with. There is nothing to do but to bury him in the river. Sewed him up in the flaps of the tent, and covered him with my flag. Got tea ready, and with one half ounce alcohol we will try to make out to bury him. But we are all so weak that I do not see how we are going to move.

At 12.40 p.m. read the burial service and carried our departed shipmate's body down to the river, where, a hole having been cut in the ice, he was buried; three volleys from our two Remingtons being fired over him as a funeral honor.

A board was prepared with this cut on it:

IN MEMORY
H. H. ERICKSEN,
Oct. 6, 1881.
U.S.S. *Jeannette*.

and this will be stuck in the river bank abreast his grave.

His clothing was divided up among his messmates. Iversen has his Bible and a lock of his hair. Kaack has a lock of his hair.

Supper at five p.m. – one half pound dog meat and tea.

7 October, Friday

One hundred and seventeenth day. Breakfast, consisting of our last one half pound dog meat and tea. Our last grain of tea was put in the kettle this morning, and we are now about to undertake our journey of twenty-five miles with some old tea-leaves and two quarts alcohol. However, I trust in God, and I believe that He who has fed us thus far will not suffer us to die of want now.

Commenced preparations for departure at 7.10. Our Winchester rifle being out of order is, with one hundred and sixty-one rounds ammunition, left behind. We have with us two Remingtons and two hundred and forty-three rounds ammunition. Left the following record in the hut:

Friday, 7 October 1881.

The undermentioned officers and men of the late U.S. Steamer *Jeannette* are leaving here this morning to make a forced march to Ku Mark Surka, or some other settlement on the Lena River. We reached here on Tuesday, October 4th, with a

disabled comrade, H. H. Ericksen (seaman), who died yesterday morning, and was buried in the river at noon. His death
resulted from frost-bite and exhaustion, due to consequent
exposure. The rest of us are well, but have no provisions left –
having eaten our last this morning.

Under way at 8.30 and proceeded until 11.20, by which time
we had made about three miles. Here we were all pretty well done
up, and, moreover, seemed to be wandering in a labyrinth. A
large lump of wood swept in by an eddy seemed to be a likely
place to get hot water, and I halted the party. For dinner we had
one ounce alcohol in a pot of tea. Then went ahead, and soon
struck what seemed like the river again. Here four of us broke
through the ice in trying to cross, and fearing frost-bite I had a
fire built on the west bank to dry us. Sent Alexey off meanwhile
to look for food, directing him not to go far nor to stay long; but at
3.30 he had not returned, nor was he in sight. Light S.W. breeze,
hazy; mountains in sight to southward.

At 5.30 Alexey returned with one ptarmigan, of which we made
soup, and with one half ounce alcohol had our supper. Then
crawled under our blankets for a sleep. Light W. breeze; full
moon; starlight. Not very cold. Alexey saw river a mile wide with
no ice in it.

8 October, Saturday

One hundred and eighteenth day. Called all hands at 5.30.
Breakfast, one ounce alcohol in a pint of hot water. Doctor's
note: Alcohol proves of great advantage; keeps off craving for
food, preventing gnawing at stomach, and has kept up the
strength of the men, as given, – three ounces per day as estimated,
and in accordance with Dr Anstie's experiments.

Went ahead until 10.30; one ounce alcohol 6.30 to 10.30; five
miles; struck big river; 11.30 ahead again; sand bank. Meet small
river. Have to turn back. Halt at five. Only made advance one
mile more. Hard luck. Snow; S.S.E. wind. Cold camp; but little
wood, one half ounce alcohol.

9 October, Sunday

One hundred and nineteenth day. All hands at 4.30 one ounce alcohol. Read divine service. Send Nindemann and Noros ahead for relief; they carry their blankets, one rifle, forty rounds ammunition, two ounces alcohol. Orders to keep west bank of river until they reach settlement. They started at seven; cheered them. Under way at eight. Crossed creek. Broke through ice. All wet up to knees. Stopped and built fires. Dried clothes. Under way again at 10.30. Lee breaking down. At one strike river bank. Halt for dinner – one ounce alcohol. Alexey shot three ptarmigans. Made soup. We are following Nindemann's track, though he is long since out of sight. Under way at 3.30. High bluff. Ice running rapidly to northward in river. Halt at 4.40 upon coming to wood. Find canoe. Lay our heads on it and go to sleep; one half ounce alcohol for supper.

10 October, Monday

One hundred and twentieth day. Last half ounce alcohol at 5.30; at 6.30 send Alexey off to look for ptarmigan. Eat deerskin scraps. Yesterday morning ate my deerskin foot-nips. Light S.S.E. airs. Not very cold. Under way at eight. In crossing creek three of us got wet. Built fire and dried out. Ahead again until eleven. Used up. Built fire. Made a drink out of the tea-leaves from alcohol bottle. On again at noon. Fresh S.S.W. wind, drifting snow, very hard going. Lee begging to be left. Some little beach, and then long stretches of high bank. Ptarmigan tracks plentiful. Following Nindemann's tracks. At three halted, used up; crawled into a hole in the bank, collected wood and built fire. Alexey away in quest of game. Nothing for supper except a spoonful of glycerine. All hands weak and feeble, but cheerful. God help us.

11 October, Tuesday

One hundred and twenty-first day. S.W. gale with snow. Unable to move. No game. One spoonful glycerine and hot water for food. No more wood in our vicinity.

12 October, Wednesday

One hundred and twenty-second day. Breakfast; last spoonful glycerine and hot water. For dinner we tried a couple of handfuls of Arctic willow in a pot of water and drank the infusion. Everybody getting weaker and weaker. Hardly strength to get firewood. S.W. gale with snow.

13 October, Thursday

One hundred and twenty-third day. Willow tea. Strong S.W. wind. No news from Nindemann. We are in the hands of God, and unless He intervenes we are lost. We cannot move against the wind, and staying here means starvation. Afternoon went ahead for a mile, crossing either another river or a bend in the big one. After crossing, missed Lee. Went down in a hole in the bank and camped. Sent back for Lee. He had turned back, lain down, and was waiting to die. All united in saying Lord's Prayer and Creed after supper. Living gale of wind. Horrible night.

14 October, Friday

One hundred and twenty-fourth day. Breakfast, willow tea. Dinner, one half teaspoonful sweet oil and willow tea. Alexey shot one ptarmigan. Had soup. S.W. wind, moderating.

15 October, Saturday

One hundred and twenty-fifth day. Breakfast, willow tea and two old boots. Conclude to move on at sunrise. Alexey breaks down, also Lee. Come to empty grain raft. Halt and camp. Signs of smoke at twilight to southward.

16 October, Sunday

One hundred and twenty-sixth day. Alexey dying. Doctor baptized him. Read prayers for sick. Mr Collins' birthday – forty years old. About sunset Alexey died. Exhaustion from starvation. Covered him with ensign and laid him in the crib.

18 October, Tuesday

One hundred and twenty-eighth day. Calm and mild, snow falling. Buried Alexey in the afternoon. Laid him on the ice of the river, and covered him over with slabs of ice.

19 October, Wednesday

One hundred and twenty-ninth day. Cutting up tent to make foot gear. Doctor went ahead to find new camp. Shifted by dark.

20 October, Thursday

One hundred and thirtieth day. Bright and sunny, but very cold. Lee and Kaack done up.

21 October, Friday

One hundred and thirty-first day. Kaack was found dead about midnight between the doctor and myself. Lee died about noon. Read prayers for sick when we found he was going.

22 October, Saturday

One hundred and thirty-second day. Too weak to carry the bodies of Lee and Kaack out on the ice. The doctor, Collins and I carried them around the corner out of sight. Then my eye closed up.

23 October, Sunday

One hundred and thirty-third day. Everybody pretty weak. Slept or rested all day, and then managed to get enough wood in before dark. Read part of divine service. Suffering in our feet. No foot gear.

24 October, Monday

One hundred and thirty-fourth day. A hard night.

25 October, Tuesday

One hundred and thirty-fifth day.

26 October, Wednesday

One hundred and thirty-sixth day.

27 October, Thursday

One hundred and thirty-seventh day. Iversen broken down.

28 October, Friday

One hundred and thirty-eighth day. Iversen died during early morning.

29 October, Saturday

One hundred and thirty-ninth day. Dressler died during night.

30 October, Sunday

One hundred and fortieth day. Boyd and Gortz died during night. Mr Collins dying.

Presumably De Long died shortly afterwards. Nindemann and Noros reached habitation but too late to save any of their comrades. Meanwhile, the first successful navigation of the Northeast Passage had been achieved by the Swede, Adolf Erik Nordenskiold in the Vega, 1878–9.

Nansen of the North

Fridtjof Nansen & Hjalmar Johansen

*The doyen of Arctic explorers, the debut trip Northwards of Nor-
wegian Fridtjof Nansen was as zoologist aboard the sealer* Viking,
*which he followed up in 1888 by sensationally leading the first
crossing of Greenland. Inspired by the discovery that the relics of
De Long's* Jeannette *had drifted across the Arctic Ocean, Nansen in
August 1893 started his great experiment – he intentionally let his
boat* Fram *become stuck in the Arctic ice and allowed the drift to
take him North. Which it did, to 84°04'.*

Pressure

Saturday 27 January 1894 . . . Severe pressure has been going on
this evening. It began at 7.30 astern in the opening, and went on
steadily for two hours. It sounded as if a roaring waterfall were
rushing down upon us with a force that nothing could resist. One
heard the big floes crashing and breaking against each other.
They were flung and pressed up into high walls, which must now
stretch along the whole opening east and west, for one hears the
roar the whole way. It is coming nearer just now; the ship is
getting violent shocks; it is like waves in the ice. They come on us
from behind, and move forward. We stare out into the night, but
can see nothing, for it is pitch-dark. Now I hear cracking and
shifting in the hummock on the starboard quarter; it gets louder
and stronger, and extends steadily. At last the waterfall roar
abates a little. It becomes more unequal; there is a longer interval
between each shock. I am so cold that I creep below.

But no sooner have I seated myself to write, than the ship
begins to heave and tremble again, and I hear through her sides
the roar of the packing. As the bear-trap may be in danger, three

men go off to see to it, but they find that there is a distance of 50 paces between the new pressure-ridge and the wire by which the trap is secured, so they leave it as it is. The pressure-ridge was an ugly sight, they say, but they could distinguish nothing well in the dark.

Most violent pressure is beginning again. I must go on deck and look at it. The loud roar meets one as one opens the door. It is coming from the bow now, as well as from the stern. It is clear that pressure-ridges are being thrown up in both openings, so if they reach us we shall be taken by both ends and lifted lightly and gently out of the water. There is pressure near us on all sides. Creaking has begun in the old hummock on the port quarter; it is getting louder, and, so far as I can see, the hummock is slowly rising. A lane has opened right across the large floe on the port side; you can see the water, dark as it is. Now both pressure and noise get worse and worse; the ship shakes, and I feel as if I myself were being gently lifted with the stern-rail, where I stand gazing out at the welter of ice-masses, that resemble giant snakes writhing and twisting their great bodies out there under the quiet, starry sky, whose peace is only broken by one aurora serpent waving and flickering restlessly in the north-east. I once more think what a comfort it is to be safe on board the *Fram*, and look out with a certain contempt at the horrible hurly-burly nature is raising to no purpose whatever; it will not crush us in a hurry, nor even frighten us.

To the Limit

On 14 March 1895, Nansen left the Fram *and, accompanied by Hjalmar Johansen (1867–1913), pushed on across the ice in a bid for the North Pole. In the beginning they made good progress of 20 miles a day, but then the unevenness of the ice and its southwards drift began to take its toll.*

3 April. Got under way yesterday about three in the afternoon. The snow was in first-rate condition after the southeast wind, which continued blowing till late in the day. The ice was tolerably passable, and everything looked more promising; the weather was fine, and we made good progress. But after several level tracts with old humpy ice, came some very uneven ones, intersected by lanes and pressure-ridges as usual. Matters did not grow any better as time went on, and at midnight or soon after we were stopped by some bad ice and a newly frozen lane which would not bear. As we should have had to make a long detour, we encamped, and Russen was killed (this was the second dog to go). The meat was divided into 26 portions, but eight dogs refused it, and had to be given pemmican. The ice ahead does not look inviting. These ridges are enough to make one despair, and there seems to be no prospect of things bettering. I turned out at midday and took a meridian observation, which makes us in 85°59′N. It is astonishing that we have not got farther; we seem to toil all we can, but without much progress. Beginning to doubt seriously of the advisability of continuing northwards much longer. It is three times as far to Franz Josef Land as the distance we have now come. How may the ice be in that direction? We can hardly count on its being better than here, or our progress quicker. Then, too, the shape and extent of Franz Josef Land are unknown, and may cause us considerable delay, and perhaps we shall not be able to find any game just at once. I have long seen that it is impossible to reach the Pole itself or its immediate vicinity over such ice as this, and with these dogs. If only we had more of them! What would I not give now to have the Olenek dogs? We must turn sooner or later. But as it is only a question of time, could we not turn it to better account in Franz Josef Land than by travelling over this drift-ice, which we have now had a good opportunity of learning to know? In all probability it will be exactly the same right to the Pole. We cannot hope to reach any considerable distance higher before time compels us to turn. We certainly ought not to wait much longer.

8 April. No, the ice grew worse and worse, and we got no way. Ridge after ridge, and nothing but rubble to travel over. We made a start at two o'clock or so this morning, and kept at it as long as we could, lifting the sledges all the time; but it grew too bad at last. I went on a good way ahead on snow-shoes, but saw no reasonable prospect of advance, and from the highest hummocks only the same kind of ice was to be seen. It was a veritable chaos of ice-blocks, stretching as far as the horizon. There is not much sense in keeping on longer; we are sacrificing valuable time and doing little. If there be much more such ice between here and Franz Josef Land, we shall, indeed, want all the time we have.

I therefore determined to stop, and shape our course for Cape Fligely.

On this northernmost camping-ground we indulged in a banquet, consisting of lobscouse, bread-and-butter, dry chocolate, stewed "tytlebær", or red whortleberries, and our hot whey drink, and then, with a delightful and unfamiliar feeling of repletion, crept into the dear bag, our best friend. I took a meridian observation yesterday, by which I see that we should be in latitude 86°10′N, or thereabouts.

Nansen later corrected his latitude to 86° 13′06″ – a new Northing record by almost three degrees.

Sledging homewards

11 July 1895. A monotonous life this on the whole, as monotonous as one can well imagine it – to turn out day after day, week after week, month after month, to the same toil over ice which is sometimes a little better, sometimes a little worse – it now seems to be steadily getting worse – always hoping to see an end to it, but always hoping in vain, ever the same monotonous range of vision over ice, and again ice. No sign of land in any direction and no open water, and now we should be in the same latitude as Cape Fligely, or at most a couple of minutes farther north. We do not know where we are, and we do not know when this will end. Meanwhile our provisions are dwindling day by day, and the number of our dogs is growing seriously less. Shall we reach land while we yet have food, or shall we, when all is said, ever reach it? It will soon be impossible to make any way against this ice and snow: the latter is only slush, the dogs sink through at every step; and we ourselves splash through it up above our knees when we have to help the dogs or take a turn at the heavy sledges, which happens frequently. It is hard to go on hoping in such circum-

stances, but still we do so; though sometimes, perhaps, our hearts fail us when we see the ice lying before us like an impenetrable maze of ridges, lanes, brash, and huge blocks thrown together pell-mell, and one might imagine one's self looking at suddenly congealed breakers. There are moments when it seems impossible that any creature not possessed of wings can get farther, and one longingly follows the flight of a passing gull, and thinks how far away one would soon be could one borrow its wings. But then, in spite of everything, one finds a way, and hope springs eternal. Let the sun peep out a moment from the bank of clouds, and the ice-plains glitter in all their whiteness; let the sunbeams play on the water, and life seems beautiful in spite of all, and worthy a struggle.

Land, at last

24 July 1895. At last the marvel has come to pass – land, land, and after we had almost given up our belief in it! After nearly two years, we again see something rising above that never-ending white line on the horizon yonder – a white line which for countless ages has stretched over this lonely sea, and which for millenniums to come shall stretch in the same way. We are leaving it, and leaving no trace behind us; for the track of our little caravan across the endless plains has long ago disappeared. A new life is beginning for us; for the ice it is ever the same.

It has long haunted our dreams, this land, and now it comes like a vision, like fairy-land. Drift-white, it arches above the horizon like distant clouds, which one is afraid will disappear every minute . . . While I was on ahead at one time yesterday morning, Johansen went up on to a hummock to look at the ice, and remarked a curious black stripe over the horizon; but he supposed it to be only a cloud, he said, and I thought no more about the matter. When, some while later, I also ascended a hummock to look at the ice, I became aware of the same black stripe; it ran obliquely from the horizon up into what I supposed to be a white bank of clouds. The longer I looked at this bank and stripe the more unusual I thought them, until I was constrained to fetch the glass. No sooner had I fixed it on the black part than it struck me at once that this must be land, and that not far off. There was a large snow-field out of which black rocks projected. It was not long before Johansen had the glass to his eye, and convinced himself that we really had land before us. We both of us naturally became highly elated. I then saw a similar white arching outline, a little farther east; but it was for the most part covered with white mist from which it could hardly be distinguished, and moreover was continually changing form. It soon, however, came out entirely, and was considerably larger and higher than the former, but there was not a black speck to be seen on it. So this was what land looked like now that we had come to it! I had imagined it in many forms, with high peaks and glittering glaciers, but never like this. There was nothing kindly about this, but it was indeed no less welcome, and on the whole we could not expect it to be otherwise than snow-covered, with all the snow which falls here.

The terra firma *before the pair was an unknown corner of Franz Josef Land.*

Bear

An incident of 5 August 1895, recounted by Johansen.

Nansen had just brought his sledge to the edge of the water and stood holding it, as the ice inclined down towards the water. My sledge and kayak were standing a little way back, and I went across to fetch it. I leant down to pick up the drag-rope, when I suddenly observed an animal just behind the kayak. I thought at first that it was "Suggen" [one of the dogs], but the next moment I discovered that it was not he, but a bear sitting in a crouching position ready to spring at me. Before I had time to get up from my stooping position, it was right upon me, pressing me backwards with its two legs down a slight incline to a fresh-water pool. The bear then dealt me a blow on the right cheek with one of its powerful fore-paws, making the bones rattle in my head, but fortunately it did not stun me. I fell over on my back, and there I lay between the bear's legs. "Get the gun," I shouted to Nansen, who was behind me, while at the same instant I saw the butt end of my own loaded gun sticking out of the kayak by my side, my fingers itching to get hold of it. I saw the bear's jaws gaping just over my head, and the terrible teeth glistening. As I fell I had seized the brute's throat with one hand, and held on to it for dear life. The bear was somewhat taken aback at this. It could not be a seal, it must have thought, but some strange creature to which it was unaccustomed – and to this slight delay I no doubt owed my life. I had been waiting for Nansen to shoot, and I noticed the bear was looking in his direction. Thinking that Nansen was taking his time, I shouted to him as I lay in the bear's embrace, "Look sharp, or you'll be too late." The bear lifted one of its paws a little, and strode across me, giving "Suggen", who stood close by barking, and watching us, a blow which sent him sprawling and howling over the ice. "Caiaphas" was served in the same way. I had let go my hold of the bear's throat and, taking advantage of the bear's inattention, I wriggled myself away from between its paws. Getting on my legs I seized my gun, when Nansen fired two shots and the bear fell down dead beside the pool.

Nansen had, of course, made haste to my assistance, but when he saw me lying under the bear and went to get his gun, which was lying in its case on the top of the kayak, the sledge with the kayak slipped right out into the water. There I lay under the bear, and there stood Nansen, and out on the kayak lay the gun. His first thought was to throw himself into the water and to fire from over the kayak, but he soon gave up this idea, as he might just as likely hit me as the bear. He had then to begin and pull the whole concern up onto the ice again, which did not, of course, take up much time, but to me, situated as I was, it was an age. The bear fell down dead at the first charge.

White Christmas

Sunday 1 December 1895. Wonderfully beautiful weather for the last few days, one can never weary of going up and down outside, while the moon transforms the whole of this ice world into a fairy-land. The hut is still in shadow under the mountain which hangs above it, dark and lowering; but the moonlight floats over ice and fjord, and is cast back glittering from every snowy ridge and hill. A weird beauty, without feeling, as though of a dead planet, built of shining white marble. Just so must the mountains stand there, frozen and icy cold; just so must the lakes lie congealed beneath their snowy covering; and now as ever the moon sails silently and slowly on her endless course through the lifeless space. And everything so still, so awfully still, with the silence that shall one day reign, when the earth again becomes desolate and empty, when the fox will no more haunt these moraines, when the bear will no longer wander about on the ice out there, when even the wind will not rage – infinite silence! In the flaming aurora borealis, the spirit of space hovers over the frozen waters. The soul bows down before the majesty of night and death . . .

Thursday 5 December. It seems as if it would never end. But patience a little longer, and spring will come, the fairest spring that earth can give us. There is furious weather outside, and snow, and it is pleasant to lie here in our warm hut, eating steak, and listening to the wind raging over us. . . .

Thursday 12 December. Between 6 and 9 this morning there were a number of shooting stars, most of them in Serpentarius. Some came right from the Great Bear; afterwards they chiefly came from the Bull, or Aldebaran, or the Pleiades. Several of them were very bright, and some drew a streak of shining dust after them. Lovely weather. But night and day are now equally dark. We walk up and down, up and down, on the level, in the darkness. Heaven only knows how many steps we shall take on that level before the winter ends. Through the gloom we could see faintly only the black cliffs, and the rocky ridges, and the great stones on the beach, which the wind always sweeps clean. Above us the sky, clear and brilliant with stars, sheds its peace over the earth; far in the west falls shower after shower of stars, some faint, scarcely visible, others bright like Roman candles, all with a message from distant worlds. Low in the south lies a bank of clouds, now and again outlined by the gleam of the northern lights; but out over the sea the sky is dark; there is open water there. It is quite pleasant to look at it; one does not feel so shut in; it is like a connecting link with life that dark sea, the mighty artery of the world, which carries tidings from land to land, from people to people, on which civilisation is borne victorious through the earth; next summer it will carry us home.

Kayaks adrift

12 June 1896. In the evening we put in to the edge of the ice, so as to stretch our legs a little; they were stiff with sitting in the kayak all day, and we wanted to get a little view over the water to the west, by ascending a hummock. As we went ashore the question arose as to how we should moor our precious vessel. "Take one of the braces," said Johansen; he was standing on the ice. "But is it strong enough?" "Yes," he answered; "I have used it as a halyard on my sledge-sail all the time." "Oh, well, it doesn't require much to hold these light kayaks," said I, a little ashamed of having been so timid, and I moored them with the halyard, which was a strap cut from a raw walrus-hide. We had been on the ice a little while, moving up and down close to the kayaks. The wind had dropped considerably, and seemed to be more westerly, making it doubtful whether we could make use of it any longer, and we went up on to a hummock close by to ascertain this better.

As we stood there, Johansen suddenly cried: "I say! the kayaks are adrift!" We ran down as hard as we could. They were already a little way out, and were drifting quickly off; the painter had given way. "Here, take my watch!" I said to Johansen, giving it to him; and as quickly as possible I threw off some clothing, so as to be able to swim more easily: I did not dare to take everything off, as I might so easily get cramp. I sprang into the water, but the wind was off the ice, and the light kayaks, with their high rigging, gave it a good hold. They were already well out, and were drifting rapidly. The water was icy cold, it was hard work swimming with clothes on, and the kayaks drifted farther and farther, often quicker than I could swim. It seemed more than doubtful whether I could manage it. But all our hope was drifting there; all we possessed was on board; we had not even a knife with us; and whether I got cramp and sank here, or turned back without the kayaks, it would come to pretty much the same thing; so I exerted myself to the utmost. When I got tired I turned over, and swam on my back, and then I could see Johansen walking restlessly up and down on the ice. Poor lad! He could not stand still, and thought it dreadful not to be able to do anything. He had not much hope that I could do it, but it would not improve matters in the least if he threw himself into the water too. He said afterwards that these were the worst moments he had ever lived through. But when I turned over again, and saw that I was nearer the kayaks, my courage rose, and I redoubled my exertions. I felt, however, that my limbs were gradually stiffening and losing all feeling, and I knew that in a short time I should not be able to move them. But there was not far to go now; if I could only hold out a little longer, we should be saved – and I went on. The strokes became more and more feeble, but the distance became shorter and shorter, and I began to think I should reach the kayaks. At last I was able to stretch out my hand to the snow-shoe, which lay across the sterns; I grasped it, pulled myself in to the edge of the kayak – and we were saved. I tried to pull myself up, but the whole of my body was so stiff with cold, that this was an impossibility. For a moment I thought that after all it was too late; I was to get so far, but not be able to get in. After a little, however, I managed to swing one leg up on to the edge of the sledge which lay on the deck, and in this way managed to tumble up. There I sat, but so stiff with cold, that I had difficulty in paddling. Nor was it easy to paddle in the double vessel, where I first had to take one or two strokes on one side, and then step into the other kayak to take a few strokes on the other side. If I had been able to separate them, and row in one while I towed the other, it would have been easy enough; but I could not undertake that piece of work, for I should have been stiff before it was done; the thing to be done was to keep warm by rowing as hard as I could. The cold had robbed my whole body of feeling, but when the gusts of wind came they seemed to go right through me as I stood there in my thin, wet woollen shirt. I shivered, my teeth chattered, and I was numb almost all over; but I could still use the paddle, and I should get warm when I got back on to the ice again.

Two auks were lying close to the bow, and the thought of having auk for supper was too tempting; we were in want of food now. I got hold of my gun, and shot them with one discharge.

Johansen said afterwards that he started at the report, thinking some accident had happened, and could not understand what I was about out there, but when he saw me paddle and pick up two birds he thought I had gone out of my mind. At last I managed to reach the edge of the ice, but the current had driven me a long way from our landing-place. Johansen came along the edge of the ice, jumped into the kayak beside me, and we soon got back to our place. I was undeniably a good deal exhausted, and could barely manage to crawl on land. I could scarcely stand, and while I shook and trembled all over Johansen had to pull off the wet things I had on, put on the few dry ones I still had in reserve, and spread the sleeping-bag out upon the ice. I packed myself well into it, and he covered me with the sail and everything he could find to keep out the cold air. There I lay shivering for a long time, but gradually the warmth began to return to my body.

Nansen, I presume

17 June 1896. It was past midday on 17 June when I turned out to prepare breakfast. I had been down to the edge of the ice to fetch salt water, had made up the fire, cut up the meat, and put it in the pot, and had already taken off one boot preparatory to creeping into the bag again, when I saw that the mist over the land had risen a little since the preceding day. I thought it would be as well to take the opportunity of having a look round, so I put on my boot again, and went up on to a hummock near to look at the land beyond. A gentle breeze came from the land, bearing with it a confused noise of thousands of bird-voices from the mountain there. As I listened to these sounds of life and movement, watched flocks of auks flying to and fro above my head, and as my eye followed the line of coast, stopping at the dark, naked cliffs, glancing at the cold, icy plains and glaciers in a land which I believed to be unseen by any human eye and untrodden by any human foot, reposing in arctic majesty behind its mantle of mist – a sound suddenly reached my ear, so like the barking of a dog, that I started. It was only a couple of barks, but it could not be anything else. I strained my ears, but heard no more, only the same bubbling noise of thousands of birds. I must have been mistaken, after all; it was only birds I had heard; and again my eye passed from sound to island in the west. Then the barking came again, first single barks, then full cry; there was one deep bark, and one sharper; there was no longer any room for doubt.

At that moment, I remembered having heard two reports the day before, which I thought sounded like shots, but I had explained them away as noises in the ice. I now shouted to Johansen that I heard dogs farther inland. Johansen started up from the bag where he lay sleeping, and tumbled out of the tent. "Dogs?" He could not quite take it in, but had to get up and listen with his own ears, while I got breakfast ready. He very much doubted the possiblity of such a thing, yet fancied once or twice that he heard something which might be taken for the barking of dogs; but then it was drowned again in the bird-noises, and, everything considered, he thought that what I had heard was nothing more than that. I said he might believe what he liked, but I meant to set off as quickly as possible, and was impatient to get breakfast swallowed. I had emptied the last of the Indian meal into the soup, feeling sure that we should have farinaceous food enough by the evening. As we were eating we discussed who it could be, whether our countrymen or Englishmen. If it was the English expedition to Franz Josef Land which had been in contemplation when we started, what should we do? "Oh, we'll just have to remain with them a day or two," said Johansen, "and then we'll have to go on to Spitzbergen, else it will be too long before we get home." We were quite agreed on this point; but we would take care to get some good provisions for the voyage out of them. While I went on, Johansen was to stay behind and mind the kayaks, so that we should run no risk of their drifting away with the ice. I got out my snow-shoes, glass, and gun, and was ready. Before starting, I went up once more to listen, and look out a road across the uneven ice to the land. But there was not a sound like the barking of dogs, only noisy auks, harsh-toned little auks, and screaming kittiwakes. Was it these, after all, that I had heard? I set off in doubt.

Then in front of me I saw the fresh tracks of an animal. They could hardly have been made by a fox, for if they were, the foxes here must be bigger than any I had ever seen. But dogs? Could a dog have been no more than a few hundred paces from us in the night without barking, or without our having heard it? It seemed scarcely probable; but whatever it was, it could never have been a fox. A wolf, then? I went on, my mind full of strange thoughts, hovering between certainty and doubt. Was all our toil, were all our troubles, privations, and sufferings, to end here? It seemed incredible, and yet . . . Out of the shadowland of doubt, certainty was at last beginning to dawn. Again the sound of a dog yelping reached my ear, more distinctly than ever; I saw more and more tracks which could be nothing but those of a dog. Among them were foxes' tracks and how small they looked! A long time passed, and nothing was to be heard but the noise of the birds. Again arose doubt as to whether it was all an illusion. Perhaps it was only a dream. But then I remembered the dogs' tracks; they, at any rate, were no delusion. But if there were people here, we could scarcely be on Gillies Land or a new land, as we had believed all the winter. We must after all be upon the south side of Franz Josef Land, and the suspicion I had had a few days ago was correct, namely, that we had come south through an unknown sound and out between Hooker Island and Northbrook Island, and were now off the latter, in spite of the impossibility of reconciling our position with Payer's map.

It was with a strange mixture of feelings that I made my way in towards land among the numerous hummocks and inequalities. Suddenly I thought I heard a shout from a human voice, a strange voice, the first for three years. How my heart beat, and the blood rushed to my brain, as I ran up on to a hummock, and hallooed with all the strength of my lungs. Behind that one human voice in the midst of the icy desert, this one message from life, stood home and she who was waiting there; and I saw nothing else as I made my way between bergs and ice-ridges. Soon I heard another shout, and saw, too, from an ice-ridge, a dark form moving among the hummocks farther in. It was a dog; but farther off came another figure, and that was a man. Who was it? Was it Jackson or one of his companions, or was it perhaps a fellow-countryman? We approached one another quickly; I waved my hat: he did the same. I heard him speak to the dog, and I listened. It was English, and as I drew nearer I thought I recognized Mr Jackson, whom I remembered once to have seen.

I raised my hat; we extended a hand to one another, with a

hearty "How do you do?" Above us a roof of mist, shutting out the world around, beneath our feet the rugged, packed drift-ice, and in the background a glimpse of the land, all ice, glacier, and mist. On one side the civilized European in an English check suit and high rubber water-boots, well shaved, well groomed, bringing with him a perfume of scented soap, perceptible to the wild man's sharpened senses; on the other side the wild man, clad in dirty rags, black with oil and soot, with long, uncombed hair and shaggy beard, black with smoke, with a face in which the natural fair complexion could not possibly be discerned through the thick layer of fat and soot which a winter's endeavours with warm water, moss, rags, and at last a knife had sought in vain to remove. No one suspected who he was or whence he came.

Jackson: "I'm immensely glad to see you."

"Thank you, I also."

"Have you a ship here?"

"No; my ship is not here."

"How many are there of you?"

"I have one companion at the ice-edge."

As we talked, we had begun to go in towards land. I took it for granted that he had recognized me, or at any rate understood who it was that was hidden behind this savage exterior, not thinking that a total stranger would be received so heartily. Suddenly he stopped, looked me full in the face, and said quickly:

"Aren't you Nansen?"

"Yes, I am."

"By Jove! I am glad to see you!"

And he seized my hand and shook it again, while his whole face became one smile of welcome, and delight at the unexpected meeting beamed from his dark eyes.

"Where have you come from now?" he asked.

"I left the *Fram* in 84°N lat., after having drifted for two years, and I reached the 86°15′ parallel, where we had to turn and make for Franz Josef Land. We were, however, obliged to stop for the winter somewhere north [of] here, and are now on our route to Spitzbergen."

"I congratulate you most heartily. You have made a good trip of it, and I am awfully glad to be the first person to congratulate you on your return."

Once more he seized my hand, and shook it heartily. I could not have been welcomed more warmly; that hand-shake was more than a mere form. In his hospitable English manner, he said at once that he had "plenty of room" for us, and that he was expecting his ship every day. By "plenty of room" I discovered afterwards that he meant that there were still a few square feet on the floor of their hut that were not occupied at night by himself and his sleeping companions. But "heart-room makes house-room," and of the former there was no lack.

As soon as I could get a word in, I asked how things were getting on at home, and he was able to give me the welcome intelligence that my wife and child had both been in the best of health when he left two years ago. Then came Norway's turn, and Norwegian politics; but he knew nothing about that, and I took it as a sign that they must be all right too. He now asked if we could not go out at once, and fetch Johansen and our belongings; but I thought that our kayaks would be too heavy for us to drag over this packed-up ice alone, and that if he had men enough it would certainly be better to send them out. If we only gave Johansen notice by a salute from our guns, he would wait patiently; so we each fired two shots. We soon met several men: Mr Armitage, the second in command, Mr Child, the photographer, and the doctor, Mr Koetlitz. As they approached, Jackson gave them a sign, and let them understand who I was; and I was again welcomed heartily. We met yet others: the botanist, Mr Fisher, Mr Burgess, and the Finn Blomqvist (his real name was Melenius). Fisher has since told me that he at once thought it must be me when he saw a man out on the ice; but he quite gave up that idea when he met me, for he had seen me described as a fair man, and here was a dark man, with black hair and beard. When they were all there, Jackson said that I had reached 86°15′N lat., and from seven powerful lungs I was given a triple British cheer, that echoed among the hummocks.

Where the *Eagle* Dared

Salomon Andrée

On 11 July 1897 the Swedish balloonist Salomon Andrée and two companions, Nils Strindberg and Knud Fraenkel, boarded the balloon Ornen (Eagle) *on Danes Island, off Spitzbergen. Their destination was the North Pole. From the outset, the voyage fared ill, with the loss of a guide-rope on launch. Other disasters followed. The unpowered balloon was carried the wrong way by the wind and the silk skin consistently leaked hydrogen. Just three days later the* Eagle *crashed on the ice of the Arctic Ocean at 82°56'N:*

12 July 1897

Although we could have thrown out ballast, and although the wind might, perhaps, carry us to Greenland, we determined to be content with standing still. We have been obliged to throw out very much ballast to-day and have not had any sleep nor been allowed any rest from the repeated bumpings, and we probably could not have stood it much longer. All three of us must have a rest, and I sent Strindb. and Fr. to bed at 11.20 o'cl. (5567), and I mean to let them sleep until 6 or 7 o'cl. if I can manage to keep watch until then. Then I shall try to get some rest myself. If either of them should succumb it might be because I had tired them out.

It is not a little strange to be floating here above the Polar Sea. To be the first that have floated here in a balloon. How soon, I wonder, shall we have successors? Shall we be thought mad or will our example be followed? I cannot deny but that all three of us are dominated by a feeling of pride. We think we can well face death, having done what we have done. Is not the whole, perhaps, the expression of an extremely strong sense of individuality which cannot bear the thought of living and dying like a man in the ranks, forgotten by coming generations? Is this ambition?

The rattling of the guide-lines in the snow and the flapping of the sails are the only sounds heard, except the whining in the basket.

14 July

11 o'cl. p.m. we jumped out of the balloon. The landing . . . Worn out and famished but 7 hours' hard work had to be done before we could recreate ourselves.

22 July

6.45 p.m. break camp. Nisse's sledge turned over and lay there in the water. 4 hr. march. Night-camp. Sunshine beautiful ice . . .

23 July

Break camp 2 p.m. Difficulties at once. Astr. obs. meteorol. Follow bear-tracks. Ferrying across with the sledges extremely risky. 4 little auks 2 ivory gulls 1 fulmar. Weather misty and windy. Snow moister. The leads more difficult. The hummocks inconsiderable. Ice on the pools. Tenting at 11 p.m. in lee of a big hummock. Nisse's cooking exp. bread, rousseau, butter, pease, soup-tablets. Hammarspik's poems. 24/7 broke camp 2.10 o'cl. several bad leads and ice-humps. The travelling bad and we were extremely fatigued. Dangerous ferryings and violent twistings, etc., of the sledges among the hummocks, etc. Followed the edge of a large lead almost the whole time.

25 July

Breaking camp delayed by rain. New method of travelling: along leads and on smoother ice, wet snow and bad going. Gull with red belly. Wings blue underneath and above. Dark ring around neck. Seals often in openings, never in herds. talked rot about seals. Nisse fell in and was in imminent danger of drowning. He was dried and wrung out and dressed in knickerbockers. Stopped short at a lead.

Load on my sledge the 26th on altering load

	Kilo	(before) lbs.
4 ice-planks	8.50	18.7
3 bamboo-p (oles)	2.00	4.4
1 carrying-ring plank	1.00	2.2
1 boat-hook	1.50	3.3
1 bottom-tarpauling	1.00	2.2
1 sack private	17.5	38.5
1 △ basket	29.00	64.–
1 pot boot-grease	3.5	7.75
1 hose	3.5	7.75
1 large press	8.00	17.5
1 shovel and 1 reserve cross-piece	1.8	4.–
1 basket with contents	65.00	143.–
1 d:o	66.5	146.–
	208.8	459.3
Grapnel with rope	2.00	4.4
	210.8	463.7

26 July

At [?] o'cl. p.m. we began with the rafting. 1 big & 1 little bear visit during night around the tent. Northerly wind, hurra. Place-determination Long. 30° 15′–30° 47′ and Lat. 82° 36′. Strindberg's bear. Bear-beef immensely good. Meat 1 hour in seawater then all well. Sledges broken. Iron-sheathing as experiment. Mending and examination of weight and considerable reduction.

Revision of plan of journey. No time for sledge-pulling. Equipment for 45 days. Strange feelings and great indulgence in food on making reduction. To sleep at last about 7 a.m. on the 27 July.

28 July

8 p.m. turned out, sheathing sledges. Begin with snow-shoes. Repair of Fraenkel's gear. Paradise; large smooth ice-floes without hummocks or leads or more melted snow-water than was needed for drinking. *"Parade-ice"* Fr. "what old mammy sends us is always confoundedly good, anyway." Terrible under foot to begin with but in the evening magnificent ice and magnificent weather. The wind is felt much but is always welcome when it drives towards S E. To-day we have crossed a number of bear-tracks but not a single lead. Now however we have come to a broad beast which we must get [. . .] tomorrow. Now we have turned in 12 o'cl. noon the 29 after having thus been at work 16 hours. We learn the poor man's way: to make use of *everything*. We also learn the art of living from one day to the other.

Describe in detail. Difficulties with the ice, the hummocks, melted snow-water, the (melted snow) pools and the leads and the floes of broken ice.

31 July

5 o'cl. a.m. start. "Tramp" on our knees in deep snow. "Tramp – tramp" on our knees. Discoverer of attractions of flopping = Nisse. Cut our way. The constant fog prevents us from choosing good road. Ever since the start we have been in very difficult country. The Polar dist. is certainly the birthplace of the principle of the greatest stumbling-blocks. 10 leads during the first 6 hours.

2 August

At 12 o'cl. midd. We broke camp. The last bear-meat was cut into small pieces so that it might at least *look like* being a lot.

Thickness of ice 1.2 m. (3.96 ft.). Scarcely an hour after breaking camp we got a new bear. It was an old worn-out male animal with rotten teeth. I brought it down by a shot in the chest at a distance of 38 m. (125 ft.) S-g and Fr-1 both fired outers. Clear calm and hot the whole day but the country extraordinarily difficult. I do not think we made 2 km. (2,200 yds.) in 10 hours. Axe destroyed. 1 skua visible and 2 gulls circling around the body of the bear. We did not get into our berths before 2 a.m. the 3 Aug. I washed my face for the first time since the 11 July and in the evening I mended a stocking. We hope that one bear will be enticed to follow us by the remains of the one shot, and so on so that we shall always have fresh meat at our heels. This time we took from the one we shot the fillet too (close in to the back) and the kidneys (1½ kilo – 3¼ lbs) and the tongue and ribs. The 3 Aug. at 12 o'cl. we rose after being much plagued by the heat in the tent. We have determined to "lie outdoors" today . . . It is so warm that we do the pulling without any coats on. The ice horrible. Clothes-drying on a large scale. I made a fork for Fraenkel.

5 August

Stock-taking of provisions

Hard bread 11b. of 1.1 (2.4 lbs)	12.1 (20.4 lbs)
12 biscuits 12 bl of	15.5 (34.1 lbs)
+5 Mellin's food	15.00 (33 lbs)
butter 17 b. of 900 (2 lbs)	15.30 (34 lbs)
Chocolate powder 9 b. of 1 (2.2 lbs) extr.	9.00 (20 lbs)
milk 10 b. of 250 (½ lb)	2.5 (5 lbs)
Lact scr. 10 b. of	2.5 (5 lbs)
Pemmican	3.0 (6.5 lbs)
Sugar	5.00 (11 lbs)
1 tin Stauffer prep	4.5 (10 lbs)
Coffee	2.00 (4.5 lbs)
1 tin chocolate	
3 b. Lime-juice tablets	
Whortleberry jam	1.00 (2.2 lbs)
9 tins sardines	
3 tins paste	

Soup tablets 3½ tins
2 bottles syrup
1 bottle port-wine
6 snowflake
flour   1. (2.2 lbs)

This stocktaking shows that we must be careful especially with
the bread.

Temp. falling still lower and each degree makes us creep
deeper down into the sleeping-sack. Bad day to-day the first
with course N 40° W = Seven Islands.

9 August

[. . .] At 7.30 o'cl. I saw a hummock formed in a lane which was
at right angles to the direction of the wind which led to a
pressure. The country consists of large uneven fields full of
brown ice small hummocks with snow-sludge and water-pools
but not many large sea-leads. It is extremely tiring. F. has
diarrhœa for 2nd time and there does not seem much left of his
moral strength. The sweet-water leads were often not so very
"sweet" to cross. A black guillemot visible. A fine beautiful
bear approached us but fled before we had a chance to shoot.
This was a great grief for us and a pity too for soon we shall
have no more bear's meat left. S. and F. went after him but in
vain. We were tired out and F. was ill. I gave him opium for the
diarrhœa. Afterwards we had several hours' work getting S's
gun in order. Its mechanism is dreadfully carelessly constructed. We have been awake and busy for 18 hours when
at 8 o'cl. p.m. we creep down into the sleeping-sack. The course
always S 40° W. The 10 at 6.10 o'cl. a.m. all up. Load on *my
sledge*

1 little sack	3.5	(7.7 lbs.)
1 front basket	37.1	81.7
1 rear basket	37.3	82.
1 private sack	15.5	34
1 medicine chest	9.00	20

1 tent	9.0	20
2 tentp	1.5	3.3
meat	5.0	11
	117.9	259.7
1 gun	1.6	3.5
	119.5	263.2
1 b. ammunition . . .	6.5	14.3
	126.0 kilo	277.5 lbs.
1 sext.	2.2	4.8
1 sack	6.0 photog.	13.2
	134.2	295.5

The ground extraordinarily difficult. absolutely untrafficable sludge-pools encountered today. they consist of broad channels filled with small lumps of ice and snow? Neither sledge nor boat can be moved forward there. In consequence of the place-determination given above the course was altered to S 50°W. (to the Seven Islands). It is remarkable that we have travelled so far in latitude in spite of the wind having been right against us for several days. In consequence of our having come below 82 we have to-day had a feast with sardines for dinner and a Stauffer-cake for supper. The going to-day has been good although the road is bad. We assume that we have gone 3 kilometers (1.8 mile) or possib. 2 minutes . . .

11 August

was a regular Tycho Brahe-day [unlucky day]. At once in the morning I came into the water and so did my sledge so that nearly everything became wet through. S. ran in to F's sledge and broke the boat with the grapnel. All the sledges turned somersaults repeatedly during the course of the day. Mine was twice turned completely up and down. The going was good but the country terrible . . . A peculiar incident happened on crossing a lead. We stood quite at a loss what to do for the edges of the ice were wretched and the channel so shallow that the boat could not float. Our ordinary methods failed us altogether. Then while we were speaking the ice-floe broke beneath Fraenkel and so we obtained a bit of ice of considerable size and with the assistance of this piece we then made the crossing quite cleverly. We have not been able to keep the course but have been obliged to go both to the north and to the east but endeavour to go S 50° W. Our distance to-day probably did not exceed 3.5 km. (2.1 miles).

At 4.30 p.m. our longitude was 30° E. At midday our latitude was 81° 54′ 7. F. thought he saw land and it was really so like land that we changed the course in that direction but it was found to be merely a peculiarly shaped large hummock.

13 August

5 p.m. start . . . Tried in vain to get a seal. The ice reasonably good. In a fissure found a little fish which was pretty unafraid and seemed to be astonished at sight of us. I killed him with the shovel . . . Just when we had passed the fissure S-g cried "three bears". We were at once in motion and full of excited expectation. Warned by our preceding disappointments we now went to work carefully. We concealed ourselves behind a hummock and waited but no bears came. Then I chose myself as a bait and crept forward along the plain whistling softly. The she-bear became attentive, came forward winding me but turned round again and lay down. At last it was too cold for me to lie immovably in the snow and then I called out to the others that we should rush up to the bears. We did so. Then the she-bear came towards me but was met by a shot which missed. I sprang up however and shot again while the bear that were fleeing, stopped for a moment then the she-bear was wounded at a distance of 80 paces but ran a little way whereupon I dropped her on the spot at 94 paces. My 4th shot dropped one cub. Then the third one ran but was wounded by Fraenkel and dropped by Strindberg who had had a longer way to go and so could not come up as quickly as I. There was great joy in the caravan and we cut our bears in pieces with pleasure and loaded our sledges with not less than 42 kilogrammes (138 lbs) i.e., with fresh meat for 23 days. Among the experiences we made with regard to the value of the parts of the bear it may be mentioned that we found the heart, brain and kidneys very palatable. The tongue too is well worth taking.

The meat on the ribs is excellent. In the evening I shot an ivory gull. The work of cutting up the bears, etc. gave us so much to do that we did not march much this day. The wind has now swung round to S E so that we hope to drift westwards. Today the weather has been extremely beautiful and that is a good thing for otherwise the work would have been ticklish. When a bear is hit he brings out a roar and tries to flee as quick as he can. We have been butchers the whole day.

22 August

[. . .] The country today has been terrible and I repeat what I wrote yesterday that we have not previously had such a large district with ice so pressed. There can scarcely be found a couple of square meters (yards) of ice which does not present evident traces of pressure and the entire country consisting of a boundless field of large and small hummocks. One cannot speak of any regularity among them. The leads to-day have been broken to pieces and the floes small, but in general it has been easy to get across. Now they are so frozen that neither ferrying nor rafting can now be employed. To-day a lead changed just when we had come across it (5 minutes later and it would have been impossible) and we had an opportunity of seeing a very powerful pressing. The floes came at a great speed and there was a creaking round about us. It made a strange and magnificent impression. The day has been extremely beautiful. Perhaps the most beautiful we have had. With a specially clear horizon we have again tried to catch sight of Gillis Land but it is impossible to get a glimpse of any part of it. Our course has been S 60° W as on the previous days and the day's-march has probably brought us about 3 min. in the direction of our course. The clear air was utilized by S-g to take lunar distances. He saw haloes on the snow . . . Magnificent Venetian landscape with canals between lofty hummock edges on both sides, water-square with ice-fountain and stairs down to the canals. Divine. Bear-ham several days old exquisite. I massaged F's foot. He had been pulling so that his knee went out of joint but it slipped in again but he had no bad effects of it. S-g had a pain in one toe, cause still unknown.

29 August

[. . .] The ice as before but the leads are still very extensive and broke so that they are very difficult to cross. It now begins to feel cold. We have seen a bear to-day but unfortunately he went off at a gallop when he saw that he was noticed. S's sledge badly broken and we could only just manage to mend it. We come slowly onwards and I imagine we shall have to make a late autumn journey to reach Mossel bay. The ice and the snow on it are becoming as hard as glass and it is difficult to pull the sledges across it. Today we have tried to go S 45° W as S's lunar observations showed that we were rather more to the westward than we had imagined. But to keep a tolerably steady course among the leads is on my word no easy task however. Tonight was the first time I thought of all the lovely things at home. S. and F. on the contrary have long spoken about it. The tent is now always covered with ice inside and the bottom, which is double, feels pretty hard when it is being rolled together. I sweep it clean morning and evening before and after the cooking.

30 August

5 o'cl. p.m. Start. The ice as before and the course too but this was hard to keep for the leads have been difficult to get across. Two Ross' gulls visible. At last we found ourselves on a floe from which we could not come without rafting. As we had not more than 20 min. left of our march-time we determined to pitch our tent and see if the ice possibly moved during the night. Scarcely had we erected the tent before S. cried out "a bear on top of us". A bear then stood 10 paces from him. I was lying inside the tent sweeping the floor and so could do nothing but F. who was outside caught hold of a gun and gave the bear a shot that made him turn, badly wounded. To save cartridges he was allowed to run a bit but at last he had to be finished off with 3 more shots. The bear however had managed to get down into a broad lead and rolled himself about there but he could not swim far. I threw a grapnel past him and brought him in to the edge of the ice. This however was so thin that we hardly dared to stand on it but at last

I succeeded in putting a noose around his neck and one around a foreleg. S. prised with a boat-hook and so we hauled him up on to the ice pretty easily. The situation was photographed and the bear was cut up. Once more we have 30 kilo (66 lbs) of meat i.e. meat for 14 days if we calculate 0.9 kilo (2 lbs) each morning and evening and 300 (11 oz) for dinner. These quantities are carried next to the body so as not to be frozen. Two Ross' gulls visible.

31 August

[. . .] The sun touched the horizon at midnight. The landscape on fire. The snow a sea of fire. The country fairly good. We could for the first time [sledge] over broad new ice. First I crept across on all fours to test if it would hold. Then we went across in several places. One ferrying had to be made. The leads were passable but the ice was in lovely movement. It is fine to work the sledges onward through the middle of the crashing ice-pressures round about us. Sometimes a lead closes just when we need it, sometimes it opens suddenly the moment before or after a crossing. I had diarrhœa badly perhaps in consequence of a chill. F.'s sledge badly broken and had to be repaired on the spot. In the evening I took both morphine and opium . . .

3 September

[. . .] Today we found ourselves surrounded by broad water-channels of great extent and found ourselves obliged to trust ourselves entirely to the boat. We succeeded in loading everything on it and then rowed for 3 hours at a pretty good pace towards the Seven Islands (our goal). It was with a rather solemn feeling when at 1h 50 o'cl. p.m. we began this new way of travelling gliding slowly over the mirror-like surface of the water between large ice-floes loaded with giant-like hummocks. Only the shriek of ivory gulls and the splashing of the seals when they dived and the short orders of the streersman broke the silence. We knew that we were moving onwards more quickly than usual and at every turn of the leads we asked ourselves in silence if we might not possibly journey on in this glorious way to the end. We called it glorious for the everlasting hauling of the sledges had become tiring I fancy the last few days and it would be a great relief for us to travel some days in another way. But at 5 o'cl. our joy came to an end; we then entered a bay in the ice which immediately afterwards was closed by a floe so that we could go neither onwards nor backwards. We were satisfied however for things had gone well, the boat was excellent and there was room for all our luggage.

9 September

[. . .] Our meat supply is beginning to come to an end and we shoot two ivory gulls to supplement it. We do not like to shoot unless we can get at least two ivory gulls at one shot. They are delicate birds but I think they cost a lot of ammunition. For the last few days F. has had a pain in his left foot. I give him massage morning and evening and rub on liniment. Today (the 9 in p.m.) I have opened a large pus-blister washed it with sublimate solution and put on a bandage. Now I hope it will heal for it is hard for us to be without F's full strength. This is more than needful with our trying work. Our attacks of diarrhœa seem to have stopped. Yesterday I had a motion for the first time for at least 4 days but in spite of that did not notice any diarrhœa. The amount of the excretion was moderate and of normal consistence. F. has frequent motions and the consistency seems to be rather fluid but he does not complain of pains in the stomach and of diarrhœa as he has done almost constantly before . . .

Just now I had to leave off writing in order to fire a shot and drop two ivory gulls. Such birds always gather around our camp. Oh if we could shoot a seal or a bear just now. We need it so much . . . 6 O'cl.

F's foot is now so bad that he cannot pull his sledge but can only help by pushing. S. and I take it in turns to go back and bring up F's sledge. This tries our strength. We could not manage more than 6 hours' march especially as the country was extremely difficult. Just when we stopped I happened to fall into the water, for an ice-floe which to all appearance and on being tested with the boat-hook seemed to be solid and on which

I jumped down proved to consist of nothing but a hard mass of ice-sludge which went to pieces when I landed on it. I flung myself on my back and floated thus until the others reached me a couple of oars with the help of which I crawled up again . . .

17 September

Since I wrote last in my diary much has changed in truth. We laboured onwards with the sledges in the ordinary way but found at last that the new-fallen snow's . . . character did not allow us to continue quickly enough. F's foot which still did not allow him to pull compelled me and S to go back in turns and pull forward F's sledge too. One of S's feet was also a little out of order. Our meat was almost at an end and the crossings between the floes became more and more difficult in consequences of the ice-sludge. But above all we found that the current and the wind irresistibly carried us down into the jaws between North East Land and Franz Joseph's Land and that we had not the least chance to reach North East Land. It was during the 12th and 13th Sept. when we were obliged to lie still on account of violent N W wind that we at last discovered the necessity of submitting to the inevitable i.e. and wintering on the ice . . .

Our first resolution was to work our way across to a neighbouring ice-floe which was bigger and stronger and richer in ice-humps than that on which we were which was low and small and full of saltwater pools, showing that it was composed of small pieces which would probably easily separate in the spring. We came to the new floe by rafting with the boat and soon found a suitable building-plot consisting of a large piece of ice which we hollowed out to some extent. The sides and the parts that were missing we supplied by filling up with blocks of ice and snow over which we threw water and thus made solid and durable. On the 15th we at last succeeded in getting a seal, as I had the luck to put a ball right through its head so that it was killed on the spot and could easily be brought "ashore".

Every part of the seal tastes very nice (fried). We are especially fond of the meat and the blubber. May we but shoot some score of seals so that we can save ourselves. The bears seem to have disappeared and of other game there are visible only ivory gulls, which, it is true, are not to be despised, but which cost too much ammunition. The ivory gulls come and sit on the roof of the tent. Remarkably enough the fulmars seem to have disappeared and of other birds only a little auk or possibly a young black guillemot have been visible during the last few days. F's foot is better now but will hardly be well before a couple of weeks. S's feet are also bad. I have made in order a landing-net to catch plankton or anything else that can be found in the water we shall see how it succeeds; a fortunate result of the attempt may I think somewhat improve our difficult position. Our humour is pretty good although joking and smiling are not of ordinary occurrence. My young comrades hold out better than I had ventured to hope. The fact that during the last few days we have drifted towards the south at such a rate contributed essentially I think to keeping up our courage. Our latitude on the 12th Sept. was 81° 21' and on the 15th we had drifted with a strong N W wind down to 80° 45'. Longitude in the latter case is I am certain considerably more easterly. Thus our drift in 72 hours amounts to about ⅔ of a degree of latitude and since then the wind has blown fresh from the same or a more northerly direction. Possibly we may be able to drive far southwards quickly enough and obtain our nourishment from the sea. Perhaps too it will not be so cold on the sea as on the land. He who lives will see. Now it is time to work. The day has been a remarkable one for us by our having seen land to-day for the first time since 11 July. It is undoubtedly New Iceland that we have had before our eyes . . .

There is no question of our attempting to go on shore for the entire island seems to be one single block of ice with a glacier border. It appears however not to be absolutely inaccessible on the east and west points. We saw a bear under the land and in the water I saw a couple of flocks (of 4) of those "black guillemot youngsters". I think a couple of little auks were also visible. The ivory gulls are seen half a score together. On the other hand the water seems to be poor in small animals for dragging gave no result (landing-net). A seal was seen but it was much terrified. We have seen no walrus. Our arrival at New Iceland is remarkable because it points to a colossal drift viz. of more than 1 degree of latitude since 12 Sept. If we drift in this way some weeks more perhaps we may save ourselves on one of the islands east of Spitzbergen. It makes us feel anxious that we have not more game within shooting-distance. Our provisions must soon and richly be supplemented if we are to have any prospect of being able to hold out for a time.

19 September

[. . .] Today S. has been very busy house-building in accordance with a method he has invented. This consists of snow and fresh water being mixed after which the entire mass is built up into a wall and allowed to freeze. The work is both solid and neat. In a couple of days we shall probably have the baking-oven (i.e., the sleeping room) ready . . . The thickness of the ice of our floe at "the great cargo-quay" has been measured and found to be 1.4–1.3–1.5m (4.6–4.3–4.95 ft) . . .

23 September

Today all three of us have been working busily on the hut cementing together ice-blocks. We have got on very well and the hut now begins to take form a little. After a couple more days of such weather and work it should not take long until we are able to move in. We can probably carry our supplies in there the day after tomorrow. This is very necessary, as mortar we employ snow mixed with water and of this mass, which is handled by S. with great skill he is also making a vaulted roof over the last parts between the walls. We have now a very good arrangement of the day with 8 hours' work beginning with 2½ hours' work, thereupon breakfast ¾ and afterwards work until 4.45 o'cl. when we dine and take supper in one meal. We have now also tried the meat of the great seal and have found that it tastes excellent. One of the very best improvements in the cooking is that of adding blood to the sauce for the steak. This makes it thick and it tastes as if we had bread. I cannot believe but that blood contains much carbohydrate, for our craving for bread is considerably less since we began to use blood in the food. We all think so. We have also found everything eatable both as regards bear, great seal, seal and ivory gull (bear-liver of course excepted). For want of time we have not yet been able to cut up and weigh our animal but I think we now have meat and ham until on in the spring. We must however shoot more so as to be able to have larger rations and to get more fuel and light.

29 September

[. . .] Our floe is diminished in a somewhat alarming degree close to our hut. The ice pressings bring the shores closer and closer to us. But we have a large and old hummock between the hut and the shore and hope that this will stop the pressure. This sounds magnificent when there is pressure but otherwise it does not appeal to us.

Thickn. of ice 1.1–1.2–1.5–1.9 (3.6–3.9–4.95–6.27 ft) have been measured by a new fissure which has arisen in our floe. Yesterday evening the 28 we moved into our hut which was christened "the home". We lay there last night and found it rather nice. But it will become much better of course. We must have the meat inside to protect ourselves against the bears. The ice in N.I. glacier is evidently stratified in a horizontal direction. The day before yesterday it rained a great part of the day which I suppose ought to be considered extremely remarkable at this time of the year and in this degree of latitude.

1 October

[. . .] The 1 Oct. was a good day. The evening was as divinely beautiful as one could wish. The water was allied with small animals and a bevy of 7 black-white "guillemots youngsters" were swimming there. A couple of seals were seen too. The work with the hut went on well and we thought that we should have the outside ready by the 2nd. But then something else happened. At 5.30 o'cl. (local time) in the morning of the 2 we heard a crash and thunder and water streamed into the hut and when we rushed out we found that our large beautiful floe had been splintered into a number of little floes and that one fissure had divided the floe just outside the wall of the hut. The floe that remained to us had a diam. of only 24 meter (80 ft) and one wall of the hut might be said rather to hang from the roof than to support it. This was a great alteration in our position and our prospects. The hut and the floe could not give us shelter and still we were obliged to stay there for the present at least. We were frivolous enough to lie in the hut the following night too. Perhaps it was because the day was rather tiring. Our belongings were scattered among several blocks and these were driving here and there so that we had to hurry. Two bear-bodies, representing provisions for 3–4 months were lying on a separate floe and so on. Luckily the weather was beautiful so that we could work in haste. No one had lost courage; with such comrades one should be able to manage under, I may say, any circumstances.

The trio landed on White Island on 5 October, where they expired shortly afterwards.

Despite several searches for Andrée's party, their bodies were not discovered until thirty years later when a walrus-hunting party stumbled upon them. Found with the corpses were the expedition's journals, letters, and a cache of photo stock which later proved developable. Almost everything is known about the Andrée expedition – except why the men died. They were still well provisioned. The likeliest culprits for the trio's demise are hypothermia or trichonosis, a parasitic disease caused by the undercooking of certain meats. Carbon-dioxide poisoning from a faulty cooker has also been suggested as the agent of their doom.

Stefansson in "The Friendly Arctic"

Vilhjalmur Stefansson

Stefansson, a Canadian ethnologist, was the last explorer to discover significant new lands in the North American Arctic, adding as much as 100,000 square miles to the map. He famously promoted the notion of "The Friendly Arctic", including by a book of that title, where the well-prepared white man could survive as well as the Inuit – from whom Stefansson himself had learned survivalist skills during a four-year sojourn in northern Alaska.

Ten Thousand Years Back in Time

In the Dolphin and Union Straits region in 1908 Stefansson found a tribe who had never before encountered a white man.

Our first day among the Dolphin and Union Straits Eskimo was the day of all my life to which I had looked forward with the most vivid anticipations, and to which I now look back with equally vivid memories, for it introduced me, a student of mankind and of primitive men especially, to a people of a bygone age. Mark Twain's Connecticut Yankee went to sleep in the 19th century and woke up in King Arthur's time among knights who rode in clinking mail to the rescue of fair ladies; we, without going to sleep at all, had walked out of the 20th century into the country of the intellectual and cultural contemporaries of a far earlier age than King Arthur's. These were not such men as Caesar found in Gaul or in Britain; they were more nearly like the still earlier hunting tribes of Britain and of Gaul living contemporaneous to but oblivious of the building of the first pyramid in Egypt. Their existence on the same continent with our populous cities was an anachronism of ten thousand years in intelligence and material development. They gathered their food with the weapons of the men of the Stone Age, they thought their simple, primitive thoughts and lived their insecure and tense lives – lives that were to me the mirrors of the lives of our far ancestors whose bones and crude handiwork we now and then discover in river gravels or in prehistoric caves. Such archæological remains found in various parts of the world of the men who antedated the knowledge of the smelting of metals, tell a fascinating story to him whose scientific imagination can piece it together and fill in the wide gaps; but far better than such dreaming was my present opportunity. I had nothing to imagine; I had merely to look and listen; for here were not remains of the Stone Age, but the Stone Age itself, men and women, very human, entirely friendly, who welcomed us to their homes and bade us stay.

Kommana, in order to buy my favor, brought me a present which he knew I would appreciate: a knife of ancient pattern and with a well-attested history. There had been a man in the Point Atkinson community some forty years ago who became intolerable to his fellows, and three of the most energetic and public-spirited men volunteered to execute him. This matter had the complete approval of the community, and was the knowledge of every one except the victim. One day the three men took him aside and of a sudden the most resolute, the owner of the knife, stabbed the man in the back with this very knife. The Eskimo system of government, which is really no system at all (or in other words a communistic anarchy), has but this one punishment, except that the power of public opinion is so much stronger with them than with us that the mere knowledge of having displeased the community would be severe punishment in itself. It seems then, on the face of it, that removing an intolerable man in the manner just described is not a bad way of dealing with a difficult situation; and it would not be if the story ended there. But the weak point of the system is that no matter if the man's relations may have been loudest of all in denouncing him and demanding that he should be killed, still the moment that any one kills him it becomes the duty of his relatives to take blood revenge on some member of the family of those who helped do the killing. Some one has to be killed, though it need not be the man directly responsible – it may quite as well be his decrepit mother or his little niece; and even that does not square things, for as soon as the relation has been killed in revenge for the execution, it becomes the duty of the executioner and his family to take revenge again upon the family of the man originally executed, so that there commences a blood feud which has no ending until the tribe divides in two sections, one of which moves to a distant place quite out of the reach of the other. This is the general way things run, but it seems that in the particular case with which our story of the knife is concerned, the relations of the executed man made it known that they intended to kill all the executioners, and within four or five years they had succeeded in killing two of them. But the third man, the owner of the knife, had been so watchful and had carried this long knife around with him so constantly that he had not yet been killed when a severe epidemic of measles swept off most of the family of the avengers, with the result that the owner of the knife lived for many years and finally died a natural death.

Most travellers who have visited the Arctic lands have commented upon the fact that Eskimo children are never punished, or, in fact, forbidden anything. The explanations offered have been various, and usually such offhand ones as the "common sense" of the observer has suggested to him. In dealing with primitive people, however, "common sense" is an exceedingly dangerous thing. It is a frail reed indeed to rely upon, for scarcely anything that the primitive man does is done without a religious motive, and we in these later days are so prone to neglect the religious aspect of things that the chances are necessarily small of the right reason being divined . . .

One family of Eskimo were the servants of the expedition for its whole four years and I had known them also on previous expeditions. This family consists of the man Ilavinirk, his wife Mamayak, and their daughter Noashak. When I first knew Noashak I formed the opinion that she was the worst child I had ever known and I retained that opinion for over six years, or until she was a young woman of perhaps twelve years. (Some Eskimo girls are fully developed at the age of twelve or thirteen.) In spite of her badness Noashak was never punished.

The two stock explanations of why Eskimo do not punish their children are: first, that the children themselves are so good that they do not need being punished (but that scarcely applied to Noashak's case); or that the Eskimo are so fond of their children that they cannot bear to punish them, which is not true, either, for they show in many ways that they are no fonder of their children than we are.

During the entire time that Noashak's family was with us she was the undisputed ruler of our establishment. My plan of work was such that I could not get along without the help of Eskimo, and I had continually before me the choice of doing as Noashak wanted or else losing the services of her parents. They were both excellent people of whom I was personally very fond, and they were more useful to me than any one else whom I could hope to secure in their places; besides, most Eskimo families have children, and to dispose of the family of which Noashak was head would only have compelled me to engage some other family of which some other child was master. True, I was allowed to decide upon the broad policy of the expedition, but any little details were liable to change without notice at Noashak's option.

It was during the absence of the sun in December, 1909, that this family and I were travelling up Horton River. We had been several days without anything to eat except sea-oil; our dogs were tired and weak from hunger and had ceased pulling. Ilavinirk and I were harnessed to the sled on either side, breaking our backs to pull it forward, and Mamayak was walking ahead breaking trail for the sled. Noashak, then a fat and sturdy girl of eight, was on top of the load, which was heavy enough in all conscience without her. Whenever we stopped to rest she would immediately jump off the sled, run up some cut-bank and slide down it, run up again and slide down again, and so on as long as we stayed. The moment we started she would jump on the load and ride.

One day when her father and I were more tired than usual and getting weaker from long fasting, I asked Ilavinirk whether he did not think it would be a good idea if Noashak got off and walked a little (we had, by the way, saved food for Noashak so that she had something to eat when the rest of us did not). He put the matter to her, telling her that it was his opinion that walking would really do her good; he told her how tired he and I were getting, and wanted to know if his dear daughter was not willing to walk now and then so as to enable us to travel a little farther each day and to reach our destination, where plenty of food waited for us, that much sooner. But she said she did not feel like walking, and that ended the discussion.

Later on when we stopped to rest again and Noashak started her old tactics of running uphill and sliding down, I again suggested to her father that she might rest while we rested and then she would no doubt feel like walking when we started travelling again. He put the case to her as before. Evidently his sympathies were on my side and he was as anxious to have her walk as I was, but her curt decision that she would rather slide downhill than walk beside the sled settled the matter.

I am unable to remember now whether I had any theory by which I explained to myself why it was that Noashak was never forbidden anything and never punished, but I know now that if I had a theory it must have been a wrong one . . .

I had noticed ever since I knew them that Mamayak in speaking to Noashak always addressed her as "mother" When one stops to think of it, it was of course a bit curious that a woman of twenty-five should address a girl of eight as "mother" I suppose, if I thought about the matter at all, I must have put this practice of theirs in the same category with that which we find among our own people, where we often hear a man addressing his wife as "mother".

One day another Eskimo family came to visit us, and strangely enough, the woman of the family also spoke to Noashak and called her "mother". Then my curiosity was finally aroused, and I asked: "Why do you two grown women call this child your mother?" Their answer was: "Simply because she is our mother", an answer which was for the moment more incomprehensible to me that the original problem. I saw, however, that I was on the track of something interesting, and both women were in a communicative mood, so it was not long until my questions brought out the facts, which (pieced together with what I already knew) make the following coherent explanation, which shows not only why these women called Noashak "mother", but shows also why it was that she must never under any circumstances be forbidden anything or punished.

When a Mackenzie Eskimo dies, the body is taken out the same day as the death occurs to the top of some neighboring hill and covered with a pile of drift-logs, but the soul (*nappan*) remains in the house where the death occurred for four days if it is a man, and for five days if it is a woman. At the end of that time a ceremony is performed by means of which the spirit is induced to leave the house and to go up to the grave, where it remains with the body waiting for the next child in the community to be born.

When a child is born, it comes into the world with a soul of its own (*nappan*), but this soul is as inexperienced, foolish, and feeble as a child is and looks. It is evident, therefore, that the child needs a more experienced and wiser soul than its own to do the thinking for it and take care of it. Accordingly the mother, so soon as she can after the birth of the child, pronounces a magic formula to summon from the grave the waiting soul of the dead to become the guardian soul of the new-born child, or its *atka*, as they express it.

Let us suppose that the dead person was an old wise man by the name of John. The mother then pronounces the formula which may be roughly translated as follows: "Soul of John, come here, come here, be my child's guardian! Soul of John, come here, come here, be my child's guardian!" (Most magic formulæ among the Eskimo must be repeated twice.)

When the soul of John, waiting at the grave, hears the summons of the mother, it comes and enters the child. From that time on it becomes the business of this acquired soul not only to do the thinking for the child, but to help in every way to keep it strong and healthy: to assist it in learning to walk, to keep it from becoming bow-legged, to assist it in teething, and in every way to look after its welfare, things which the child's own soul with which it was born could not possibly do for the child, on account of its weakness and inexperience.

The spirit of John not only teaches the child to talk, but after the child learns to talk it is really the soul of John which talks to you and not the inborn soul of the child. The child, therefore, speaks with all the acquired wisdom which John accumulated in the long lifetime, plus the higher wisdom which only comes after death. Evidently, therefore, the child is the wisest person in the family or in the community, and its opinions should be listened to accordingly. What it says and does may seem foolish to you, but that is mere seeming and in reality the child is wise beyond your comprehension.

The fact that the child possesses all the wisdom of the dead John is never forgotten by its parents. If it cries for a knife or a pair of scissors, it is not a foolish child that wants the knife, but the soul of the wise old man John that wants it, and it would be presumptuous of a young mother to suppose she knows better than John what is good for the child, and so she gives it the knife. If she refused the knife (and this is the main point), she would not only be preferring her own foolishness to the wisdom of John, but also she would thereby give offense to the spirit of John, and in his anger John would abandon the child. Upon the withdrawal of his protection the child would become the prey to disease and would probably die, and if it did not die, it would become stupid or hump-backed or otherwise deformed or unfortunate. John must, therefore, be propitiated at every cost, and to deliberately offend him would be in fact equivalent to desiring the child's misfortune or death and would be so construed by the community; so that a man is restrained from forbidding his child or punishing it, not only by his own interest in the child's welfare, but also by the fear of public opinion, because if he began to forbid his child or to punish it, he would at once become known to the community as a cruel and inhuman father, careless of the welfare of his child . . .

As the child grows up the soul with which he was born (the *nappan*) gradually develops in strength, experience, and wisdom, so that after the age of ten or twelve years it is fairly competent to look after the child and begins to do so; at that age it therefore becomes of less vital moment to please the guardian spirit (*atka*), and accordingly it is customary to begin forbidding children and punishing them when they come to the age of eleven or twelve years. People say about them then: "I think the *nappan* is competent now to take care of him and it will be safe to begin teaching him things."

Caribou Hunt

An incident from 1917, when Stefansson was leading an expedition to the Canadian Far North; it is perhaps as well to add that Stefansson was not always so considerate to the members of his expeditions as he appears here; he had previously abandoned the young William Laird McKinley (see page 164) and the other members of the Karluk *expedition to a cold fate.*

Apart from the islands actually discovered by my expedition, there is no known country in the northern hemisphere that has been so little visited as Isachsen Land, in north latitude 79°, west longitude 103°. We feel sure that no Eskimos ever saw that island. From the beginning of the world to our own time it had been visited only once – by Captain Isachsen in 1901. Isachsen made a hurried sledge trip round the island. The journey took him about a week. In one place he saw some caribou tracks, and I think he may have seen some caribou at a distance, but he did not try to hunt them. The next visitors were my sledge party in 1916, and on that occasion we saw no caribou and had to feed ourselves and our dogs entirely on seals.

My second visit, and the third visit of human beings to the island, was in 1917. We were then on the most dangerous adventure that has ever fallen to our lot. By the road we had to travel we were some five hundred miles away from the nearest Eskimos and six hundred miles away from our own base camp. Four of us had been on a long journey out on the moving sea-ice to the north-west. When we were more than a hundred miles north-west from Isachsen Land two of my three companions were taken seriously ill. We turned towards shore immediately, and it was a hard fight to make land. When we got there after a struggle of two weeks we found ourselves with one man so sick that he could not walk, another who could barely walk, but was of no use otherwise, and with two teams of dogs that were exhausted with hard work and so thin from short rations during the forced march towards shore that they were little more than skeletons. It had been my pride through many years never to lose a dog. Furthermore, I was exceedingly fond of every one of these dogs, for they had worked for me faithfully for years. I was concerned for their safety, and still more concerned for the safety of the sick men. By that time, however, my confidence in our ability to make a living in the Arctic had become so strong through eight years of experience that I felt more worry for the lives of the men on the score of illness than for fear they might actually die of hunger.

But the first day on Isachsen Land was a depressing contradiction of my hopes and expectations. The one man in good health and the two men who were sick had to make their way as best they could along the coast while I hunted inland parallel to their course. I walked that day twenty miles across one of the very few stretches of entirely barren land that I have seen in the Arctic. Under foot was gravel without a blade of grass. Much of the land was lightly covered with snow, as in other typical Arctic lands in winter, and I looked in vain in the snow for track or other sign of any living thing.

That evening my men were depressed, partly because of their illness and also because it looked as if we had at last come into a region as barren as many people think the polar countries generally are. It was clear that if we saw game the next day we should simply have to have it. Where game is plentiful you may lose one chance and soon get another; but where it is scarce you must not allow any opportunity to slip through your fingers.

I am telling this particular hunting story rather than any other to illustrate the principle of how you must hunt caribou in the polar regions if it is essential that you should get every animal you see. It certainly was essential in this case, for I wanted not only to stave off immediate hunger, but to secure meat enough to enable us to camp in one place for several weeks and give the sick men a chance to become well.

On our second day at Isachsen Land the men again followed the coastline with the sledges, cutting across the shortest distance from point to point, while I walked a much longer course inland. I had gone but a few miles when I came upon the tracks of a band of caribou. You can seldom be sure from the tracks of the minimum number in a band if there are more than ten animals, for caribou have a way of stepping in each other's footprints. There are always likely to be more animals in a band than you have been able to make out from the tracks.

The trail showed that these caribou were travelling into the wind, as they usually do. There were only light airs, and the snow had on it a crust that broke underfoot with a crunching noise. Under such conditions the band were likely to hear me four or five hundred yards away. The country now was a rolling prairie – not barren gravel as yesterday. It was impossible to tell which ridge might hide the caribou from me, so instead of following the trail ahead I went back along it for about half a mile, studying the tracks to see just how fast they had been moving. They had been travelling in a leisurely way and feeding here and there. I estimated that their average rate of progress would not be more than three or four miles per day. I could not rely on this, however, for a wolf may turn up any time and begin a pursuit which takes a band twenty-five or fifty miles away. Should a wolf pass to windward of them, so that they got his smell without his knowing about them, they would be likely to run from five to ten miles.

When I had made up my mind that these caribou were moving slowly I went to the top of a neighbouring hill and through my glasses studied the landscape carefully. With good luck I might have seen some of them on top of some hill, and the problem would have become definite. But I watched for half an hour and saw nothing. Clearly they were either feeding in some low place or else they were lying down, for caribou are like cattle in their habit of lying down for long periods. I now commenced a cautious advance, not along the actual trail, but criss-crossing it from high hill-top to high hill-top, hoping to get a view of the animals while they were at least half a mile from me and while I was beyond the range of their eyesight, for they cannot see a man even under the most favourable conditions farther off than half a mile. Under ordinary conditions they would not see you much beyond a quarter of a mile.

Finally I saw the band lying quietly on some flat land. There was no cover to enable me to approach safely within five hundred yards, and that is too far for good shooting. I thought these might be the only caribou in the whole country. We had thirteen hungry dogs and two sick men, and now that I had a large band before me it was my business to get enough food at one time to enable us to spend at that place two or three weeks, while the men had a chance to regain their health and the dogs to regain their flesh and strength.

On a calm day, when caribou can hear you farther than you can shoot, there is only one method of hunting. You must study their movements from afar until you make up your mind in which direction they are going. Then you must walk in a wide curve round them until you are in the locality toward which they are moving and well beyond earshot. This takes judgment, for they usually travel nearly or quite into the wind, and you must not allow them to scent you. You therefore have to choose a place which you think is near enough to their course for them to pass within shooting distance, and still not directly enough in front to enable them to smell you.

On this occasion the glaring light on the snow had been so hard on my eyes that I did not feel they were in perfect condition, and no one can shoot well if his eyes are not right. Unless there is a change of wind caribou are not likely to turn their course back along the trail by which they have come. I accordingly selected a hill across which they had walked that morning and half a mile away from where they now were. On the top of this hill, where I could see them, although they could not see me (because my eyes were better than theirs) I lay down, covered my head with a canvas hunting-bag to keep the sun away, and went to sleep. Sleeping is the best possible way of passing time, but my object now was not only to pass the time until the caribou began moving, but also to get my eyes into perfect condition.

When you go to sleep at twenty below zero you have in the temperature an automatic alarm clock. My clothes were amply warm enough to keep me comfortable while I was awake, but I knew that when I went to sleep my circulation would slow down. This reduces the body temperature, and the same weather that will not chill you when you are awake will chill you enough to wake you from a sleep.

In this case the chill woke me in about half an hour to an unpleasant situation. A fog had set in, and I could not see the caribou, nor had I any means of knowing whether they were still lying down or whether they had started to move. If this had been a good game-country I might have taken chances on advancing through the fog a little, but I was so impressed with the possibility that these were the only animals within a hundred miles that carelessness was not to be considered. At this time of year we had twenty-four hours of daylight. The fog was bound to lift sooner or later, and whenever it did I would commence the hunt over again.

The fog did lift in about two hours, and I did have to commence the hunt all over again, for the caribou were gone. I was to the north of them, and I felt sure that they had not gone by near me; so they must have gone east, west, or south. I was probably so near them that I could not with safety go on top of any of the adjoining hills, so I went back north half a mile and climbed a high hill there. From that hill I saw nothing, and went half a mile to one side to another hill. Then I saw the caribou. They were now feeding half a mile south of where they had been when the fog covered them up. In the meantime the breeze had stiffened, so that now there was no longer danger of my being heard. I did not, therefore, have to circle them and lie in wait in front, but could follow up directly behind.

Eventually I got within about three hundred yards. But I wanted to get within two hundred, so I lay still and waited for them to move into a more favourable locality. During my wait an exceedingly thick fog-bank rolled up, but with it the wind did not slacken. Under cover of this fog I felt safe in crawling ahead a hundred yards, for I knew that I could see through the fog quite as well as the animals, and that they could not hear me because of the wind. The reason I had not approached them in the previous fog was that the weather then had been nearly calm and they would have heard me.

At 200 yards I was just able to make out the outline of the nearest caribou. I did not dare to go closer, and, of course, I could not begin shooting with only one or two animals in sight when I wanted to get them all. I had before now counted them carefully. There were twenty-one, which I estimated would be enough to feed our men and dogs between two and three weeks, giving them a chance to recuperate.

After about half an hour the fog began gradually to clear, and in another half-hour I could see all the animals. I was near the top of a hill and they were in a hollow, the nearest of them about a hundred and fifty yards away and the farthest about three hundred.

In winter the ground in any cold country will split in what we call frost-cracks. These are cracks in the frozen surface of what in summer is mud. They are ordinarily only half an inch or so wide, but I have seen cracks four or five inches wide. These cracks form when the mercury is dropping and with a noise that resembles a rifle-shot. Under the same conditions the ice on the small lakes cracks similarly. These loud noises are so familiar to the caribou, and the report of a rifle is so similar, that the mere sound of a rifle does not scare them. Of course, we have smokeless powder, so they cannot see where the shots come from. What does scare them is the whistle of the bullet and the thud as it strikes the ground. It is instinctive with all animals to run directly away from the source of any noise that frightens them. It is another instinct of caribou when they are alarmed to run towards the centre of the herd. A band that has been scattered while feeding will bunch up when they take fright. When you know these two principles it is obvious that the first caribou to kill is the one farthest away from you. On some occasions when I have been unable to get within good shooting distance of a band, I have commenced by firing a few shots into a hill on the other side of them, hoping that the noise of the striking bullets would scare them towards me. Frequently it works. On this occasion, however, I merely took careful aim at an animal about three hundred yards away. It dropped so instantaneously that although the sound of the bullet striking it induced the other caribou to look up, they recognized no sign of real danger. They were, however, alert, and when they saw the second caribou fall they ran together into a group and moved somewhat towards me. I now shot animals on the outer margin of the group, and as each fell the others would run a little away from that one. Their retreat in any direction was stopped by my killing the foremost animal in the retreat, whereupon the band would turn in the opposite direction.

It would not have been difficult for me to kill the whole band alone, but I was not shooting alone. From a point somewhere above and behind me I could hear other shots, and some animals I was not aiming at were dropping. Without looking round I knew what this meant. My companions travelling along shore on the ice had seen the caribou, and had waited for some time until they began to fear that I might have missed the band. The two sick men had been left behind in camp, while their Eskimo companion had come inland to try to get the caribou. When he got near he saw that I was approaching them, and very wisely did not interfere. There is nothing so likely to spoil a caribou-hunt as two hunters whose plans conflict. Even when they have a chance to consult at the beginning of the hunt, two men are less likely to be successful than one. For one thing, caribou may see a black dot on the landscape and take no warning from it, but if they see two black dots and later notice that they are either close together or farther apart than they were a moment before, this makes a danger signal which they understand. That is the main reason why I always hunt alone. If there are two hunters to go out from the same camp on any given day, they should go in opposite directions. In this way they double the chance of finding game, and each has a fair chance of getting the animals he does find.

On our journeys we never kill more animals than we need, but in this case we needed the whole twenty-one. The Eskimo and I went down to the ice with my hunting-bag filled with the tongues of the caribou. This gave the sick men a more appetizing meat than they had had for a long time. The dogs had to wait for their food until we were able to move camp right to where the caribou had been shot. Although they were thin and tired, they became so excited at the smell of the fresh-killed caribou which they got from our clothes that they pulled towards shore as if they had been well fed and of full strength.

On the hill from which I had shot the caribou we pitched camp. During the next two weeks the invalids rapidly gained in health. We called the place Camp Hospital. Few hospitals have ever been more successful. When we left it three weeks later the dogs were fat and the men well.

Cook Attains the Pole . . .

Frederick A. Cook

An American physician, born in New York State, Frederick Cook took his first polar journey as a member of the 1891 expedition to Greenland led by Robert E. Peary. Two further expeditions to the Arctic followed, together with a Belgian expedition to the Antarctic, before Cook made his claim to be the first man to reach the North Pole – on 21 April 1908. Initially feted as a hero, Cook was then the object of campaign of vilification by his rival Peary, who asserted that his visit on 6 April 1909 was the first to the Pole. An investigation by Copenhagen University discredited Cook, whose case was undermined by his evidently specious claim to have been the first to ascend Mount McKinley. Cook's reputation sank still further when he was gaoled for stock-fraud, and even though he was eventually pardoned he never recovered his public standing. He died on 5 August 1940, leaving behind a voice recording: "I state emphatically that I, Frederick A. Cook, discovered the North Pole." In all probability he didn't, but then neither in all probability did Peary.

With the Pole only 29 miles distant, more sleep was quite impossible. We brewed an extra pot of tea, prepared a favorite broth of pemmican, dug up a surprise of fancy biscuits and filled up on good things to the limit of the allowance for our final feast days. The dogs, which had joined the chorus of gladness, were given an extra lump of pemmican. A few hours more were agreeably spent in the tent. Then we started out with new spirit for the uttermost goal of our world.

Bounding joyously forward, with a stimulated mind, I reviewed the journey. Obstacle after obstacle had been overcome. Each battle won gave a spiritual thrill, and courage to scale the next barrier. Thus had been ever, and was still, in the unequal struggles between human and inanimate nature, an incentive to go onward, ever onward, up the stepping-stones to ultimate success. And now, after a life-denying struggle in a world where every element of Nature is against the life and progress of man, triumph came with steadily measured reaches of fifteen miles a day!

We were excited to fever heat. Our feet were light on the run. Even the dogs caught the infectious enthusiasm. They rushed along at a pace which made it difficult for me to keep a sufficient advance to set a good course. The horizon was still eagerly searched for something to mark the approaching boreal center. But nothing unusual was seen. The same expanse of moving seas of ice, on which we had gazed for five hundred miles, swarmed about us as we drove onward.

Looking through gladdened eyes, the scene assumed a new glory. Dull blue and purple expanses were transfigured into plains of gold, in which were lakes of sapphire and rivulets of ruby fire. Engirdling this world were purple mountains with gilded crests. It was one of the few days on the stormy pack when all Nature smiled with cheering lights.

As the day advanced beyond midnight and the splendor of the summer night ran into a clearer continued day, the beams of gold on the surface snows assumed a more burning intensity. Shadows of hummocks and ice ridges became dyed with a deeper purple, and in the burning orange world loomed before us Titan shapes, regal and regally robed.

From my position, a few hundred yards ahead of the sleds, with compass and axe in hand, as usual, I could not resist the temptation to turn frequently to see the movement of the dog train with its new fire. In this backward direction the color scheme was reversed. About the horizon the icy walls gleamed like beaten gold set with gem-spots of burning colors; the plains represented every shade of purple and blue, and over them, like vast angel wings outspread, shifted golden pinions. Through the sea of palpitating color, the dogs came, with spirited tread, noses down, tails erect and shoulders braced to the straps, like chariot horses. In the magnifying light they seemed many times their normal size. The young Eskimos, chanting songs of love, followed with easy, swinging

steps. The long whip was swung with a brisk crack. Over all arose a
cloud of frosted breath, which, like incense smoke, became silvered
in the light, a certain signal of efficient motive power.

We all were lifted to the paradise of winners as we stepped over
the snows of a destiny for which we had risked life and willingly
suffered the tortures of an icy hell. The ice under us, the goal for
centuries of brave, heroic men, to reach which many had suffered
terribly and terribly died, seemed almost sacred. Constantly and
carefully I watched my instruments in recording this final reach.
Nearer and nearer they recorded our approach. Step by step, my
heart filled with a strange rapture of conquest.

   At last we step over colored fields of sparkle, climbing walls of
purple and gold – finally, under skies of crystal blue, with flaming
clouds of glory, we touch the mark! The soul awakens to a definite
triumph; there is sunrise within us, and all the world of night-
darkened trouble fades. We are at the top of the world! The flag is
flung to the frigid breezes of the North Pole!

In building our igloo the boys frequently looked about expec-
tantly. Often they ceased cutting snowblocks and rose to a
hummock to search the horizon for something which, to their
idea, must mark this important spot, for which we had struggled
against hope and all the dictates of personal comforts. At each
breathing spell their eager eyes picked some sky sign which to
them meant land or water, or the play of some god of land or sea.
The naive and sincere interest which the Eskimos on occasions
feel in the mystery of the spirit-world gives them an imaginative
appreciation of nature often in excess of that of the more material
and skeptical Caucasian.

   Arriving at the mysterious place where, they felt, something
should happen, their imagination now forced an expression of
disappointment. In a high-keyed condition, all their superstitions
recurred to them with startling reality.

   In one place the rising vapor proved to be the breath of the
great submarine god – the "*Ko-Koyah.*" In another place, a
motionless little cloud marked the land in which dwelt the
"*Turnah-huch-suak*", the great Land God, and the air spirits
were represented by the different winds, with sex relations.

Ah-weh-lah and E-tuk-i-shook, with the astuteness of the aborigine, who reads Nature as a book, were sharp enough to note that the high air currents did not correspond to surface currents; for, although the wind was blowing homeward, and changed its force and direction, a few high clouds moved persistently in a different direction.

This, to them, indicated a warfare among the air spirits. The ice and snow were also animated. To them the whole world presented a rivalry of conflicting spirits which offered never-ending topics of conversation.

As the foot pressed the snow, its softness, its rebound, or its metallic ring indicated sentiments of friendliness or hostility. The ice, by its color, movement or noise, spoke the humor of its animation, or that of the supposed life of the restless sea beneath it. In interpreting these spirit signs, the two expressed considerable difference of opinion. Ah-we-lah saw dramatic situations and became almost hysterical with excitement; E-tuk-i-shook saw only a monotone of the normal play of life. Such was the trend of interest and conversation as the building of the igloos was completed.

Contrary to our usual custom, the dogs had been allowed to rest in their traces attached to the sleds. Their usual malicious inquisitiveness exhausted, they were too tired to examine the sleds to steal food. But now, as the house was completed, holes were chipped with a knife in ice-shoulders, through which part of a trace was passed, and each team was thus securely fastened to a ring cut in ice-blocks. Then each dog was given a double ration of pemmican. Their pleasure was expressed by an extra twist of the friendly tails and an extra note of gladness from long-contracted stomachs. Finishing their meal, they curled up and warmed the snow, from which they took an occasional bite to furnish liquid for their gastric economy. Almost two days of rest followed, and this was the canine celebration of the Polar attainment.

We withdrew to the inside of the dome of snowblocks, pulled in a block to close the doors, spread out our bags as beds on the platform of leveled snow, pulled off boots and trousers, and slipped half-length into the bristling reindeer furs. We then discussed, with chummy congratulations, the success of our long drive to the world's end.

While thus engaged, the little Juel stove piped the cheer of the pleasure of ice-water, soon to quench our chronic thirst. In the meantime, Ah-we-lah and E-tuk-i-shook pressed farther and farther into their bags, pulled over the hoods, and closed their eyes to an overpowering fatigue. But my lids did not easily close. I watched the fire. More ice went into the kettle. With the satisfaction of an ambition fulfilled, I peeped out occasionally through the pole-punched port, and noted the horizon glittering with gold and purple.

Quivers of self-satisfying joy ran up my spine and relieved the frosty mental bleach of the long-delayed Polar anticipation.

In due time we drank, with grateful satisfaction, large quantities of ice-water, which was more delicious than any wine. A pemmican soup, flavored with musk ox tenderloins, steaming with heat – a luxury seldom enjoyed in our camps – next went down with warming, satisfying gulps. This was followed by a few strips of frozen fresh meat, then by a block of pemmican. Later, a few squares of musk ox suet gave the taste of sweets to round up our meal. Last of all, three cups of tea spread the chronic stomach-folds, after which we reveled in the sense of fulness of the best meal of many weeks.

With full stomachs and the satisfaction of a worthy task well performed, we rested.

We had reached the zenith of man's Ultima Thule, which had been sought for more than three centuries. In comfortable berths of snow we tried to sleep, turning with the earth on its northern axis.

But sleep for me was impossible. At six o'clock, or six hours after our arrival at local noon, I arose, went out of the igloo, and took a double set of observations. Returning, I did some figuring, lay down on my bag, and at ten o'clock, or four hours later, leaving Ah-we-lah to guard the camp and dogs, E-tuk-i-shook joined me to make a tent camp about four miles to the magnetic south. My object was to have a slightly different position for subsequent observations.

Placing our tent, bags and camp equipment on a sled, we pushed it over the ice field, crossed a narrow lead sheeted with young ice, and moved on to another field which seemed to have much greater dimensions. We erected the tent not quite two hours later, in time for a midnight observation. These sextant readings of the sun's altitude were continued for the next twenty-four hours.

In the idle times between observations, I went over to a new break between the field on which we were camped and that on which Ah-weh-lah guarded the dogs. Here the newly-formed sheets of ice slid over each other as the great, ponderous fields stirred to and fro. A peculiar noise, like that of a crying child, arose. It came seemingly from everywhere, intermittently, in successive crying spells. Lying down, and putting my fur-cushioned ear to the edge of the old ice, I heard a distant thundering noise, the reverberations of the moving, grinding pack, which, by its wind-driven sweep, was drifting over the unseen seas of mystery. In an effort to locate the cry, I searched diligently along the lead. I came to a spot where two tiny pieces of ice served as a mouthpiece. About every fifteen seconds there were two or three sharp, successive cries. With the ice-axe I detached one. The cries stopped; but other cries were heard further along the line.

The time for observations was at hand, and I returned to take up the sextant. Returning later to the lead, to watch the seas breathe, the cry seemed stilled. The thin ice-sheets were cemented together, and in an open space nearby I had an opportunity to study the making and breaking of the polar ice.

That tiny film of ice which voiced the baby cries spreads the world's most irresistible power. In its making we have the nucleus for the origin of the polar pack, that great moving crust of the earth which crunches ships, grinds rocks, and sweeps mountains into the sea. Beginning as a mere microscopic crystal, successive crystals, by their affinity for each other, unite to make a disc. These discs, by the same law of cohesion, assemble and unite. Now the thin sheet, the first sea ice, is complete, and either rests to make the great field of ice, or spreads from floe to floe and from field to field, thus spreading, bridging and mending the great moving masses which cover the mid-polar basin.

There was about us no land. No fixed point. Absolutely nothing upon which to rest the eye to give the sense of location or to judge distance.

Here everything moves. The sea breathes, and lifts the crust of ice which the wind stirs. The pack ever drifts in response to the pull of the air and the drive of the water. Even the sun, the only fixed dot in this stirring, restless world, where all you see is, without your seeing it, moving like a ship at sea, seems to have a rapid movement in a gold-flushed circle not far above endless fields of purple crystal; but that movement is never higher, never lower – always in the same fixed path. The instruments detect a slight spiral ascent, day after day, but the eye detects no change.

After a midnight observation – of April 22 – we returned to camp. When the dogs saw us approaching in the distance they rose, and a chorus of howls rang over the regions of the Pole – regions where dogs had never howled before. All the scientific work being finished, we began hastily to make final preparations for departure.

We had spent two days about the North Pole. After the first thrills of victory, the glamor wore away as we rested and worked. Although I tried to do so, I could get no sensation of novelty as we pitched our last belongings on the sleds. The intoxication of success had gone. I suppose intense emotions are invariably followed by reactions. Hungry, mentally and physically exhausted, a sense of the utter uselessness of this thing, of the empty reward of my endurance, followed my exhilaration.

Ninety Degrees North

Robert E. Peary

Of all the seekers of the North Pole, US naval officer Robert Edwin Peary was the most obsessive. He led his first expedition to the Arctic, a cautious reconnoitre of west Greenland, in 1886, aged 30. Thereafter, he went North almost annually. "I must *have fame," he wrote to his mother on one such trip; on another, he lost his toes to frostbite, declaring "a few toes aren't much to give to achieve the Pole." All in all, these early trips were failures; it was not until 1906 he even achieved a Northing record, 87° 06′N. Three years later, on 6 April 1909, Peary claimed the Pole. His "Peary System" of a dog-sled dash supported by relay camps needed the help of a whole Inuit community. On the last leg, however, Peary was only accompanied by his black manservant, Matthew Henson, and four Inuit, Ooqueah, Seegloo, Egingwah and Ootah.*

Perhaps a man always thinks of the very beginning of his work when he feels it is nearing its end. The appearance of the ice-fields to the north this day, large and level, the brilliant blue of the sky, the biting character of the wind – everything excepting the surface of the ice, which on the great cap is absolutely dead level with a straight line for a horizon – reminded me of those marches of the long ago . . .

Near the end of the march I came upon a lead which was just opening. It was ten yards wide directly in front of me; but a few hundred yards to the east was an apparently practicable crossing where the single crack was divided into several. I signalled to the sledges to hurry; then, running to the place, I had time to pick a road across the moving ice cakes and return to help the teams across before the lead widened so as to be impassable. This passage was effected by my jumping from one cake to another, picking the way, and making sure that the cake would not tilt under the weight of the dogs and the sledge, returning to the former cake where the dogs were, encouraging the dogs ahead while the driver steered the sledge across from cake to cake, and threw his weight from one side to the other so that it could not overturn. We got the sledges across several cracks so wide that while the dogs had no trouble in jumping, the men had to be pretty active in order to follow the long sledges. Fortunately the sledges were of the new Peary type, twelve feet long. Had they been of the old Eskimo type, seven feet long, we might have had to use ropes and pull them across hand over hand on an ice cake.

It is always hard to make the dogs leap a widening crack, though some of the best dog drivers can do it instantly, using the whip and the voice. A poor dog driver would be likely to get everything into the water in the attempt. It is sometimes necessary to go ahead of the dogs, holding the hand low and shaking it as though it contained some dainty morsel of food, thus inspiring them with courage for the leap.

Perhaps a mile beyond this, the breaking of the ice at the edge of a narrow lead as I landed from a jump sent me into the water nearly to my hips; but as the water did not come above the waistband of my trousers, which were water-tight, it was soon scraped and beaten off before it had time to freeze.

This lead was not wide enough to bother the sledges.

As we stopped to make our camp near a huge pressure ridge, the sun, which was gradually getting higher, seemed almost to have some warmth. While we were building our igloos, we could see, the water clouds lying to the east and south-east of us some miles distant, that a wide lead was opening in that direction. The approaching full moon was evidently getting in its work.

As we had travelled on, the moon had circled round and round the heavens opposite the sun, a disk of silver opposite a disk of gold. Looking at its pallid and spectral face, from which the brighter light of the sun had stolen the colour, it seemed hard to realize that its presence there had power to stir the great ice-fields around us with restlessness – power even now, when we were so near our goal, to interrupt our pathway with an impassable lead.

The moon had been our friend during the long winter, giving us light to hunt by for a week or two each month. Now it seemed no longer a friend, but a dangerous presence to be regarded with fear. Its power, which had before been beneficent, was now malevolent and incalculably potent for evil.

When we awoke early in the morning of 3 April after a few hours' sleep, we found the weather still clear and calm. There were some broad heavy pressure ridges in the beginning of this march, and we had to use pickaxes quite freely. This delayed us a little, but as soon as we struck the level old floes we tried to make up for lost time. As the daylight was now continuous we could travel as long as we pleased, and sleep as little as we must. We hustled along for ten hours again, as we had before, making only twenty miles because of the early delay with the pickaxes and another brief delay at a narrow lead. We were now half-way to the 89th parallel, and I had been obliged to take up another hole in my belt.

Some gigantic rafters were seen during this march, but they were not in our path. All day long we had heard the ice grinding and groaning on all sides of us, but no motion was visible to our eyes. Either the ice was slacking back into equilibrium, sagging northward after its release from the wind pressure, or else it was feeling the influence of the spring tides of the full moon. On, on we pushed, and I am not ashamed to confess that my pulse beat high, for the breath of success seemed already in my nostrils . . .

The last march northward ended at ten o'clock of the forenoon of 6 April. I had now made the five marches planned from the point at which Bartlett turned back, and my reckoning showed that we were in the immediate neighbourhood of the goal of all our striving. After the usual arrangements for going into camp, at approximately local noon, on the Columbia meridian, I made the first observation at our polar camp. It indicated our position as 89° 57′.

We were now at the end of the last long march of the upward journey. Yet with the Pole actually in sight I was too weary to take the last few steps. The accumulated weariness of all those days and nights of forced marches and insufficient sleep, constant peril and anxiety, seemed to roll across me all at once. I was actually too exhausted to realize at the moment that my life's purpose had been achieved. As soon as our igloos had been completed, and we

had eaten our dinner and double-rationed the dogs, I turned in
for a few hours of absolutely necessary sleep, Henson and the
Eskimos having unloaded the sledges and got them in readiness
for such repairs as were necessary. But, weary though I was, I
could not sleep long. It was, therefore, only a few hours later
when I woke. The first thing I did after awaking was to write
these words in my diary: "The Pole at last. The prize of three
centuries. My dream and goal for twenty years. Mine at last! I
cannot bring myself to realize it. It seems all so simple and
commonplace."

Everything was in readiness for an observation at 6 p.m.,
Columbia meridian time, in case the sky should be clear, but
at that hour it was, unfortunately, still overcast. But as there were
indications that it would clear before long, two of the Eskimos
and myself made ready a light sledge carrying only the instruments, a tin of pemmican, and one or two skins; and drawn by a
double team of dogs, we pushed on an estimated distance of ten
miles. While we travelled, the sky cleared, and at the end of the
journey, I was able to get a satisfactory series of observations at
Columbia meridian midnight. These observations indicated that
our position was then beyond the Pole.

Nearly everything in the circumstances which then surrounded
us seemed too strange to be thoroughly realized, but one of the
strangest of those circumstances seemed to me to be the fact that,
in a march of only a few hours, I had passed from the western to
the eastern hemisphere and had verified my position at the
summit of the world. It was hard to realize that, on the first
miles of this brief march, we had been travelling due north, while,
on the last few miles of the same march, we had been travelling
south, although we had all the time been travelling precisely in
the same direction. It would be difficult to imagine a better
illustration of the fact that most things are relative. Again, please
consider the uncommon circumstance that, in order to return to
our camp, it now became necessary to turn and go north again for
a few miles and then to go directly south, all the time travelling in
the same direction.

As we passed back along that trail which none had ever seen
before or would ever see again, certain reflections intruded
themselves which, I think, may fairly be called unique. East,

west, and north had disappeared for us. Only one direction remained and that was south. Every breeze which could possibly blow upon us, no matter from what point of the horizon, must be a south wind. Where we were, one day and one night constituted a year, a hundred such days and nights constituted a century. Had we stood in that spot during the six months of the Arctic winter night, we should have seen every star of the northern hemisphere circling the sky at the same distance from the horizon, with Polaris (the North Star) practically in the zenith.

Four months later Peary reached habitation, the Inuit settlement of Etah in Greenland – only to hear the bitter news that Frederick Cook had already claimed the Pole. Nothing daunted, Peary insisted that the Pole was his. A bitter feud broke out and eventually Peary and his powerful sponsors, including the National Geographic Society destroyed Cook's claim. Gradually, though, doubts surfaced over Peary's own claim since his calculations were so few and his supposed rate of travel over the ice so great (at 30 miles plus per day). Most likely, Peary did not reach the Pole, only its near vicinity. Perhaps it does not matter. Peary was not a good man but was, indisputably, a great explorer.

Sledge-Tracks

Ejnar Mikkelsen

Accompanied by a dog-sled team and two companions, Iversen and Jørgensen, Ejnar Mikkelsen set off across Greenland to recover the maps and diaries of a previous expedition, lost in the desolate inland ice-fields. The year was 1909.

It was a long way we had to go, and the dogs were almost dead beat. Two of them died while we were at Lamberts Land, and when we set off back southwards several others were unable to tighten their traces; they staggered as they walked and stumbled repeatedly. They could not go on. One of them lay motionless on the sledge and would soon be dead. Three dogs died on the first day of our homeward journey, and the next morning while we were cooking our spartan breakfast in the tent and Iversen was busied outside preparing for departure, I heard him exclaim: "Now devil take me, have you ever seen the like of that? Max, God help me, has eaten Devil!"

I knew well enough that the dogs were dreadfully hungry, but that they were so hungry that they would attack a weaker fellow and eat its thin body was a thing I had never experienced before, nor thought possible. It was ghastly and boded us no good.

Devil was dead, and that was not such a loss, for he was a bad dog who stole from his companions and shirked his work, if he could see his way to do so; but what was much worse was that Max, a big, strong and willing dog, one of our best, over-ate himself on Devil and died of it before the day was out.

To add to the day's difficulties we had a violent snowstorm. The snow swirled across the ice covering it with a thick, soft layer, through which we and the dogs had to wade, laboriously dragging the sledges behind us. Even worse was in store, for when we camped we discovered that our last tin of paraffin had leaked and a considerable quantity of the precious stuff run out on to the snow. This meant that until we reached our most northerly depot and could get more paraffin, we must have hot food and drink only once a day. That was almost the worst of all.

It was a ghastly journey. We pressed on as hard as we could, fully conscious of the fact that we were fighting for our lives; and when you are doing that, you can accomplish wonders. Our provisions were almost at an end and our strength was not what it had been. When at length we reached Danmarks Havn with its hut, warmth and food, we even expressed a hope that a storm might compel us to stay there for a day or two, both for the dogs' sakes and our own. Scarcely had the words crossed our lips than a storm was howling and racing across land and ice in violent gusts, flinging pebbles and crust-ice against the hut, while we sat snugly indoors with the dogs, resting, eating and sleeping, enjoying the savage fury of the storm which increased till it reached hurricane force. It was not until the ninth day after reaching Danmarks Havn that we were able to continue our journey.

By this time we were really anxious. The darkness was lengthening at a disturbing pace, and it was going to be very difficult groping our way across the pitfalls of the ice – if indeed there was any ice, for it seemed more than probable that the violent storm had broken it all up and swept it far out to sea. If the ice were not broken, however, we ought to be able to make a fairly quick journey back to Shannon, for the long rest had allowed the dogs to recover. They were comparatively brisk and frisky as we harnessed them to the sledges and hopefully set off towards the faint gleam of light that, like a beacon in the darkness, showed us the direction in which we should go. In the centre of that gleam lay our ship, some 130 miles away in the south.

Our hopes of a quick end to that journey, on which everything had gone against us right from the very first, were disappointed as soon as we got outside the Danmarks Havn and came to the storm-tossed sea ice, where soft white snow was lying several feet deep between the great packs of ice that we had to cross, and we sank deep into it. Although the dogs were well rested, they could not haul the sledges through the soft snow, scarcely even with a man to help, and things went black before our eyes as the three of us hauled on the sledges to move them no more than a few yards. This was such a labour and we were so fagged that, despite the cold and our anxiety to press on, we had to stop for a breather nearly every ten minutes.

So we toiled southwards yard by yard, and the twilight had turned into the deep darkness of night long before exhaustion forced us to stop and pitch our tent only very few miles from Danmarks Havn. The shortness of the distance we had covered was bad enough, but that was not the extent of the day's worries. Once the dogs had been fed and we had gobbled up our pemmican and got ready for bed by pulling off our moccasins and stockings, it was discovered that both of Jørgensen's feet were badly frost-bitten. All the toes and the beginning of the foot were swollen and of the yellow, waxen colour of a corpse; rime crystals glittered on the skin.

Horrified, we asked how he could have got so badly frostbitten. He thought that it must have been shortly after we set out that morning, when he had trodden through into a fissure filled with water, and the water had run into his moccasins. He had not paid particular attention to it, especially as the first searing pain in his feet quickly passed off; and even though his feet had seemed to become strangely insensible afterwards, he had said nothing so as not to waste precious time.

We spent most of the night rubbing his feet and warming them, and by degrees we did get a little life back into some of the toes. But when we had done all that could be done and crept into our sleeping bags, I felt pretty certain that Jørgensen would not be able to come on the big sledge journey across the inland ice that we planned for the spring.

I was quite certain of this when we removed the bandages a week later and saw the blue-coloured toes that were the all too evident signs of frost-bite. Iversen thought the same as I did, for a while later, as I sat on a hummock of ice during one of our all too frequent rests, he came up to me in the gloom and asked if I thought Jørgensen's feet would be all right by the spring. Unfortunately, I replied, I replied, I did not. Iversen paused, thumped his leg with his whip once or twice, then said: "That's what I thought. But if you like, I'll gladly go with you across the inland ice to Danmarks Fjord. It can't be much worse a journey than the one we can almost see the end of now."

A stout fellow, Iversen!

We toiled and struggled southwards, sledging in storms, snow and darkness so black that I had to let my leader dog go ahead on a long trace and leave her to find the best way through the jumble of ice. By doing that I could be sure of warning in time and not drive into deep holes or vainly try to force the sledge up packs that were yards high, yet impossible to see in that darkness without shadows. We waded through deep, soft snow which would bear neither us, the dogs, nor the sledges which sank deep into the yielding stuff and were continually capsizing, when it took the combined efforts of Iversen and myself to right them. We sledged over old ice with hummocks yards high and holes yards deep. We hauled the sledges across new ice that was solid enough, but covered with slush saturated with salt, and this penetrated the soles of our moccasins, through our thick wool socks, right to our icy feet that winced at the cold. It was good that they did, for then we knew that our toes had not yet become frost-bitten. That salt ice was a hell both for us and for the few dogs we still had left; but there was no escaping it, for in the darkness we could not see whether we should go to the right or to the left to avoid its sting. We just had to keep a more or less straight course towards our goal beneath the twinkling stars in the south, and take what the ice had to offer us with what equanimity we could muster – which was not much.

Our dogs were utterly exhausted. Although we had stayed too long in Danmarks Havn, the rest had not been long enough to restore the dogs' strength, and one after the other dropped in its traces, killed by the wet and by the effort of helping us to haul the sledges those last seventy miles or so of the seven hundred we had sledged. Dead, they were skinned and cut up and given to the others which still had spirit enough to wish to eat. It was not much exaggeration when, one day after a rest, Iversen called out to me as I moved off: "Hi! Wait a bit! Don't go off into the dark till I've got my dogs propped on their feet and can induce them to move."

My leader dog, the incomparable Girly, and I were in the lead, trying to find the easiest way through the darkness. Behind me I could make out the second sledge, driven by Iversen, who flung his weight into the trace over his shoulder whenever the sledge had to negotiate the slightest unevenness, toiled and fought to keep up with the lighter, leading sledge. In the rear came Jørgensen who had to cling to the uprights in order not to fall, for his feet would scarcely carry him and were so painful that every step was like being cut with knives.

We were a pitiable little procession. The dogs no longer whined, did not even snarl at each other; only now and again did plaintive gasps come from the poor brutes when the going became too heavy or the salt slush too biting. My two companions had still not lost their sense of humour, for now and again Iversen would strike up, and Jørgensen bravely join in and intone some lines of an old psalm used at weddings: "How lovely it is together, together . . ."

Naturally it was. At any rate it was better than being quite alone in that hell of darkness, ice, snow, storm and cold; but, as things were, it took a good deal of courage and confidence to be able to sing at all. I felt no desire to do so.

At length we caught a glimpse of the mountains on Shannon during the twilight of noon, and that spurred us to renewed efforts. For the next two or three days the land seemed to get no nearer, but then all at once the black mass of mountain had heaved itself up over the horizon and blotted out the lowest of the stars. It could not be long now; one more night in our sleeping bags that were frozen when we got in and later running with moisture, and then . . . ? The toil, the effort and the struggle to get through had been so great that we could scarcely believe that it would soon be over, let alone rejoice at the prospect. All sense of joy had been tortured out of us.

We knew that now we had only a few miles left, yet every star had long been kindled in the sky before we reached the crossing place. There we left one sledge, and with Jørgensen on the other, well covered with our stiff-frozen sleeping-bags and warmed by the weakest of our dogs, Iversen and I flung ourselves into the traces and hauled, hauled for all we were worth, cracked our whips to get our few dogs to make a final spurt, inciting them with yells and cries that we hoped would also be heard by our companions out there in the darkness. Thus, on 17 December, after fifteen days toil from Danmarks Havn, our eighty-six days long sledge journey finally ended; for suddenly, in the pitch dark night, with the aurora borealis flaming above our heads, the solid outline of the ship loomed in front of us like a section of denser night.

A light or two gleamed in the darkness; then we heard a dog howl and at that our poor brutes also understood that rest was near. They gave short joyful barks, such as we had not heard for a long time, pricked their ears and in joyful anticipation of all that now was within hearing and smelling distance, they picked up their tails and pulled as they had not pulled for a long time. They managed quite a speed, and with Iversen and I lumbering stiff-leggedly alongside in a weird kind of gallop we reached *Alabama*, while the others came hurrying to meet us with lanterns to light the last bit of the way of our seven-hundred-mile long journey through the darkness to Lamberts Land and back.

We stumbled aboard and down into the cabin, where glad companions thrust great mugs of scalding coffee into our hands and wonderful thick slices of white bread with mountains of butter. And meanwhile, the ice in our clothes melted. We dripped water, and pools formed under us. Then, to the others' amazement, we began to peel off our sledging clothes, layer after layer, and all as dirty and wet as a floorcloth fit to be thrown away.

Nor were our dogs forgotten in the joy of our homecoming; they were given as much as they could eat and more. Of the twenty-three fit dogs we had had harnessed to our sledges when we left the ship on 26 September, only seven returned with us; the rest of the faithful creatures had died on the way of exhaustion, hunger and cold. A sledge dog's life is a harsh one.

Thin Ice

W. Elmer Ekblaw

The American geographer W. Elmer Ekblaw (1890–1956) was a member of the 1913–17 Crocker Land Arctic Expedition to Thule, northwest Greenland.

Spring had come to Thule. The daily temperatures still sank below freezing, but the daily sunlight approached the 24-hour maximum. In the sunlit niches among the rocks, the snow was fast evaporating. Every day the open water was breaking in toward the land. The spring hunting was on. At the first opportunity, Mene, Sechmann and I had set out from North Star Bay for a hunting trip at Cape Parry.

When we arrived, we found other hunters already rendezvoused there, comfortably quartered in snow houses along the shore and well stocked with walrus and seal that they had killed. We stayed with them three days and then started back toward North Star Bay, hunting along the edge of the ice as we sledged southward toward Saunders Island in the mouth of Wolstenholme Sound.

Halfway between Beechwood Point and the northern point of Saunders Island, but well out to sea, we came upon a deep re-entrant of the open water, where a large herd of walrus were disporting themselves along the edge of a patch of hummocky old ice – an irresistible lure for Mene and Sechmann, who would not go on without a try at this game. By a stroke of good fortune all too in frequent in an Eskimo hunter's experience, Mene sank his harpoon at the first cast deep into the flank of a big cow walrus that swam up to the low berg behind which he had stalked the herd.

In due time we "landed" the huge carcass, cut it up on the ice and, after feeding the dogs all they could eat, set up our tent and made ready to turn in for a sleep, while the dogs settled the meal they had eaten. It was well after midnight. The sun had hardly set. In the soft night light, the pale moon swung high in the sky, almost invisible. Flocks of fulmars, guillemots and eiders, but lately returned to the north, winged their ways still farther northward. The sky was well-nigh cloudless, the water rippled calm and dark before our tent and the ice toward the land gleamed solid and white as far as we could see.

Yet Sechmann shook his head and seemed uneasy – the sky in the south did not please him. Mene and I could detect nothing dubious and made light of his fears. Tired as he was, Sechmann got into his sleeping-bag reluctantly and, while Mene and I made the most of the chance to rest, he kept restless vigil.

Early forenoon came. The sun had risen well into the sky when Sechmann called us urgently. We turned out at once. A gray glare hung in the sky over the open water seaward and gusts of eddying winds swirled the loose snow about. The dogs were stirring uneasily. Not a bird was in sight on the water or in the air.

But it was none of these signs that had alarmed Sechmann enough to call us; he directed our attention to a long, wraith-like horizontal pennant of cloud flung out like a weather-vane from the tip of a lone monadnock rising high above the plateau back of North Star Bay. To the Polar Eskimo, this pennant of cloud is a dread warning of the approach of a violent southerly gale and storm that will carry the ice out to sea. The moment Mene, who knew full well its grave import, saw this, he excitedly yelled to us to waste not a single moment in getting away.

We untied our dogs and hitched them to the sledges in less time than it takes to tell. We left our tent, our sleeping-bags, our heap of walrus meat and, with our whips snapping in angry staccato, raced away as fast as our well-fed dogs could carry us. We headed straight for North Star Bay, dodging the patches of rough ice as best we could, straining our eyes for the smoothest going ahead, running behind our sledges to lighten the loads for the dogs. The dogs sensed the alarm we felt. As the wind strengthened and the snow sifting before it rose higher and struck harder, they increased their speed rather than slowed down.

For an hour or more we raced along, hardly calling a word to one another – Mene, with the biggest and best dogs, in the lead; Sechmann, with poorer dogs but a better driver, close behind Mene's sledge; and I close behind Sechmann, merely because my dogs would not let the others get away.

And then came the crisis.

Spread black and threatening before us, a dark lead of new, thin ice stretched across the whole sound. How wide it was, we could not see in the haze of wind-driven snow. How thin it was, we could readily see, as our killing-irons broke through it of their own weight. How far it extended, we could only guess, but probably it reached from shore to shore.

During our absence the ice had parted under the urge of the ebbing spring tide and had drifted seaward. The water had frozen again over the lead, but only a thin film of ice had formed – so recently that no frost had yet whitened it. There it lay, barring our way, a dark, treacherous band that we had to cross. We could not tarry a moment, for not far behind us the storm was rolling in, a dark mass of tumbling cloud and wind-tossed snow.

As Sechmann drew his dogs back from the lead for a good running start, Mene moved along the lead a half hundred yards and drew back a little farther than Sechmann had done and I took my position still farther along the lead and still farther back; for, as Sechmann explained, we must not strike the ice at the same time or near together.

As Mene and I held our dogs back to give Sechmann a chance to get started, we waved to each other but neither spoke a word – our feelings were too tense. As Sechmann's dogs struck out across the thin ice, they spread wide apart in the line; low and swift, with feet wide-spread, they ran; astride and well back on his sledge, Sechmann cracked his whip fast and furiously, encouraging but not striking his dogs. It was easy to see that they realized as well as he the danger they faced. Beneath the runners of his sledge, the yielding ice bent down; it rose in a wave-like fold before and behind.

Almost before Sechmann's dogs had got well out on the thin ice, Mene's team was on its way toward the edge. As his sledge struck the dark band, I saw, as I had not seen with Sechmann's sledge, that, while the rounded front part of the runners was holding up on the ice as the dogs sped along, the sharp, square corners at the back were cutting through and little jets of water were spraying up on either side of the runner. The runners were actually cutting two narrow lanes through the ice.

My own dogs had already dashed forward and, as my sledge neared the black, thin ice, I dared hardly hope that it would hold me, for I weighed at least fifty pounds more than either Mene or Sechmann. But my runners were shod a quarter-inch wider and, though the ice bent deep under the sledge, this extra width carried my greater weight. My dogs were doing their best to keep pace with Mene's and Sechmann's, so I had no need of using my whip.

With my heart in my mouth, scarcely daring to breathe, I sat rigid, watching the water spraying out from the sides of both runners; at times half the runners were cutting through. If a dog had stumbled, or bumped into another, to slow the sledge a moment, we should have dropped through. But not a dog faltered; every one knew as well as I what would happen if he did. Never had my team made such speed. The first moments were the most perilous. The young ice was thin, but it was also smooth as glass and we gathered momentum as we raced on; yet, even so, the minutes seemed hours. The lead proved to be over half a mile wide and it seemed an age before we got across.

As he struck the solid ice, Sechmann gave a wild yell of relief; Mene gave another as he achieved it a moment later; but, until I had taken a breath or two, I could not even whisper. To them, particularly to Sechmann, who came from the hazardous ice of the Disko region, it was an old, oft-repeated adventure; to me – well, I vowed it was my last hazard over such thin ice.

We could not take time to greet each other and congratulate ourselves on the safe outcome of our decision. The storm still raged and there might be other such leads ahead. We could lose no time. We drove relentlessly on through the gathering blizzard and finally made shore just within Cape Abernathy. There we built a snow shelter and stayed till the storm swept by.

Rescue from Wrangel Island

William Laird McKinlay

As a young Glasgow schoolteacher in 1913 McKinlay signed up with the Canadian Arctic Expedition led by the anthropologist Vihjalmur Stefansson. A more slapdash or irresponsible polar leader than Stefansson it is difficult to conjure; when the expedition's ship, Karluk, became trapped in Arctic ice, Stefansson went off on a caribou hunt, declaring he would be "back to the ship in ten days"; in fact, he wandered for five years. Meanwhile, the Karluk, like the Jeanette and Fram before her, drifted with the pack ice. Eventually, the Karluk was crushed and sank but, led by the ship's commander, Robert Bartlett (who had captained Peary's ship on his 1909 pole attempt), all the ship's complement of twenty-five escaped over the ice to Wrangel Island. From there Bartlett made a 700-mile journey to fetch help. McKinlay was one of the party left behind on the island; of these eight died trying to escape over the ice, two died of malnutrition, and one committed suicide. The survivors owed their lives to the Inuit family with the Karluk expedition, Kuralak, Kiruk ("Auntie"), Helen and Mugpi.

Although I kept as active as I could I was becoming more and more conscious of my physical weakness. Every step was taken by sheer effort of will. I could not have walked to Rodger's Harbour*, let alone to Siberia. What worried me even more than the steady decline in my physical well-being was an increasing sense of loneliness. My difference with Munro had shaken me badly. I had nothing in common with my companions in the other tent except our common distress; my only contact with them was when they were engaged in argument with Hadley over food, and

* Rodger's Harbour: a camp set up by some of the Karluk party on the south of Wrangel Island.

I felt I no longer had any influence with them. At times I felt weighed down with weariness, wretchedness, and an anguish which I knew I must keep in check.

Then gradually it dawned on me that I had been concentrating on the purely material and had lost sight of what had previously been my mainstay – that inscription in my Bible, Psalm 121. At once my spirits lifted. It was not simply that I stopped worrying about the future; it was an acceptance of the fact that the future was not in my hands. It was the acceptance of "Thy will be done". I was still acutely conscious of my depressing physical weakness. I was still determined to do all in my power to counter it, but the wretchedness of spirit was gone. I felt much more contented. I was ready to face whatever was to come.

Keeping in mind the need to conserve ammunition Kuraluk tried every method his native skill could contrive to get food. He killed a bird or two with a spear. He practised with a "throwing" stick, but without any luck. When the ice filled the bay there was nothing, not a living thing to be seen. A large flock of geese flew over one day, but all we had of them was the sound of their flight. On 26 August Kuraluk saw the tracks of a bear. On the twenty-eighth Hadley and I saw a pod of five walrus far out on the ice, but when he and Kuraluk went up the hill to pinpoint them they were gone. Everything seemed to be against us.

Hadley, Kuraluk and I were determined to do everything possible to preserve our supply of dried meat intact, for it seemed our only insurance against starvation. But we had still to put up with the improvidence of our colleagues. One day when we three were out of camp they tried to persuade Auntie to give them some of our walrus hide. They had finished theirs a week before. Their share of the three *ugruks* – half the catch, although they were only three to our six – would last them only three more days, and they had made no effort to preserve any of it. Our share was still drying on the rack. It looked as if we would have to keep them going on our ration.

Then Williamson suddenly announced his intention of visiting Rodger's Harbour. We were absolutely astonished. He had never walked a mile from camp since the day we landed on the island. Yet he set out on the morning of 18 August and returned on the morning of the twenty-first. It just did not make sense that a man who had been inactive for so long should be capable of covering between sixty and seventy miles in that short period. I could not have done it at that time. He reported that the three men at Rodger's Harbour were all well and in good spirits. They had had five seals and a large number of duck eggs, but were now living on sealskin. The ice was still around the south coast, but as Williamson was leaving it had started moving under the influence of a south-west gale, and Munro was not expecting a ship before the end of the month. Williamson brought back a .45 Colt revolver and 36 cartridges belonging to the cook. Hadley wrote in his diary: "I told him he had better not have any more accidents with guns in that Tent because I would not stand for any more."

In the eternal search for food the Eskimos had introduced a new item to our diet, the roots of a plant unknown to us, long and fibrous, and looking and tasting like what I, as a boy, had known as "liquorice stick". It had to be boiled for a long time and required a great deal of chewing. With this and scurvy grass and the rotting scraps from our meat tin, we continued to keep our dried meat intact. What we ate had little or no sustenance in it, but it prevented the violent muscular contractions of an empty stomach and deadened the sickening hunger pains. But the liquorice root also gave us acute constipation. In spite of plenty of seal oil, our bowels simply ceased to function. In fact my entire internal mechanism seemed to be in complete disarray.

On 22 August Williamson asked for some of our precious dried meat. Hadley noted: "Meat all gone we started on our Dried meat and that will soon be gone we've to feed both parties now with it and then we will start on the skins." We decided to give each man in the other tent a daily ration which would not be increased under any circumstances. In return we asked for a share of their tea tablets; ours had been finished for some time, but they still had plenty, because they had the remainder of the rations of Munro, Maurer and Breddy. I had never recovered my ration from Mamen, so Munro had a good supply at Rodger's Harbour. Williamson had brought back 300 tablets from there. He gave us 88 tablets, and while we drank our first mug of tea Hadley grimly announced that from then on he would "prove as good a horse-trader as the next fellow!"

Since I had gone to live with Hadley and the Eskimos the

routine at mealtimes had never varied. We all sat round with the dish in the middle and helped ourselves, dipping each morsel in a separate dish of seal oil. This practice did not, of course, ensure an equal distribution. If one happened to be a slow eater it was just too bad. Now, as we started on the dried meat, Auntie started to divide it up at each meal and give us separate portions. When the meal was over we noticed that each of the Eskimos kept back a little from his or her plate and put it in a closed tin. Hadley and I were intrigued, and his reaction was typical of his attitude to the Eskimos – "I'm damned if I'm going to let a dirty Indian beat me, even at saving meat!" So we both started a savings bank of our own. However, just when I had saved enough for one meal my tin fell off the meat rack and the dogs got my savings.

We tried to eke out the dried meat by having meatless days. On those days a typical menu was: Breakfast, a mug of soup from the rotting scraps in our "starvation" tin; lunch, a mug of tea with a piece of walrus hide and some decomposed blubber from the "poke"; supper, cooked roots with tea. But I finally decided to give up roots. My digestive organs could stand no more.

For four weeks after the killing of the three *ugruks* not one living thing fell to our hunters. On 28 August the ice was back in the bay and we were scouting round hopefully. Here and there were a few pools of water in which crowbills were swimming around with their young. We could not afford ammunition to shoot them, but Kuraluk had a brilliant idea. Why not net them? We dug out a net which had lain neglected under a snow-drift. With infinite care we disposed ourselves round a hole filled with birds and with a mighty heave cast the net over them. Not a bird escaped us. Our first day's catch was 30 old birds and 60 of their offspring. The following day we got 120 all told. We were jubilant. The haul was not to be compared to an *ugruk*, or a walrus, or a bear, but it was such an unexpected windfall, and all achieved without the expenditure of a single cartridge. Our spirits rose. We forgot for the time being that August had ended and hope of rescue had dwindled almost to vanishing point.

September opened fine and fair, with clear skies, bright sun and a very light southerly air. Kuraluk killed thirty crowbills with his throwing stick. Hadley sat at a seal hole for hours and was just about to give up when the seal's snout appeared. He killed it, but it sank like a stone, and Kuraluk refused to try to find it. Hadley tried to grapple for it himself and he managed to bring the seal to the surface, but before he could get his hands on it, it slipped off the hook and disappeared.

It was bitterly cold next day, but Hadley sat at a seal hole all day, and the day after, becoming more and more despondent. Sitting beside a hole for six hours on end with nothing happening was a depressing occupation. There was not a sign of any living thing, except the odd young fox. There were several of these around from time to time, quite unafraid and very inquisitive. They would sit watching us at a distance of not more than ten feet. If we made any move towards them they would trot off, stop when we stopped, then turn and resume their watching. Williamson fired thirteen shots at one little fox with his Colt .45, and at the end of the barrage the fox was still sitting staring at him.

We were hungry, almost desperately hungry. Our birds were finished, our dried meat was gone, and sealskin could do no more than stave off starvation. We caught one young fox in a trap, but it merely proved tantalizing. Hadley said that foxes were not usually eaten, because they were too rank in flavour, but I could find no fault with that little fellow. I kept busy making and setting traps, not just for meat, but also for skins. I was optimistic enough to think I might get enough to make a fur shirt for the winter.

We were now having heavy snow again, and we were all doing what we could to improve our clothing, though some of us had little hope of keeping warm. Kuraluk went along the beach and cut off a large slab of whalebone from part of a skeleton he found. With this he intended to shoe a sledge which he would build during the winter for use on our long journey to Siberia in the spring. What optimists we were!

By 6 September we had decided that there was no prospect of bigger game in the area and we would move next day to our new camp site and start building a hut for the winter. That afternoon Hadley and Kuraluk returned dragging a seal. It was a mere infant, not more than enough to provide one main meal. Unashamedly we gorged on seal meat and blood soup, stifling our conscience with the excuse that we would be fitter for the strenuous work of moving house next day. And we finished off the banquet with a helping of fish, the first we had caught during our stay on the island. Auntie and Helen had seen these small tomcod, about fifteen inches long, in a crack in the beach ice, and caught them by "jigging" for them. The jig was merely a bent pin fastened to a length of sinew. This was lowered into the crack and held stationary until a fish swam over it. Then, with an upward jerk, the fish was impaled on the pin. They caught about two dozen, and they were so delicious that we decided to get up early next morning and go "jigging" for our breakfast before the big move.

So, at daybreak on 7 September everybody in our tent was out with a bent pin on the end of a line, and the tomcod catch was slowly piling up. After a few hours we three men returned to the tent to get on with preparations for the removal. Then Kuraluk went out to find a piece of wood to make a spear for Hadley. He was hardly outside when he startled us with a mighty shout:

"*Umiakpik kunno!*" ("Maybe a ship!")

Hadley and I tumbled out, and I got my glasses on the object which was causing Kuraluk's excitement. It was three miles off to the east, at the edge of the ice which filled the bay and beyond. And without any doubt it was a ship, a small schooner. She seemed to be steaming northwest, and we could not tell whether she was a relief ship, or just a walrus-hunter chasing the large herd we had seen on the ice a few days before.

When we saw her hoist her sail our hearts missed a beat. She wasn't looking for us! She was on her way north! As one man we started shouting, and the noise must have scared every seal in the Arctic, though I doubt if anyone heard it three miles away on the ship. Hadley blazed away precious ammunition with his revolver, and we sent Kuraluk racing over the ice in the hope of heading her off.

Then we saw her lower her sail, and as we watched, hardly able to believe our eyes, a party of men disembarked on the ice and began walking towards the beach. We were saved! Captain Bartlett had got through!

We were in a daze. Stupified by shock and disbelief, we could only think of one thing – food. We called to Auntie and the kids and found that they had collected about two pounds of tomcod.

Keeping our camp routine to the last, we traded some of the fish with Williamson for tea tablets. As our rescuers were crossing the ice to reach us we were putting on the pots for a meal of fish and tea, determined to eat our tomcod before we left. We didn't rush out with glad cries to meet the men who trudged up to our tents. We were shy and too dazed to speak. It was all so unreal, like a dream. We shook hands, and they told us they were from the schooner *King and Winge*. They were on their way to trade and to hunt walrus, but their owner, Olaf Svenson, had promised to look for us if he could get near enough Wrangel Island. They had called first at Rodger's Harbour and had Munro, Maurer and Templeman on board.

Obediently we stood and posed for a cinematograph cameraman, who had joined the *King and Winge* in the hope of a rescue story. He followed us everywhere as we stumbled about, gathering our bits and pieces together. We left our tents standing, with conspicuous notes fixed on poles in case any other search vessel should arrive. (In fact the *Corwin* managed to reach the island not long after we left.)

We staggered out across the ice for the last time. We were sure we could walk unaided the three miles to the ship, but the cameraman insisted that each of us should be supported by two of the ship's company. I think it made a better picture. The men told us that Captain Bartlett had organized a rescue operation after reaching Siberia, and he was now on the United States Revenue Cutter *Bear*, which was also making for Wrangel Island.

Someone told us that all the world except the United States was at war, but the news made almost no impact on our reeling brains. We were more interested in the prospect of the meal waiting for us when we got on board the *King and Winge* at 1.30 pm. This was something we had been dreaming about for months. A thousand times we had imagined how we would relish those first mouthfuls of real food. It would be a memorable meal. But it was nothing like that. We ate mechanically, still in a dream. The first thing I ate was bread and butter, but when we had finished our meal I could hardly remember what I had eaten.

Then came a hot bath, and that really was luxury. There was no use pretending that one bath could move all the dirt and grease caked on different parts of our bodies; it would take many soakings to do that. But we did feel cleaner when we donned new clothing from the ship's "slop chest". We mooned around, or lay down on beds of skins spread on the deck. We got up again and drank coffee in the galley, where the coffee pot was kept continuously bubbling on the stove for our special benefit. We smoked and smoked. We lay down again, got up again, drank more coffee. Sleep was impossible.

During the short night we tied up to an ice floe, and at 4 a.m. we got under way again. The ice had thickened up, but strangely enough the risk of being frozen in again never crossed my mind. After a great deal of bucking and twisting and turning, we reached loose ice and steamed towards Herald Island. We wanted to make one last attempt to look for traces of the Mate's party. But we came up against ice which was solid and impenetrable, and we could not get near the island.

At 11.30 a.m. on 8 September, as we turned southwards, we spotted the smoke of a steamship, which was coming towards us. It was the *Bear*. She hove to, and as she came alongside, we saw a familiar figure on the deck. It was Captain Bartlett.

McKinlay returned from his experiences in the Arctic to serve as an officer on the Western Front. With the peace he once again became a teacher, and it was only in 1976 that McKinlay committed the truth of Stefansson's Karluk *expedition to paper. He died in 1983, aged 95.*

"At last! At last! People":
Rasmussen Encounters Eskimo

Knud Rasmussen

*Born in 1879, the Danish ethnologist Rasmussen journeyed widely
across Greenland and the North American Arctic in support of his
theory that the Eskimo (Inuit) were descended from migratory Asian
tribes. The encounter below, from Rasmussen's Fifth Thule Expedition (1921–4), took place in northwest Greenland ("Knud Rasmussen Land"), where the Inuit were still almost untouched by
modern culture.*

We had reached our goal!

But one of our number was dangerously ill, and we were
powerless to relieve him; the people we had hoped to meet with
at Cape York settlement had left their houses, and our famished
dogs were circling madly round us; we had hardly enough food
left for one good meal, even for ourselves. To lighten our sledges
we had stored our chests of supplies at Cape Murdoch, and a
considerable proportion of the provisions that we had calculated
would suffice for the journey thence to Cape York had been
devoured by the dogs.

The forced pace of the last two days and nights had greatly
exhausted us; for the moment, however, we were so much struck
by all the new sights around us, by the strange, primitive human
dwellings, that we forgot our fatigue in exploring the settlement.
But it was not long before we flung ourselves down by our sledges
and dropped asleep.

It is but a short rest, though, that a traveller can permit himself
under critical circumstances. One of us soon woke again and
roused the others. A more careful examination of the snow huts
then revealed that it could not have been long since their owners

had left them. In one of them there was a large seal, not cut up, which provided our dogs with a very welcome feast.

There were numerous sledge-tracks running north-ward, with only a light powdering of snow upon them; consequently men could not be far away.

I remembered a story told us by an old Greenlander whom we had visited in Danish West Greenland, on our way north.

He knew that they had kinsmen a long way north; but no one was certain exactly whereabouts. It was so far away. The following tradition he had heard as a child:

"Once upon a time there was a man who lived farther north than any of the settlements. He hunted bears every spring on a dogsledge.

"Once, during the chase, he came upon strange sledge-tracks, and made up his mind to seek out the people who had made them. So he set out on his bear-hunts the next year earlier than he was wont to do. The third day he came to houses different in appearance from those to which he was accustomed. But he met with no people; fresh tracks, though, showed that the settlement had been only recently left.

"When the bear-hunter drove off the following year he took wood with him, as a gift to the strangers; for he thought they must suffer greatly from the want of wood, as they used narwhal's tusks for the roof-beams of their houses.

"But he did not meet with the strangers on his second visit either. True, the tracks were newer than they had been the last time, but he did not dare to follow them up, and thus put a still greater distance between himself and his own village. He contented himself with burying the wood he had brought with him in the snow near the houses, and then, having presented his gifts, he went home.

"The third year he raised the best team of dogs that he had ever had, and earlier than was his custom he drove north after bears and the strange people. When at last he reached the village it was just as it had been the other years; the inhabitants had gone; but in the snow, where he had left his wood, they had hidden a large bundle of walrus tusks, and inside, in the entrance passage, lay a magnificent bitch and puppies. These were the return gifts of the strangers.

"He put them on his sledge and drove back home; but the people who lived north of all other men he never found."

And now, just as had been the case then, many sledge-tracks ran north, and again, as in the legend, it could not have been many days since they had been made.

It was an odd experience, creeping through the long, low tunnel entrances into the houses; with our furs on we could hardly pass. At the end, we came to a hole up through which we had to squeeze ourselves, and then we were in the house. There was a strong smell of raw meat and fox inside.

The first time one sees a house of this description one is struck by the little with which human beings can be content. It is all so primitive, and has such an odour of paganism and magic incantation. A cave like this, skilfully built in arch of gigantic blocks of stone, one involuntarily peoples mentally with half supernatural beings. You see them, in your fancy, pulling and tearing at raw flesh, you see the blood dripping from their fingers, and you are seized yourself with a strange excitement at the thought of the extraordinary life that awaits you in their company.

We walked round, examining all these things, which, in their silent way, spoke to us of the men and women who lived their lonely life up here. A little way from the houses, in a circle, were some large round stones, shining with stale grease. "Here they must have had their meals," suggested one of our Greenlanders. Already our imagination was at work.

Farther up, just under the overhanging cliff, lay a kayak with all its appurtenances, covered over with stones. Behind it was a sledge, with dead dogs harnessed to it, almost wholly hidden by the drifting snow. There, then, men lay buried with all their possessions, as Eskimo custom prescribes.

All that we saw was new to us and absorbingly interesting. At last we were on Polar Eskimo ground, and our delight at having reached our goal was unmeasured. If only we had been spared the calamity of our comrade's serious illness! He lay dazed and feverish, unable to stir, and had to be fed when he required to eat. At a council among ourselves, it was agreed that Mylius-Erichsen should remain with him, keeping the two seal-hunters, while Jörgen Brönlund and I drove on north as fast as our almost exhausted dogs could take us, to look for people. We calculated that at a distance of about sixty-four English miles from Cape York we ought to come across Eskimos at Saunders Island, and if not there, then at Natsilivik, some forty English miles farther north. All the provisions we could take were a few biscuits and a box of butter. Still we had our rifles to fall back upon.

The sealers had gone out to try their luck, and we waited for them to return – which they did empty-handed. Then we drank a little cocoa, and drove off along the glorious rocky coast, into the clear, light night.

In the neighbourhood of Cape Atholl we discovered fresh sledge-tracks, which we followed up. They led to a stone cairn, under a steep wall of rock, which cairn contained a large deposit of freshly-caught bearded seal. Ah! then we could not be far from human beings. The intense suspense of it! For it almost meant our comrade's life.

We had driven all night – some twelve hours, and a little way beyond Cape Atholl were obliged to pull up, to give the dogs a rest and breathing time. We had covered about 56 English miles at full gallop, and, should we be forced to drive all the way to Natsilivik, should have to make reasonable allowance for the empty stomachs of our poor animals. We flung ourselves down on the ice, discussed our prospects, ate a little butter – we simply dared not eat our biscuits – lay down on our sledges and went to sleep.

After three hours' rest we went on again.

We had only driven a little way when a black dot became visible in front. It developed and grew into a sledge.

"Jörgen! – Knud! – Jörgen! – Knud!"

We were half mad with relief and delight, and could only call out each other's names.

Speed signal! The dogs drop their tails and prick up their ears. We murmur the signal again between our teeth, and the snow swirls up beneath their hind legs. A biting wind cuts us in the face. At last! At last! People, other people, the new people – the Polar Eskimos!

A long narrow sledge is coming towards us at full speed, a whip whistles through the air, and unfamiliar dog-signals are borne on the wind to our ears. A little fur-clad man in a pair of glistening white bearskin trousers springs from the sledge and runs up to his

team, urging the dogs on still faster with shouts and gesticula-
tions. Behind him, sitting astride the sledge, sits another person,
dressed in blue fox, with a large pointed hat on her head: that is
his wife.

Our dogs begin to bark, and the sledges meet to the accompaniment of loud yelps. We spring off and run up to each other,
stop and stare at one another, incapable of speech, both parties
equally astonished.

I explain to him who we are, and where we come from.

"White men! White men!" he calls out to his wife. "White men
have come on a visit!"

We have no difficulty in understanding or making ourselves
understood.

I hasten to the woman, who has remained seated on the sledge.
All sorts of strange emotions crowd in upon me, and I do not
know what to say. Then, without thinking what I am doing, I
hold out my hand. She looks at me, uncomprehending, and
laughs. And then we all laugh together.

The man's name is Maisanguaq (the little white whale skin),
his wife Meqo (the feather); they live at Igfigsoq, from twelve to
sixteen English miles south of our meeting-place, and we learn
that three or four other families live at the same place.

In our eagerness to arrive at Agpat (Saunders Island) we had
cut across outside the bay on which Igfigsoq lies.

The snow on the ice at the entrance to the bay being hard, we
had not been able to detect sledge-tracks which might have led us
to enter it. But when we heard that there were far more people at
Agpat, and that the hunting and sealing there were particularly
good, I decided to drive straight on, and, by sledge post, advise
my comrades to do the same.

Maisanguaq promptly seated himself across my sledge, his wife
driving theirs, and we all set off together towards Agpat, carrying
on the liveliest conversation meanwhile. The two ought really to
have been at home by this time, but had turned back to show us
the way.

Meqo was a capital dog-driver, and wielded her long whip as
well as any man. In West Greenland you never see a woman
drive, so I expressed my surprise; Maisanguaq laughed out with
pride, and called out to her gaily to lash hard with her whip, it

amused the white men, and Meqo swung her whip, and off we dashed, she leading.

"*Tugto! tugto!*" she cried, and the dogs bounded forward, and soon we began to near the high-lying little island on which Agpat lay.

Maisanguaq then told me that "many" people lived at Agpat: there were three stone houses and five snow huts; and he burst into peals of laughter each time he thought of the surprise he was going to witness. "White men! White men!" he called out, whenever an instant's pause in the conversation occurred, and rubbed his hands with glee.

Suddenly he stopped short and listened, then jumped up in my sledge and looked behind. Another sledge had come in sight a long way to our rear.

"*Aulavte! aulavte!*" he called out. (That is the signal for a halt.) But my dogs did not understand him, and I had to come to the rescue by whistling to them.

Then he jumped out on the one side, and began to hop up in the air and slap himself on the legs. He continued to indulge in these extraordinary antics till he was quite red in the face from his exertions. This was an indication that something unusual was going on. The strange sledge came on at a gallop; as it approached, two young fellows sprang out and ran alongside, shouting. Maisanguaq began to yell too, and continued to flounder about like a madman.

At last the sledge came up to ours and stopped. The two young men were named Qulutana and Inukitsoq. First, of course, they wanted to know who we were, and Maisanguaq delivered himself of his lesson. Then the whole caravan drove on, laughing and shouting, towards Agpat.

Never in my life have I felt myself to be in such wild, unaccustomed surroundings, never so far, so very far away from home, as when I stood in the midst of the tribe of noisy Polar Eskimos on the beach at Agpat. We were not observed till we were close to the land, so the surprise and confusion created by our arrival were all the greater.

Maisanguaq recommenced his jumping antics by the side of the sledge as soon as we arrived within calling distance of the place, and then screamed out a deafening "White men! White men!"

The people, who had been moving briskly about among the houses, stood still, and the children left off their play.

"White men! White men!" repeated the young fellows who had joined us. Our dogs drooped their tails and pricked up their ears as a many-tongued roar from the land reached us. And then, like a mountain-slide, the whole swarm rushed down to the shore, where we had pulled up – a few old grey-haired men and stiff-jointed old crones, young men and women, children who could hardly toddle, all dressed alike in these fox and bear-skin furs, which create such an extraordinarily barbaric first impression. Some came with long knives in their hands, with blood-stained arms and upturned sleeves, having been in the midst of flaying operations when we arrived, and all this produced a very savage effect; at the moment it was difficult to believe that these "savages", "the neighbours of the North Pole", as Astrup called them, were ever likely to become one's good, warm friends.

Our dogs were unharnessed, and quantities of meat flung to them at once. Meat there was in abundance, and everywhere, in between the houses, you saw cooking-hearths. It was immediately apparent that these people were not suffering from privation.

On one's arrival at a settlement in Danish West Greenland, it is usual for the young women to help the newcomers off with their outdoor clothes. Now, for a moment, I forgot where I was, and as the Greenlandic custom is, stretched out my foot towards a young girl who was standing by my side, meaning her to pull off my outer boots. The girl grew embarrassed, and the men laughed. There was that winning bashfulness about her that throws attraction over all Nature's children; a pale blush shot across her cheek, like a ripple over a smooth mountain lake; she half turned away from me, and her black eyes looked uneasily out over the frozen sea.

"What is thy name?"

"Others will tell thee what my name is," she stammered.

"Aininâq is her name," put in the bystanders, laughing.

A jovial old paterfamilias then came up to her and said with gravity:

"Do what the strange man asks thee!" And she stooped down at once and drew off my boots.

"Move away; let me come!" called out an old woman from the crowd, and she elbowed the people aside and forced her way through to my sledge.

"It was my daughter thou wast talking to!" she burst out eagerly. "Dost thou not think her beautiful?" and she rolled her little selfconscious eyes around.

But Aininâq had slipped quietly away from the crowd of curious beholders and hidden herself. It was only later that I learnt my request to her had been construed into a proposal of marriage.

Jörgen and I were now conducted up to the houses. Sheltering walls of snow had been built up here and there to form cooking-places, and round these the natives clustered. A young fellow came up carrying a frozen walrus liver, raw, which was our first meal; all the men of the village ate of it with us, to show their hospitable intent. Curious youngsters gaped at us greedily from every side, and ran away when we looked at them.

When the pot had boiled, we were called in to the senior of the tribe, the magician Sagdloq ("The Lie"); the boiled meat was placed on the floor, and a knife put in our hands.

A lively conversation got under way. The people were not difficult to understand, as their dialect differed but little from the ordinary Greenlandic; they were surprised themselves at the ease with which they understood us, who yet came from such a distance.

After the meal, they immediately set about building us a snow hut.

"There is a sick man with you, so you must be helped quickly," they said.

They hewed large blocks out of the hard snow: those were to be the walls of our new house. Then they set it up in a hollow in the snow, and in the course of half an hour it stood complete.

A sledge was sent for our comrades, and by early morning we were all together.

The reception these pagan savages gave us was affectingly cordial; it seemed that they could not do enough for us. And just as they were on our arrival – helpful as they could possibly be, and most generous with their gifts – so they remained the whole time that we spent among them . . .

Wings Over the Pole

Richard E. Byrd

A graduate of the US Naval Academy at Annapolis, Byrd turned to aviation in 1916 following an injury which ended his military career. On the night of 8 May 1926 Byrd, together with his pilot Floyd Bennett, set off from Spitzbergen for the North Pole in a triple-engined Fokker:

With a total load of nearly 10,000 pounds we raced down the runway. The rough snow ahead loomed dangerously near but we never reached it. We were off for our great adventure!

Beneath us were our shipmates – every one anxious to go along, but unselfishly wild with delight that we were at last off – running in our wake, waving their arms, and throwing their hats in the air. As long as I live I can never forget that sight, or those splendid fellows. They had given us our great chance.

For months previous to this hour, utmost attention had been paid to every detail that would assure our margin of safety in case of accident, and to the perfection of our scientific results in the case of success.

We had a short-wave radio set operated by a hand dynamo, should we be forced down on the ice. A hand-made sledge presented to us by Amundsen was stowed in the fuselage, on which to carry our food and clothing should we be compelled to walk to Greenland. We had food for ten weeks. Our main staple, pemmican, consisting of chopped-up dried meat, fat, sugar and raisins, was supplemented by chocolate, pilot-bread, tea, malted milk, powdered chocolate, butter, sugar and cream cheese, all of which form a highly concentrated diet.

Other articles of equipment were a rubber boat for crossing open leads if forced down, reindeer-skin, polar-bear and seal fur clothes, boots and gloves, primus stove, rifle, pistol, shotgun and ammunition; tent, knives, axe, medical kit and smoke bombs – all as compact as humanly possible.

If we should come down on the ice the reason it would take us so long to get back, if we got back at all, was that we could not return Spitzbergen way on account of the strong tides. We would have to march Etah way and would have to kill enough seal, polar-bear and musk-ox to last through the Arctic nights.

The first stage of our navigation was the simple one of dead reckoning, or following the well-known landmarks in the vicinity of Kings Bay, which we had just left. We climbed to 2,000 feet to get a good view of the coast and the magnificent snow-covered mountains inland. Within an hour of taking [to] the air we passed the rugged and glacier-laden land and crossed the edge of the polar ice pack. It was much nearer to the land than we had expected. Over to the east was a point where the ice field was very near the land.

We looked ahead at the sea ice gleaming in the rays of the midnight sun – a fascinating scene whose lure had drawn famous men into its clutches, never to return. It was with a feeling of exhilaration that we felt that for the first time in history two mites of men could gaze upon its charms, and discover its secrets, out of reach of those sharp claws.

Perhaps! There was still that "perhaps", for if we should have a forced landing disaster might easily follow.

It was only natural for Bennett and me to wonder whether or not we would ever get back to this small island we were leaving, for all the airmen explorers who had preceded us in attempts to reach the Pole by aviation had met with disaster or near disaster . . .

As we sped along over the white field below I spent the busiest and most concentrated moments of my life. Though we had confidence in our instruments and methods, we were trying them for the first time over the Polar Sea. First, we obtained north and south bearings on a mountain range on Spitzbergen which we could see for a long distance out over the ice. These checked fairly well with the sun-compass. But I had absolute confidence in the sun-compass.

We could see mountains astern gleaming in the sun at least a hundred miles behind us. That was our last link with civilization. The unknown lay ahead.

Bennett and I took turns piloting. At first Bennett was steering, and for some unaccountable reason the plane veered from the course time and time again, to the right. He could glance back where I was working, through a door leading to the two pilots' seats. Every minute or two he would look at me, to be checked if necessary, on the course by the sun-compass. If he happened to be off the course I would wave him to the right or left until he got on it again. Once every three minutes while I was navigating I checked the wind drift and ground speed, so that in case of a change in wind I could detect it immediately and allow for it.

We had three sets of gloves which I constantly changed to fit the job in hand, and sometimes removed entirely for short periods to write or figure on the chart. I froze my face and one of my hands in taking sights with the instruments from the trapdoors. But I noticed these frostbites at once and was more careful thereafter. Ordinarily a frostbite need not be dangerous if detected in time and if the blood is rubbed back immediately into the affected parts. We also carried leather helmets that would cover the whole face when necessary to use them.

We carried two sun-compasses. One was fixed to a trapdoor in the top of the navigator's cabin; the other was movable, so that when the great wing obscured the sun from the compass on the trapdoor, the second could be used inside the cabin, through the open windows.

Every now and then I took sextant sights of the sun to see where the lines of position would cross our line of flight. I was very thankful at those moments that the Navy requires such thorough navigation training, and that I had made air navigation my hobby.

Finally, when I felt certain we were on our course, I turned my attention to the great ice pack, which I had wondered about ever since I was a youngster at school. We were flying at about 2,000 feet, and I could see at least 50 miles in every direction. There was no sign of land. If there had been any within 100 miles' radius we would have seen its mountain peaks, so good was the visibility.

The ice pack beneath was criss-crossed with pressure ridges, but here and there were stretches that appeared long and smooth enough to land on. However, from 2,000 feet pack ice is extraordinarily deceptive.

The pressure ridges that looked so insignificant from the plane varied from a few feet to 50 or 60 feet in height, while the average thickness of the ice was about 40 feet. A flash of sympathy came over me for the brave men who had in years past struggled northward over that cruel mass.

We passed leads of water recently opened by the movement of the ice, and so dangerous to the foot traveler, who never knows when the ice will open up beneath and swallow him into the black depths of the Polar Sea.

I now turned my mind to wind conditions, for I knew they were a matter of interest to all those contemplating the feasibility of a polar airway. We found them good. There were no bumps in the air. This was as we had anticipated, for the flatness of the ice and the Arctic temperature was not conducive to air currents, such as are sometimes found over land. Had we struck an Arctic gale, I cannot say what the result would have been as far as air roughness is concerned. Of course we still had the advantage of spring and 24-hour daylight.

It was time now to relieve Bennett again at the wheel, not only that he might stretch his legs, but so that he could pour gasoline into the tanks from the five-gallon tins stowed all over the cabin. Empty cans were thrown overboard to get rid of the weight, small though it was.

Frequently I was able to check myself on the course by holding the sun-compass in one hand and steering with the other.

I had time now leisurely to examine the ice pack and eagerly sought signs of life, a polar-bear, a seal, or birds flying, but could see none.

On one occasion, as I turned to look over the side, my arm struck some object in my left breast pocket. It was filled with good-luck pieces!

I am not superstitious, I believe. No explorer, however, can go off without such articles. Among my trinkets was a religious medal put there by a friend. It belonged to his fiancée and he firmly believed it would get me through. There was also a tiny horseshoe made by a famous blacksmith. Attached to the pocket was a little coin taken by Peary, pinned to his shirt, on his trip to the North Pole.

When Bennett had finished pouring and figuring the gasoline consumption, he took the wheel again. I went back to the incessant navigating. So much did I sight down on the dazzling snow that I had a slight attack of snow blindness. But I need not have suffered, as I had brought along the proper kind of amber goggles.

Twice during the next two hours I relieved Bennett at the wheel. When I took it the fourth time, he smiled as he went aft. "I would rather have Floyd with me," I thought, "than any other man in the world."

We were now getting into areas never before viewed by mortal eye. The feelings of an explorer superseded the aviator's. I became conscious of that extraordinary exhilaration which comes from looking into virgin territory. At that moment I felt repaid for all our toil.

At the end of this unknown area lay our goal, somewhere beyond the shimmering horizon. We were opening unexplored regions at the rate of nearly 10,000 square miles an hour, and were experiencing the incomparable satisfaction of searching for new land. Once, for a moment, I mistook a distant, vague, low-lying cloud formation for the white peaks of a far-away land.

I had a momentary sensation of great triumph. If I could explain the feeling I had at this time, the much-asked question would be answered: "What is this Arctic craze so many men get?"

The sun was still shining brightly. Surely fate was good to us, for without the sun our quest of the Pole would have been hopeless.

To the right, somewhere, the rays of the midnight sun shone down on the scenes of Nansen's heroic struggles to reach the goal that we were approaching with the ease of an eagle at the rate of nearly 100 miles an hour. To our left, lay Peary's oft-traveled trail.

When I went back to my navigating, I compared the magnetic compass with the sun-compass and found that the westerly error in the former had nearly doubled since reaching the edge of the ice pack, where it had been eleven degrees westerly.

When our calculations showed us to be about an hour from the

Pole, I noticed through the cabin window a bad leak in the oil tank of the starboard motor. Bennett confirmed my fears. He wrote: "That motor will stop."

Bennett then suggested that we try a landing to fix the leak. But I had seen too many expeditions fail by landing. We decided to keep on for the Pole. We would be in no worse fix should we come down near the Pole than we would be if we had a forced landing where we were.

When I took to the wheel again I kept my eyes glued on that oil leak and the oil-pressure indicator. Should the pressure drop, we would lose the motor immediately. It fascinated me. There was no doubt in my mind that the oil pressure would drop any moment. But the prize was actually in sight. We could not turn back.

At 9.02 a.m., 9 May 1926, Greenwich civil time, our calculations showed us to be at the Pole! The dream of a lifetime had at last been realized.

We headed to the right to take two confirming sights of the sun, then turned and took two more.

After that we made some moving and still pictures, then went on for several miles in the direction we had come, and made another larger circle to be sure to take in the Pole. We thus made a non-stop flight around the world in a very few minutes. In doing that we lost a whole day in time and of course when we completed the circle we gained that day back again.

Time and direction became topsy-turvy at the Pole. When crossing it on the same straight line we were going north one instant and south the next! No matter how the wind strikes you at the North Pole it must be travelling north and however you turn your head you must be looking south and our job was to get back to the small island of Spitzbergen which lay somewhere south of us!

There were two great questions that confronted us now. Were we exactly where we thought we were? If not – and could we be absolutely certain? – we would miss Spitzbergen. And even if we were on a straight course, would that engine stop? It seemed certain that it would.

As we flew there at the top of the world, we saluted the gallant, indomitable spirit of Peary and verified his report in every detail.

Below us was a great, eternally frozen, snow-covered ocean, broken into ice fields or cakes of various sizes and shapes, the boundaries of which were the ridges formed by the great pressure of one cake upon another. This showed a constant ice movement and indicated the non-proximity of land. Here and there, instead of a pressing together of the ice fields, there was a separation, leaving a water-lead which had been recently frozen over and showing green and greenish-blue against the white of the snow. On some of the cakes were ice hummocks and rough masses of jumbled snow and ice.

At 9.15 a.m. we headed for Spitzbergen, having abandoned the plan to return via Cape Morris Jessup on account of the oil leak.

But, to our astonishment, a miracle was happening. That motor was still running. It is a hundred to one shot that a leaky engine such as ours means a motor stoppage. It is generally an oil lead that breaks. We afterward found out the leak was caused by a rivet jarring out of its hole, and when the oil got down to the level of the hole it stopped leaking. Flight Engineer Noville had put an extra amount of oil in an extra tank.

The reaction of having accomplished our mission, together with the narcotic effect of the motors, made us drowsy when we were steering. I dozed off once at the wheel and had to relieve Bennett several times because of his sleepiness.

I quote from my impressions cabled to the United States on our return to Kings Bay:

The wind began to freshen and change direction soon after we left the Pole, and soon we were making over 100 miles an hour.

The elements were surely smiling that day on us, two insignificant specks of mortality flying there over that great, vast, white area in a small plane with only one companion, speechless and deaf from the motors, just a dot in the centre of 10,000 square miles of visible desolation.

We felt no larger than a pinpoint and as lonely as the tomb; as remote and detached as a star.

Here, in another world, far from the herds of people, the smallnesses of life fell from our shoulders. What wonder that we felt no great emotion of achievement or fear of death that lay stretched beneath us, but instead, impersonal, disembodied. On, on we went. It seemed forever onward.

Our great speed had the effect of quickening our mental processes, so that a minute appeared as many minutes, and I realized fully then that time is only a relative thing. An instant can be an age, an age an instant.

We were aiming for Grey Point, Spitzbergen, and finally when we saw it dead ahead, we knew that we had been able to keep on our course! That we were exactly where we had thought we were!

It was a wonderful relief not to have to navigate any more. We came into Kings Bay flying at about 4,000 feet. The tiny village was a welcome sight, but not so much so as the good old *Chantier* that looked so small beneath. I could see the steam from her welcoming and, I knew, joyous whistle.

It seemed but a few moments until we were in the arms of our comrades, who carried us with wild joy down the snow runway they had worked so hard to make.

Among the first to meet us had been Captain Amundsen and Lincoln Ellsworth, two good sports.

Byrd returned to America to a hero's ticker-tape reception and the awarding of a Congressional Medal of Honour. Over the years, however, doubts were raised as to whether Byrd and Bennett had actually reached the North Pole; Byrd himself is alleged to have admitted in private that he flew short of the goal but in sight of it.

Too Close to the Ice

Umberto Nobile

Commander of the airship **Norge**, *which overflew the North Pole on the Amundsen-Ellsworth expedition of 1926, Nobile returned to the Arctic two years later with another airship, the* **Italia**. *This time Colonel Nobile's intention was to explore the unknown north of Greenland, and from there chart a new course to the Pole.*

On the morning of 25 May the bitter struggle against the wind went on without respite.

For nearly 30 hours a stiff head-wind of 24 or 30 m.p.h. had been blowing. We advanced with difficulty, swerving now to one side, now to the other. It had become extremely difficult to keep on our course. Often the squalls got the upper hand of our helmsman, producing deviations of 20 or even 30 degrees.

Wind and fog. Fog and wind. Incessantly. And from time to time flurries of snow.

Everyone on board went about his business in silence. Some looked tired. The damp, grey, chilly atmosphere surrounding us weighed on our spirits. For a whole day and more we travelled thus. Not a glimmer of light through the fog above us; fog and cloud all the time. And below us, the colourless, monotonous pack.

Zappi and Mariano had charge of the route, dividing their attention between the steering-wheel, the speed-measuring apparatus, and the table on which the charts were spread. Trojani and Cecioni took turns at the elevator. Malmgren helped the Naval officers, taking long spells at the steering-wheel. Behounek, calm and impassive as ever, was beside his instruments. Pontremoli and Lago had gone to sleep some hours before in the fur bags laid down towards the stern. I was supervising everything, more or less, but for some time my attention had been given to checking the speed and to the radio-goniometrical reports, which served to determine our position.

There was great uncertainty as to this. We were making far less headway than our speed measurements indicated. Obviously, the zigzag course into which we were driven diminished our actual progress along the route. Only so could it be explained that we had not yet seen the land that ought to have been sighted some hours previously.

It was a really difficult situation. But – as always in similar circumstances – the difficulties had excited my energy: I did not feel tired, but even more alert than usual.

I divided my time between the navigation table, the wireless cabin, and speed measurements. When I got Biagi's reports I myself marked them on the map. Now and again I went into the front of the pilot-cabin to see that everything was all right. Then passing by my child's photograph – an old photograph which had already accompanied me on the *Norge* and had been fixed up again on the wall this time – I gave it a rapid glance. Maria's lovely eyes looked back at me. I was struck by the sadness of their expression – they seemed to be misted with tears.

Given the uncertainty as to our position, the radio-goniometrical data had assumed a vital importance. The trouble was that the radio did not tell us the exact spot where we were, but only the direction in which the *Città di Milano* heard our signals most strongly. So one could trace a bearing on the chart, somewhere along which the airship was at that moment; but where on this line, we did not know.

Towards seven in the morning my anxiety at not yet seeing land grew still keener. By this time, if we could rely on our calculations – according to which at 1.30 a.m. we had been 100 miles NE of Moffen Island – we should have already sighted the coast. But there was nothing to be seen. In front of us, to the extreme limit of the horizon, nothing but frozen sea.

I felt more than ever the need of checking our position: we must reckon with the drain on our petrol caused by the forced speed at which we were travelling; that was still my chief worry.

I was anxious to put an end to this uncertainty, somehow or other. So it occurred to me to order that for half an hour at least, we should travel westwards, at right angles to the line given by these reports, instead of straight along it, as we had done until then. The angle between the two observations made at the beginning and end of this course, would give us an approximate idea of our position on the line, and so of our distance from King's Bay.

At 7.40 a.m. we were on a radius from King's Bay passing about 10 miles NE of Moffen Island. I gave orders to steer westwards. At 8.10 the new observation showed that the radius had approached the island by 3 or 4 miles. This experiment had not lasted long enough to give a reliable result, but I dared not go on with it because the wind, blowing hard on the bow, reduced our speed too much.

So we resumed our course towards North-East Land, steering southwards. The wind seemed even stronger.

At 9.25 I was standing by the door of the wireless cabin waiting for news when suddenly I heard someone cry: "The elevator wheel has jammed!" I ran up at once and saw Trojani – who had been for some time at this helm – trying to turn the wheel, to raise the nose. But he could not manage it. The controls of the helm were blocked.

I realized the gravity of the danger. We were at a height of 750 ft. The ship, being down by the nose, was dropping. In a few minutes we should strike the pack.

There was nothing to be done but to stop the engines – which I did at once. When I looked out and saw the three propellers at a standstill I breathed once more. There was nothing now to fear, for the ship was so light that soon it would stop sinking and go up again.

As I had foreseen, the moment the engines were stopped the descent slowed down abruptly, and about 250 ft from the pack it ceased altogether. We began to rise gently.

In the meantime Cecioni – who had been asleep in the keel – came down into the cabin, and by my orders paid out the ballast chain, which was lying on the floor. As the chain was heavy this little operation took some time, and I thought it would be much better to let the chain hang out, ready in case of need. At that moment I had not the faintest idea how soon the event would justify this small precaution.

While we were slowly rising, Viglieri had released the elevator by a sharp blow. I ordered Cecioni to take it to pieces and examine the mechanism. As he worked, the airship went on rising. Some time before I had opened all the air-valves, so that the gas-pressure had been reduced below zero. Now it showed signs of going up again. I kept an eye on the pressure-gauges.

Soon we were swallowed up in fog. At this moment Mariano came to me and said: "Don't you think, sir, we might take the opportunity of getting above the fog and taking the height of the sun?"

I agreed, all the more readily because the fog around us was becoming steadily more luminous, showing that it was thinning out. Besides, Cecioni had not yet finished his work.

During the ascent I saw the pressure-gauges register a slight rise. At a certain point I noticed that the pressure in the last compartment of the stern was much higher than in the others. I then let out a little gas, to equalize the pressure in this compartment with that of the others. We were still going up.

At 2,700 ft we at last emerged from the fog and found blue sky. A glorious sun flooded the cabin with its rays. Mariano and Zappi made their observations.

Cecioni had finished. On dismounting the casing of the elevator he had found nothing wrong with it, so probably the obstruction had been caused by ice forming on the inside. In any case, the helm was now working perfectly well.

We were at 3,300 ft by this time. The gas began to dilate, making the liquid rise rapidly in the pressure-gauges; but before they reached the height at which they were normally kept when flying, I ordered two engines to be started – the centre and the left.

It was 9.55 a.m.

We set off again, and flew for a few minutes longer above the fog, scanning the horizon in front to see if by any chance the highest peaks of the Svalbard were rising up in the far distance out of the mist. But there was nothing to be seen. Nothing, as far as our field-glasses would reach, except the sea and the fog.

I then decided to come down to the height at which we had until lately been sailing. It was essential to find the pack again, so that we could go on checking our drift and speed.

We plunged back into the fog and slowly descended until
the frozen sea appeared clearly in sight. We were about 900 ft
up.

The Crash

My first thought was to measure our speed. We had only two
engines working, but it seemed to me all the same that we were
making a bit more headway than before.

Our first measurement, in fact, showed a velocity in relation
to the pack of about 30 m.p.h. The wind had gone down, then, and
there was no need to start the third engine. I was relieved at this,
for it deferred our anxiety about the petrol. I was also glad not to
have to go on straining the ship by an excessive speed.

Once more I turned my attention to the course, with Mariano
and Viglieri. Combining the position given by the recent height
measurement with the radio-goniometrical report at 10 o'clock,
we had located our position with approximate certainty. We were
apparently 45 miles NE of the Ross Islands and 180 miles NE of
King's Bay.

On the basis of this distance I calculated that we should reach
the Bay between three and four in the afternoon, and intended to
announce this by wireless a little later on.

Everything on board was now in order and each man had
resumed his post. Malmgren was at the helm, with Zappi giving
him instructions from time to time. Cecioni had not left the
elevator since he had tested its casing. Beside him, between the
pressure-gauges and the engine controls, stood Trojani.

In the rear of the cabin with me, sitting round the navigation
table, were Mariano and Viglieri. One of them was taking speed
measurements with the Goertz apparatus clamped to the side of
the table. Behounek stood behind us, making observations with
his instruments. Pontremoli and Lago, as I said before, had been
asleep for some hours up in the stern.

The mechanics were all awake, in their respective engine-
boats, Arduino, helped by Alessandrini, was in the gangway,
superintending the inside of the ship.

We were flying between 600 and 900 ft up. The dirigible was

still light, so to keep it at the proper height we had to hold the nose down.

At 10.30 I again ordered a speed measurement. When this had been taken I walked to the front of the cabin and looked out of the right-hand porthole, between the steering-wheel and the elevator. To test the height, I dropped a glass ball full of red liquid, and stood there, timing its fall with a stop-watch.

While I was attending to this, I heard Cecioni say excitedly: "We are heavy!"

I turned with a start to look at the instruments.

The ship was right down by the stern, at an angle of 8 degrees to the horizon; nevertheless, we were rapidly falling.

The peril was grave and imminent. A short distance below us stretched the pack. I at once gave the orders which had to be given, the only ones that could save the ship in this emergency – if that was possible: to accelerate the two engines, start the third, and at the same time lift the nose of the dirigible still higher. I hoped by these means to overcome the unexpected heaviness.

Simultaneously, I shouted to Alessandrini to run out on the top of the ship and inspect the stern valves, as I thought gas might be escaping – the only explanation that occurred to me at the moment of this serious and rapid increase in weight.

Meanwhile, the mechanics had carried out my orders. Pomella and Caratti had speeded their engines up to 1,400 revolutions and Ciocca, with surprising promptness, had started his own. The ship began to move faster, and tilted at an angle of 15 or 20 degrees.

The dynamic lift obtained in this way must certainly have represented several hundredweight.

But unfortunately we went on falling. The variometer – on which my eyes were fixed – confirmed it; in fact, we seemed to be dropping even faster.

I realized that there was nothing more to be done. The attempt to combat the increased weight by propulsion had failed . . . A crash was now inevitable; the most we could do was to mitigate its consequences.

I gave the necessary orders: to stop the engines at once, so as to avoid fire breaking out as we crashed; and to drop the ballast-chain. Sending Cecioni to do this, I put Zappi in his place.

It was all that could have been ordered; it was ordered promptly and with absolute calm. The perfect discipline on board was unbroken, so that each man carried out my orders as best he could, in the vertiginous rapidity of the event.

In the meantime the pack was approaching at a fearful speed. I saw that Cecioni was finding it difficult to untie the rope which held the chain. "Hurry up! Hurry up!" I shouted to him. Then noticing that the engine on the left, run by Caratti, was still working. I leaned out of a porthole on that side, and at the top of my voice – echoed, I think, by one of the officers – repeated the order: "Stop the engine!" At that moment I saw the stern-boat was only a few tens of yards from the pack. I drew back into the cabin.

The recollection of those last terrible instants is very vivid in my memory. I had scarcely had time to reach the spot near the two rudders, between Malmgren and Zappi, when I saw Malmgren fling up the wheel, turning his startled eyes on me. Instinctively I grasped the helm, wondering if it were possible to guide the ship on a snow-field and so lessen the shock . . . Too late! . . . There was the pack, a few yards below, terribly uneven. The masses of ice grew larger, came nearer and nearer . . . A moment later we crashed.

There was a fearful impact. Something hit me on the head, then I was caught and crushed. Clearly, without any pain, I felt some of my limbs snap. Some objects falling from a height knocked me down head foremost. Instinctively I shut my eyes, and with perfect lucidity and coolness formulated the thought: "It's all over!" I almost pronounced the words in my mind.

It was 10.33 on 25 May.

The fearful event had lasted only 2 or 3 minutes!

After the Crash

When I opened my eyes I found myself lying on the ice, in the midst of an appalling pack. I realized at once that others had fallen with me.

I looked up to the sky. Towards my left the dirigible, nose in air, was drifting away before the wind. It was terribly lacerated around the pilot-cabin. Out of it trailed torn strips of fabric, ropes, fragments of metal-work. The left wall of the cabin had remained attached. I noticed a few creases in the envelope.

Upon the side of the crippled, mutilated ship stood out the black letters ITALIA. My eyes remained fixed on them, as if fascinated, until the dirigible merged in the fog and was lost to sight.

It was only then that I felt my injuries. My right leg and arm were broken and throbbing; I had hurt my face and the top of my head, and my chest seemed all upside down with the violence of the shock. I thought my end was near.

Suddenly I heard a voice – Mariano's – asking: "Where is the General?" And I looked around me.

I had never seen such a terrible pack: a formless, contorted jumble of pointed ice-crags, stretching to the horizon.

Two yards away on the right, Malmgren was sitting, and a little farther off lay Cecioni, moaning aloud. Next him was Zappi. The others – Mariano, Behounek, Trojani, Viglieri, and Biagi – were standing up. They appeared unhurt, except for Trojani, whose face was stained by a few patches of blood.

Here and there one could see wreckage – a dreary note of grey against the whiteness of the snow. In front of me a strip of bright red, like blood which had flowed from some enormous wound, showed the spot where we had fallen. It was the liquid from the glass balls.

I was calm. My mind was perfectly clear. But now I was feeling the seriousness of my injuries – worst of all, a terrible convulsion in my chest. Breathing was a great effort. I thought I had probably sustained some grave internal injury. It seemed that death was very near – that maybe I had only 2 or 3 hours to live.

I was glad of this. It meant that I should not have to watch the despair and slow death-agony of my comrades. What hope was there for them? With no provisions, no tent, no wireless, no sledges – nothing but useless wreckage – they were lost, irremediably lost, in this terrible wilderness of ice.

The fate of the downed airship gripped the western world. Among those who searched for the Italians was Roald Amundsen, whose seaplane was lost in the doing. Eventually, the Italia *airmen were rescued by the Soviet ice-breaker* Krasin. *Reviled by the Italian fascist regime for the* Italia *disaster, Colonel Nobile exiled himself for many years. He published his memoirs,* My Polar Flights, *in 1961. Nobile died on 19 July 1978, at the age of ninety-three.*

White Devils

David Haig-Thomas

In 1938, accompanied by an Eskimo hunter, Haig-Thomas sledged from Thule in Greenland across Ellesmere Island to Amund Ringnes Island where, while mapping the coastline, he discovered a new island. His account of his expedition was published in 1939 as Tracks in the Snow.

I had stopped to rest – in fact, I thought of taking a little nap in the sun – when I heard the distant bark of a dog. I strained my ears. There it was again. It was a bark mixed with fear and rage. My mind flew to the little bitch and the three puppies which we had left near the tent. I ran to the shore and climbed a little knoll, from which I could see the tent through my glasses. Just as I had thought! There were two large white wolves not five yards away from the bitch. I could see her head over the rock. She was showing her teeth and snarling defiance. If these white devils killed my dog I would be even with them; and, dropping down on to the ice-foot, I ran as hard as I could.

I knew I was out of sight of the wolves, and should be able to come up within a hundred yards without their seeing me. Several times I slipped on the ice and dropped into a walk, for I mustn't be out of breath when I arrived. I wanted to shoot straight. For the last few yards I crept up on my hands and knees; and all the time the barking was growing louder. The bitch must have been keeping the wolves off for half an hour, and they were not likely to attack in the next few seconds if they had already waited so long. I was pretty certain that they were the two wolves that Nookap and I had observed from the tent. We had seen them sleeping on the ice close to the remains of a seal which they had killed and eaten.

I took off my reindeer coat, folded it up, and rested my rifle on it: then slowly drew up my head. There they were about one hundred yards away, standing within a few feet of the little bitch. I looked to see that the sights were right. I changed the soft-nosed bullet for a hard one, for I didn't wish to damage the skin more than possible, knowing that the Museum would be overjoyed to have them. Now, you bloodthirsty brutes, I whispered to myself; and squeezed the trigger.

One of the wolves sprang into the air and dropped dead, while its mate bounded away up the hillside. For a short time the empty case refused to eject; then out it came and another cartridge was slipped into the barrel.

The wolf was now a good four hundred yards away. I turned round, rested the rifle and fired again. I saw a little puff of snow below the wolf – evidently I had under-estimated the distance. The animal stood motionless, perhaps wondering why its mate hadn't followed. I didn't think there would be time to alter the sights, so fired five or six feet over its back. An answering plop told me I had found my mark. The wolf spun round, snapped at its side, then loped off, leaving a trail of blood behind it. It was now too far off for me to waste any more cartridges on. I thought that at any moment it would fall dead; but through my glasses I could see a large red splash too far back: the bullet had gone through its stomach.

That any animal should suffer a slow death is horrible; yet I was glad I had not missed altogether when I remembered how many musk-oxen's calves I had probably saved, and when I thought of the brutal way the wolves kill the musk-oxen, by tearing out their stomachs from between their legs when they are still alive and leaving them to die a slow, lingering death. Then I felt ashamed of myself; for, after all, in what other way could a wolf kill a musk-ox? It wouldn't be able to tear out its throat, for the musk-ox's horns are very sharp; and anyway the long hair and wool on its neck would probably be ample protection. It is strange what cruel methods Nature teaches to her children.

Hunting in the Land of the Long Day

Doug Wilkinson

*For more than a year in the early 1950s the Canadian photographer
Doug Wilkinson lived at Aulatseevik (pop. 31) on north Baffin
Island. He did so as a member of an Inuit family, with no outside
resources. The Inuit named Wilkinson "Kingmik," meaning "dog",
because of the similarity of the sounds "dog" and "Doug".*

Every day in July the hunters of Aulatseevik, myself among them,
roamed far and wide over the ice in the never-ending hunt for
food. Usually we went off in pairs, each pair with sled and dogs
moving off in a different direction, to be gone sometimes for only
a day, sometimes for three or four before coming back to the
camp for a rest. On such hunts we lived completely off the land,
or rather off the products of the sea, eating most of the meat raw,
caching what we and the dogs could not eat in some convenient
place so that it would serve as dog food during the long winter
night to come.

On a few occasions all the adults and most of the children at the
camp went out together on an organized hunt, five or six sleds
moving over the ice together. On such organized hunts we would
be gone for as little as a day, or as much as three days, and rarely
did anyone think of sleep in that time. It was hunt and eat, from
the time we left, until the time we returned to camp, everyone
completely stuffed, thoroughly exhausted, and soaking wet from
splashing through the deep puddles on the ice.

The main purpose of these hunts is to get the skins of the young
seals. The skin is the property of the man making the kill while all
meat and fat is communal property.

The weapon generally used on such hunts is the seal harpoon.
It consists of a long steel shaft about shoulder high that is

rounded off at one end and has a sealskin line wound about the other to form a rough handle. Onto the rounded end is fitted the harpoon head which is readily detachable. The head is made of steel fashioned to form a broad flat point that tails off into flanged flukes curving back from the main axis. Attached to this head is a long sealskin line. The steel head has a ball socket which fits over the rounded end of the harpoon handle. With the head held in place, the sealskin line is run along the handle to a spot about two thirds of the way to the top where a small metal loop is fastened. At this point on the sealskin line a tiny thong of sealskin has been sewn. This thong is threaded into the metal loop, the main line pulled taut and the thong wedged under the loop. The harpoon head is now firmly attached to the handle, yet a quick tug on the line is all that is needed to free the small thong and allow the head to drop free of the handle.

When harpooning a seal the harpoon handle is gripped in one hand and the coiled line in the other. Standing over the seal hole waiting for the seal to rise, the hunter, if he is right-handed, holds the harpoon head to the left across his knees. Both feet are kept flat on the ice, and together. There must be no movement of the feet as a sound could easily carry down through the ice and frighten the seal. The hunter stands back about two feet from the hole, invisible to a seal rising up from below. He rests by bending over from the waist, and putting his elbows on his knees; otherwise he stands upright, eyes glued to the hole ready to spot the tell-tale rise of water in the hole that signifies the approach of a seal. When this happens, he slowly raises the harpoon high, arm straight above the head. The moment the seal's head breaks the surface, down goes the arm and, if he is a good hunter, the harpoon head enters the seal's body at the thick neck.

Such accuracy comes only after long practice. Eskimo men and boys play games to ensure that they get practice without having to wait for seals. In one such game a broomstick is used for a harpoon. The player stands on a patch of clear snow or earth, both feet together, knees straight. About two feet to the front and slightly to one side the broom handle is thrust into the snow, making a neat round hole. Then without moving his feet he raises the broom handle high and tries to plunge it down into the same hole, putting all the force he can into the drive.

When the harpoon head enters the seal's body, thrust in deep through the layers of fat, the hunter gives a sharp tug on the line held in his other hand. The line comes free of the handle which is quickly withdrawn leaving the harpoon head buried deep under the fat and flesh. By this time the seal has taken off for the depths. The hunter drops the harpoon handle, grabs the line with both hands, and hangs on. When the seal reaches the limit of the line, it is pulled up short. The harpoon head is pulled backward and the curved flukes pull it flat under the skin. The seal is safely hooked.

My first organized hunt was one of the most unusual events of my life as an Eskimo. We had five sleds, each with four or five hunters, ranging in age from old Akomalik and his wife to little Noahkudluk, Idlouk's youngest son. As we moved off from the camp there was a lot of confusion and laughter; dog teams became tangled and people ran from sled to sled, pushing one another off onto the ice and sometimes into the water. About three miles out on the frozen surface of Eclipse Sound, all sleds stopped by a large frozen-in iceberg, while the male hunters climbed the berg and with their telescopes searched the ice around looking for the best spot to go after the young seals. To the north and west lay much rough ice, ideal places for the seals to have their *aglos* as the Eskimos call the openings under the snow in which the young are raised. Here and there black dots that were sleeping seals were visible on the ice, a few of them being identified as young seals.

Once the area was decided upon, everyone readied his harpoon, then jumped aboard a sled. In a moment five sleds were racing over the ice toward a nearby area of rough broken ice about a mile away. Here three young seals had been spotted asleep on the ice. Speed was essential now for the first sled on the spot might get in a quick shot at a seal before it went down, and then would have first chance at covering the best holes in the area to await the seal coming up.

Faster and faster the sleds flew over the ice, dogs urged on by voice and whip. The sleds slammed down into puddles of water throwing up sheets of ice-cold water over the occupants at the front. They did not mind; being up front they would be first off the sled in the race for the holes. I was with Idlouk on his big sled along with Oodleteetuk and a visiting Eskimo, Kyaklooapik. Our sled slowly drew ahead of the others as we approached the nearest seal.

The seals had seen us coming from some distance off. Being young, their curiosity got the better of their caution and they squirmed around on the ice, necks craning into the air as they attempted to make out what we could be. The sight of the onrushing sleds was too much for two of the seals; they quickly dived into the holes, but the third one was curious. It stayed out on the ice as if hypnotized by the fast-approaching sled.

When we came within three hundred yards, it was still there, straining for a better look. Now we all started to shout at the top of our lungs. The seal rolled over and over, almost standing on hind flippers. Two hundred yards and it was still there. Then the dogs caught sight of it and the sled leaped forward with a jerk. When a hundred yards off, I dropped my harpoon and snatched up the rifle from the sled. With a running jump, I leaped clear and ran quickly to one side so as to get a clear line of fire. Dropping to one knee I took quick aim and fired. No luck, the shot went wild. I had not time for another, for at that moment the dogs reached the seal.

They were on him in a flash. The careening sled, with nothing to hold it back, slammed into the fighting, snarling dogs. Idlouk and Kyaklooapik leaped into the fray. Both had dropped their harpoons and were trying to catch the madly squirming seal with their bare hands and keep it clear of the dogs. What a mêlée! Idlouk, Kyaklooapik, joined by Oodleteetuk and myself, ten dogs and the seal all fighting like fiends in a raceway of rushing water about one foot deep beside the seal hole.

Idlouk got the seal by a front flipper, but the seal and a dog bit his hand and he had to let go. Then Kyaklooapik dropped on it and tried to pin it down beneath his weight, while we kicked and slashed at the dogs to get them away. But the seal was strong and slippery. It squirmed out from under Kyaklooapik, rolled under two or three dogs and reached the edge of the hole. Idlouk grabbed a hind flipper as it started to slide into the hole, while Oodleteetuk and I fell on him to keep him from being dragged into the hole. But Idlouk couldn't keep his grip. With a mighty flip and a splash the seal was gone, leaving us lying in a heap in the foot-deep water.

By this time the other sleds had come up. Quickly everyone ran off over the ice, searching out the other breathing holes in the vicinity. In five minutes twenty hunters were scattered over the ice in an area of about a square mile, each motionless over a seal hole waiting for the seal to come up. Idlouk, Oodleteetuk, Kyaklooapik and I retrieved our harpoons from the overturned sled, and covered off holes but the best ones were taken by people from the other sleds. Now all we could do was wait. It was only a matter of time until the seal came up in one of the holes.

Five minutes went by and there was no sign of the seal. Not a sound could be heard as everyone stood motionless. Then, a shout rang out from my left. Kitchooalik had spotted the seal's head in a hole no one had noticed. Quickly one of the small boys nearby moved over to cover that hole. All was quiet again.

I stood motionless, eyes glued to the tiny whirlpool in the hole at my feet. Small chips of ice bobbed and chuckled in the swiftly racing water, sucked under from time to time only to bob up again in a different spot. I was soaked to the skin, water dripped from my clothes hitting the ice in a steady rhythm of musical pings. With such noises I was sure no seal would come my way, but, already a little more like an Eskimo, I stood patiently, no thought for anything but the seal.

As I waited I became conscious of another sound. Far off to the south where the sheer rock cliffs of our island lay deep in the shadow of the afternoon sun, a dull muted roar grew in volume until it filled the air all about. It was an awe-inspiring sound. Heavy and pulsating it came, as if giant machines were grinding rocks and stone, rending the earth to dust. The air about me quivered and trembled, tremors ran through the ice under my feet. I looked about with apprehension, half expecting to see the far-off land sink into oblivion or suddenly disappear in a flash of flame. Near me stood Agnowyah, Idlouk's old mother. As the sound built up, she dropped her harpoon to the ice and looked wildly about. She shrank down to the ice, eyes gazing terror-stricken at the distant land. All the hunters' heads turned to watch.

We could see nothing, but we knew it was a landslide. Tremendous at it was, we were too far out from shore to do anything but note the direction from whence the sound came. Later I visited the place of the slide on the north shore of our island, and I found an entirely new valley. The slide had started in a small snow field near the top of the island. At first it had been all snow, but as it gained momentum and weight the slide tore off rocks and soil, ripping a tortuous path that gradually widened from three yards to over three hundred, rushing between rocky cliffs at express-train speed until finally it poured off the land onto the sea ice which cracked and buckled beneath the massive weight.

Slowly the sound died. Fitfully it flared up once or twice, then was heard no more. Agnowyah rose to her feet and picked up the harpoon, her normally brown face pale. She looked over in my direction, but appeared not to see me. I could see her lips moving as if in prayer, and I wondered if she prayed to the God the white men had brought to her land, or if she prayed to Seela, a god she knew well in her youth, the shadowy being who lives somewhere between earth and sky, and threatens mankind with all the mighty powers of nature.

Another five minutes went by and still we waited by the holes. Then out of the corner of my eye I saw movement. Fifty yards away stood Kadluk, slowly raising his harpoon. For thirty seconds he stood motionless, harpoon held high above his head, while I watched, my breath caught in my throat. Suddenly, in a movement too fast to follow, his arm flashed down, and his shout ripped through the quiet air. I saw the released shaft of his harpoon drop to the ice as he grasped the taut line with both hands and braced himself for the pull.

As I ran over, he started to haul in the line. Hand over hand the line came slowly reeling in. The seal was not a big one, and pulling it was not a difficult job. With a splash the seal's head broke clear of the water; Kadluk dragged it, fighting, out onto the ice. He pulled it clear of the hole and stepped up close to its side. Stooping over slightly he waved his left hand inches away from its nose. The seal's head lifted and the jaws opened as if to bite. Quickly Kadluk swung a roundhouse right, hitting the seal flush on the top of its upraised head. The seal collapsed on the ice, killed instantly by the single, crushing blow.

For the next three hours we continued to hunt seals on the ice. Kadluk got another and Idlouk got three. No seals came up to the holes I watched, although they came to holes close by. It was a cold job, standing motionless by the hole watching and waiting for the seals to come. The wind dried my outer clothing, but I was still wet to the skin. Kitchooalik stepped onto a snow-covered hole and went in the water up to his hips. That made five of us with clothes wet through.

After Idlouk's second kill everyone agreed that it was time for lunch. Three primus stoves were lit, and Kadluk prepared to cut up one of the tender young seals. He and Kitchooalik first removed the skin, working very carefully so as not to damage it with knife cuts. The skinned carcass was then slit from throat to hind flippers, and the ribs pulled back and pressed flat. Then everyone gathered around the kill and started in to feed on raw meat cut right out of the carcass within half an hour of the kill. As I was new to this type of feast, Idlouk showed me how to sample all the better portions, parts considered by the Eskimos to be the tastiest of them all. First there was a small slice of heart, followed by a snack of the steaming liver. With each piece of meat taken, a small square of fat was eaten too, and this gave piquancy to the taste. Next I tried the meat from the shoulder, or the flipper as it is often called. This was delicious, but a little difficult to separate from the bone. I refused an eyeball, taking instead a section of the lower ribs with bits of meat and fat attached.

We stood around the seal in a circle, eating and talking, moving around constantly, always searching out a tastier piece of meat or fat. The younger boys dashed back and forth between the carcass and the primus stoves, getting them lit, filling the kettles with fresh water from the surface pools on the sea ice, putting in the tea, and letting it boil. Good-natured banter flew back and forth, no small part of it directed at me.

"Perhaps Kingmik finds Eskimo food too much for his stomach. I noticed he refused an eyeball."

"Ah, but he's still a white man. We have to make allowances. Give him a little time."

When all had eaten their fill, mugs were filled with strong black tea. Tobacco pouches came out and everyone relaxed sitting on the sleds, sipping tea and smoking, belching slightly as they talked. Beside the sled lay the remains of the devoured seal, now a heap of fat with some small bits of meat and bone. These the dogs would clear up before we pulled away. Sitting on the sled beside me, Idlouk asked if I would like to try one of the old-style dishes, one that not many Eskimos bothered with today, as it takes too long to prepare. I said yes, I would like to try.

Putting down his cup of tea, he retrieved the head from the remains of the seal. Smashing the skull, he extracted the brains and laid them on the ice. Next he took the remaining eyeball, and put it beside the brains. From the thick layer of fat that once enclosed the seal's entire body, he cut a slab some six inches square. Putting the brains and the eyeball onto the fat, he proceeded to chop it up with his big snowknife. For about fifteen minutes he worked very carefully, chopping and mixing until brains and eyeball had been reduced to a pale yellow mush thoroughly flavoured with bits of fat.

Taking a bit on the tip of his knife, he tasted it, paused for a moment, and then added a small square of fat and chopped this well into the mixture. Then he tried it again. This time he was pleased at the result. Looking at me with a sly grin he said, "Now you try it."

Although I had not liked the sight of the eyeball as it was being chopped in, I was intrigued by the mixture. Tentatively I took a small quantity on the tip of my knife and popped it into my mouth. I rolled it around to get the flavour and then swallowed. The mixture had a pleasant taste, quite sweet, but unlike anything I had ever eaten before.

I tried another bit, then another. Idlouk helped me and in ten minutes we cleaned up the lot. By the time I was finished, I thought the taste delicious, and I have never changed my opinion to this day.

Top of The World

Wally Herbert

On 21 February 1968 Wally Herbert set out on what he called the "one pioneer journey" left to Man on the surface of the Earth – the journey across the top of the world. Accompanying Herbert on the British Trans-Arctic Expedition were Allan Gill, Roy Koerner, Kenneth Hedges and 34 huskies.

Polar Bears

It had been a perfect day with not a cloud in the sky except those clouds on the horizon in the direction of land. It was also the first day we were bothered by polar bears. A couple of polar bears came up behind us whilst we were sledging and were effectively shooed away. But from then onwards we encountered polar bears all the way to the landfall. They were becoming a menace. Every day we saw at least two, and we were also meeting at that time a lot more broken ice than we had met previously. The floes were pretty cracked up with the pressure building up. The surface was also getting bad by that time and there was quite a lot of slush around. So it was almost touch and go whether we were going to get on to land anyway. The sledging season was quickly ending and we were journeying then as fast as we possibly could. But we were only making about eight to ten miles a day.

The land was taking a long time to get closer and there were many whiteouts. When the weather cleared we always expected to see the land much closer, but it seemed just as far away. We seemed to be travelling and travelling but making no progress. The distraction, however, was the polar bears and we killed three during those three days. Sometimes they would come down-wind, but usually they approached us from behind and they just kept coming. There was one occasion when a polar bear came in sight and Fritz was in an awkward position: he was trying to cross a stretch of very tricky ice, weak, sloppy ice, with rotten small pans of ice in the middle of it, and suddenly a polar bear came along. The dogs of course took off and dragged the sledge into the water. The sledge didn't go right down but it rocked into the water. It was pulled out with a great deal of difficulty. And all this time the polar bear kept on coming, and Fritz didn't know what to do: whether to shoot it with a gun, shoot it with a camera, or try and rescue the sledge. All the other dog teams were going berserk and it was absolute chaos. We had only three guns, so one of us had no means of self-defence, myself on this occasion. I had the camera with a telephoto lens and was taking pictures as fast as I could. But the polar bear was approaching the lead sledge from ahead, and Fritz and Ken were up by the dogs in front. Allan was just behind with his dogs, keeping them under control, and I was at the back taking pictures of the whole scene. Fritz and Ken fired a couple of shots, but it wouldn't go away. It just kept coming. It didn't actually attack – it just kept walking. You've got to shoot them sometimes otherwise they would come right on and hit you, and there is no way of knowing how close they will come before they turn round and walk away – if they do walk away at all.

Crack Up

It was about 6.30 a.m. on the morning of 24 February when we were having breakfast. We were all packed up and ready to go but we still had several odds and ends to sort out and the hut was in a mess. Just as we started breakfast we heard a salvo of shots, twangy sounds which we knew from previous experience were caused by a floe splitting up. We dropped everything and made a dash for the door. All four of us tumbled outside to find the floe splitting and cracking up all around us. One crack, the nearest one to the hut, was about twelve feet away. We weren't really dressed for outside work and the temperature was minus 40° with a slight breeze blowing, but we were separated from our dogs and sledges and much of our gear. So we scattered. I leaped across the crack and tried to get the dogs back on to our side. There was only time for Fritz to get one team of dogs across. The crack was opening so quickly that we all had to leap back on to the hut side before it eventually opened up to about 45 feet wide.

Meanwhile, the whole area started to gyrate. Pressure was building in some places, leads opening wider in others. We weren't in any immediate danger, because once a crack has occurred the pressure usually relaxes a little, and nothing else happens until the floes get off line from each other and come together again. Then you get pressure building up and cracks occurring at right angles. This is what we really feared after the initial crack. It had gone straight underneath one of the two tents which had collapsed into the lead and was now lying in the water. From then on, everything was chaotic.

We rushed back into the hut. Obviously we had to get away as quickly as we possibly could, but there were several last-minute things that had to be done, such as packing up the radio set and sorting out one or two pots and pans. We didn't have time, nor did we dare, to carry on with breakfast. All the time we were inside the hut we were in danger, so we took it in turns to stay outside on guard. We threw everything into boxes and just chucked them outside. We had intended leaving the hut spick and span, sorting out all the expensive items of equipment we were going to leave behind and putting them all on the table so that if an aircraft could land at some later date, they'd be able to take the equipment away. As it turned out, everyone was in such a rush that this stuff was thrown all over the place to make room. I even had to take a hand-axe to the furniture which had taken so many days to construct, and smash it all up in order to get at the various other items of gear which were tucked away out of sight and easy reach.

It was still fairly dark outside so that every time someone left the hut, they had to take one of our two lamps, which plunged the hut into semi-darkness. All the time we were in the hut we could hear the noises of the pressure outside, and the tension grew. We eventually threw everything into four piles and started sorting it out roughly into sledge loads. The sledges had already been partly loaded a couple of days before; we had sorted out the amount of dog food and man rations we had to take, and loaded all the personal gear. The problem now was to try to get the dogs across to our part of the floe. Each man went after his own team of dogs. He had to leap from one floe to another, hitch them all up, and get them back again. The route we had taken across to the dogs was impossible to retrace because the floes were moving all the time. Some of the floes were small enough to tilt and rock when we jumped on them. One of the standard techniques for getting across leads is on a very small floe, a very small pan of ice, which can be used as a raft to ferry stuff across. You can put a sledge on to a raft of ice and get a rope on either end, with one man standing on the raft and the other towing him across with the rope.

In this way we managed to get the dogs across.

Dead Reckoning

Navigating by dead reckoning on the Arctic Ocean is complicated by the fact that the ice is drifting, and if you see no sun for several days you really have no exact idea where you might be. You know roughly in which direction you are going, but you don't know which way the ice is drifting; you don't know exactly how far you've travelled, because you have had to make so many detours. In the Antarctic where you're travelling across fairly flat, featureless country, you can tow along a sledge wheel which ticks off the distance in miles you've travelled. You cannot do this across the ice pack of the Arctic Ocean; the wheel would buckle before it had recorded ten miles, so you have no choice but to guess. Usually the guesses were quite good. We compared each other's guesses of the distance at the end of the day and it was seldom that our guesses were more than a mile from the mean. Our final approach to the Pole was made on dead-reckoning using a very hazy sun for a general direction.

On 5 April we pitched our camp, feeling sure that we must be within two miles of the Pole. Overnight a blizzard blew up which obscured the sun altogether; there was no chance of a fix. In the very early hours of the morning, however, the wind died down, the sky cleared, the sun came out and every couple of hours I'd go outside and do a sun shot. I could not compute these fixes – Allan had all the tables in his tent and I didn't want to wake him up. I felt in any case that there would be time enough later that morning to confirm the position, and sent out by radio the following message to Her Majesty the Queen:

I have the honour to inform your Majesty that today, 5 April, at 0700 hours Greenwich Mean Time, the British Trans-Arctic Expedition by dead reckoning reached the North Pole 407 days after setting out from Point Barrow, Alaska. My companions of the crossing party, Allan Gill, Major Kenneth Hedges, R.A.M.C., and Dr Roy Koerner, together with Squadron Leader Church, R.A.F., our radio relay officer at Point Barrow, are in good health and spirits and hopeful that by forced marches and a measure of good fortune the Expedition will reach Spitzbergen by Mid-summer's Day of this year, thus concluding in the name of our Country the first surface crossing of the Arctic Ocean. (Signed W. W. Herbert, Expedition Leader.)

Allan came across with the computed position just after I had finished transmitting and had switched off the radio. I was shaken to find that we were seven miles short of the Pole, instead of only about a mile and a half. Feeling that one ought to be at least within two miles of the Pole before saying that by dead reckoning one has reached it, we packed up immediately, broke camp and got going to try and put ourselves where we had said we were. It was about 9 a.m. We had several hours to go before the G.M.T. date changed, and there was a pretty good chance that in that time we'd get to the Pole.

Navigation in the vicinity of the Pole is a problem. If your calculation of the longitude is slightly out, then the time at which the sun crosses your meridian – in other words that time at which the sun is due north – is wrong, and so you head in the wrong direction. And of course, if you head in the wrong direction, you increase your errors in your dead reckoning longitude. Your azimuth then is thrown even further into error and you increase your errors progressively until you spiral into almost a complete circle. This is what happened to us on this particular day.

We set off and travelled for what we estimated was seven miles and stopped. We set up the theodolite, did a rough calculation, and found that we were still seven miles from the Pole. It was unbelievable. We had used up a lot of our time in getting there – the G.M.T. date was going to change within the next seven hours and we were still seven miles short of our goal. We couldn't understand where we had gone wrong. How could one travel seven miles in the direction of the North Pole and still be seven miles from it? The only possible answer was that we must have been travelling parallel to the dateline and were thus passing the Pole. We concluded there must have been something very wrong with our azimuth taken from the position we had computed that morning; so we went into the computations again, and found an error in the longitude. We did another series of observations, all of which took time, and set off again. We travelled hard for three hours, set up a theodolite yet again, and found that we were three miles south of the Pole and on longitude zero. With Spitzbergen as our goal and being still three weeks behind schedule, we should really have carried straight on and not gone back.

But one cannot with a clear conscience say one is at the Pole when one is three miles short of it – more especially since we had told Her Majesty that by dead reckoning we had reached it. So we set off yet again, travelling on a very precise azimuth. We chopped through every single pressure ridge that came our way, cutting ourselves a dead straight line due north. But it was slow progress and the drift was going against us. We were, in fact, hardly making any progress at all. After about four hours we'd come less than a mile.

In desperation, we off-loaded the sledges, laid a depot and took on with us only the barest essentials, just enough for one night's camp. It was a risk, the only time during the whole journey that we took such a risk. But it paid off. With the lighter sledges we made faster progress, and after about three hours estimated that we must surely be at the Pole, possibly even beyond it. So we stopped, set up our tents, and did a final fix which put us at 89° 59′ N, one mile south of the North Pole on longitude 180. In other words, we'd crossed the Pole about a mile back along our tracks. But the drift was now with us, so we must surely cross the Pole a second time as we drifted overnight. We got into our sleeping-bags and fell asleep.

The pad marks of thirty-five Eskimo huskies, the broad tracks of four heavy Eskimo-type sledges, and the four sets of human footprints which had approached the North Pole and halted one mile beyond it on the morning of Easter Sunday, 1969, no longer mark the spot where we took our final sun shots and snatched a few hours' rest. For even while we were sleeping, our camp was slowly drifting; and the Pole, by the time we had reloaded our sledges a few hours later and set course for the island of Spitzbergen, lay north in a different direction.

It had been an elusive spot to find and fix. At the North Pole, two separate sets of meridians meet and all directions are south. The temperature was minus 35° Fahrenheit. The wind was from the south-west, or was it from the north-east? It was Sunday, or was it Saturday? Maybe it was Monday. It was a confusing place to be – a place which lay on our course from Barrow to Spitzbergen and which had taken us 408 days to reach.

Trying to set foot upon it had been like trying to step on the shadow of a bird that was circling overhead. The surface across which we were moving was itself a moving surface on a planet that was spinning about an axis. We were standing approximately on that axis, asleep on our feet, dog tired and hungry. Too tired to celebrate our arrival on the summit of this super-mountain around which the sun circles almost as though stuck in a groove.

We set up our camera and posed for some pictures – 36 shots at different exposures. We tried not to look weary, tried not to look cold. We tried only to huddle, four fur-clad figures, in a pose that was vaguely familiar – for what other proof of the attainment could we bring back than a picture posed in this way?

Reaching the North Pole was a major objective for the expedition – for, with the exception of Ralph Plaisted's 1968 skidoo voyage, they were the first to make an undisputed surface crossing to 90°N – but they still had a minimum of 600 nautical miles to reach land. And, with the onset, of the Spring thaw the ice was beginning to thin and crack up. Eventually, on 29 May two of the expedition party landed

WALLY HERBERT

on Small Blackboard Island, northeast of Spitzbergen, to clinch the first surface crossing of the Arctic Ocean. The expedition had travelled 3620 miles – "a feat of endurance which ranks with any in polar history" said Prime Minister Harold Wilson. For his service to polar exploration, Herbert was knighted in 1999.

Satan's Cauldron

Ranulph Fiennes

Sir Ranulph Twisleton-Wykeham-Fiennes was educated at Eton, and served with the Royal Scots Greys and 21 SAS. Dubbed the "World's Greatest Living Explorer" by the Guinness Book of Records, Fiennes has led over 20 expeditions, not least the epic Transglobe Expedition of 1979–82, which achieved the first circumpolar navigation of the Earth. Accompanying Fiennes for the round trip was Charlie Burton.

Hole in the Day

So we set off into a curtain of snow blown from the north west which settled over the many slits and trenches freshly opened up by the wind. I could see very little to my front due to flying ice particles that stung my eyes. Twice I lurched down into camouflaged patches of sticky *nilas* and held my breath as the skidoo tracks slithered and clawed for purchase. Both these places were invisible due to a dusting of blown snow. I should have been warned but it was so good to be moving again that I carried on into the gathering gloom of dusk. Each time a new split caught me unawares I signalled wildly to Charlie who shoved a hand up to acknowledge the warning and took care to avoid my route.

The canals began to proliferate and widen. Soon there was a spider's web of open canals cunningly concealed by the poor light and the newly fallen snow. From time to time I turned to check the whereabouts of Charlie in the twilit murk. This I did once too often and narrowly missed a wide canal zig-zagging across my front.

No sooner did I come clear of this cutting than a divergent channel with four-foot high banks barred my new course. Again I swerved. This time too late. Skidoo and sledge skidded into the trough flinging me towards the far bank. My legs broke through the snow's crust and water filled my boots but my chest was against the further wall and I scrambled out.

The skidoo was beyond my reach and already settling fast like a cow caught in a quagmire. Within minutes it was gone, its 900 pounds laden weight pointing down at the black ocean floor far below. Slowly the steel sledge tilted despite the air trapped between items inside the sledge boxes. The front of the sledge was just within reach and I grabbed at a lashing strap. With a twist around my leather mitt, the strap could not slip.

I shouted for Charlie. He was twenty yards away unaware of my problem and unable to hear me above the noise of his skidoo. I could not stand up to attract his attention but did so lying down with my free hand. Charlie saw this and came up at once. "She's going down," I shouted somewhat unnecessarily. "Try to save the tent."

The tent was in a rear-mounted box. Each box had a separate lashing strap and, since the sledge had already been briefly immersed in salt water ditches that day, the straps were covered with a sheen of hard ice.

Charlie found he could only just reach the rear of the sledge and with thick mitts could not unlash the straps which held the tent box. So he took his mitts off, a thing we *very* rarely do outside our tent, and began to work at the frozen strap.

As he did so the sledge settled slowly but surely and my arm began to feel stretched to its limit. I could not hold on much longer. My body, laid out on the ice bank, was slowly pulled over the edge.

With my free hand I opened the second box and pulled free the radio and search beacon.

Charlie could not get at the tent but he loosened the lashing of another box and retrieved my theodolite. He also removed a bundle of tent rods tied separately to the sledge. But by then one of his hands had lost all feeling and my own arm could take it no more.

"I'm letting go," I warned him and did so. If my arms had been measured just then and turned out to have been of equal length I would not have believed it. Within a minute the sledge had silently disappeared. The tent went with it.

We had long ago learnt that warmth must be very quickly applied to frozen limbs. Warmth meant a tent even though it was unusually mild that day, −33°C with a twenty-two-knot breeze. I connected the long aluminium tent poles and pushed their ends into the snow to form the skeleton of a small igloo. Over this I flung the light tarpaulin with which Charlie normally covered our skidoos at camps. With Charlie's shovel I covered the tarpaulin's edges with snow to keep it taut over the skeleton. All cooking equipment and half the rations were on my sledge somewhere below us, but Charlie carried a spoon, mug, a spare tin pot and a spare petrol cooker. Also a spare set of navigation almanacs.

Whilst I fixed up the shelter Charlie worked hard to keep his worse hand alive, flinging it from side to side trying to force some blood down his arm and into the white unfeeling fingers. Once the spare cooker was alight we bundled what gear we had into the shelter and Charlie began the wonderful but painful process of regaining his fingers.

The temperature fell back to −40°C during the night.

Two of us could in no way fit into Charlie's down sleeping bag but it came with an outer waterproof cover and an inner cloth liner both of which Charlie gave me and this kept some of the cold at bay. There was much chattering of teeth that night and halfway through it I made us a cup of coffee.

Charlie's face staring at me in the dim light from a candle balanced between us looked skull-like.

"You look half dead," I told him.

"Thanks. You don't look too healthy yourself."

I had made a stupid mistake and we both knew it. In my zeal to press north whatever the conditions, I had lost precious equipment and, very nearly, some of Charlie's fingers. Each day since we had left the coast I had recorded details of the ice conditions, incidence of open water, dimensions of major pressure walls and apparent age of floe systems. All my records had sunk along with my photo of Ginnie, personal gear and spare clothing. Gone, too, was my oilskin container with the only two items to have travelled every foot of the way with me, Gnome Buzzard and Eddie Pike's china mouse.

Still, we were both alive and no further from our goal. We had certainly fared better than a Thule Eskimo hunter whose story we had heard of. He fell through sea-ice close to his sledge. Searchers found the place later the same night through the howling of his dogs. The moon lit up an expanse of ice fragments made during his last struggles. His body was retrieved with hooks and his torn nails showed how, clutching at the ice, he had fought to climb out.

Sludge

During the night of 28 March we awoke sweating inside our damp bags. The atmosphere was oppressive and there was deathly silence. I thought briefly of a line from Wally's doggerel: "Beware the calm that follows the storm." As I moved outside in the morning I knew at once that something unusual was happening. Our rubble-strewn paddock was entirely surrounded by mottled marshes of steaming sludge. The light of the sun, a sickly yellow, appeared to flutter and fade from minute to minute. Neither of us spoke as we raised camp and tightened the lashings of our sledges.

To the north east a brown-skinned lake disappeared into the gloom. Elsewhere the marsh was broken by floes similar to lumps of melted cheese on the surface of onion soup. I heaved a lump of ice on to the skin of this marsh. It settled slowly into the jellied crust then, in a leisurely manner, disappeared. I looked at Charlie. His eyebrows lifted and he shook his head slowly. We walked to the eastern side of our island and slung a chunk out into the brownish skin of the lake. There was a rippling motion away from the point of impact but no break-through. Again I looked at Charlie. He remained expressionless. I shrugged and we made for the skidoos.

There followed five hours of hell. God was exceptionally good to us that morning. By rights we should not have tried to travel. Our route was about as straight as a pig's tail and went where the perils of the moment dictated. To stop would mean to sink. For a thousand yards we moved over this first lake, which was in reality more like a wide river, with a sludge wash spreading out in front of our slow advance. The brown-skinned lane ended in open water which hissed with curling vapour on both sides of us. A solitary floe chunk with one low edge gave us brief respite. From it we listened for signs of what lay ahead in the yellow murk.

A soft squeaking and grinding emanated from nowhere in particular. Satan's private cauldron could hardly have produced so evil an aspect. Often that morning we lost sight of each other in the fog. Sometimes we moved on foot, Charlie waiting on some bump suspended in the marsh half-way from the skidoos and shouting to guide me back. We were frightened lest a new fracturing cut us off from the sledges. If that happened we could not expect to live for long. By noon we were weary with apprehension since the marsh, for all we knew, stretched on for many miles. Then the mist grew less dense and in a while, thank God, it cleared away altogether and fourteen miles of *solid* ice rewarded our morning's efforts.

I felt wonderfully good and forgot about my chin and nose and toes and all the vast distance ahead. For nothing could surely ever be so bad again. If we could travel over that marsh we could cross anything. Such a sense of elation and conceit did not last long but was fine whilst it did.

Cold Reality

David Hempleman-Adams

Born in Wiltshire, England, in 1956, David Hempleman-Adams became the first person to reach the four magnetic and geographical poles and the highest summits of all seven continents. Below he recounts a rare failure, his 1983 attempt to walk solo to the North Pole:

I knew the trip was over on day 32, on the 87th Parallel, and still over 200 miles to the North Pole. I was climbing up a high pressure ridge, straining to drag my sledge behind me. I reached the top of the ridge some fifteen feet above the flat ice around it when the ridge suddenly collapsed beneath my feet. I landed on my side with a heavy bump and immediately doubled up in pain. I did not know it at the time, but I had just cracked two ribs.

I tried to catch my breath, hoping against hope that I had just badly winded myself, and waited for the pangs to ease. They did not. In excruciating pain, it took me two hours to erect the tent, an exercise that normally took me ten minutes, now that I was well-practised. I then remembered something the picture editor of the *Sunday Express* magazine, to whom I was relaying the story of the trip, told me before I left, that the best pictures in the world are often the ones you do not want to take. I set up the camera, slumped back on my sledge, and took a photo, thinking that this might be the last picture of me alive.

I waited three hours to make sure that it really was the end, and then contacted Eureka. Mac said stop mucking about, but I told him I was badly injured and needed to get out. Steve radioed down to a doctor in Resolute, and then began to relay a series of questions back up to me. The main question, to see if I had punctured a lung, was whether I was coughing up blood. I was taking pain killers, but they seemed to have no effect. Lying down flat and straight was especially painful, so I stayed fixed in a foetal position during the radio call and after.

The nearest plane was at Resolute, but a storm had set in down there and they would not be able to move for two days. If there was a danger of me dying out there, then they might be able to use a military plane, but as they reckoned everything was relatively okay I would have to wait. Everything was not okay. I was in complete agony. I was also utterly dejected, missed home and Claire terribly, and just wanted to return to warmth and comfort. Instead, I knew that I would be stuck out there alone, the most northerly man on earth, for at least the next two days. Still, I tried to reason, it was better to be a living failure than a dead hero.

The storm at Resolute moved on, as predicted, after two days, but straight up to Eureka where the plane was scheduled to stop in order to refuel. The message that crackled over the radio was not what I wanted to hear: "Hang in there, we've got to wait for the storm at Eureka to clear." I was beginning to run out of food and fuel now, and I could feel the ice beginning to drift. A cold fear began to creep back inside me: if my radio batteries went flat I would not be able to give the pilot a weather report from where I was, which could result in him flying all the way up to me, only to turn back again in storm conditions. At £10,000 a flight, I would have to pocket the bill, knowing that I had no money at home. If the batteries went down on the Argos then they would have to find me blind. It would be like trying to find the proverbial needle in a haystack. Then, of course, there was a very clear danger that the ice around me would break up.

Outside the wind began to whip up until, in a very short space of time, I found myself in storm conditions. The radio blasted out that the weather was fine now at Eureka, and a plane would be coming to get me shortly. I had to radio them back telling them to forget it because the howling storm was now with me. This was to last for four days. The wind tugged incessantly at the tent's flysheet, producing spindrift so fine that it was blasting into my tent through the sewing-needle holes in the fabric. Now I began to pray for the storm to stop. My life, I reckoned, was now completely in the lap of the gods.

When the storm eventually died down I heard the depressing news that another storm had arrived at Eureka. Now I was seriously worried. My food supplies had just about gone, I was rapidly losing weight, still suffering from enormous pain from my ribs which prevented me from moving, and growing increasingly colder. It was clear that unless I was rescued immediately I would die out there, in the frozen wastes of the Arctic Ocean.

After ten days out in the wilderness, Steve and Mac managed to persuade Operation Caesar to lend their plane, which happened to be only 60 miles away out on the floating ice station on the polar shelf. Mac's voice told me the reassuring news over the radio. Half an hour later he returned over the airwaves: "A plane should be over you at any moment now." Even as he said this, I could hear the wonderful hum of an aircraft engine. I crawled out of my tent and saw a Twin Otter landing close by. To say it was an emotional moment would be an understatement. Barely able to stand up, a lump appeared in my throat and the tears began to pour from my eyes. My nightmare was almost over. I was going to survive the ordeal.

The pilot jumped out of the plane, walked over to me, shook my hand and said, "Congratulations."

"What on earth for?" I asked, surprised by his response. As far as I was concerned, I had been a total failure.

"Well, you've walked 230 miles and spent 42 days out here on your own and lived," he said. "That's success to me."

I remember muttering: "I'll be back." The pilot then lifted all my gear on to the plane, while I slowly climbed in. They took me back to the Operation Caesar base where I was met by a Dr Webber who found me a bunk and then took me to the kitchen. I must have eaten everything I could lay my hands on. The scientists there were all very kind to me. They seemed to appreciate what I had just been through and could relate to me. After a brief stop I was then flown back to Resolute, to join up with Steve and Mac who had come down from Eureka. They were pleased to see me, and although disappointed that the trip did not work out, seemed eager to get back home.

The doctor at Resolute had a good look at me and diagnosed two cracked ribs. Steve watched all this and laughed as I was bandaged up. "No pain, no gain," he smirked. I then took a series of telephone calls from the press. One reporter asked me what it was like to be a failure. This question obviously hurt, but I replied by repeating what I had told myself back in the tent out on the ice: "At least I'm a living failure."

It was good just to be getting out of the ice and cold of the Arctic. On arriving at Montreal airport we discovered that, having been flown out to Canada first class by Canadian Pacific, the airline had decided to return us to Britain in economy. The eventual flight was half empty, but we were still made to wait at the back of the queue until they were sure they had three stand-by tickets. Nobody likes a loser.

During the long flight back to London I began to tell myself a few home truths. I was immensely inexperienced in polar travel, and had been completely foolhardy even to have attempted the walk. Much of the equipment was wrong, and the very best I could say about the trip was that it proved to be a valuable training exercise. It was a warm May evening as I arrived at Stansted airport. It was so good to be back, away from the cold, and to see the lush green fields of England. It was even better to see Claire.

Over the next few days I received a complete pasting from the mountaineering press in particular, but also from the world of adventuring. The final straw was when I was interviewed by BBC South-West. "Was it not just the case that you simply were not man enough to complete the trek?" asked the reporter. This was probably true, although being "man enough" had much less to do with the failure of the trip than just the simple, but crucial, factor that I was not experienced or prepared enough for what the North Pole was going to throw at me. Despite the living hell I had experienced over the past couple of months, I was not finished. I vowed to myself that I would return to the Arctic and, one day, would make it to the North Pole itself.

The following year, 1984, Hempleman-Adams walked solo and unsupported to the magnetic North Pole; in 1992, he led a party to the geomagnetic North Pole; in 1998 he finally gained the geographical North Pole.

Blood on the Dream

Barry Lopez

The celebrated American traveller and nature-writer joins the Yup'ik people of St Lawrence Island, Alaska, on a walrus hunt:

The mountain in the distance is called Sevuokuk. It marks the north-west cape of Saint Lawrence Island in the Bering Sea. From where we are on the ice, this eminence defines the water and the sky to the east as far as we can look. Its western face, a steep wall of snow-streaked basalt, rises above a beach of dark cobbles, riven, ice-polished, ocean-rolled chips of Sevuokuk itself. The village of Gambell is there, the place I have come from with the Yup'ik men, to hunt walrus in the spring ice.

We are, I believe, in Russian waters; and also, by a definition to them even more arbitrary, in "tomorrow", on the other side of the international date line. Whatever political impropriety might be involved is of little importance to the Yup'ik, especially while they are hunting. From where blood soaks the snow, then, and piles of meat and slabs of fat and walrus skin are accumulating, from where ivory tusks have been collected together like exotic kindling, I stare toward, the high Russian coast. The mental categories, specific desires, and understanding of history among the people living there are, I reflect, nearly as different from my own as mine are from my Yup'ik companions'.

I am not entirely comfortable on the sea ice butchering walrus like this. The harshness of the landscape, the vulnerability of the boat, and the great size and power of the hunted animal combine to increase my sense of danger. The killing jars me, in spite of my regard for the simple elements of human survival here.

We finish loading the boats. One of the crews has rescued two dogs that have either run off from one of the Russian villages or been abandoned out here on the ice. Several boats gather gunnel to gunnel to look over the dogs. They have surprisingly short hair and seem undersize to draw a sled, smaller than Siberian huskies. But the men assure me these are typical Russian sled dogs.

We take our bearing from the far prominence of Sevuokuk and turn home, laden with walrus meat, with walrus hides and a few seals, with crested auklets and thick-billed murres, with ivory and Russian dogs. When we reach shore, the four of us put our shoulders to the boat to bring it high up on the beach. A young man in the family I am staying with packs a sled with what we have brought back. He pulls it away across the snow behind his Honda three-wheeler, toward the house. Our meals. The guns and gear, the harpoons and floats and lines, the extra clothing and portable radios are all secured and taken away. I am one of the last to leave the beach, still turning over images of the hunt.

No matter what sophistication of mind you bring to such events, no matter what breadth of anthropological understanding, no matter your fondness for the food, your desire to participate, you have still seen an animal killed. You have met the intertwined issues – What is an animal? What is death? – in those large moments of blood, violent exhalation, and thrashing water, with the acrid odor of burned powder in the fetid corral smells of a walrus haul-out. The moments are astounding, cacophonous, also serene. The sight of men letting bits of meat slip away into the dark green water with mumbled benedictions is as stark in my memory as the suddenly widening eyes of the huge, startled animals.

I walk up over the crest of the beach and toward the village, following a set of sled tracks. There is a narrow trail of fresh blood in the snow between the runners. The trial runs out at a lattice-work of drying racks for meat and skins. The blood in the snow is a sign of life going on, of other life going on. Its presence is too often confused with cruelty.

I rest my gloved fingers on the driftwood meat rack. It is easy to develop an affection for the Yup'ik people, especially when you are invited to participate in events still defined largely by their own traditions. The entire event – leaving to hunt, hunting, coming home, the food shared in a family setting – creates a sense of well-being easy to share. Viewed in this way, the people seem fully capable beings, correct in what they do. When you travel with them, their voluminous and accurate knowledge, their spiritual and technical confidence, expose what is insipid and groundless in your own culture.

I brood often about hunting. It is the most spectacular and succinct expression of the Eskimo's relationship with the land, yet one of the most perplexing and disturbing for the outsider to consider. With the compelling pressures of a cash-based economy to contend with, and the ready availability of modern weapons, hunting practices have changed. Many families still take much of their food from the land, but they do it differently now. "In-authentic" is the criticism most often made of their methods, as though years ago time had stopped for the Yup'ik.

But I worry over hunting for another reason – the endless reconciliation that must be made of Jacob with his brother Esau. The anguish of Gilgamesh at the death of his companion En-kidu. We do not know how exactly to bridge this gap between civilized man and the society of the hunter. The Afrikaner writer Laurens van der Post, long familiar with Kalahari hunting peoples as archetypal victims of our prejudice, calls the gap between us "an abyss of deceit and murder" we have created. The existence of such a society alarms us. In part this is a trouble we have with writing out our history. We adjust our histories in order to elevate ourselves in the creation that surrounds us; we cut ourselves off from our hunting ancestors, who make us uncomfortable. They seem too closely aligned with insolent, violent predatory animals. The hunting cultures are too barbaric for us. In condemning them, we see it as "inevitable" that their ways are being eclipsed. Yet, from the testimony of sensitive visitors among them, such as van der Post and others I have mentioned in the Arctic, we know that something of value resides with these people.

I think of the Eskimos compassionately as *hibakusha* – the Japanese word for "explosion-affected people", those who continue to suffer the effects of Hiroshima and Nagasaki. Eskimos are trapped in a long, slow detonation. What they know about a good way to live is disintegrating. The sophisticated, ironic voice of civilization insists that their insights are only trivial, but they are not.

I remember looking into a herd of walrus that day and thinking: do human beings make the walrus more human to make it comprehensible or to assuage loneliness? What is it to be estranged in this land?

It is in the land, I once thought, that one searches out and eventually finds what is beautiful. And an edge of this deep and rarefied beauty is the acceptance of complex paradox and the forgiveness of others. It means you will not die alone.

Musher

Alistair Scott

Alistair Scott, a Briton, arrived in Alaska in 1987 with the dream of driving a dog-sled team through the far north wastes. After five months of learning sledging techniques – and the personalities of his dogs, Silver, Rosco, Kavik, Sisco, Duran, Sensor, Alf and Nanook – Scott set out in mid-winter on an 700 mile journey along the Arctic Circle. His route shadowed that of the Iditarod, the famous trans-Alaska dog-sled race.

The dogs padded across a tabletop of ice, the opposite of the wild surface we had seen the previous day. The sun hit them obliquely and their shadow sides remained frosted for hours. Ice beards formed on their faces, and the front runners required belly covers against the constant chill. However, boredom was their main complaint. The hills to our right were low whalebacks and almost invisible at dog-level, the ones in front never seemed to get any larger, and there was little else on which they could focus their attention. The ravens came and went. Otherwise there was only me. Every so often a dog would turn to see what I was doing. As I was staring at them, we stared at each other, exchanging long glances. Then I began singing to them, as I had read of antarctic mushers doing this to lift their dogs' spirits on long monotonous hauls. My song didn't last long. It was obvious my dogs preferred monotony and low spirits. So I swapped my feet on the runners and turned round to face the way we had come, crouched down in the wind shadow of the sled bag, tied myself to the handlebars and dozed for a mile or two while catching some sun. One of the beauties of mushing is that its autopilot is the most sophisticated system in the world. It was not uncommon for Eskimos to climb into their sled furs and go to sleep on trails their dogs knew well, waking up when the motion stopped to find themselves at home.

We reached Koyuk early in the evening. Its blue fuel-storage tanks had been visible for some time, and gradually its houses had grown out of a wooded patch of hillside. I had been given a name to contact here, but decided not to risk imposing myself on another stranger. I would sleep rough ("siwash" in gold-rush terminology) beside my sled. While preparing to do this beside a fish rack with six intact seals lying frozen at its base, I was approached by a youth on a snow machine. His father had sent him to see if I wanted a place to sleep. Scarcely five minutes had passed since my arrival.

In keeping with all settlements of Eskimo founding, Koyuk was sited for its proximity to good fishing and hunting. Then gold and coal were found to the north and at the turn of the century it became a supply point for miners, and a depot for the extracted coal awaiting shipment to Nome. Tests for oil had proved positive in Norton Bay, I was told, but development had been abandoned in deference to hunting and fishing interests which still provided the mainstay of the village economy. Koyuk was alcoholically "dry", a factor which appeared to have a bearing on its firefighters. They were sent as far afield as Idaho and California and had an excellent reputation, unlike their counterparts in Unalakleet and Shaktoolik who were notorious for quenching their thirsts before their fires.

Ken Tewey liked dogs. He said anyone who ran dogs was welcome at his home. He had twelve himself and they cost eighty dollars a week to feed. Commercial dog food sold for twice its Fairbanks price here, as did most commodities. A small lighter could freight in supplies from Nome in summer, but it was expensive. The cheapest snow machine cost $4,250 delivered to Koyuk. A replacement track cost $700. Petrol sold for $2.15 per gallon. Ken believed people soon wouldn't be able to afford snow machines any more and would *have* to go back to dogs. He said this with relish because he was trying to preserve some of "the old way". "Kids have it soft now. My kids won't haul water without a snow machine or three-wheeler. They don't walk any more," he complained. Only he and his cousin kept dogs – other than odd pets – in a village of 200 people.

Ken was about fifty-five but his round wind-furrowed face looked older. He wore large, dark-tinted glasses and walked with a cumbersome gait. He was of average height and with a bulk which disguised the brawn of a carpenter's, hunter's and fisherman's life. Divorced fifteen years earlier he had since raised his five children on his own. His house was kept spotless and seemed twice as large as the one of my previous host. Franklin, it transpired, was his cousin and Franklin's wife was his aunt.

"I got a twenty-eight-foot boat but a permit only three days a week. Fish 'n' Game don't like natives. They tell us we can't hunt, but we just ignore them. We always lived here. We never killed off what we hunt, an' they come an' tell us how much to take. We don't go tell them how to live." He talked fast and with little intonation. Words were clipped, sentences seemed to run uphill and hit a wall. Native speech forced me to listen hard at first, and so it took time to appreciate its finer qualities, a meaty directness and stark sincerity.

We sat talking in a kitchen expansive enough to take a beluga broadside. Ken smoked incessantly and seemed to want to talk. I asked why it was I saw so few teenagers about the villages.

"Huh!" he exclaimed. "Why don't anybody see them? They've turned into night people – sleep all day, party all night. Kids don't have no respect now, not for elders, not for parents, not for strangers." He pointed at his small granddaughter who was playfully hitting my leg. "In my day we have to wait at the door until they call us in to meet a stranger. Eskimo culture is going out."

In his day, he recalled, the Covenanter Church was full on Sundays. No one worked on the Sabbath. He remembered women making raincoats from the intestines of bowhead whales, and men stretching walrus stomachs over wooden frames for ceremonial drums. His mother had been widowed young and had raised her five children on her own. They had worn Salvation Army clothes, but once he had been given a new pair of overalls. They were such a treasure he had only worn them on Sundays, until a relative had told him he would soon grow out of them – after that he had worn them every day. Drums, Sabbaths, whale-gut raincoats and Salvation Army overalls – he sketched a vivid picture of the pattern of change. In general, a change for the worse, he believed, and the Settlement Act had accelerated the deterioration of family and village bonds with its sudden influx of money and squabbles.

Ken went to the fridge and brought out a bowl of "Eskimo ice cream", *akutug*. He made it from seal oil, caribou or reindeer fat, sugar and water, all fluffed up into a sorbet and served in a sea of berries. Seal oil is an acquired taste and I hadn't fully acquired it by them, but I was working hard at it. *Akutug* was said to provide blizzard-proof warmth.

"In summer it gets real hot here. Ninety-two degrees sometimes. Too hot, we get headaches. We like −30° better. We need lots of ice cream at −30°." He smoked and talked late into the night. Finally he asked:

"Would you like an Eskimo name? When you have an Eskimo name, you become one of us."

I felt deeply honoured. "I'd love one."

He wrote down my new name. Arpiq. "It means 'salmonberry'. I give it to you because your face is the same colour."

"What colour are salmonberries?"

He pointed to some of the berries in the remaining *akutug*. They were bright orange.

The next morning my sunburn was still glowing as I set off for Elim. I had only gone fifty yards when I heard my new name.

"ARPIQ!" Ken yelled. I plunged down the brake and stopped. "There's many Eskimo girls between here and Nome. Maybe you'll be lucky. It's leap year. In leap years Eskimo girls go out and get the men . . ."

The trail had turned inland to reach White Mountain and here it offered a choice. To reach the mining district of Council, twenty miles away, a musher followed the Fish River and headed north. To reach Nome, seventy-seven miles away, the westbound traveller was led back to the coast. The "modern" Iditarod trail did not head for the sea directly but stayed inland and swung round to the coast at Topkok Head. The last of the Seward Peninsula's trees were on this route and they stood ranked by size, a downward projection from the tallest at White Mountain, through the lesser and sparser to nothing at Mile 15.

The "old" Iditarod trail did not visit White Mountain but branched off at Golovin, hopped over a headland and reached the

coast long before Topkok Head. It passed a mining community at
Bluff, on Daniels Creek (a name I was to hear mentioned later),
and it was here that Stuck once came across an enterprise of
wondrous ingenuity. Miners had sunk an "ice shaft" to the
seabed through twelve feet of water. They had hollowed out a
hole in the surface ice and stopped when there was only a thin
skin remaining before reaching the water. Overnight frost would
build up new ice underneath, allowing them to excavate several
inches deeper, and again they would stop before breaking
through. In this way they had reached the bottom inside a
cylindrical wall of ice. "They had a curious chute, like a ship's
ventilator, to catch the wind and funnel cold air down the shaft"
to prevent it from thawing.

Topkok Hill was another nasty Iditaspot, a sharp climb followed by a long exposed summit. A cold wind drove straight into
our faces and maintained a moving blanket of snow close to the
ground. Fortunately the sky was clear and the visibility good. A
musher I'd met in Galena, Gary Guy, had got caught here in the
previous year's Iditarod. He and a fellow racer were beset by 30 to
50 knot winds for two days. The temperature was −20°F which
equated to an extreme of −90°F in terms of wind-chill. They had
cocooned themselves in their sleeping bags in the lee of their
sleds. Their dogs survived with no protection, for the wind blew
away any snow that might have built up to afford some insulation.
Gary was unable to feed them during the ordeal. On the third day
conditions improved and they made it to a shelter cabin, spent
several hours cooking and eating and then carried on to Nome.

Half-way across the top we passed this shelter cabin, and found
it transformed into an ice sculpture. It was an A-frame hut with a
wedge of snow at one end, the entrance end. The wedge was too
steep to climb without a struggle and the only way into the hut
was through an eighteen-inch hole scraped through the top of the
wedge. We drove on, over a surface striated by furrows, and came
to the end of Topkok, the drop down to sea-level. The view
showed a clear coast for a couple of miles and then the world
ended in a whiteout. Our run of good weather was coming to an
end just fifty miles from home.

When we entered the storm it was hard to tell whether snow
was actually falling, or just being whipped up by the wind. The

trail ran along a raised beach strewn with logs and stumps but was regularly marked by tall tripods. The wind was bitterly cold and it came knifing in from right to left. It forced a way into every gap in my clothing and found zips no obstacle at all. I stopped to put belly covers on the dogs. The warmth evaporated from my hands in seconds and my fingers turned clumsy and muddling. At first visibility stayed at a hundred yards, which was the minimum to see the markers; then it began falling.

Even with my parka hood narrowed to a slit the wind penetrated and forced me to turn my head and squint through the hairs of the ruff. It was worse for the dogs. Their eyes watered and knuckles of ice built up around the lids. Every fifteen minutes I had to remove these by pulling gently and thawing the side frozen to their fur with what warmth was in my fingers. After a couple of miles of this the sled struck an end of driftwood. There was a splitting sound and the handlebars went loose. I called the dogs to a halt.

A crosspiece bracing the handlebars had cracked and was no longer giving any support. The damage was not severe but it affected my control of the sled and I feared that a sudden wrench would break the handlebars completely. The twenty minutes it took to lash a temporary repair, with frequent stops to warm my hands, felt like hours.

Visibility was fluctuating between 50 and 80 yards, though there were moments when Duran and Rosco in lead were barely discernible. I had to stop frequently to look for tripods, sometimes leaving the dogs and walking ahead on foot. Then Duran decided he wanted to run with the wind behind him and kept pulling off to the left. When I gee'd the leaders over Rosco would respond for a while but gradually Duran would pull him aside. I replaced them with Silver and Alf.

The wind had transformed Alf into a peculiar shape. He was completely flat on one side and all billowing hairiness on the other. But he was no good either. I swapped him with Sensor. Sensor was a timid dog and usually went wherever Silver indicated. For several hundred yards he endured the discomfort, but then began pulling back. Silver turned and snapped at him – her usual form of discipline when a companion was disputing her control – but Sensor was more intimidated by the wind. I stopped

yet again, added an extra section of gangline and put Silver in
single lead. I felt nervous about giving the command to go, for
this was my last resort.

"All right. GEE, GEE."

In retrospect, I suppose, it was only a small manoeuvre, and
perhaps my predicament wasn't as serious as I imagined at the
time, but I will never forget the way that dog immediately turned
into the wind. She flattened her ears and headed into the blast
without any hesitation. The snow continued to fly and ice still
formed around the dogs' eyes, and still Silver gee'd and hawed on
a single word and we wove a zigzag course along the elusive line of
markers. It is easy to become maudlin about dogs and I daresay
every musher has a shared moment treasured above all others.
This is mine, this is how I see Silver yet, leading us through a
whiteout on the last leg to Nome.

Perfect Storm

Bear Grylls

At the age of 23 Bear Grylls became the youngest Briton to summit Everest. Five years later, Grylls led a British attempt to cross the North Atlantic in an open rigid inflatable boat (RIB). On the night of 7 August 2003, 300 miles off the coast of Iceland, The Arnold and Son Explorer *and her five-man crew encountered a devastating storm:*

By 3 a.m., Mick and I were still firing on adrenalin in our determination to keep the RIB level. Every sinew in our exhausted bodies was reacting to the sea beneath us.

Suddenly, though, the boat was struck by two waves simultaneously. Two converging walls of water collided over us. The *Arnold and Son Explorer* lurched violently to star-board and began to corkscrew. I clearly remember thinking she was going over. But she rose up again. The three bodies in the sardine tin were lifted at least 4 inches off the soaking wet thin foam covering, then landed in a heap as the boat crashed back into the water.

Mick was literally washed off his seat, and the force of the water threw him on top of me. We both clutched at anything solid around us. In the dark, and in blind panic, I grabbed hold of the wheel again and frantically tried to guess where the next freak wave was coming from. We were like blind men in a boxing ring, alone and afraid, taking punches from every direction.

Over and over again we were picked up like a feather on the swell and then dropped back to the water surface, with an impact equivalent to 7 tonnes of aluminium and fuel being dropped from the second storey of a house.

We had no idea how long our electrical equipment could

withstand the combined effects of the relentless physical batter-
ing and the regular drenching by water pouring over the boat.

I was more frightened than I have ever been in my life, yet I
have never wanted so desperately to live.

Our forward speed was almost zero, and we still had such a
long way to go. The weather was getting worse, not better, and I
wondered how much longer we could stay upright.

And what if we capsized?

I recalled how in diver training we had been told we would be
able to survive for about fifteen minutes in the waters of the North
Sea. We would have much less time up here in these icy seas just
south of the Arctic Circle. We knew the drill: to try to clamber to
the stern of the boat, which would then be upside down. Then keep
together. But if you were separated in the capsize, the bottom line
was that you would be lost to the waves. You would die.

I remember looking back at Charlie and seeing a look of terror
on his face. He was ashen-white. His eyes looked a million miles
away. They stared at me blankly. Empty. He didn't even bother
to spit the water away from his mouth as the spray hit him in the
face. He just lay there, beyond caring.

Nige was in the deckchair. He was holding his knife in one
hand and his flares in the other. He looked deadly serious and
truly scared. I looked back to the helm. I had seen all I needed to
in those three brief seconds.

Time was moving so slowly, but everything was hurtling
through my head at treble speed. I suddenly saw familiar faces
in the sea and the waves. I reached out to touch Mick. I just
needed to know he was there.

I was tiring. I had to be stronger.

The only light on the boat was a dull green glow from the
screen but it was enough to see what I had spotted. Glued to the
edge of the console was a small, laminated photograph of Shara,
holding our little Jesse; and she was smiling at me.

I had never felt in such danger of not seeing them again. I felt
sick. I stared at Jesse, my little son. It broke my heart. "How have
I got into this situation?" I murmured. "I promise you I will
come home. I will see you again."

I started muttering even louder to myself, almost talking out
loud. I was speaking to Shara. My love.

"I will get this boat back safely. I will get back to you. Watch me, baby, this one last time."

Shara has always believed in me. She thinks I am stronger than I am. She thinks I am nicer than I am. She defends me and always takes my side. If I am annoyed with someone, so is she. If I am exhausted, she soothes me. She makes me calm when I am nervous. And I have always loved her. She's my buddy. I would not break the promise I had made her at Heathrow.

Together, we had the world to live for. We had a son.

My mind raced back to that afternoon when little Jesse was born. I remember so vividly how people had warned me against watching my wife give birth: "It's so animalistic," they said.

It was a strange word. Yet every ounce of me wanted to be alongside her. It was our time, the biggest moment of our lives, and I knew we should be together.

It felt as though the world was standing still. I sat there and held her as she writhed in pain. In her weakness, she somehow looked so strong, so feminine, so pretty. Not animalistic. I was witnessing so much more than the birth of a child; I was also watching the birth of a woman. Shara.

This was my family, all I had ever dreamed of, and the two of them both looked so frail as they lay there wiped out, exhausted. We had always wanted to call him Jesse. Shara said it was after King David's father in the Bible. King David had been quite a player. He even killed a giant called Goliath when he was only a kid. I liked the name though because it reminded me of Uncle Jesse in *The Dukes of Hazzard* – in dungarees, with a big white dirty beard.

But Jesse also means "God's gift". That felt so right to us.

As I watched them both sleep in the hospital, I was over-whelmed by a feeling of protectiveness. I would do anything for them; I would even die for them. I had never felt that before.

And right here, in the pitch black of the storm, utterly drained, sodden and frightened, I felt as though I was being asked, "Could I now live for them?"

"Come on, Bear, we'll get through this," Mick shouted in my ear, thumping me on the back. "We've been through worse than this

and come out alive. We'll do it again. We'll just get through this
. . . then we'll never go anywhere again!" And he slapped me
once more.

Then Mick rummaged through the sodden food sack and
pulled out another can of Red Bull. He swigged at it, then lifted
my visor. I opened my mouth and tilted my head back so he could
pour the liquid caffeine down my throat. It went everywhere.

"Come on, Bear, you're doing great, keep going! We can do
this, buddy. Just keep going."

Adrenalin was still surging through our bodies as on and on,
through the night, we kept shouting at each other, punching
each other, encouraging each other. And somehow we kept
going.

Ever since Mick and I were eight years old, playing around in
the Isle of Wight, there has been a bond between us. That bond
was built through school, strengthened on the cold south-east
ridge of Everest when he so nearly died; and now it was being
reforged in the icy, choppy waters of the frozen North Atlantic.

While we were fighting our own battles at the console, there
were three other men on that boat, huddled in the sardine tin,
desperately trying to cope with their own worlds of terror inside
their heads.

Charlie recalls:

For ten hours or so, I was absolutely convinced I was going to
die. It was not just a question of being afraid; rather, an utter
conviction that I was near the end.

It was not a question of "if"; it was rather a matter of
"when", because I really believed the boat was going to flip.

Strangely, I had thought about this kind of near-death
experience in advance. Before the expedition, I would get
fit by running in the streets around my home in Manchester
and, whenever I needed to motivate myself to push harder, I
just imagined I had been thrown into the freezing water and I
was swimming to get back to the boat. That image was very
clear in my mind, and now it seemed to be about to happen,
for real.

In some ways, the thought of drowning had always sounded
quite relaxing. That's a bit morbid, I know, but the idea of

being in the water, floating away, being numb to everything, thinking how nice it was not to have to worry about the bank manager – I must admit that I found that whole concept to be quite relaxing.

However, when it came to the crunch, the human instinct for preservation did kick in. I remember deciding I really did want to do quite a lot of things before I die. I didn't want to die here and now. I was not going to give up lightly. I was quite surprised by this. I thought of my immediate family: that kicked in, and very strongly. It was practical, not emotional. It was my decision: I didn't want to die. I wanted to get through this.

For me, time passed quite quickly. If you tell someone to sit in the corner, the first ten minutes go slowly, but then the hours pass quickly; and I wasn't really aware of Bear and Mick although I could see them hitting each other and shouting at each other. When things had started getting serious, they had gone all military; they were both practical and impressive, but I was still terrified.

Huddled beside Charlie, almost indistinguishable in a cold, wet heap, Nige shook with the cold and with his thoughts.

He recalls:

I understood Bear's decision to helm through the night. He felt that was what he had to do in the circumstances, and, from my point of view, well, it meant I didn't have to move – it was a bit of a result.

My main concern, though, was that the boat would flip, and I was trying to plan how I would get out of the boat from where I was lying. I imagined it would happen very quickly, and my strategy was to get myself around the back of the boat, pull the life raft out from where it was stowed and then help any of the guys who might be caught inside. We would set off our EPIRB distress signals, and call for help on the VHF radio.

This was my plan, but, lying there in the sardine tin, I knew it would be futile. If that boat flipped, there was no doubt at all that there would have been five dead bodies in the ocean. That is for certain. We were more than 200 miles from land, and there was no sign of any other shipping in our vicinity.

I didn't know exactly what it would take to make the boat go over, but it felt as if it was going to go over at every wave. It was going upright, and slamming down; then we would get hit from the side. I have never wanted to be somewhere else so much. I'm not religious, but I did find myself asking for someone to help us.

I prayed. We all prayed. We were praying for our lives.

And, somehow, we kept the boat upright.

Dawn seemed never to arrive. It was the blackest night I had ever seen. Mick and I would imagine the dawn ahead of us, to the east. We would then be convinced we could see it. But it was always an illusion; or worse, another wall of white water.

We knew that dawn would bring the light with it, and that would mean we would be able to read the seas once more.

Finally, though, the night sky began to brighten in the east. Together, shoulder to shoulder, Mick and I watched as dawn crept slowly over the distant horizon. The wind was just as strong, and the waves were just as menacing; we were still in danger, but we knew that our greatest enemy, the darkness, was disappearing before us.

My eyes settled on one of the laminated sayings stuck around the boat. It had been placed on the console just beside the photograph of Shara and Jesse and read, "Each day ends so that a new beginning can be made."

As the early morning of Friday, 8 August 2003 dawned over the Denmark Strait, it was indeed a new beginning.

I asked Mick to get all the guys up and huddle round. I wanted to encourage them. We could get through this now. There was hope. We had been through hell together, but I felt we were emerging out the other side.

So we cramped together, all of us freezing cold, the others squatting behind us on the edge of the sardine tin. I felt the cold chill of dawn on my face as I turned to them. It was 5.15 a.m. We were all exhausted and bedraggled, wearing full gear and helmets, squashed on this small boat in the midst of a still-heaving ocean.

"OK, guys," I began, shouting again to make myself heard. "First of all, I am sorry that I broke the rota. I found a way of handling the boat, using the bucket to control her, so I wanted to keep going rather than stop in the middle of the night and have to explain how we could each do this.

"I know it's been a tough and bloody cold night for everyone, but we're going to get through this. It's daylight now. The sea has just lost its greatest ally – the darkness. There is no reason why we shouldn't make it out of this. We're going to reach Iceland.

"Only two things will stop us.

"The first is that we run out of fuel. But there is no need for this to happen. Andy has control of this, and we have enough to reach Iceland. But, Charlie, help him. Look out for him. Get him something to eat. Help him manage the fuel systems. Andy, we need all your skill and attention for these last few hundred miles."

Andy nodded.

"The second is that we flip the boat. But I am telling you, we will not flip her if we concentrate and helm her correctly. We *will* flip if anyone loses concentration. Whoever is helming needs to be 120 per cent alert. There was margin for helming error before; that does not exist in this sea state.

"From now on, we go back to the rota. Everybody will helm for only half an hour at a time now, and we must help each other. We must all dig deeper than ever before. If we do this, we *will* reach Iceland before nightfall."

Then I took a couple of minutes with everyone in turn, to show them how we could minimize the slamming by adjusting the position of the bucket over the jet. They all saw our defiant, plucky RIB respond, hugging the breaking waves as she punched through them.

Charlie later described my whole speech as "almost Churchillian". I'm not sure that's quite true, but I was just trying to keep everyone hanging on in there, just a little bit longer.

Mick and I were exhausted by now, and we collapsed into the sardine tin. Nige and Andy began to share the helming. Charlie had told me he didn't want to take the responsibility at this stage. I respected him for saying that. It was time for Andy and Nige to become the most important men on the boat, with our lives in

their hands. And Charlie, as ever, kept their spirits up by feeding
them chocolate and water.

Together, we had survived our longest night.

*The TransAtlantic Arctic Expedition successfully completed its
3000 mile crossing of the North Atlantic.*

PART TWO

The South Pole

"I for one had come to that point of suffering at which I did not really care if only I could die without much pain. They talk of the heroism of the dying – they little know – it would be so easy to die, a dose of morphia, a friendly crevasse, and blissful sleep. The trouble is to go on . . ."

Apsley Cherry-Garrard, *The Winter Journey*, 1911

Introduction: the South Pole

The South Pole, the southern end of the earth's axis, lies within Antarctica, the world's most hostile continent. This Geographical South Pole, distinct from the Magnetic South Pole (currently wandering Antarctica's Adelie Coast), is at an elevation of 9,300 feet, with 8,850 of those feet comprised of ice. James Cook, the English naval officer and explorer, was the first to cross the Antarctic Circle, a blasting berg-strewn experience which caused him to remark in his *A Voyage Towards the South Pole* (1777) that "no man will ever venture further than I have done". Cook was wrong: *A Voyage Towards the South Pole* caught the European imagination and created a self-denying prophecy. Man upon man clamoured to sail South to see the sights described by Cook – and to best his Southing record. There was money in it, too, for Cook had discovered seal- and whale-rich grounds around South Georgia. In 1820 Fabian Bellinghausen of Russia and Edward Bransfield of England, both sighted the Antarctic continent itself. James Ross's Royal Navy expedition of 1839 made the first Antarctic landfall, after which the British took a markedly proprietorial view of the white continent, just as they did of the Arctic. Thus the Norwegian Amundsen's successful attempt on the South Pole in 1911, beating Scott of the Royal Navy, was a national tragedy, all the more so because Scott and his companions died in the doing. (There was also the British lament that Amundsen's bid was not quite "proper", for he had used dogs, rather than man-hauling his sledges as the British did). Scott's journal of his last expedition – assuredly one of the true masterpieces of travel-writing – recorded an epic struggle against bad luck and Nature and preserved, to this day, the public opinion of the Antarctic as the fantasy ice palace of Heroes.

Which, of course, is not wide of the mark. Mawson, Shackleton, and Byrd – to pick three post-Scott explorers at random – all endured extraordinary struggles against the white death with a resoluteness of body and soul that can only inspire. But there is more to seek in Antarctica than the physical and mental limits of humankind. Scott's own expedition was (almost) as much about scientific research as it was polar conquest; to the very end Scott and his companions pulled along their weighty geological specimens. Today, the uninhabited continent is inhabited by some 20 scientific bases, prime among them the Amundsen-Scott base at 90° South, established to understand Antarctica's geology, ecosystem and weather. There is irony, even tragedy, in the scientific exploration of Antarctica: As David Halverg finds in "Melting Point", global warming is causing sections of the Antarctic iceshelves to break off and glaciers to retreat. Where the Edwardian Antarctic explorers landed on a foreshore of ice, the modern visitor can step onto rocky beach. The immortal Antarctica of the heroes, in other words, is disappearing – literally – before our eyes.

Farthest South

Ernest Shackleton

*Of all the Antarctic explorers from the "Heroic Age" the reputation
of Shackleton has stood highest longest. Scott has been found wanting
for his amateurism, Amundsen – perversely – for his clinical pro-
fessionalism, but of Shackleton the only complaint is the occasional
peccadillo. So high, indeed, is Shackleton's stock that he is a
curriculum subject in US business schools for those wanting to learn
leadership skills.*

*Born in 1874 in County Kildare, Shackleton was apprenticed to
the Merchant Navy and became a junior officer under Robert F.
Scott during the 1901–4 expedition to the South Pole. Shackleton, to
his chagrin, was invalided home. In 1907 Shackleton led his own
expedition to Antarctica on the whaler* Nimrod. *After wintering at
Cape Royds on the Ross Sea, the expedition discovered the Magnetic
South Pole, climbed 12,500-foot Mount Erebus – and then, as
Shackleton relates below, pushed further South than any had gone
before.*

26 November

A day to remember, for we have passed the "farthest South"
previously reached by man. Tonight we are in latitude 82° 18½′
South, longitude 168° East, and this latitude we have been able to
reach in much less time than on the last long march with Captain
Scott, when we made latitude 82° 16½′ our "farthest South". We
started in lovely weather this morning, with the temperature plus
19°F, and it has been up to plus 20°F during the day, giving us a
chance to dry our sleeping bags. We were rather anxious at
starting about Quan, who had a sharp attack of colic, the result
no doubt of his morbid craving for bits of rope and other odds

and ends in preference to his proper food. He soon got well enough to pull, and we got away at 7:40 a.m., the surface still very soft. There are abundant signs that the wind blows strongly from the south southeast during the winter, for the sastrugi are very marked in that direction. There are extremely large circular crystals of snow on the Barrier surface, and they seem hard and brittle. They catch the light from the sun, each one forming a reflector that dazzles the eyes as one glances at the million points of light. As each hour went on today, we found new interest to the west, where the land lies, for we opened out Shackleton Inlet, and up the inlet lies a great chain of mountains, and far into the west appear more peaks; to the west of Cape Wilson appears another chain of sharp peaks about 10,000 ft high, stretching away to the north beyond the Snow Cape, and continuing the land on which Mount A. Markham lies. To the south south-east ever appear new mountains. I trust that no land will block our path. We celebrated the breaking of the "farthest South" record with a four-ounce bottle of Curacao, sent us by a friend at home. After this had been shared out into two tablespoonfuls each, we had a smoke and a talk before turning in. One wonders what the next month will bring forth. We ought by that time to be near our goal, all being well.

Note. It falls to the lot of few men to view land not previously seen by human eyes, and it was with feelings of keen curiosity, not unmingled with awe, that we watched the new mountains rise from the great unknown that lay ahead of us. Mighty peaks they were, the eternal snows at their bases, and their rough-hewn forms rising high toward the sky. No man of us could tell what we would discover in our march south, what wonders might not be revealed to us, and our imaginations would take wings until a stumble in the snow, the sharp pangs of hunger, or the dull ache of physical weariness brought back our attention to the needs of the immediate present. As the days wore on, and mountain after mountain came into view, grimly majestic, the consciousness of our insignificance seemed to grow upon us. We were but tiny black specks crawling slowly and painfully across the white plain, and bending our puny strength to the task of wresting from nature secrets preserved inviolate through all the ages. Our anxiety to learn what lay beyond was nonetheless keen, however, and the long days of marching over the Barrier surface were saved from monotony by the continued appearance of new land to the southeast.

27 November

Started at 8 a.m., the ponies pulling well over a bad surface of very soft snow. The weather is fine and clear save for a strong mirage, which throws all the land up much higher than it really is. All day we have seen new mountains arise, and it is causing us some anxiety to note that they trend more and more to the eastward, for that means an alteration of our course from nearly due south. Still they are a long way off, and when we get up to them we may find some strait that will enable us to go right through them and on south. One speculates greatly as we march along, but patience is what is needed. I think that the ponies are feeling the day in, day out drudgery of pulling on this plain. Poor beasts, they cannot understand, of course, what it is all for, and the wonder of the great mountains is nought to them, though one notices them at times looking at the distant land. At lunch time I took a photograph of our camp, with Mount Longstaff in the background. We had our sledge flags up to celebrate the breaking of the southern record. The long snow cape marked on the chart as being attached to Mount Longstaff is not really so. It is attached to a lower bluff mountain to the north of Mount Long-staff. The most northerly peak of Mount Longstaff goes sheer down into the Barrier, and all along this range of mountains are very steep glaciers, greatly crevassed. As we pass along the mountains the capes disappear, but there are several well marked ones of which we have taken angles. Still more mountains appeared above the horizon during the afternoon, and when we camped tonight some were quite clearly defined, many, many miles away. The temperature has been up to plus 22°F today, and we took the opportunity of drying our sleeping bags, which we turned inside out and laid on the sledges. Tonight the tempera-ture is plus 13°F. We find that raw frozen pony meat cools one on the march, and during the ten minutes' spell after an hour's march we all cut up meat for lunch or dinner; in the hot sun it thaws well. This fresh meat ought to keep away scurvy from us. Quan seems much better today, but Grisi does not appear fit at all. He seems to be snow blind. Our distance today was 16 miles 1200 yards.

28 November

Started at 7:50 a.m. in beautiful weather, but with a truly awful surface, the ponies sinking in very deeply. The sledges ran easily, as the temperature was high, plus 17° to plus 20°F, the hot sun making the snow surface almost melt. We halted at noon for a latitude observation, and found our latitude to be 82° 38′ South. The land now appears more to the east, bearing southeast by south, and some very high mountains a long way off with lower foothills, can be seen in front, quite different to the land abeam of us, which consists of huge sharp pointed mountains with crevassed glaciers moving down gullies in their sides. Marshall is making a careful survey of all the principal heights. All day we have been traveling up and down long undulations, the width from crest to crest being about one and a half miles, and the rise about 1 in 100. We can easily see the line by our tracks sometimes being cut off sharp when we are on the down gradient and appearing again a long way astern as we rise. The first indication of the undulation was the fact of the mound we had made in the morning disappearing before we had traveled a quarter of a mile. During the afternoon the weather was very hot. A cool breeze had helped us in the forenoon, but it died away later. Marshall has a touch of snow blindness, and both Grisi and Socks were also affected during the day. When we camped tonight Grisi was shot. He had fallen off during the last few days, and the snow blindness was bad for him, putting him off his feed. He was the one chosen to go at the depot we made this evening. This is Depot C, and we are leaving one week's provisions and oil, with horse meat, to carry us back to Depot B. We will go on tomorrow with 1200 lb. weight (nine weeks' provisions), and we four will pull with the ponies, two on each sledge. It is late now, 11 p.m., and we have just turned in. We get up at 5:30 every morning. Our march for the day was 15 miles 1500 yards statute.

29 November

Started at 8:45 a.m. with adjusted loads of 630 lb. on each sledge. We harnessed up ourselves, but found that the ponies would not pull when we did, and as the loads came away lightly, we untoggled our harness. The surface was very soft, but during the morning there were occasional patches of hard sastrugi, all pointing south southeast. This is the course we are now steering, as the land is trending about southeast by east. During the day still more great mountains appeared to the southeast, and to the west we opened up several huge peaks, 10,000 to 15,000 ft in height. The whole country seems to be made up of range after range of mountains, one behind the other. The worst feature of today's march was the terribly soft snow in the hollows of the great undulations we were passing. During the afternoon one place was so bad that the ponies sank in right up to their bellies, and we had to pull with might and main to get the sledges along at all. When we began to ascend the rise on the southern side of the undulation it got better. The ponies were played out by 5:45 p.m., especially old Quan, who nearly collapsed, not from the weight of the sledge, but from the effort of lifting his feet and limbs through the soft snow. The weather is calm and clear, but very hot, and it is trying to man and beast. We are on a short allowance of food, for we must save all we can, so as to help the advance as far as possible. Marshall has taken the angles of the new land today. He does this regularly. The hypsometer readings at 1 p.m. are very high now if there is no correction, and it is not due to weather. We must be at about sea level. The undulations run about east by south, and west by west, and are at the moment a puzzle to us. I cannot think that the feeding of the glaciers from the adjacent mountains has anything to do with their existence. There are several glaciers, but their size is inconsiderable compared to the vast extent of Barrier affected. The glaciers are greatly crevassed. There are enormous granite cliffs at the foot of the range we are passing, and they stand vertically about 4000 to 5000 ft without a vestige of snow upon them. The main bare rocks appear to be like the schists of the western mountains opposite our winter quarters, but we are too far away, of course, to be able to tell with any certainty. Down to the south are mountains

entirely clear of snow, for their sides are vertical, and they must
be not less than 8000 to 9000 ft in height. Altogether it is a weird
and wonderful country. The only familiar thing is the broad
expanse of Barrier to the east, where as yet no land appears. We
did 14 miles 900 yards (statute) today, and are tired. The snow
came well above our ankles, and each step became a labor. Still we
are making our way south, and each mile gained reduces the
unknown. We have now done over 300 miles due south in less
than a month.

30 November

We started at 8 a.m. this morning. Quan very shaky and seemingly on his last legs, poor beast. Both he and Socks are snow
blind, so we have improvised shades for their eyes, which we trust
will help them a little. We took turns of an hour each hauling at
Quan's sledge, one at each side, to help him. Socks, being faster,
always gets ahead and then has a short spell, which eases him
considerably. We advanced very slowly today, for the surface was
as bad as ever till the afternoon, and the total distance covered
was 12 miles 150 yards. Quan was quite played out, so we camped
at 5:45 p.m. We give the ponies ample food, but they do not eat it
all, though Quan whinnies for his every meal time. He is particularly fond of the Maujee ration, and neglects his maize for it.
Again today we saw new land to the south, and unfortunately for
our quick progress in that direction, we find the trend of the coast
more to the eastward. A time is coming, I can see, when we will
have to ascend the mountains, for the land runs round more and
more in an easterly direction. Still after all we must not expect to
find things cut and dried and all suited to us in such a place. We
will be thankful if we can keep the ponies as far as our next depot
which will be in latitude 84° South. They are at the present
moment lying down in the warm sun. It is a beautifully calm clear
evening; indeed as regards weather we have been wonderfully
fortunate, and it has given Marshall the chance to take all the
necessary angles for the survey of these new mountains and
coastline. Wild is cook this week, and my week is over so I am
now living in the other tent. We are all fit and well, but our

appetites are increasing at an alarming rate. We noticed this tonight after the heavy pulling today. A great deal of the land we are passing seems to consist of granite in huge masses, and here and there are much crevassed glaciers pouring down between the mountains, perhaps from some inland ice sheet similar to that in the north of Victoria Land. The mountains show great similarity in outline, and there is no sign of any volcanic action at all so far. The temperature for the day has ranged between plus 16° and plus 12°F, but the hot sun has made things appear much warmer.

1 December

Started at 8 a.m. today. Quan has been growing weaker each hour, and we practically pulled the sledge. We passed over three undulations, and camped at 1 p.m. In the afternoon we only did four miles, Quan being led by Wild. He also led Socks with one sledge, whilst Adams, Marshall, and I hauled 200 lb. each on the other sledge, over a terribly soft surface. Poor old Quan was quite finished when we came to camp at 6 p.m., having done 12 miles 200 yards, so he was shot. We all felt losing him, I particularly, for he was my special horse ever since he was ill last March. I had looked after him, and in spite of all his annoying tricks he was a general favourite. He seemed so intelligent. Still it was best for him to go, and like the others he was well fed to the last. We have now only one pony left, and are in latitude 83° 16′ South. Ahead of us we can see the land stretching away to the east, with a long white line in front of it that looks like a giant Barrier, and nearer a very crusted-up appearance, as though there were great pressure ridges in front of us. It seems as though the Barrier end had come, and that there is now going to be a change in some gigantic way in keeping with the vastness of the whole place. We fervently trust that we will not be delayed in our march south. We are living mainly on horsemeat now, and on the march, to cool our throats when pulling in the hot sun, we chew some raw frozen meat. There was a slight breeze for a time today, and we felt chilly, as we were pulling stripped to our shirts. We wear our goggles all the time, for the glare from the snow surface is intense and the sky is cloudless. A few wisps of fleecy cloud settle on the tops of the loftiest mountains, but that is all. The surface of the Barrier still sparkles with the million frozen crystals which stand apart from the ordinary surface snow. One or two new peaks came in sight today, so we are ever adding to the chain of wonderful mountains that we have found. At one moment our thoughts are on the grandeur of the scene, the next of what we would have to eat if only we were let loose in a good restaurant. We are very hungry these days, and we know that we are likely to be for another three months. One of the granite cliffs we are nearing is over 6000 ft sheer, and much bare rock is showing, which must have running water on it as the hot sun plays down. The moon was visible in the sky all day and it was something familiar, yet far removed from these days of hot sunshine and wide white pathways. The temperature is now plus 16°F, and it is quite warm in the tent.

2 December

Started at 8 a.m., all four of us hauling one sledge, and Socks following behind with the other. He soon got into our regular pace, and did very well indeed. The surface during the morning was extremely bad and it was heavy work for us. The sun beat down on our heads and we perspired freely, though we were working only in shirts and pajama trousers, whilst our feet were cold in the snow. We halted for lunch at 1 p.m., and had some of Quan cooked, but he was very tough meat, poor old beast. Socks, the only pony left now, is lonely. He whinnied all night for his lost companion. At 1 p.m. today we had got close enough to the disturbance ahead of us to see that it consisted of enormous pressure ridges, heavily crevassed and running a long way east, with not the slightest chance of our being able to get southing that way any longer on the Barrier. So after lunch we struck due south in toward the land, which is now running in a southeast direction, and at 6 p.m. we were close to the ridges off the coast. There is a red hill about 3000 ft in height, which we hope to ascend tomorrow, so as to gain view of the surrounding country. Then we will make our way if possible, with the pony up a glacier ahead of us on to the huge ice, and on to the Pole if all goes well. It is an anxious time for us, for time is precious and food more so; we will be greatly relieved if we find a good route through the mountains. Now that we are close to the land we can see more clearly the nature of the mountains. From Mount Longstaff in a southeast direction, the land appears to be far more glaciated than further north, and since the valleys are very steep, the glaciers that they contain are heavily crevassed. These glaciers bear out in a northeast direction into the Barrier. Immediately opposite our camp the snow seems to have been blown off the steep mountain sides. The mountain ahead of us, which we are going to climb tomorrow, is undoubtedly granite, but very mildly weathered. In the distance it looked like volcanic rock, but now there can be no doubt that it consists of granite. Evidently the great ice sheet has passed over this part of the land, for the rounded forms could not have been caused by ordinary weathering. Enormous pressure ridges that run out from the south of the mountain ahead must be due to a glacier far greater in extent than any we have yet met. The glacier that comes out of Shackleton Inlet makes a disturbance in the Barrier ice, but not nearly as great as the disturbance in our immediate neighborhood at the present time. The glacier at Shackleton Inlet is quite a short one. We have now closed in to the land, but before we did so we could see the rounded tops of great mountains extending in a southeasterly direction. If we are fortunate enough to reach the summit of the mountain tomorrow, we should be able to see more clearly the line of these mountains to the southeast. It would be very interesting to follow along the Barrier to the southeast, and see the trend of the mountains but that does not enter into our program. Our way lies to the south. How one wishes for time and unlimited provisions. Then indeed we could penetrate the secrets of this great lonely continent. Regrets are vain, however, and we wonder what is in store for us beyond the mountains if we are able to get there. The closer observation of these mountains ought to give geological results of importance. We may have the good fortune to discover fossils, or at any rate to bring back specimens that will determine the geological history of the country and prove a connection between the granite boulders lying on the slopes of Erebus and Terror and the land lying to the far south. Our position tonight is latitude 83° 28' South, longitude 171° 30' East. If we can get on the mountain tomorrow, it will be the pioneer landing in the far south. We traveled 11 miles 1450 yards (statute) today, which was not bad, seeing that we were pulling 180 lb. per man on a bad surface. We got a photograph of the wonderful red granite peaks close to us, for now we are only eight miles or so off the land. The temperature is plus 20°, with a high barometer. The same fine weather continues, but the wind is cold in the early morning, when we turn out at 5:30 a.m. for breakfast.

4 December

Unable to write yesterday owing to bad attack of snow blindness, and not much better tonight, but I must record the events of the two most remarkable days that we have experienced since leaving the winter quarters. After breakfast at 5:30 a.m. yesterday, we started off from camp, leaving all camp gear standing and a good feed by Socks to last him the whole day. We got under way at 9 a.m., taking four biscuits, four lumps of sugar, and two ounces of chocolate each for lunch. We hoped to get water at the first of the rocks when we landed. Hardly had we gone one hundred yards when we came to a crevasse, which we did not see very distinctly, for the light was bad, and the sun obscured by clouds. We roped up and went on in single file, each with his ice-pick handy. I found it very difficult to see clearly with my goggles, and so took them off, and the present attack of snow blindness is the result, for the sun came out gloriously later on. We crossed several crevasses filled with snow except at the sides, the gaps being about 2 ft wide, and the whole crevasses from 10 to 20 ft across. Then we were brought up all standing by an enormous chasm of about 80 ft wide and 300 ft deep which lay right across our route. This chasm was similar to, only larger than, the one we encountered in latitude 80° 30′ South when on the southern journey with Captain Scott during the *Discovery* expedition. By making a detour to the right we found that it gradually pinched out and became filled with snow, and so we were able to cross and resume our line to the land, which very deceptively appeared quite close but was really some miles away.

Crossing several ridges of ice pressure and many more crevasses, we eventually at 12:30 p.m. reached an area of smooth blue ice in which were embedded several granite boulders, and here we obtained a drink of delicious water formed by the sun playing on the rock face and heating the ice at the base. After traveling for half a mile, we reached the base of the mountain which we hoped to climb in order to gain a view of the surrounding country. This hill is composed of granite, the red appearance being no doubt due to iron. At 1 p.m. we had a couple of biscuits and some water, and then started to make our way up the precipitous rock face. This was the most difficult part of the whole climb, for the granite was weathered and split in every direction, and some of the larger pieces seemed to be just nicely balanced on smaller pieces, so that one could almost push them over by a touch. With great difficulty we clambered up this rock face, and then ascended a gentle snow slope to another rocky bit, but not so difficult to climb. From the top of this ridge there burst upon our view an open road to the south, for there stretched before us a great glacier running almost south and north between two huge mountain ranges. As far as we could see, except toward the mouth, the glacier appeared to be smooth, yet this was not a certainty, for the distance was so great. Eagerly we clambered up the remaining ridges and over a snow slope, and found ourselves at the top of the mountain, the height being 3350 ft according to aneroid and hypsometer. From the summit we could see the glacier stretching away south inland till at last it seemed to merge in high inland ice. Where the glacier fell into the Barrier about northeast bearing, the pressure waves were enormous, and for miles the surface of the Barrier was broken up. This was what we had seen ahead of us the last few days, and we now understood the reason of the commotion on the Barrier surface. To the southeast we could see the lofty range of mountains we had been following still stretching away in the same direction, and we can safely say that the Barrier is bounded by a chain of mountains extending in a south-easterly direction as far as the 86th parallel South. The mountains to the west appear to be more heavily glaciated than the ones to the eastward. There are some huge granite faces on the southern sides of the mountains, and these faces are joined up by cliffs of a very dark hue. To the south southeast, toward what is apparently the head of the glacier, there are several sharp cones of very black rock, eight or nine in all. Beyond these are red granite faces, with sharp, needlelike spurs, similar in appearance to the "cathedral" rocks described by Armitage in connection with the *Discovery* expedition to the western mountains. Further on to the south the mountains have a bluff appearance, with long lines of stratification running almost horizontally. This bluff mountain range seems to break about sixty miles away, and beyond can be seen dimly other mountains. Turning to the west, the mountains on that side appeared to be rounded and covered with huge masses of ice, and glaciers showing the lines of crevasses. In the far distance there is what looked like an active volcano. There is a big mountain with a cloud on the top, bearing all the appearance of steam from an active cone. It would be very interesting to find an active volcano so far south. After taking bearings of the trend of the mountains, Barrier and glacier, we ate our frugal lunch and wished for more, and then descended. Adams had boiled the hypsometer and taken the temperature on the top, whilst Marshall, who had carried the camera on his back all the way up, took a couple of photographs. How we wished we had more plates to spare to get a record of the wonderful country we were passing through. At 4 p.m. we began to descend, and at 5 p.m. we were on the Barrier again. We were rather tired and very hungry when, at 7 p.m., we reached our camp. After a good dinner, and a cupful of Maujee ration in the hoosh as an extra, we turned in.

Today, December 4, we got under way at 8 a.m. and steered into the land, for we could see that there was no question as to the way we should go now. Though on the glacier, we might encounter crevasses and difficulties not to be met with on the Barrier, yet on the latter we could get no further than 86° South, and then would have to turn in toward the land and get over the mountains to reach the Pole. We felt that our main difficulty on the glacier route would be with the pony Socks, and we could not expect to drag the full load ourselves as yet without relay work. Adams, Marshall, and I pulled one sledge with 680 lb. weight, and Wild followed with Socks directly in our wake, so that if we came to a crevasse he would have warning. Everything went on well except that when we were close in to land, Marshall went through the snow covering of a crevasse. He managed to hold himself up by his arms. We could see no bottom to this crevasse. At 1 p.m. we were close to the snow slope up which we hoped to reach the interior of the land and thence get on to the glacier. We had lunch and then proceeded, finding, instead of a steep, short slope, a long, fairly steep gradient. All the afternoon we toiled at the sledge, Socks pulling his load easily enough, and eventually, at 5 p.m., reached the head of the pass, 2000 ft above sea level. From that point there was a gentle descent toward the glacier, and at 6 p.m. we camped close to some blue ice with granite boulders embedded in it, around which were pools of water. This water saves a certain amount of our oil, for we have not to melt snow or ice. We turned in at 8 p.m., well satisfied with the day's work. The weather now is wonderfully fine, with not a breath of wind, and a warm sun beating down on us. The temperature was up to plus 22°F at noon, and is now plus 18°F. The pass through which we have come is flanked by great granite pillars at least 2000 ft in height and making a magnificent entrance to the "Highway to the South." It is all so interesting and everything is on such a vast scale that one cannot describe it well. We four are seeing these great designs and the play of nature in her grandest moods for the first time, and possibly they may never be seen by man again. Poor Marshall had another four miles' walk this evening, for he found that he had lost his Jaeger jacket off the sledge. He had therefore to tramp back uphill for it, and found it two miles away on the trail. Socks is not feeding well. He seems lonely without his companions. We gave him a drink of thaw water this evening, but he did not seem to appreciate it, preferring the snow at his feet.

5 December

Broke camp sharp at 8 a.m. and proceeded south down an icy slope to the main glacier. The ice was too slippery for the pony, so Wild took him by a circuitous route to the bottom on snow. At the end of our ice slope, down which the sledge skidded rapidly, though we had put on rope brakes and hung on to it as well as we could, there was a patch of soft snow running parallel with the glacier, which here trended about southwest by south. Close ahead of us were the massed up, fantastically shaped and split masses of pressure across which it would have been impossible for us to have gone, but, fortunately, it was not necessary even to try, for close into the land was a snow slope free from all crevasses, and along this gentle rise we made our way. After a time this snow slope gave place to blue ice, with numberless cracks and small crevasses across which it was quite impossible for the pony to drag the sledge without a serious risk of a broken leg in one of the many holes, the depth of which we could not ascertain. We therefore unharnessed Socks, and Wild took him over this bit of ground very carefully, whilst we others first hauled our sledge and then the pony sledge across to a patch of snow under some gigantic granite pillars over 2000 ft in height, and here, close to some thaw water, we made our lunch camp. I was still badly snow blind, so stayed in camp whilst Marshall and Adams went on to spy out a good route to follow after lunch was over. When they returned they informed me that there was more cracked-up blue ice ahead, and that the main pressure of the glacier came in very close to the pillar of granite that stood before us, but that beyond that there appeared to be a snow slope and good going. The most remarkable thing they reported was that as they were walking along a bird, brown in color with a white line under each wing, flew just over their heads and disappeared to the south. It is, indeed, strange to hear of such an incident in latitude 83° 40′ South. They were sure it was not a skua gull, which is the only bird I could think of that would venture down here, and the gull might have been attracted by the last dead pony, for when in latitude 80° 30′ South, on my last southern trip, a skua gull arrived shortly after we had killed a dog.

After lunch we started again, and by dint of great exertions managed, at 6 p.m., to camp after getting both sledges and then the pony over another couple of miles of crevassed blue ice. We then went on and had a look ahead, and saw that we are going to have a tough time tomorrow to get along at all. I can see that it will, at least, mean relaying three or four times across nearly half a mile of terribly crevassed ice, covered in places with treacherous snow, and razor edged in other places, all of it sloping down toward the rock debris-strewn shore on the cliff side. We are camped under a wonderful pillar of granite that has been arounded by the winds into a perfectly symmetrical shape, and is banded by lines of gneiss. There is just one little patch of snow for our tents, and even that bridges some crevasses. Providence will look over us tonight, for we can do nothing more. One feels that at any moment some great piece of rock may come hurtling down, for all around us are pieces of granite, ranging from the size of a hazelnut to great boulders twenty to forty tons in weight, and on one snow slope is the fresh track of a fallen rock. Still we can do no better, for it is impossible to spread a tent on the blue ice, and we cannot get any further tonight. We are leaving a depot here. My eyes are my only trouble, for their condition makes it impossible for me to pick out the route or do much more than pull. The distance covered today was 9 miles with 4 miles relay.

6 December

Started at 8 a.m. today in fine weather to get our loads over the half mile of crevassed ice that lay between us and the snow slope to the south south-west. We divided up the load and managed to get the whole lot over in three journeys, but it was an awful job, for every step was a venture, and I, with one eye entirely blocked up because of snow blindness, felt it particularly uncomfortable work. However, by 1 p.m. all our gear was safely over, and the other three went back for Socks. Wild led him, and by 2 p.m. we were all camped on the snow again. Providence has indeed looked after us. At 3 p.m. we started south southwest up a long slope to the right of the main glacier pressure. It was very heavy going, and we camped at 5 p.m. close to a huge crevasse, the snow bridge of which we crossed. There is a wonderful view of the mountains, with new peaks and ranges to the southeast, south and southwest. There is a dark rock running in conjunction with the granite on several of the mountains. We are now over 1700 ft up on the glacier, and can see down on to the Barrier. The cloud still hangs on the mountain ahead of us; it certainly looks as though it were a volcano cloud, but it may be due to condensation. The lower current clouds are traveling very fast from south southeast to north northwest. The weather is fine and clear, and the temperature plus 17°F.

7 **December**

Started at 8 a.m., Adams, Marshall and self pulling one sledge. Wild leading Socks behind. We traveled up and down slopes with very deep snow, into which Socks sank up to his belly, and we plunged in and out continuously, making it very trying work. Passed several crevasses on our right hand and could see more to the left. The light became bad at 1 p.m., when we camped for lunch, and it was hard to see the crevasses, as most were more or less snow covered. After lunch the light was better, and as we marched along we were congratulating ourselves upon it when suddenly we heard a shout of "help" from Wild. We stopped at once and rushed to his assistance, and saw the pony sledge with the forward end down a crevasse and Wild reaching out from the side of the gulf grasping the sledge. No sign of the pony. We soon got up to Wild, and he scrambled out of the dangerous position, but poor Socks had gone. Wild had a miraculous escape. He was following up our tracks, and we had passed over a crevasse which was entirely covered with snow, but the weight of the pony broke through the snow crust and in a second all was over. Wild says he just felt a sort of rushing wind, the leading rope was snatched from his hand, and he put out his arms and just caught the further edge of the chasm. Fortunately for Wild and us, Socks' weight snapped the swingle-tree of the sledge, so it was saved, though the upper bearer is broken. We lay down on our stomachs and looked over into the gulf, but no sound or sign came to us; a black bottomless pit it seemed to be. We hitched the pony sledge to ourselves and started off again, now with a weight of 1000 lb. for the four of us. Camped at 6:20 p.m., very tired, having to retreat from a maze of crevasses and rotten ice on to a patch where we could pitch our tents. We are indeed thankful for Wild's escape. When I think over the events of the day I realize what the loss of the sledge would have meant to us. We would have had left only two sleeping bags for the four of us, and I doubt whether we could have got back to winter quarters with the short equipment. Our chance of reaching the Pole would have been gone. We take on the maize to eat ourselves. There is one ray of light in this bad day, and that is that, anyhow we could not have taken Socks on much further. We would have had to shoot him tonight, so that although his loss is a serious matter to us, for we had counted on the meat, still we know that for traction purposes he would have been of little further use. When we tried to camp tonight we stuck our ice axes into the snow to see whether there were any more hidden crevasses, and everywhere the axes went through. It would have been folly to have pitched our camp in that place, as we might easily have dropped through during the night. We had to retreat a quarter of a mile to pitch the tent. It was very unpleasant to turn back, even for this short distance, but on this job one must expect reverses.

8 December

Started at 8 a.m. and immediately began dodging crevasses and pits of unknown depth. Wild and I were leading, for, thank heaven, my eyes are fit and well again. We slowly toiled up a long crevassed slope, and by lunch time were about 1900 ft up the glacier. We had covered 6 miles 150 yards of an uphill drag, with about 250 lb. per man to haul. After lunch we still traveled up, but came on to blue glacier ice almost free from crevasses, so did much better, the sledges running easily. We camped at 6 p.m., the day's journey having been 12 miles 150 yards. The slope we went up in the morning, was not as bad as we had anticipated, but quite bad enough for us to be thankful that we are out, at any rate for a time, from the region of hidden crevasses. The hypsometer tonight gave our height as 2300 ft above sea level. It is beautifully fine still. We have been wonderfully fortunate in this, especially in view of the situation we are in.

9 December

Another splendid day as far as the weather is concerned, and much we needed it, for we have had one of our hardest day's work and certainly the most dangerous so far. We started at 7:45 a.m. over the blue ice, and in less than an hour were in a perfect maze of crevasses, some thinly bridged with snow and others with a thicker and therefore more deceptive covering. Marshall went

through one and was only saved by his harness. He had quite
disappeared down below the level of the ice, and it was one of
those crevasses that open out from the top, with no bottom to be
seen, and I daresay there was a drop of at least 1000 ft. Soon after,
Adams went through, then I did. The situation became momen-
tarily more dangerous and uncertain. The sledges, skidding
about, came up against the sheer, knife-like edges of some of
the crevasses, and thus the bow of the second sledge, which had
been strained when Socks fell, gave way. We decided to relay our
gear over this portion of a glacier until we got on to safer ground,
and it was well past eleven o'clock before we had got both sledges
on to better ice. We camped at 11:45 a.m. to get the sun's
meridian altitude, and, to save time while watching the sun's
rise and fall, decided to lunch at noon. The latitude we found to
be 84° 2′ South, which is not so bad considering that we have been
hauling our heavy load of 250 lb. per man uphill for the last two
days. At noon we were nearly 2500 ft above sea level. In the
afternoon we had another heavy pull, and now are camped
between two huge crevasses, but on a patch of hard snow. We
pitched camp at 6 p.m., very tired and extremely hungry after
dragging uphill all the afternoon for over five hours. It is 8 p.m.
now, and we are nearly 3000 ft above sea level. Low cumulus
clouds are hanging to the south of us, as they have done for many
days past, obscuring any view in that direction. We are anxiously
hoping to find soon a level and inland ice sheet so that we can put
on more speed. The distance today was 11 miles 1450 yards plus
two miles relay. The talk now is mainly about food and the things
we would like to eat, and at meal times our hoosh disappears with
far too great speed. We are all looking forward to Christmas Day,
for then, come what may, we are going to be full of food.

10 December

Falls, bruises, cut shins, crevasses, razor edged ice, and a heavy
upward pull have made up the sum of the day's trials, but there
has been a measure of compensation in the wonderful scenery, the
marvelous rocks and the covering of a distance of 11 miles 860
yards toward our goal. We started at 7:30 a.m. amongst crevasses,

but soon got out of them and pulled up a long slope of snow. Our altitude at noon was 3250 ft above sea level. Then we slid down a blue ice slope, after crossing crevasses. Marshall and I each went down one. We lunched at 1 p.m. and started at 2 p.m. up a long ridge by the side moraine of the glacier. It was heavy work, as the ice was split and presented knife-like edges between the cracks, and there were also some crevasses. Adams got into one. The going was terribly heavy, as the sledges brought up against the ice edges every now and then, and then there was a struggle to get them started again. We changed our foot gear, substituting ski boots for the finnesko, but nevertheless had many painful falls on the treacherous blue ice, cutting our hands and shins. We are all much bruised. We camped on a patch of snow by the land at 6 p.m. The rocks of the moraine are remarkable, being of every hue and description. I cannot describe them, but we will carry specimens back for the geologists to deal with. The main rocks of the "Cloud Maker", the mountain under which we are camped, appear to be slates, reef quartz and a very hard, dark brown rock, the name of which I do not know. The erratics of marble, conglomerate, and breccia are beautiful, showing a great mass of wonderful colors, but these rocks we cannot take away. We can only take with us small specimens of the main rocks, as weight is of importance to us, and from these small specimens the geologists must determine the character of the land. This mountain is the one we thought might be an active volcano when we saw it from the mountain at the foot of the glacier, but the cloud has blown away from its head today, and we can see definitely that it is not a volcano. It is a remarkable sight as it towers above us with the snow clinging to its sides. Tonight there is a cold north wind. I climbed about 600 ft up the mountain and got specimens of the main rocks in situ. The glacier is evidently moving very slowly, and not filling as much of the valley as it did at some previous date, for the old moraines lie higher up in terraces. Low cumulus clouds to the south are hiding some of the new land in that direction. We are all very hungry and tired tonight after the day's fight with glacier. Whilst I went up the mountain to spy out the land the others ground up the balance of the maize, brought for pony feed, between flat stones, in order that we may use it ourselves to eke out our supply of food. The method of prepara-

tion was primitive, but it represented the only way of getting it fit
to cook without the necessity of using more oil than we can spare
for lengthy boiling. The temperature was plus 12°F at noon
today, and is plus 14° now at 8 p.m. We are getting south,
and we hope to reach the inland ice in a couple of days; then
our marching will be faster. The weather is still fine.

11 December

A heavy day. We started away at 7:40 a.m. and tried to keep
alongside the land, but the ice of the glacier sloped so much that
we had to go on to the ridge, where the sledges could run without
side slipping. This slipping cuts the runners very badly. We
crossed the medial moraine, and found rock there with what
looked like plant impressions. We collected some specimens.

In the afternoon we found the surface better, as the cracks were
nearly all filled up with water turned to ice. We camped for lunch
on rubbly ice. After lunch we rounded some pressure ridges fairly
easily, and then pulled up a long ice slope with many sharp
points. All the afternoon we were passing over ice in which the
cracks had been closed up, and we began to have great hopes that
the end of the glacier was in sight, and that we would soon be able
to put in some good marches on the plateau. At 5 p.m. we found
more cracks and a mass of pressure ice ahead and land appeared as
the clouds ahead lifted. I cannot tell what it means, but the
position makes us anxious. The sledges will not stand much more
of this ice work, and we are still 340 geographical miles away from
the Pole. Thank God the weather is fine still. We camped at 6
p.m. on hard ice between two crevasses. There was no snow to
pack round the tents, so we had to put the sledges and the
provision bags on the snow cloths. We made the floor level inside
by chipping away the points of ice with our ice axes. We were
very hungry after hoosh tonight. Awkward features about the
glacier are the little pits filled with mud, of which I collected a
small sample.* It seems to be ground down rock material, but
what the action has been I cannot tell. The hot sun, beating down

---

* These pits are known as cryoconite holes.

on this mud, makes it gradually sink into the body of the glacier, leaving a rotten ice covering through which we often break. It is like walking over a cucumber frame, and sometimes the boulders that have sunk down through the ice can be seen 3 to 4 ft below the surface. The ice that has formed above the sunken rocks is more clear than the ordinary glacier ice. We are 3700 ft up, and made 8 miles 900 yards to the good today. We have the satisfaction of feeling that we are getting south, and perhaps tomorrow may see the end of all our difficulties. Difficulties are just things to overcome after all. Every one is very fit.

12 December

Our distance – three miles for the day – expresses more readily than I can write it the nature of the day's work. We started at 7:40 a.m. on the worst surface possible, sharp edged blue ice full of chasms and crevasses, rising to hills and descending into gullies; in fact, a surface that could not be equaled in any polar work for difficulty in traveling. Our sledges are suffering greatly, and it is a constant strain on us both to save the sledges from breaking or going down crevasses, and to save ourselves as well. We are a mass of bruises where we have fallen on the sharp ice, but, thank God, no one has even a sprain. It has been relay work today, for we could only take on one sledge at a time, two of us taking turns at pulling the sledge whilst the others steadied and held the sledge to keep it straight. Thus we would advance one mile, and then return over the crevasses and haul up the other sledge. By repeating this today for three miles we marched nine miles over a surface where many times a slip meant death. Still we have advanced three miles to the south, and tonight we are camped on a patch of névé. By using our ice axes we made a place for the tent. The weather is still splendidly fine, though low clouds obscure our horizon to the south. We are anxiously hoping to cross the main pressure tomorrow, and trust that we will then have better traveling. Given good traveling, we will not be long in reaching our goal. Marshall is putting in the bearings and angles of the new mountains. They still keep appearing to the west and east. Distance 3 miles 500 yards, with relays 9 miles 1500 yards.

13 December

We made a start at 8 a.m. and once again went up hill and down
dale, over crevasses and blue, ribbed ice, relaying the sledges. We
had covered about a mile when we came to a place where it
seemed almost impossible to proceed. However, to our right,
bearing about southwest by south, there seemed to be better
surface and we decided to make a detour in that direction in
order, if possible, to get round the pressure. While returning for
one of the sledges I fell on the ice and hurt my left knee, which
was a serious matter, or rather might have been. I have had a
bandage on all the afternoon while pulling, and the knee feels
better now, but one realizes what it would mean if any member of
our party were to be damaged under these conditions and in this
place. This afternoon we came on to a better surface, and were
able to pull both sledges instead of relaying. We are still gradually
rising, and tonight our hypsometer gives 203.7, or 4370 ft up.
There is a cool southerly wind; indeed, more than we have had
before, and as we have only a patch of névé on the glacier for our
tents, we had to take the provision bags and gear off the sledges to
keep the tent cloths down. The temperature is plus 19°F. New
mountains are still appearing to the west southwest as we rise. We
seem now to be going up a long yellow track, for the ice is not so
blue, and we are evidently traveling over an old moraine, where
the stones have sunk through the ice when its onward movement
has been retarded. I am sure that the bulk of the glacier is growing
less, but the onward movement still continues, though at a much
slower pace than at some previous period. The gain for the day
was five miles, and in addition we did four miles relay work.

14 December

This has been one of our hardest day's work so far. We have been
steering all day about south southwest up the glacier, mainly in
the bed of an ancient moraine, which is full of holes through
which the stones and boulders have melted down long years ago.
It has been snowing all day with a high temperature, and this has
made everything very wet. We have ascended over 1000 ft today,

our altitude at 6 p.m. being 5600 ft above sea level, so the
mountains to the west must be from 10,000 to 15,000 ft in height,
judging from their comparative elevation. My knee is better
today. We have had a heavy pull and many falls on the slippery
ice. Just before camping, Adams went through some snow, but
held up over an awful chasm. Our sledges are much the worse for
wear, and the one with the broken bow constantly strikes against
the hard, sharp ice, pulling us up with a jerk and often flinging us
down. At this high altitude the heavy pulling is very trying,
especially as we slip on the snow covering the blue ice. There has
evidently been an enormous glaciation here, and now it is dwindling away. Even the mountains show signs of this. Tonight our
hopes are high that we are nearly at the end of the rise and that
soon we will reach our longed for plateau. Then southward
indeed! Food is the determining factor with us. We did $7\frac{1}{2}$ miles
today.

15 December

Started at 7:40 a.m. in clear weather. It was heavy going uphill on
the blue ice, but gradually we rose the land ahead, and it seemed
as though at last we were going to have a change, and that we
would see something new. At lunchtime we were on a better
surface, with patches of snow, and we could see stretching out in
front of us what was apparently a long, wide plain. It looked as
though now really we were coming to the level ground for which
we have longed, especially as the hypsometer gave us an altitude
of 7230 ft, but this altitude at night came down to 5830 ft so the
apparent height may be due to barometric pressure and change of
weather, for in the afternoon a stiff breeze from the southwest
sprang up. The temperature was plus 18°F at noon, and when the
wind came up it felt cold, as we were pulling in our pajama
trousers, with nothing underneath. We have been going steadily
uphill all the afternoon, but on a vastly improved surface, consisting of hard névé instead of blue ice and no cracks, only
covered in crevasses, which are easily seen. Ahead of us really
lies the plateau. We can also see ahead of us detached mountains,
piercing through the inland ice, which is the road to the south for

us. Huge mountains stretch out to the east and west. After last week's toil and anxiety the change is delightful. The distance covered today was 13 miles 200 yards.

16 December

We started at 7 a.m., having had breakfast at 5:30 a.m. It was snowing slightly for the first few hours, and then the weather cleared. The surface was hard and the going good. We camped at noon and took sights for latitude, and ascertained that our position was 84° 50′ South. Ahead of us we could see a long slope, icy and crevassed, but we did 13 miles 1650 yards for the day. We camped at 5:30 p.m., and got ready our depot gear. We have decided to travel as lightly as possible, taking only the clothes we are wearing, and we will leave four days' food, which I calculate should get us back to the last depot on short ration. We have now traversed nearly one hundred miles of crevassed ice, and risen 6000 ft on the largest glacier in the world. One more crevassed slope, and we will be on the plateau, please God. We are all fit and well. The temperature tonight is plus 15°F, and the wind is blowing freshly from the southwest. There are splendid ranges of mountains to the west southwest, and we have an extended view of glacier and mountains. Ahead of us lie three sharp peaks, connected up and forming an island in what is apparently inland ice or the head of the glacier. The peaks lie due south of us. To the eastward and westward of this island the ice bears down from the inland ice sheet, and joins the head of the glacier proper. To the westward the mountains along the side of the glacier are all of the bluff type, and the lines of stratification can be seen plainly. Still further to the westward, behind the frontal range, lie sharper peaks, some of them almost perfect cones. The trend of the land from the "Cloudmaker" is about south southwest. We are traveling up the west side of the glacier. On the other side, to the east, there is a break in the bluff mountains, and the land beyond runs away more to the southeast. The valley is filled with pressure ice, which seems to have come from the inland ice sheet. The mountains to the southeast also show lines of stratification. I hope that the photographs will be clear enough to give an idea of the character of this land. These mountains are not beautiful in the ordinary acceptance of the term, but they are magnificent in their stern and rugged grandeur. No foot has ever trod on their mighty sides, and until we reached this frozen land no human eyes had seen their forms.

17 December

We made a start at 7:20 a.m. and had an uphill pull all the morning over blue ice with patches of snow, which impeded our progress until we learned that the best way was to rush the sledges over them, for it was very difficult to keep one's footing on the smooth ice, and haul the sledges astern over the snow. By 1 p.m. we had done eight miles of this uphill work, and in the afternoon we did four more. We had worked from 7:23 a.m. until 6:40 p.m. with one hour's rest for lunch only and it seems as though twelve miles was not much, but the last two hours' going was very stiff. We had to take on one sledge at a time up the icy slope, and even then we had to cut steps with our ice axes as we went along. The work was made more difficult by the fact that a strong southerly wind was dead in our faces. The second sledge we hauled up the rise by means of the alpine rope. We made it fast to the sledge, went on with the first sledge till the rope was stretched out to its full length, then cut a place to stand on, and by our united efforts hauled the sledge up to where we stood. We repeated this until we had managed to reach a fairly level spot with both the sledges, and we pitched our tents on a small patch of snow. There was not enough of the snow to make fast the snow cloths of the tents, and we had to take the gear off the sledges and pile that round to supplement the snow. We have burned our boats behind us now as regards warm clothing, for this afternoon we made a depot in by the rocks of the island we are passing, and there left everything except the barest necessaries. After dinner tonight Wild went up the hillside in order to have a look at the plateau. He came down with the news that the plateau is in sight at last, and that tomorrow should see us at the end of our difficulties. He also brought down with him some very interesting geological specimens, some of which certainly look like coal. The quality may be poor, but I have little doubt that the stuff is coal. If that proves to be the case, the discovery will be most interesting to the scientific world. Wild tells me that there are about six seams of this dark stuff, mingled with sandstone, and that the seams are from 4 in. to 7 or 8 ft in thickness. There are vast quantities of it lying on the hillside. We took a photograph of the sandstone, and I wish very much that we could spare time to examine the rocks more thoroughly. We may be able to do this on the way back. We have but little time for geological work, for our way is south and time is short, but we found that the main rock is sandstone and on our way back we will collect some. I expect that this will be the most southerly rock that we shall obtain, for we ought to reach the plateau tomorrow, and then there will be no more land close to us. It is gusty tonight, but beautifully clear. The altitude, according to the hypsometer, is 6100 ft.

NOTE. When I showed the specimens to Professor David after our return to the *Nimrod*, he stated definitely that some of them were coal and others "mother of coal."

18 December

Almost up: The altitude tonight is 7400 ft above sea level. This has been one of our hardest days, but worth it, for we are just on the plateau at last. We started at 7:30 a.m., relaying the sledges, and did 6 miles 600 yards, which means nearly 19 miles for the day of actual traveling. All the morning we worked up loose, slippery ice, hauling the sledges up one at a time by means of the alpine rope, then pulling in harness on the less stiff rises. We camped for lunch at 12:45 p.m. on the crest of a rise close to the pressure and in the midst of crevasses, into one of which I managed to fall, also Adams. Whilst lunch was preparing I got some rock from the land, quite different to the sandstone of yesterday. The mountains are all different just here. The land on our left shows beautifully clear stratified lines, and on the west side sandstone stands out, greatly weathered. All the afternoon we relayed up a long snow slope, and we were hungry and tired when we reached camp. We have been saving food to make it spin out, and that increases our hunger; each night we all dream of foods. We save two biscuits per man per day, also pemmican and sugar, eking out our food with pony maize, which we soak in water to make it less hard. All this means that we have now five weeks' food, while we are about 300 geographical miles from the Pole, with the same distance back to the last depot we left yesterday, so we must march on short food to reach our goal. The temperature is plus 16°F tonight, but a cold wind all the morning cut our faces and broken lips. We keep crevasses with us still, but I think that tomorrow will see the end of this. When we passed the main slope today, more mountains appeared to the west of south, some with sheer cliffs and others rounded off, ending in long snow slopes. I judge the southern limit of the mountains to the west to be about latitude 86° South.

19 December

Not on the plateau level yet, though we are tonight 7888 ft up, and still there is another rise ahead of us. We got breakfast at 5 a.m. and started at 7 a.m. sharp, taking on one sledge. Soon we got to the top of a ridge, and went back for the second sledge, then hauled both together all the rest of the day. The weight was about 200 lb. per man, and we kept going until 6 p.m., with a stop of one hour for lunch. We got a meridian altitude at noon, and found that our latitude was 85° 5′ South. We seem unable to get rid of the crevasses, and we have been falling into them and steering through them all day in the face of a cold southerly wind, with a temperature varying from plus 15° to plus 9°F. The work was very heavy, for we were going uphill all day, and our sledge runners, which have been suffering from the sharp ice and rough traveling, are in a bad way. Soft snow in places greatly retarded our progress, but we have covered our ten miles, and now are camped on good snow between two crevasses. I really think that tomorrow will see us on the plateau proper. This glacier must be one of the largest, if not the largest, in the world. The sastrugi seem to point mainly to the south, so we may expect head winds all the way to the Pole. Marshall has a cold job tonight, taking the angles of the new mountains to the west, some of which appeared today. After dinner we examined the sledge runners and turned one sledge end for end, for it had been badly torn while we were coming up the glacier, and in the soft snow it clogged greatly. We are still favored with splendid weather, and that is a great comfort to us, for it would be almost impossible under other conditions to travel amongst these crevasses, which are caused by the congestion of the ice between the headlands when it was flowing from the plateau down between the mountains. Now there is comparatively little movement, and many of the crevasses have become snow-filled. Tonight we are 290 geographical miles from the Pole. We are thinking of our Christmas dinner. We will be full that day, anyhow.

20 December

Not yet up, but nearly so. We got away from camp at 7 a.m., with a strong head wind from the south, and this wind continued all day, with a temperature ranging from plus 7° to plus 5°. Our beards coated with ice. It was an uphill pull all day around pressure ice, and we reached an altitude of over 8000 ft above sea level. The weather was clear, but there were various clouds, which were noted by Adams. Marshall took bearings and angles at noon, and we got the sun's meridian altitude, showing that we were in latitude 85° 17′ South. We hope all the time that each ridge we come to will be the last, but each time another rises ahead, split up by pressure, and we begin the same toil again. It is trying work and as we have now reduced our food at breakfast to one pannikin of hoosh and one biscuit, by the time the lunch hour has arrived, after five hours' hauling in the cold wind up the slope, we are very hungry. At lunch we have a little chocolate, tea with plasmon, a pannikin of cocoa, and three biscuits. Today we did 11 miles, 950 yards (statute), having to relay the sledges over the last bit, for the ridge we were on was so steep that we could not get the two sledges up together. Still, we are getting on; we have only 279 more miles to go, and then we will have reached the Pole. The land appears to run away to the southeast now, and soon we will be just a speck on this great inland waste of snow and ice. It is cold tonight. I am cook for the week, and started tonight. Every one is fit and well.

21 December

Midsummer Day, with 28° of frost! We have frostbitten fingers and ears, and a strong blizzard wind has been blowing from the south all day, all due to the fact that we have climbed to an altitude of over 8000 ft above sea level. From early morning we have been striving to the south, but six miles is the total distance gained, for from noon, or rather from lunch at 1 p.m., we have been hauling the sledges up, one after the other, by standing pulls across crevasses and over great pressure ridges. When we had advanced one sledge some distance, we put up a flag on a bamboo to mark its position, and then roped up and returned for the other. The wind, no doubt, has a great deal to do with the low temperature, and we feel the cold, as we are going on short commons. The altitude adds to the difficulties, but we are getting south all the time. We started away from camp at 6:45 a.m. today, and except for an hour's halt at lunch, worked on until 6 p.m. Now we are camped in a filled-up crevasse, the only place where snow to put around the tents can be obtained, for all the rest of the ground we are on is either névé or hard ice. We little thought that this particular pressure ridge was going to be such an obstacle; it looked quite ordinary, even a short way off, but we have now decided to trust nothing to eyesight, for the distances are so deceptive up here. It is a wonderful sight to look down over the glacier from the great altitude we are at, and to see the mountains stretching away east and west, some of them over 15,000 ft in height. We are very hungry now, and it seems as cold almost as the spring sledging. Our beards are masses of ice all day long. Thank God we are fit and well and have had no accident, which is a mercy, seeing that we have covered over 130 miles of crevassed ice.

22 December

As I write of today's events, I can easily imagine I am on a spring sledging journey, for the temperature is minus 5°F and a chilly southeasterly wind is blowing and finds its way through the walls of our tent, which are getting worn. All day long, from 7 a.m., except for the hour when we stopped for lunch, we have been relaying the sledges over the pressure mounds and across crevasses. Our total distance to the good for the whole day was only four miles southward, but this evening our prospects look brighter, for we must now have come to the end of the great glacier. It is flattening out, and except for crevasses there will not be much trouble in hauling the sledges tomorrow. One sledge today, when coming down with a run over a pressure ridge, turned a complete somersault, but nothing was damaged, in spite of the total weight being over 400 lb. We are now dragging 400 lb. at a time up the steep slopes and across the ridges, working with the alpine rope all day, and roping ourselves together when we go back for the second sledge, for the ground is so treacherous that many times during the day we are saved only by the rope from falling into fathomless pits. Wild describes the sensation of walking over this surface, half ice and half snow, as like walking over the glass roof of a station. The usual query when one of us falls into a crevasse is! "Have you found it?" One gets somewhat callous as regards the immediate danger, though we are always glad to meet crevasses with their coats off, that is, not hidden by the snow covering. Tonight we are camped in a filled-in crevasse. Away to the north down the glacier a thick cumulus cloud is lying, but some of the largest mountains are standing out clearly. Immediately behind us lies a broken sea of pressure ice. Please God, ahead of us there is a clear road to the Pole.

23 December

Eight thousand eight hundred and twenty feet up, and still steering upward amid great waves of pressure and ice falls, for our plateau, after a good morning's march, began to rise in higher ridges, so that it really was not the plateau after all. Today's crevasses have been far more dangerous than any others we have crossed, as the soft snow hides all trace of them until we fall through. Constantly today one or another of the party has had to be hauled out from a chasm by means of his harness, which had alone saved him from death in the icy vault below. We started at 6:40 a.m. and worked on steadily until 6 p.m., with the usual lunch hour in the middle of the day. The pony maize does not swell in the water now, as the temperature is very low and the water freezes. The result is that it swells inside after we have eaten it. We are very hungry indeed, and talk a great deal of what we would like to eat. In spite of the crevasses, we have done thirteen miles today to the south, and we are now in latitude 85° 41' South. The temperature at noon was plus 6°F and at 6 p.m. it was minus 1°F, but it is much lower at night. There was a strong southeast to south southeast wind blowing all day, and it was cutting to our noses and burst lips. Wild was frostbitten. I do trust that tomorrow will see the end of this bad traveling, so that we can stretch out our legs for the Pole.

24 December

A much better day for us; indeed, the brightest we have had since entering our Southern Gateway. We started off at 7 a.m. across waves and undulations of ice, with some one or other of our little party falling through the thin crust of snow every now and then. At 10:30 a.m. I decided to steer more to the west, and we soon got on to a better surface, and covered 5 miles 250 yards in the forenoon. After lunch, as the surface was distinctly improving, we discarded the second sledge, and started our afternoon's march with one sledge. It has been blowing freshly from the south and drifting all day, and this, with over 40° of frost, has coated our faces with ice. We get superficial frost bites every now and then. During the afternoon the surface improved greatly, and the cracks and crevasses disappeared, but we are still going uphill, and from the summit of one ridge saw some new land, which runs south southeast down to latitude 86° South. We camped at 6 p.m., very tired and with cold feet. We have only the clothes we stand up in now, as we depoted everything else, and this continued rise means lower temperatures than I had anticipated. Tonight we are 9095 ft above sea level, and the way before us is still rising. I trust that it will soon level out, for it is hard work pulling at this altitude. So far there is no sign of the very hard surface that Captain Scott speaks of in connection with his journey on the Northern Plateau. There seem to be just here regular layers of snow, not much wind swept, but we will see better the surface conditions in a few days. Tomorrow will be Christmas Day, and our thoughts turn to home and all the attendant joys of the time. One longs to hear "the hansoms slurring through the London mud." Instead of that, we are lying in a little tent, isolated high on the roof of the end of the world, far, indeed, from the ways trodden of men. Still, our thoughts can fly across the wastes of ice and snow and across the oceans to those whom we are striving for and who are thinking of us now. And, thank God, we are nearing our goal. The distance covered today was 11 miles 250 yards.

25 December

Christmas Day. There has been from 45° to 48° of frost, drifting snow and a strong biting south wind, and such has been the order of the day's march from 7 a.m. to 6 p.m. up one of the steepest rises we have yet done, crevassed in places. Now, as I write, we are 9500 ft above sea level, and our latitude at 6 p.m. was 85° 55′ South. We started away after a good breakfast, and soon came to soft snow, through which our worn and torn sledge-runners dragged heavily. All morning we hauled along, and at noon had done 5 miles 250 yards. Sights gave us latitude 85° 51′ South. We had lunch then, and I took a photograph of the camp with the Queen's flag flying and also our tent flags, my companions being in the picture. It was very cold, the temperature being minus 16°F, and the wind went through us. All the afternoon we worked steadily uphill, and we could see at 6 p.m. the new land plainly trending to the southeast. This land is very much glaciated. It is comparatively bare of snow, and there are well-defined glaciers on the side of the range, which seems to end up in the southeast with a large mountain like a keep. We have called it "The Castle". Behind these the mountains have more gentle slopes and are more rounded. They seem to fall away to the southeast, so that, as we are going south, the angle opens and we will soon miss them. When we camped at 6 p.m. the wind was decreasing. It is hard to understand this soft snow with such a persistent wind, and I can only suppose that we have not yet reached the actual plateau level, and that the snow we are traveling over just now is on the slopes, blown down by the south and southeast wind. We had a splendid dinner. First came hoosh, consisting of pony ration boiled up with pemmican and some of our emergency Oxo and biscuit. Then in the cocoa water I boiled our little plum pudding, which a friend of Wild's had given him. This, with a drop of medical brandy, was a luxury which Lucullus himself might have envied; then came cocoa, and lastly cigars and a spoonful of *crème de menthe* sent us by a friend in Scotland. We are full tonight, and this is the last time we will be for many a long day. After dinner we discussed the situation, and we have decided to still further reduce our food. We have now nearly 500 miles, geographical, to do if we are to get to the Pole and back to the spot where we are at the present moment. We have one month's food, but only three weeks' biscuit, so we are going to make each week's food last ten days. We will have one biscuit in the morning, three at midday, and two at night. It is the only thing to do. Tomorrow we will throw away everything except the most absolute necessities. Already we are, as regards clothes, down to the limit, but we must trust to the old sledge runners and dump the spare ones. One must risk this. We are very far away from all the world, and home thoughts have been much with us today, thoughts interrupted by pitching forward into a hidden crevasse more than once. Ah, well, we shall see all our own people when the work here is done. Marshall took our temperatures tonight. We are all two degrees subnormal, but as fit as can be. It is a fine open air life and we are getting south.

26 December

Got away at 7 a.m. sharp, after dumping a lot of gear. We marched steadily all day except for lunch, and we have done 14 miles 480 yards on an uphill march, with soft snow at times and a bad wind. Ridge after ridge we met, and though the surface is better and harder in places, we feel very tired at the end of ten hours' pulling. Our height tonight is 9590 ft above sea level according to the hypsometer. The ridges we meet with are almost similar in appearance. We see the sun shining on them in the distance, and then the rise begins very gradually. The snow gets soft, and the weight of the sledge becomes more marked. As we near the top the soft snow gives place to a hard surface, and on the summit of the ridge we find small crevasses. Every time we reach the top of a ridge we say to ourselves: "Perhaps this is the last," but it never is the last; always there appears away ahead of us another ridge. I do not think that the land lies very far below the ice sheet, for the crevasses on the summits of the ridges suggest that the sheet is moving over land at no great depth. It would seem that the descent toward the glacier proper from the plateau is by a series of terraces. We lost sight of the land today, having left it all behind us, and now we have the waste of snow all around. Two more days and our maize will be finished. Then our hooshes will be more woefully thin than ever. This shortness of food is unpleasant, but if we allow ourselves what, under ordinary circumstances, would be a reasonable amount, we would have to abandon all idea of getting far south.

27 December

If a great snow plain, rising every seven miles in a steep ridge, can be called a plateau, then we are on it at last, with an altitude above the sea of 9820 ft. We started at 7 a.m. and marched till noon, encountering at 11 a.m. a steep snow ridge which pretty well cooked us, but we got the sledge up by noon and camped. We are pulling 150 lb. per man. In the afternoon we had good going till 5 p.m. and then another ridge as difficult as the previous one, so that our backs and legs were in a bad way when we reached the top at 6 p.m., having done 14 miles 930 yards for the day. Thank heaven it has been a fine day, with little wind. The temperature is minus 9°F. This surface is most peculiar, showing layers of snow with little sastrugi all pointing south southeast. Short food make us think of plum puddings, and hard half-cooked maize gives us indigestion, but we are getting south. The latitude is 86° 19′ South tonight. Our thoughts are with the people at home a great deal.

28 December

If the Barrier is a changing sea, the plateau is a changing sky. During the morning march we continued to go up hill steadily, but the surface-was constantly changing. First there was soft snow in layers, then soft snow so deep that we were well over our ankles, and the temperature being well below zero, our feet were cold through sinking in. No one can say what we are going to find next, but we can go steadily ahead. We started at 6:55 a.m., and had done 7 miles 200 yards by noon, the pulling being very hard. Some of the snow is blown into hard sastrugi, some that look perfectly smooth and hard have only a thin crust through which we break when pulling; all of it is a trouble. Yesterday we passed our last crevasse, though there are a few cracks or ridges fringed with crystals shining like diamonds, warning us that the cracks are open. We are now 10,199 ft above sea level, and the plateau is gradually flattening out, but it was heavy work pulling this afternoon. The high altitude and a temperature of 48° of frost made breathing and work difficult. We are getting south – attitude 86° 31' South tonight. The last sixty miles we hope to rush, leaving everything possible, taking one tent only and using the poles of the other as marks every ten miles, for we will leave all our food sixty miles off the Pole except enough to carry us there and back. I hope with good weather to reach the Pole on January 12, and then we will try and rush it to get to Hut Point by February 28. We are so tired after each hour's pulling that we throw ourselves on our backs for a three minute spell. It took us over ten hours to do 14 miles 450 yards today, but we did it all right. It is a wonderful thing to be over 10,000 ft up, almost at the end of the world. The short food is trying, but when we have done the work we will be happy. Adams had a bad headache all yesterday, and today I had the same trouble, but it is better now. Otherwise we are all fit and well. I think the country is flattening out more and more, and hope tomorrow to make fifteen miles, at least.

29 December

Yesterday I wrote that we hoped to do fifteen miles today, but such is the variable character of this surface that one cannot prophesy with any certainty an hour ahead. A strong southerly wind, with from 44° to 49° of frost, combined with the effect of short rations, made our distance 12 miles 600 yards instead. We have reached an altitude of 10,310 ft, and an uphill gradient gave us one of the most severe pulls for ten hours that would be possible. It looks serious, for we must-increase the food if we are to get on at all, and we must risk a depot at seventy miles off the Pole and dash for it then. Our sledge is badly strained, and on the abominably bad surface of soft snow is dreadfully hard to move. I have been suffering from a bad headache all day, and Adams also was worried by the cold. I think that these headaches are a form of mountain sickness, due to our high altitude. The others have bled from the nose, and that must relieve them. Physical effort is always trying at a high altitude, and we are straining at the harness all day, sometimes slipping in the soft snow that overlies the hard sastrugi. My head is very bad. The sensation is as though the nerves were being twisted up with a cork-screw and then pulled out. Marshall took our temperatures tonight, and we are all at about 94°, but in spite of this we are getting south. We are only 198 miles off our goal now. If the rise would stop the cold would not matter, but it is hard to know what is man's limit. We have only 150 lb. per man to pull, but it is more severe work than the 250 lb. per man up the glacier was. The Pole is hard to get.

30 December

We only did 4 miles 100 yard today. We started at 7 a.m., but had to camp at 11 a.m., a blizzard springing up from the south. It is more than annoying. I cannot express my feelings. We were pulling at last on a level surface, but very soft snow, when at about 10 a.m. the south wind and drift commenced to increase, and at 11 a.m. it was so bad that we had to camp. And here all day we have been lying in our sleeping bags trying to keep warm and listening to the threshing drift on the tent side. I am in the cooking tent, and the wind comes through, it is so thin. Our precious food is going and the time also, and it is so important to us to get on. We lie here and think of how to make things better, but we cannot reduce food now, and the only thing will be to rush all possible at the end. We will do and are doing all humanly possible. It is with Providence to help us.

31 December

The last day of the old year, and the hardest day we have had almost, pushing through soft snow uphill with a strong head wind and drift all day. The temperature is minus 7°F, and our altitude is 10,477 ft above sea level. The altitude is trying. My head has been very bad all day, and we are all feeling the short food, but still we are getting south. We are in latitude 86° 54' South tonight, but we have only three weeks' food and two weeks' biscuit to do nearly 500 geographical miles. We can only do our best. Too tired to write more tonight. We all get iced up about our faces, and are on the verge of frostbite all the time. Please God the weather will be fine during the next fourteen days. Then all will be well. The distance today was eleven miles.

NOTE. If we had only known that we were going to get such cold weather as we were at this time experiencing, we would have kept a pair of scissors to trim our beards. The moisture from the condensation of one's breath accumulated on the beard and trickled down on to the Burberry blouse. Then it froze into a sheet of ice inside, and it became very painful to pull the Burberry off in camp. Little troubles of this sort would have seemed less serious to us if we had been able to get a decent feed at the end of the day's work, but we were very hungry. We thought of food most of the time. The chocolate certainly seemed better than the cheese, because the two spoonfuls of cheese per man allowed under our scale of diet would not last as long as the two sticks of chocolate. We did not have both at the same meal. We had the bad luck at this time to strike a tin in which the biscuits were thin and overbaked. Under ordinary circumstances they would probably have tasted rather better than the other biscuits, but we wanted bulk. We soaked them in our tea so that they would swell up and appear larger, but if one soaked a biscuit too much, the sensation of biting something was lost, and the food seemed to disappear much too easily.

1 January 1909

Head too bad to write much. We did 11 miles 900 yards (statute) today, and the latitude at 6 p.m. was 87° 6½ ' South, so we have beaten North and South records. Struggling uphill all day in very soft snow. Every one done up and weak from want of food. When we camped at 6 p.m. fine warm weather, thank God. Only 172½ miles from the Pole. The height above sea level, now 10,755 ft, makes all work difficult. Surface seems to be better ahead. I do trust it will be so tomorrow.

2 January

Terribly hard work today. We started at 6:45 A.M. with a fairly good surface, which soon became very soft. We were sinking in over our ankles, and our broken sledge, by running sideways, added to the drag. We have been going uphill all day, and tonight are 11,034 ft above sea level. It has taken us all day to do 10 miles 450 yards, though the weights are fairly light. A cold wind, with a temperature of minus 14°F, goes right through us now, as we are weakening from want of food, and the high altitude makes every movement an effort, especially if we stumble on the march. My head is giving me trouble all the time. Wild seems the most fit of us. God knows we are doing all we can, but the outlook is serious if this surface continues and the plateau gets higher, for we are not traveling fast enough to make our food spin out and get back to our depot in time. I cannot think of failure yet. I must look at the matter sensibly and consider the lives of those who are with me. I feel that if we go on too far it will be impossible to get back over this surface, and then all the results will be lost to the world. We can now definitely locate the South Pole on the highest plateau in the world, and our geological work and meteorology will be of the greatest use to science; but all this is not the Pole. Man can only do his best, and we have arrayed against us the strongest forces of nature. This cutting south wind with drift plays the mischief with us, and after ten hours of struggling against it one pannikin of food with two biscuits and a cup of cocoa does not warm one up much. I must think over the situation carefully tomorrow, for time is going on and food is going also.

3 January

Started at 6:55 a.m., cloudy but fairly warm. The temperature was minus 8°F at noon. We had a terrible surface all the morning, and did only 5 miles 100 yards. A meridian altitude gave us latitude 87° 22′ South at noon. The surface was better in the afternoon, and we did six geographical miles. The temperature at 6 p.m. was minus 11°F. It was an uphill pull toward the evening, and we camped at 6:20 p.m., the altitude being 11,220 ft above the sea. Tomorrow we must risk making a depot on the plateau, and make a dash for it, but even then, if this surface continues, we will be two weeks in carrying in through.

4 January

The end is in sight. We can only go for three more days at the most, for we are weakening rapidly. Short food and a blizzard wind from the south, with driving drift, at a temperature of 47° of frost, have plainly told us today that we are reaching our limit, for we were so done up at noon with cold that the clinical thermometer failed to register the temperature of three of us at 94°. We started at 7:40 a.m., leaving a depot on this great wide plateau, a risk that only this case justified, and one that my comrades agreed to, as they have to every one so far, with the same cheerfulness and regardlessness of self that have been the means of our getting as far as we have done so far. Pathetically small looked the bamboo, one of the tent poles, with a bit of bag sewn on as a flag, to mark our stock of provisions, which has to take us back to our depot, one hundred and fifty miles north. We lost sight of it in half an hour, and are now trusting to our footprints in the snow to guide us back to each bamboo until we pick up the depot again. I trust that the weather will keep clear. Today we have done 12½ geographical miles, and with only 70 lb. per man to pull it is as hard, even harder, work than the 100 odd lb. was yesterday, and far harder than the 250 lb. were three weeks ago, when we were climbing the glacier. This, I consider, is a clear indication of our failing strength. The main thing against us is the altitude of 11,200 ft and the biting wind. Our faces are cut, and our feet and hands are always on the verge of frostbite. Our fingers, indeed, often go, but we get them around more or less. I have great trouble with two fingers on my left hand. They had been badly jammed when we were getting the motor up over the ice face at winter quarters, and the circulation is not good. Our boots now are pretty well worn out, and we have to halt at times to pick the snow out of the soles. Our stock of sennegrass is nearly exhausted, so we have to use the same frozen stuff day after day. Another trouble is that the lamp wick with which we tie the finnesko is chafed through, and we have to tie knots in it. These knots catch the snow under our feet, making a lump that has to be cleared every now and then. I am of the opinion that to sledge even in the height of summer on this plateau, we should have at least forty ounces of food a day per man, and we are on short rations of the ordinary allowance of thirty-two ounces. We depoted our extra underclothing to save weight about three weeks ago, and are now in the same clothes night and day. One suit of under-clothing, shirt and guernsey, and our thin Burberries, now all patched. When we get up in the morning, out of the wet bag, our Burberries become like a coat of mail at once, and our heads and beards get iced-up with the moisture when breathing on the march. There is half a gale blowing dead in our teeth all the time. We hope to reach within 100 geographical miles of the Pole; I am confident that the Pole lies on the great plateau we have discovered, miles and miles from any outstanding land. The temperature tonight is minus 24°F.

5 January

Today headwind and drift again, with 50° of frost, and a terrible
surface. We have been marching through 8 in. of snow, covering
sharp sastrugi, which plays havoc with our feet, but we have done
13⅓ geographical miles, for we increased our food, seeing that it
was absolutely necessary to do this to enable us to accomplish
anything. I realize that the food we have been having has not been
sufficient to keep up our strength, let alone supply the wastage
caused by exertion, and now we must try to keep warmth in us,
though our strength is being used up. Our temperatures at 5 a.m.
were 94°F. We got away at 7 a.m. sharp and marched till noon,
then from 1 p.m. sharp till 6 p.m. All being in one tent makes our
camp work slower, for we are so cramped for room, and we get up
at 4:40 a.m. so as to get away by 7 a.m. Two of us have to stand
outside the tent at night until things are squared up inside, and
we find it cold work. Hunger grips us hard, and the food supply is
very small. My head still gives me great trouble. I began by
wishing that my worst enemy had it instead of myself, but now I
don't wish even my worst enemy to have such a headache; still, it
is no use talking about it. Self is a subject that most of us are
fluent on. We find the utmost difficulty in carrying through the
day, and we can only go for two or three more days. Never once
has the temperature been above zero since we got on to the
plateau, though this is the height of summer. We have done our
best, and we thank God for having allowed us to get so far.

6 January

This must be our last outward march with the sledge and camp
equipment. Tomorrow we must leave camp with some food, and
push as far south as possible, and then plant the flag. Today's
story is 57° of frost, with a strong blizzard and high drift; yet we
marched 13¼ geographical miles through soft snow, being helped
by extra food. This does not mean full rations, but a bigger ration
than we have been having lately. The pony maize is all finished.
The most trying day we have yet spent, our fingers and faces
being frost-bitten continually. Tomorrow we will rush south

with the flag. We are at 88° 7′ South tonight. It is our last outward march. Blowing hard tonight. I would fail to explain my feelings if I tried to write them down, now that the end has come. There is only one thing that lightens the disappointment, and that is the feeling that we have done all we could. It is the forces of nature that have prevented us from going right through. I cannot write more.

7 January

A blinding, shrieking blizzard all day, with the temperature ranging from 60° to 70° of frost. It has been impossible to leave the tent, which is snowed up on the lee side. We have been lying in our bags all day, only warm at food time, with fine snow making through the walls of the worn tent and covering our bags. We are greatly cramped. Adams is suffering from cramp every now and then. We are eating our valuable food without marching. The wind has been blowing eighty to ninety miles an hour. We can hardly sleep. Tomorrow I trust this will be over. Directly the wind drops we march as far south as possible, then plant the flag, and turn homeward. Our chief anxiety is lest our tracks may drift up, for to them we must trust mainly to find our depot; we have no land bearings in this great plain of snow. It is a serious risk that we have taken, but we had to play the game to the utmost, and Providence will look after us.

8 January

Again all day in our bags, suffering considerably physically from cold hands and feet, and from hunger, but more mentally, for we cannot get on south, and we simply lie here shivering. Every now and then one of our party's feet go, and the unfortunate beggar has to take his leg out of the sleeping bag and have his frozen foot nursed into life again by placing it inside the shirt, against the skin of his almost equally unfortunate neighbor. We must do something more to the south, even though the food is going, and we weaken lying in the cold, for with 72° of frost the wind cuts through our thin tent, and even the drift is finding its way in and on to our bags, which are wet enough as it is. Cramp is not uncommon every now and then, and the drift all round the tent has made it so small that there is hardly room for us at all. The wind has been blowing hard all day; some of the gusts must be over seventy or eighty miles an hour. This evening it seems as though it were going to ease down, and directly it does we shall be up and away south for a rush. I feel that this march must be our limit. We are so short of food, and at this high altitude, 11,600 ft, it is hard to keep any warmth in our bodies between the scanty meals. We have nothing to read now, having depoted our little books to save weight, and it is dreary work lying in the tent with nothing to read, and too cold to write much in the diary.

9 January

Our last day outwards. We have shot our bolt, and the tale is latitude 88° 23′ South, longitude 162° East. The wind eased down at 1 a.m., and at 2 a.m. we were up and had breakfast. At 4 a.m. started south, with the Queen's Union Jack, a brass cylinder containing stamps and documents to place at the furthest south point, camera, glasses, and compass. At 9 a.m. we were in 88° 23′ South, half running and half walking over a surface much hardened by the recent blizzard. It was strange for us to go along without the nightmare of a sledge dragging behind us. We hoisted Her Majesty's flag and the other Union Jack afterwards, and took possession of the plateau in the name of His Majesty. While the Union Jack blew out stiffly in the icy gale that cut us to the bone, we looked south with our powerful glasses, but could see nothing but the dead white snow plain. There was no break in the plateau as it extended toward the Pole, and we feel sure that the goal we have failed to reach lies on this plain. We stayed only a few minutes, and then, taking the Queen's flag and eating our scanty meal as we went, we hurried back and reached our camp about 3 p.m. We were so dead tired that we only did two hours' march in the afternoon and camped at 5:30 p.m. The temperature was minus 19°F. Fortunately for us, our tracks were not obliterated by the blizzard; indeed, they stood up, making a trail easily followed. Homeward bound at last. Whatever regrets may be, we have done our best.

Shackleton's feat in reaching within 97 miles of the Pole earned him a knighthood. Four years later, he returned to Antarctica with the epic Endurance *expedition (see pp 372ff).*

The Ascent of Mount Erebus

T. W. Edgeworth David

The scientific officer on Shackleton's Nimrod *expedition (see p247),
Professor David led the successful assault on Mount Erebus. David's
account of the summiting is from* Aurora Australis, *the book the
expedition produced in a hut at Camp Royd recording its exploits
and the first book to be published in Antarctica.*

The angle of ascent was now steeper than ever, being 34°, that is a
rise of 1 in 1½ . As the hard snow slopes were mostly much too
steep to climb, without resorting to the tedious expedient of
cutting steps with an ice-axe, we kept as much as possible to the
rocky arêtes. Occasionally, however, the arête would terminate
upwards in a large snow slope, and in such cases we cut steps
across the névé to any arête which seemed to persist for some
length in an upward direction. Often this second arête would end
upwards in a névé field, and then we had to cut steps as before.

Burdened as we were with our forty pound loads, and more or
less stiff after thirty continuous hours in our sleeping-bags, and
beginning besides to find respiration more difficult as the altitude
increased, we felt exhausted, while we were still 800 feet below
the rim of the main crater. Accordingly we halted at noon, thawed
some snow with the primus, and were soon revelling in cups of
delicious tea, hot and strong, which at once reinvigorated us.
Once more we tackled the ascent. When close to the top Mackay,
who had become separated from the rest of the party, started
cutting steps with his ice-axe up a long and very steep névé slope.
The task was almost impossible for one so heavily loaded as he
was, but nevertheless, he won his way unaided to the summit.

By this time we had reached the rim of the main crater. Often,
while toiling up its slopes, we had tried to picture to ourselves the

probable scenery at the summit, and had imagined an even plain of névé, or glacier ice, filling the extinct crater to the brim, and sloping up gradually to the active cone at its southern end: but we now found ourselves on the very brink of a massive precipice of black rock, forming the inner edge of the vast crater. This wall of dark lava is mostly vertical, while in places it overhangs: it is from 80 to 100 feet in height. The base of this cliff was separated from the snow plain beyond by a deep ditch, like a huge dry moat. The ditch was evidently not a "bergschrund", but was due chiefly to the action of the blizzards. These winds blowing fiercely from the south-east, and striking against the great inner wall of the old crater, give rise to a powerful back eddy at the base of the cliff, and it is this eddy which has scooped out the deep trench in the hard snow; the trench was from thirty to forty feet deep, and was bounded by more or less vertical sides.

Beyond the wall and trench was an extensive snowfield, with the active cone and crater at its south end, the latter emitting great volumes of steam; but what surprised us most were the extraordinary structures which rose every here and there above the surface of this snowfield. These were in the form of mounds and pinnacles of the most varied and fantastic appearance. Some resembled bee-hives, others were like huge ventilating cowls, others like isolated turrets, or bits of battlemented walls; others again in shape resembled various animals. We were wholly unable at first sight, to divine the origin of these remarkable objects, and the need for rest and refreshment cut short contemplation for the time. We hurried along the rampart of the old crater wall, in search of a suitable camping ground. It was at this time that our figures, thrown up against the skyline, were seen through a telescope by Armytage from our winter quarters at Cape Royds, over twelve miles distant. We selected for our camp, a little rocky gully on the north-west slope of the main cone, and fifty feet below the rim of the old crater. Here we had the satisfaction of being able to ease our shoulders at last from their burdens.

While some cooked the meal, Dr Marshall examined Brocklehurst's feet, as the latter stated that for some time past he had lost all feeling in them. We were all surprised and shocked, when his ski-boots and socks were taken off, to see that both his big toes were black, and had evidently been "gone" for several hours, and that four more toes, though less severely affected, were also frost-bitten. It must have required great pluck and determination on his part to have climbed almost continuously for nine hours, up the steep and difficult track we had followed, with his feet so badly frost-bitten. Doctors Marshall and Mackay at once set to work with a will to restore circulation in the feet, by warming and chafing them. Their efforts were, under the circumstances, eminently successful, but it was clear that recovery from so severe a frost-bite would be slow and tedious. Brocklehurst's feet having been thoroughly warmed were put into dry socks, and finneskoes stuffed with sennegraes; and then we all had lunch at about 3–30 p. m.

Leaving Brocklehurst safely tucked up in the three man sleeping bag, the remaining five of us started off to explore the floor of the old crater. Ascending to the crater rim we climbed along it, until we came to a spot where there was a practicable breach in the crater wall, and where a narrow tongue of snow bridged the névé trench at its base. As soon as we arrived on the hard snow on the far side, Mackay joined us all up with the alpine rope, and with him in the lead we advanced cautiously over the snow plain, keeping a sharp lookout for crevasses. We steered for one of the remarkable mounds which had so interested us at a distance; when we reached the nearest of them, and curious examined it, we were as far as ever from understanding how it had formed: we noticed some curious hollows, like large drains partly roofed in, running towards the mound, and at the time we supposed these to be ordinary crevasses. Pushing on slowly we reached eventually a small parasitic cone, about 1,000 feet above the level of our camp, and over a mile distant.

Here peeped from under the snow brown masses of earthy looking material, which we found to consist of lumps of lava, large felspar crystals, from one to three inches in length, and fragments of pumice; both felspar and pumice were, in many cases, coated with sulphur. We now started to return to our camp; we were no longer roped together, as we had not met with any definite crevasses on our way up. We directed our steps towards one of the ice mounds, which resembled a lion couchant. To our surprise the lion appeared now to be blowing smoke out of his mouth.

The origin of the mounds was no longer a mystery; they were the outward and visible signs of fumaroles. In ordinary climates, a fumarole, or volcanic vapour well, may be detected by the thin cloud of steam above it, like breath exhaled on a frosty day, and usually one can at once feel the warmth, by passing one's hand into the vapour column; but, in the rigour of the Antarctic climate, the fumaroles of Erebus have their vapour turned into ice as soon as it reaches the surface of the snow plain. Thus ice mounds, somewhat similar in shape to the sinter mounds formed by the geysers of New Zealand, of Iceland, and of Yellowstone Park, are built up around the orifices of the fumaroles of Erebus. When exploring one of these fumaroles, Mackay fell suddenly up to his thighs into one of its concealed conduits; he saved himself however, from falling in deeper still, with his ice axe. Marshall had a nearly similar experience at about the same time. Eventually we all arrived safely at our camp soon after 6 p. m., and found Brocklehurst progressing as well as could be expected.

As we sat on the rocks at tea, we had a glorious view to the west. While the foothills of Erebus flushed rosy red in the sunset, a vast rolling sea of cumulus cloud covered all the land from Cape Bird to Cape Royds. McMurdo Sound, now rapidly freezing over, showed warm ochreous tints, where the floe ice had formed, with dark purplish gray streaks marking the leads of open water between. Far away the Western Mountains glowed with the purest tints of greenish purple and amethyst. That night we had nothing but hard rock rubble under our sleeping-bags, and quite anticipated another blizzard; nevertheless, "weariness can snore upon the flint," and thus we slept soundly couched on Kenyte lava.

The following morning had two surprises for us; first, when we arose at 4 a.m. there was no sign of a blizzard, and next, while we were preparing breakfast, someone exclaimed, "Look at the great shadow of Erebus," and a truly wonderful sight it was. All the land below the base of the main cone, and for forty miles to the west of it, across McMurdo Sound, was a rolling sea of dense cumulus cloud. Projected obliquely on this, as on a vast magic lantern screen, was the huge bulk of the giant volcano. The sun had just risen, and flung the shadow of Erebus right across the Sound, and against the foothills of the Western Mountains.

Every detail of the profile of Erebus, as outlined on the clouds, could be readily recognized. There to the right was the great black fang, the relic of the first crater; far above and beyond that was to be seen the rim of the main crater, near our camp; then further to the left, and still higher, rose the active crater with its canopy of steam faithfully portrayed on the cloud screen. Still further to the left the dark shadow dipped rapidly down into the shining fields of cloud below. All within the shadow of Erebus was a soft bluish grey; all without was warm, bright and golden. Words fail to describe a scene of such transcendent majesty and beauty.

After breakfast while Marshall was attending to Brocklehurst's feet, the hypsometer which had become frozen on the way up, was thawed out with the heat of the primus, and a boiling point determination was made. This when reduced, and combined with the mean of our aneroid levels, made the altitude of the old crater rim, just above our camp, 11,400 feet. The highest point reached by us on the preceding evening, according to our aneroid, was about 1,000 feet above the preceding level, and thus was 12,400 feet above the sea.

At 6 a.m. we left our camp, and made all speed to reach the crater summit. As soon as we had crossed the snow trench, at the foot of the cliff, we roped ourselves together in the same order as before, and stood over towards a conspicuous fumarole. This was the one which bore some resemblance to a lion; it was about 20 feet in height; Mawson* photographed this from here, and also took a view of the active crater, about one and a half miles distant. There was considerable difficulty in taking photographs on Erebus, owing to the focal plane of the camera having become frozen. Near the furthest point reached by us on the preceding afternoon, we observed that there were several patches of ice of a lemon-yellow colour, the yellow being due to sulphur. We next ascended several rather steep slopes, formed of alternating beds of hard snow and vast quantities of large and perfect felspar crystals, mixed with pumice; all these beds dipped away from the active crater. A little further on we reached the foot of the recent

* Douglas Mawson: British-Australian geologist, later leader of the Australasian Antarctic Expedition. See pp360ff.

cone of the active crater; here we unroped, as there was no
possibility of any crevasses ahead of us.

Our progress was now painfully slow, as the altitude and cold
combined to make respiration difficult.

The cone was built up chiefly of blocks of pumice, from a few
inches up to three feet in diameter. Externally these were grey, or
often yellow, owing to incrustations of sulphur, but internally
they were of a resinous brown colour. A shout of joy and surprise
broke from the leading files, when a little after 10 a.m., the edge
of the active crater was at last reached. We had travelled only
about two and a half miles from our camp, and had ascended just
2,000 feet, and yet this had taken us, with a few short halts, just
four hours.

The scene that now suddenly burst upon us was magnificent
and awe-inspiring. We stood on the verge of a vast abyss, and at
first could neither see to the bottom, nor across it, on account of
the huge mass of steam filling the crater, and soaring aloft in a
column 500 to 1,000 feet high. After a continuous loud hissing
sound, lasting for some minutes, there would come from below a
big dull boom, and immediately afterwards a great globular mass
of steam would rush upwards to swell the volume of the snow-
white cloud which ever sways over the crater. These phenomena
recurred at intervals of a few minutes during the whole of our stay
at the crater. Meanwhile the whole of the air around us was
extremely redolent of burning sulphur.

Presently a gentle northerly breeze fanned away the steam
cloud and at once the whole crater stood revealed to us in all its
vast extent and depth.

Mawson's measurements made the depth 900 feet, and the
greatest width about half a mile. There were evidently at least
three well-like openings at the bottom of the caldron, and it was
from these that the steam explosions proceeded. Near the south-
west portion of the crater, there was an immense rift in the rim
perhaps 300 to 400 feet deep. The crater wall opposite to the one
at the top of which we were standing, presented features of special
interest. Beds of dark pumiceous lava, or pumice alternated with
white zones of snow; there was no direct evidence that the snow
was interbedded with the lava, though it is possible that such may
have been the case. From the top of one of the thickest of the lava,

or pumice beds, just where it touched a belt of snow, there rose scores of small steam jets, all in a row; they were too numerous and too close together to have been each an independent fumarole. The appearance was rather suggestive of the snow being converted into steam by the heat of the layer of rock immediately below it. While at the crater's edge we made a boiling point determination with the hypsometer, but the result was not so satisfactory as that made earlier in the morning at our camp. As the result of averaging aneroid levels, together with the hypsometer determination at our camp at the top of the old crater, calculations made by us show that the summit of Erebus is probably about 13,370 feet above sea-level.

As soon as our measurements had been made, and some photographs had been taken by Mawson, we hurried back towards our camp, as it was imperatively necessary to get Brocklehurst down to the base of the main cone that day, and this meant a descent in all, of nearly 8,000 feet. On the way back a traverse was made of the main crater, and levels taken for constructing a geological section; we also collected numerous specimens of the unique felspar crystals, and of the pumice and sulphur.

On arrival in camp we had a hasty meal, and having hurriedly packed up, shouldered our burdens once more, and started down the steep mountain slope. Brocklehurst insisted on carrying his heavy load, in spite of his frost-bitten feet. We followed a course a little to the west of the one we took when ascending. The rock was rubbly and kept slipping under our feet, so that falls were frequent. After descending a few hundreds of feet, we found that the rubbly spur of rock, down which we were floundering, ended abruptly in a long and steep névé slope.

Three courses were now open to us; either to retrace our steps to the point above us, where our rocky spur had deviated from the main arête; or to cut steps across the névé slope to this arête; or to glissade down some 500 to 600 feet to the rocky ledge below. Naturally, in our then tired state, we preferred to move in the path of least resistance offered by the glissade; accordingly we all dumped our burdens, and rearranged such as needed to be altered, so that they might all well and truly roll. We were now very thirsty, and some of us quenched our thirst, satisfactorily for the time, by gathering a little snow, squeezing it into a ball in the palm of one's hand, and then placing it on the surface of a piece of rock. Although the shade temperature was then considerably below zero, Fahr., the black rock had absorbed so much heat from the direct rays of the sun, that the snowball, when placed on it, commenced to melt almost immediately, and the thaw water started to trickle over the surface of the rock. The chill having been taken off the snowball in this way, the remainder could be safely transferred to one's mouth, and yielded a refreshing drink.

Our loads having now been modelled into the shape of sausages, we launched them down the slope, and watched them intently, as, like animated things, they bumped and bounded over the wavy ridges of the névé slope. Brocklehurst's load, consisting largely of all our cooking utensils, done up in a large bag, if not the most erratic, was certainly the noisiest, and recalled, on a small scale, Kipling's Bolivar, "clanging like a smithy shop after every roll". The battered remains of the aluminium vessels fetched up with a final big bang against the rocks below. Mackay now led the glissade, and firmly grasping his ice-axe, slid to the bottom in less than a minute; we all followed suit.

As we gathered speed on our downward course, and the chisel edge of the ice-axe bit deeper into the hard névé, it sprayed our faces and necks with a miniature shower of ice. The temperature was low, and whenever the steel of the ice-axe touched one's bare skin, it seemed to burn it like a hot iron. We all reached the bottom of the slope safely, and fired with the success of our first glissade, and finding an almost endless succession of snow slopes below us, we let ourselves go again and again, in a series of wild rushes towards the foot of the main cone. Here and there we bumped heavily against the opposing edges of hard "sastrugi", or tore our nether garments on projecting points of sharp rock. Unfortunately it was not only clothes and cookers which suffered in our wild career: a valuable aneroid was lost, and one of the hypsometer thermometers broken. It seemed as though we should never reach the bottom of the cone, but at last the slope flattened out to the gently inclined terrace, where our depôt lay; altogether we had dropped down 5,000 feet in level by glissading.

The Winter Journey

Apsley Cherry-Garrard

Cherry-Garrard was the second youngest member of Scott's epochal
Terra Nova *expedition to Antarctica. Everything "Cherry" did
thereafter – and he lived until 1959 – was an anti-climax, even
service in the First World War: "Talk of ex-soldiers," he later
wrote, "give me ex-Antarcticists, unsoured and with their ideals
intact: they could sweep the world." Cherry-Garrard paid homage
to his fellow "Antarcticists" in his only book,* The Worst Journey in
the World, 1922. *The title was perhaps misleading, for the epon-
ymous trek was not Scott's bid for 90 South but Cherry-Garrard's
own Winter Journey of June–July 1911 overland to Cape Crozier in
search of the nesting place of the Emperor penguin. No humans had
ever made the journey before, no scientist had ever retrieved the
Emperor's eggs. It was, as "Cherry" said, "the weirdest bird-nesting
expedition that has been or ever will be". Accompanying the slight,
bespectacled 25-year-old Cherry-Garrard was Dr Wilson, the expedition's scientific officer, and Lieutenant "Birdie" Bowers.*

Cape Evans to Cape Crozier

The horror of the nineteen days it took us to travel from Cape
Evans to Cape Crozier would have to be re-experienced to be
appreciated; and any one would be a fool who went again: it is not
possible to describe it. The weeks which followed them were
comparative bliss, not because later our conditions were better –
they were far worse – but because we were callous. I for one had
come to that point of suffering at which I did not really care if only I
could die without much pain. They talk of the heroism of the dying
– they little know – it would be so easy to die, a dose of morphia, a
friendly crevasse, and blissful sleep. The trouble is to go on . . .

It was the darkness that did it. I don't believe minus seventy temperatures would be bad in daylight, not comparatively bad, when you could see where you were going, where you were stepping, where the sledge straps were, the cooker, the primus, the food; could see your footsteps lately trodden deep into the soft snow that you might find your way back to the rest of your load; could see the lashings of the food bags; could read a compass without striking three or four different boxes to find one dry match; could read your watch to see if the blissful moment of getting out of your bag was come without groping in the snow all about; when it would not take you five minutes to lash up the door of the tent, and five hours to get started in the morning . . .

But in these days we were never less than four hours from the moment when Bill cried "Time to get up" to the time when we got into our harness. It took two men to get one man into his harness, and was all they could do, for the canvas was frozen and our clothes were frozen until sometimes not even two men could bend them into the required shape.

The trouble is sweat and breath. I never knew before how much of the body's waste comes out through the pores of the skin. On the most bitter days, when we had to camp before we had done a four-hour march in order to nurse back our frozen feet, it seemed that we must be sweating. And all this sweat, instead of passing away through the porous wool of our clothing and gradually drying off us, froze and accumulated. It passed just away from our flesh and then became ice: we shook plenty of snow and ice down from inside our trousers every time we changed our foot-gear, and we could have shaken it from our vests and from between our vests and shirts, but of course we could not strip to this extent. But when we got into our sleeping-bags, if we were fortunate, we became warm enough during the night to thaw this ice: part remained in our clothes, part passed into the skins of our sleeping-bags, and soon both were sheets of armourplate.

As for our breath – in the daytime it did nothing worse than cover the lower parts of our faces with ice and solder our balaclavas tightly to our heads. It was no good trying to get your balaclava off until you had had the primus going quite a long time, and then you could throw your breath about if you wished. The trouble really began in your sleeping-bag, for it was far too cold to keep a hole open through which to breathe. So all night long our breath froze into the skins, and our respiration became quicker and quicker as the air in our bags got fouler and fouler: it was never possible to make a match strike or burn inside our bags!

Of course we were not iced up all at once: it took several days of this kind of thing before we really got into big difficulties on this score. It was not until I got out of the tent one morning fully ready to pack the sledge that I realized the possibilities ahead. We had had our breakfast, struggled into our foot-gear, and squared up inside the tent, which was comparatively warm. Once outside, I raised my head to look round and found I could not move it back. My clothing had frozen hard as I stood – perhaps fifteen seconds. For four hours I had to pull with my head stuck up, and from that time we all took care to bend down into a pulling position before being frozen in.

By now we had realized that we must reverse the usual sledging routine and do everything slowly, wearing when possible the fur mitts which fitted over our woollen mitts, and always stopping whatever we were doing, directly we felt that any part of us was getting frozen, until the circulation was restored. Henceforward it was common for one or other of us to leave the other two to continue the camp work while he stamped about in the snow, beat his arms, or nursed some exposed part. But we could not restore the circulation of our feet like this – the only way then was to camp and get some hot water into ourselves before we took our foot-gear off. The difficulty was to know whether our feet were frozen or not, for the only thing we knew for certain was that we had lost all feeling in them. Wilson's knowledge as a doctor came in here: many a time he had to decide from our descriptions of our feet whether to camp or to go on for another hour. A wrong decision meant disaster, for if one of us had been crippled the whole party would have been placed in great difficulties. Probably we should all have died.

On 29 June the temperature was –50° all day and there was sometimes a light breeze which was inclined to frost-bite our faces and hands. Owing to the weight of our two sledges and the bad surface our pace was not more than a slow and very heavy plod: at our lunch camp Wilson had the heel and sole of one foot frost-bitten, and I had two big toes. Bowers was never worried by frost-bitten feet.

That night was very cold, the temperature falling to $-66°$, and it was $-55°$ at breakfast on 30 June. We had not shipped the eider-down linings to our sleeping-bags, in order to keep them dry as long as possible. My own fur bag was too big for me, and throughout this journey was more difficult to thaw out than the other two: on the other hand, it never split, as did Bill's.

We were now getting into that cold bay which lies between the Hut Point Peninsula and Terror Point. It was known from old *Discovery* days that the Barrier winds are deflected from this area, pouring out into McMurdo Sound behind us, and into the Ross Sea at Cape Crozier in front. In consequence of the lack of high winds the surface of the snow is never swept and hardened and polished as elsewhere: it was now a mass of the hardest and smallest snow crystals, to pull through which in cold tempera-tures was just like pulling through sand. I have spoken elsewhere of Barrier surfaces, and how, when the cold is very great, sledge runners cannot melt the crystal points but only advance by rolling them over and over upon one another. That was the surface we met on this journey, and in soft snow the effect is accentuated. Our feet were sinking deep at every step.

And so when we tried to start on 30 June we found we could not move both sledges together. There was nothing for it but to take one on at a time and come back for the other. This has often been done in daylight when the only risks run are those of blizzards which may spring up suddenly and obliterate tracks. Now in darkness it was more complicated. From 11 a.m. to 3 p.m. there was enough light to see the big holes made by our feet, and we took on one sledge, trudged back in our tracks, and brought on the second. Bowers used to toggle and untoggle our harnesses when we changed sledges. Of course in this relay work we covered three miles in distance for every one mile forward, and even the single sledges were very hard pulling. When we lunched the temperature was $-61°$. After lunch the little light had gone, and we carried a naked lighted candle back with us when we went to find our second sledge. It was the weirdest kind of procession, three frozen men and a little pool of light. Generally we steered by Jupiter, and I never see him now without recalling his friendship in those days.

We were very silent, it was not very easy to talk: but sledging is always a silent business. I remember a long discussion which began just now about cold snaps – was this the normal condition of the Barrier, or was it a cold snap? – what constituted a cold snap? The discussion lasted about a week. Do things slowly, always slowly, that was the burden of Wilson's leadership: and every now and then the question, Shall we go on? and the answer Yes. "I think we are all right as long as our appetites are good," said Bill. Always patient, self-possessed, unruffled, he was the only man on earth, as I believe, who could have led this journey.

That day we made 3¼ miles, and travelled 10 miles to do it. The temperature was –66° when we camped, and we were already pretty badly iced up. That was the last night I lay (I had written slept) in my big reindeer bag without the lining of eider-down which we each carried. For me it was a very bad night: a succession of shivering fits which I was quite unable to stop, and which took possession of my body for many minutes at a time until I thought my back would break, such was the strain placed upon it. They talk of chattering teeth: but when your body chatters you may call yourself cold. I can only compare the strain to that which I have been unfortunate enough to see in a case of lock-jaw. One of my big toes was frost-bitten, but I do not know for how long. Wilson was fairly comfortable in his smaller bag, and Bowers was snoring loudly. The minimum temperature that night as taken under the sledge was –69°; and as taken on the sledge was –75°. That is a hundred and seven degrees of frost.

We did the same relay work on 1 July, but found the pulling harder still; and it was all that we could do to move the one sledge forward. From now onwards Wilson and I, but not to the same extent as Bowers, experienced a curious optical delusion when returning in our tracks for the second sledge. I have said that we found our way back by the light of a candle, and we found it necessary to go back in our same footprints. These holes became to our tired brains not depressions but elevations: hummocks over which we stepped, raising our feet painfully and draggingly. And then we remembered, and said what fools we were, and for a while we compelled ourselves to walk through these phantom hills. But it was no lasting good, and as the days passed we realized that we must suffer this absurdity, for we could not do anything else. But of course it took it out of us.

During these days the blisters on my fingers were very painful. Long before my hands were frost-bitten, or indeed anything but cold, which was of course a normal thing, the matter inside these big blisters, which rose all down my fingers with only a skin between them, was frozen into ice. To handle the cooking gear or the food bags was agony; to start the primus was worse; and when, one day, I was able to prick six or seven of the blisters after supper and let the liquid matter out, the relief was very great. Every night after that I treated such others as were ready in the same way until they gradually disappeared. Sometimes it was difficult not to howl.

I *did* want to howl many times every hour of these days and nights, but I invented a formula instead, which I repeated to myself continually. Especially, I remember, it came in useful when at the end of the march with my feet frostbitten, my heart beating slowly, my vitality at its lowest ebb, my body solid with cold, I used to seize the shovel and go on digging snow on to the tent skirting while the cook inside was trying to light the primus. "You've got it in the neck – stick it – stick it – you've got it in the neck," was the refrain, and I wanted every little bit of encouragement it would give me: then I would find myself repeating "Stick it – stick it – stick it – stick it," and then "You've got it in the neck." One of the joys of summer sledging is that you can let your mind wander thousands of miles away for weeks and weeks. Oates used to provision his little yacht (there was a pickled herring he was going to have): I invented the compactest little revolving bookcase which was going to hold not books, but pemmican and chocolate and biscuit and cocoa and sugar, and have a cooker on the top, and was going to stand always ready to quench my hunger when I got home: and we visited restaurants and theatres and grouse moors, and we thought of a pretty girl, or girls, and . . . But now that was all impossible. Our conditions forced themselves upon us without pause: it was not possible to think of anything else. We got no respite. I found it best to refuse to let myself think of the past or the future – to live only for the job of the moment, and to compel myself to think only how to do it most efficiently. Once you let yourself imagine . . .

The Emperors

We roped up, and started to worry along under the cliffs, which had now changed from ice to rock, and rose 800 feet above us. The turmoil of pressure which climbed against them showed no order here. Four hundred miles of moving ice behind it had just tossed and twisted those giant ridges until Job himself would have lacked words to reproach their Maker. We scrambled over and under, hanging on with our axes, and cutting steps where we could not find a foothold with our crampons. And always we got towards the Emperor penguins, and it really began to look as if we were going to do it this time, when we came up against a wall of ice which a single glance told us we could never cross. One of the largest pressure ridges had been thrown, end on, against the cliff. We seemed to be stopped, when Bill found a black hole, something like a fox's earth, disappearing into the bowels of the ice. We looked at it: "Well, here goes!" he said, and put his head in, and disappeared. Bowers likewise. It was a longish way, but quite possible to wriggle along, and presently I found myself looking out of the other side with a deep gully below me, the rock face on one hand and the ice on the other. "Put your back against the ice and your feet against the rock and lever yourself along," said Bill, who was already standing on firm ice at the far end in a snow pit. We cut some fifteen steps to get out of that hole. Excited by now, and thoroughly enjoying ourselves, we found the way ahead easier, until the penguins' call reached us again and we stood, three crystallized ragamuffins, above the Emperors' home. They were there all right, and we were going to reach them, but where were all the thousands of which we had heard?

We stood on an ice-foot which was really a dwarf cliff some twelve feet high, and the sea-ice, with a good many ice-blocks strewn upon it, lay below. The cliff dropped straight, with a bit of an overhang and no snow-drift. This may have been because the sea had only frozen recently; whatever the reason may have been it meant that we should have a lot of difficulty in getting up again

without help. It was decided that someone must stop on the top
with the Alpine rope, and clearly that one should be I, for with
short sight and fogged spectacles which I could not wear I was
much the least useful of the party for the job immediately ahead.
Had we had the sledge we could have used it as a ladder, but of
course we had left this at the beginning of the moraine miles back.

We saw the Emperors standing all together huddled under the
Barrier cliff some hundreds of yards away. The little light was
going fast: we were much more excited about the approach of
complete darkness and the look of wind in the south than we were
about our triumph. After indescribable effort and hardship we
were witnessing a marvel of the natural world, and we were the
first and only men who had ever done so; we had within our grasp
material which might prove of the utmost importance to science;
we were turning theories into facts with every observation we
made, – and we had but a moment to give.

The disturbed Emperors made a tremendous row, trumpeting
with their curious metallic voices. There was no doubt they had
eggs, for they tried to shuffle along the ground without losing
them off their feet. But when they were hustled a good many eggs
were dropped and left lying on the ice, and some of these were
quickly picked up by eggless Emperors who had probably been
waiting a long time for the opportunity. In these poor birds the
maternal side seems to have necessarily swamped the other
functions of life. Such is the struggle for existence that they
can only live by a glut of maternity, and it would be interesting to
know whether such a life leads to happiness or satisfaction.

*After securing several Emperor eggs, the three expeditionaries then
set off on the return. The temperature dropped to –49° and seventy
miles from home a blizzard blew their tent away.*

The Loss of the Tent

I do not know what time it was when I woke up. It was calm, with
that absolute silence which can be so soothing or so terrible as
circumstances dictate. Then there came a sob of wind, and all was

still again. Ten minutes and it was blowing as though the world was having a fit of hysterics. The earth was torn in pieces: the indescribable fury and roar of it all cannot be imagined.

"Bill, Bill, the tent has gone," was the next I remember – from Bowers shouting at us again and again through the door. It is always these early morning shocks which hit one hardest: our slow minds suggested that this might mean a peculiarly lingering form of death. Journey after journey Birdie and I fought our way across the few yards which had separated the tent from the igloo door. I have never understood why so much of our gear which was in the tent remained, even in the lee of the igloo. The place where the tent had been was littered with gear, and when we came to reckon up afterwards we had everything except the bottom piece of the cooker, and the top of the outer cooker. We never saw these again. The most wonderful thing of all was that our finnesko were lying where they were left, which happened to be on the ground in the part of the tent which was under the lee of the igloo. Also Birdie's bag of personal gear was there, and a tin of sweets.

Birdie brought two tins of sweets away with him. One we had to celebrate our arrival at the Knoll: this was the second, of which we knew nothing, and which was for Bill's birthday, the next day. We started eating them on Saturday, however, and the tin came in useful to Bill afterwards.

To get that gear in we fought against solid walls of black snow which flowed past us and tried to hurl us down the slope. Once started nothing could have stopped us. I saw Birdie knocked over once, but he clawed his way back just in time. Having passed everything we could find in to Bill, we got back into the igloo, and started to collect things together, including our very dishevelled minds.

There was no doubt that we were in the devil of a mess, and it was not altogether our fault. We had had to put our igloo more or less where we could get rocks with which to build it. Very naturally we had given both our tent and igloo all the shelter we could from the full force of the wind, and now it seemed we were in danger not because they were in the wind, but because they were not sufficiently in it. The main force of the hurricane, deflected by the ridge behind, fled over our heads and appeared to form by suction a vacuum below. Our tent had either been sucked upwards into this, or had been blown away because some of it was in the wind while some of it was not. The roof of our igloo was being wrenched upwards and then dropped back with great crashes: the drift was spouting in, not it seemed because it was blown in from outside, but because it was sucked in from within: the lee, not the weather, wall was the worst. Already everything was six or eight inches under snow.

Very soon we began to be alarmed about the igloo. For some time the heavy snow blocks we had heaved up on to the canvas roof kept it weighted down. But it seemed that they were being gradually moved off by the hurricane. The tension became well-nigh unendurable: the waiting in all that welter of noise was maddening. Minute after minute, hour after hour – those snow blocks were off now anyway, and the roof was smashed up and down – no canvas ever made could stand it indefinitely.

We got a meal that Saturday morning, our last for a very long time as it happened. Oil being of such importance to us we tried to use the blubber stove, but after several preliminary spasms it came to pieces in our hands, some solder having melted; and a very good thing too, I thought, for it was more dangerous than useful. We finished cooking our meal on the primus. Two bits of the cooker having been blown away we had to balance it on the primus as best we could. We then settled that in view of the shortage of oil we would not have another meal for as long as possible. As a matter of fact God settled that for us.

We did all we could to stop up the places where the drift was coming in, plugging the holes with our socks, mitts and other clothing. But it was no real good. Our igloo was a vacuum which was filling itself up as soon as possible: and when snow was not coming in a fine black moraine dust took its place, covering us and everything. For twenty-four hours we waited for the roof to go: things were so bad now that we dare not unlash the door.

Many hours ago Bill had told us that if the roof went he considered that our best chance would be to roll over in our sleeping-bags until we were lying on the openings, and get frozen and drifted in.

Gradually the situation got more desperate. The distance between the taut-sucked canvas and the sledge on which it should have been resting became greater, and this must have been due to the stretching of the canvas itself and the loss of the snow blocks on the top: it was not drawing out of the walls. The crashes as it dropped and banged out again were louder. There was more snow coming through the walls, though all our loose mitts, socks and smaller clothing were stuffed into the worst places: our pyjama jackets were stuffed between the roof and the rocks over the door. The rocks were lifting and shaking here till we thought they would fall.

We talked by shouting, and long before this one of us proposed to try and get the Alpine rope lashed down over the roof from outside. But Bowers said it was an absolute impossibility in that wind. "You could never ask men at sea to try such a thing," he said. He was up and out of his bag continually, stopping up holes, pressing against bits of roof to try and prevent the flapping and so forth. He was magnificent.

And then it went.

Birdie was over by the door, where the canvas which was bent over the lintel board was working worse than anywhere else. Bill was practically out of his bag pressing against some part with a long stick of some kind. I don't know what I was doing but I was half out of and half in my bag.

The top of the door opened in little slits and that green Willesden canvas flapped into hundreds of little fragments in fewer seconds than it takes to read this. The uproar of it all was indescribable. Even above the savage thunder of that great wind on the mountain came the lash of the canvas as it was whipped to little tiny strips. The highest rocks which we had built into our walls fell upon us, and a sheet of drift came in.

Birdie dived for his sleeping-bag and eventually got in, together with a terrible lot of drift. Bill also – but he was better off: I was already half into mine and all right, so I turned to help Bill. "Get into your own," he shouted, and when I continued to try and help him, he leaned over until his mouth was against my ear. "*Please*, Cherry," he said, and his voice was terribly anxious. I know he felt responsible: feared it was he who had brought us to this ghastly end.

The next I knew was Bowers's head across Bill's body. "We're all right," he yelled, and we answered in the affirmative. Despite the fact that we knew we only said so because we knew we were all wrong, this statement was helpful. Then we turned our bags over as far as possible, so that the bottom of the bag was uppermost and the flaps were more or less beneath us. And we lay and thought, and sometimes we sang.

I suppose, wrote Wilson, we were all revolving plans to get back without a tent: and the one thing we had left was the floor-cloth upon which we were actually lying. Of course we could not speak at present, but later after the blizzard had stopped we discussed the possibility of digging a hole in the snow each night and covering it over with the floor-cloth. I do not think we had any idea that we could really get back in those temperatures in our present state of ice by such means, but no one ever hinted at such a thing. Birdie and Bill sang quite a lot of songs and hymns, snatches of which reached me every now and then, and I chimed in, somewhat feebly I suspect. Of course we were getting pretty badly drifted up. "I was resolved to keep warm," wrote Bowers, "and beneath my debris covering I paddled my feet and sang all the songs and hymns I knew to pass the time. I could occasionally thump Bill, and as he still moved I knew he was alive all right – what a birthday for him!" Birdie was more drifted up than we, but at times we all had to hummock ourselves up to heave the snow off our bags. By opening the flaps of our bags we could get small pinches of soft drift which we pressed together and put into our mouths to melt. When our hands warmed up again we got some more; so we did not get very thirsty. A few ribbons of canvas still remained in the wall over our heads, and these produced volleys of cracks like pistol shots hour after hour. The canvas never drew out from the walls, not an inch. The wind made just the same noise as an express train running fast through a tunnel if you have both the windows down.

I can well believe that neither of my companions gave up hope for an instant. They must have been frightened, but they were never disturbed. As for me I never had any hope at all; and when the roof went I felt that this was the end. What else could I think? We had spent days in reaching this place through the darkness in cold such as had never been experienced by human beings. We had been out for four weeks under conditions in which no man had existed previously for more than a few days, if that. During this time we had seldom slept except from sheer physical exhaustion, as men sleep on the rack; and every minute of it we had been fighting for the bed-rock necessaries of bare existence, and always in the dark. We had kept ourselves going by enormous care of our feet and hands and bodies, by burning oil, and by having plenty of hot fatty food. Now we had no tent, one tin of oil left out of six, and only part of our cooker. When we were lucky and not too cold we could almost wring water from our clothes, and directly we got out of our sleeping-bags we were frozen into solid sheets of armoured ice. In cold temperatures with all the advantages of a tent over our heads we were already taking more than an hour of fierce struggling and cramp to get into our sleeping-bags – so frozen were they and so long did it take us to thaw our way in. No! Without the tent we were dead men.

And there seemed not one chance in a million that we should ever see our tent again. We were 900 feet up on the mountain side, and the wind blew about as hard as a wind can blow straight out to sea. First there was a steep slope, so hard that a pick made little impression upon it, so slippery that if you started down in finnesko you never could stop: this ended in a great ice-cliff some hundreds of feet high, and then came miles of pressure ridges, crevassed and tumbled, in which you might as well look for a daisy as a tent: and after that the open sea. The chances, however, were that the tent had just been taken up into the air and dropped somewhere in this sea well on the way to New Zealand. Obviously the tent was gone.

Face to face with real death one does not think of the things that torment the bad people in the tracts, and fill the good people with bliss. I might have speculated on my chances of going to Heaven; but candidly I did not care. I could not have wept if I had tried. I had no wish to review the evils of my past. But the past did seem to have been a bit wasted. The road to Hell may be paved with good intentions: the road to Heaven is paved with lost opportunities.

I wanted those years over again. What fun I would have with them: what glorious fun! It was a pity. Well has the Persian said that when we come to die we, remembering that God is merciful, will gnaw our elbows with remorse for thinking of the things we have not done for fear of the Day of Judgement.

And I wanted peaches and syrup – badly. We had them at the hut, sweeter and more luscious than you can imagine. And we have been without sugar for a month. Yes – especially the syrup.

Thus impiously I set out to die, making up my mind that I was not going to try and keep warm, that it might not take too long, and thinking I would try and get some morphia from the medical case if it got very bad. Not a bit heroic, and entirely true! Yes! comfortable, warm reader. Men do not fear death, they fear the pain of dying.

And then quite naturally and no doubt disappointingly to those who would like to read of my last agonies (for who would not give pleasure by his death?) I fell asleep. I expect the temperature was pretty high during this great blizzard, and anything near zero was very high to us. That and the snow which drifted over us made a pleasant wet kind of snipe marsh inside our sleeping-bags, and I am sure we all dozed a good bit. There was so much to worry about that there was not the least use in worrying: and we were so *very* tired. We were hungry, for the last meal we had had was in the morning of the day before, but hunger was not very pressing.

And so we lay, wet and quite fairly warm, hour after hour while the wind roared round us, blowing storm force continually and rising in the gusts to something indescribable. Storm force is force 11, and force 12 is the biggest wind which can be logged: Bowers logged it force 11, but he was always so afraid of over-estimating that he was inclined to underrate. I think it was blowing a full hurricane. Sometimes awake, sometimes dozing, we had not a very uncomfortable time so far as I can remember. I knew that parties which had come to Cape Crozier in the spring had experienced blizzards which lasted eight or ten days. But this did not worry us as much as I think it did Bill: I was numb. I vaguely called to mind that Peary had survived a blizzard in the open: but wasn't that in the summer?

It was in the early morning of Saturday (22 July) that we discovered the loss of the tent. Some time during that morning we had had our last meal. The roof went about noon on Sunday and we had had no meal in the interval because our supply of oil was so low; nor could we move out of our bags except as a last necessity. By Sunday night we had been without a meal for some thirty-six hours.

The rocks which fell upon us when the roof went did no damage, and though we could not get out of our bags to move them, we could fit ourselves into them without difficulty. More serious was the drift which began to pile up all round and over us. It helped to keep us warm of course, but at the same time in these comparatively high temperatures it saturated our bags even worse than they were before. If we did not find the tent (and its recovery would be a miracle) these bags and the floor-cloth of the tent on which we were lying were all we had in that fight back across the Barrier which could, I suppose, have only had one end.

Meanwhile we had to wait. It was nearly 70 miles home and it had taken us the best part of three weeks to come. In our less miserable moments we tried to think out ways of getting back, but I do not remember very much about that time. Sunday morning faded into Sunday afternoon, – into Sunday night, – into Monday morning. Till then the blizzard had raged with monstrous fury; the winds of the world were there, and they had all gone mad. We had bad winds at Cape Evans this year, and we had far worse the next winter when the open water was at our doors. But I have never heard or felt or seen a wind like this. I wondered why it did not carry away the earth.

In the early hours of Monday there was an occasional hint of a lull. Ordinarily in a big winter blizzard, when you have lived for several days and nights with that turmoil in your ears, the lulls are more trying than the noise: "the feel of not to feel it"* I do not remember noticing that now. Seven or eight more hours passed, and though it was still blowing we could make ourselves heard to one another without great difficulty. It was two days and two nights since we had had a meal.

We decided to get out of our bags and make a search for the tent. We did so, bitterly cold and utterly miserable, though I do not think any of us showed it. In the darkness we could see very little, and no trace whatever of the tent. We returned against the wind, nursing our faces and hands, and settled that we must try and cook a meal somehow. We managed about the weirdest meal eaten north or south. We got the floor-cloth wedged under our bags, then got into our bags and drew the floor-cloth over our

* Keats.

heads. Between us we got the primus alight somehow, and by hand we balanced the cooker on top of it, minus the two members which had been blown away. The flame flickered in the draughts. Very slowly the snow in the cooker melted, we threw in a plentiful supply of pemmican, and the smell of it was better than anything on earth. In time we got both tea and pemmican, which was full of hairs from our bags, penguin feathers, dirt and debris, but delicious. The blubber left in the cooker got burnt and gave the tea a burnt taste. None of us ever forgot that meal: I enjoyed it as much as such a meal could be enjoyed, and that burnt taste will always bring back the memory.

It was still dark and we lay down in our bags again, but soon a little glow of light began to come up, and we turned out to have a further search for the tent. Birdie went off before Bill and me. Clumsily I dragged my eider-down out of my bag on my feet, all sopping wet: it was impossible to get it back and I let it freeze: it was soon just like a rock. The sky to the south was as black and sinister as it could possibly be. It looked as though the blizzard would be on us again in a moment.

I followed Bill down the slope. We could find nothing. But, as we searched, we heard a shout somewhere below and to the right. We got on a slope, slipped, and went sliding down quite unable to stop ourselves, and came upon Birdie with the tent, the outer lining still on the bamboos. Our lives had been taken away and given back to us.

We were so thankful we said nothing.

The End of the Worst Journey

We are looked upon as beings who have come from another world. This afternoon I had a shave after soaking my face in a hot sponge, and then a bath. Lashly had already cut my hair. Bill looks very thin and we are all very blear-eyed from want of sleep. I have not much appetite, my mouth is very dry and throat sore with a troublesome hacking cough which I have had all the journey. My taste is gone. We are getting badly spoiled, but our beds are the height of all our pleasures.

Another very happy day doing nothing. After falling asleep two or three times I went to bed, read *Kim*, and slept. About two hours after each meal we all want another, and after a tremendous supper last night we had another meal before turning in. I have my taste back but all our fingers are impossible, they might be so many pieces of lead except for the pins and needles feeling in them which we have also got in our feet. My toes are very bulbous and some toenails are coming off. My left heel is one big burst blister. Going straight out of a warm bed into a strong wind outside nearly bowled me over. I felt quite faint, and pulled myself together thinking it was all nerves; but it began to come on again and I had to make for the hut as quickly as possible. Birdie is now full of schemes for doing the trip again next year. Bill says it is too great a risk in the darkness, and he will not consider it, though he thinks that to go in August might be possible.

Bowers and Wilson never did make another journey to the Emperors. Instead, they joined Scott's doomed attempt on the South Pole. Cherry-Garrard was among the search party which found their corpses.

Pole Position

Roald Amundsen

It was Amundsen's intention to be the first to the North Pole but, on finding that Peary had beaten him to it, the Norwegian explorer secretly switched his efforts to 90° South. Landing in Antarctica, he outflanked the British expedition of R.F. Scott in a highly efficient eight-week sprint to the Pole by ski and dog-pulled sledge. Amundsen did not bother to dress up his explorations in the pretence of science or gentlemanly sport; he simply wanted to be first. And Amundsen was first to the Pole, reaching it a month before Scott, just as he had been the first to navigate the Northwest Passage.

In lat. 87° S. – according to dead reckoning – we saw the last of the land to the north-east. The atmosphere was then apparently as clear as could be, and we felt certain that our view covered all the land there was to be seen from that spot. We were deceived again on this occasion, as will be seen later. Our distance that day (4 December) was close upon twenty-five miles; height above the sea, 10,100 feet.

The weather did not continue fine for long. Next day (5 December) there was a gale from the north, and once more the whole plain was a mass of drifting snow. In addition to this there was thick falling snow, which blinded us and made things worse, but a feeling of security had come over us and helped us to advance rapidly and without hesitation, although we could see nothing. That day we encountered new surface conditions – big, hard snow-waves (sastrugi). These were anything but pleasant to work among, especially when one could not see them. It was of no use for us "forerunners" to think of going in advance under these circumstances, as it was impossible to keep on one's feet. Three or four paces was often the most we managed to do before falling down. The sastrugi were very high, and often abrupt; if one came on them unexpectedly, one required to be more than an acrobat to keep on one's feet. The plan we found to work best in these conditions was to let Hanssen's dogs go first; this was an unpleasant job for Hanssen, and for his dogs too, but it succeeded, and succeeded well. An upset here and there was, of course, unavoidable, but with a little patience the sledge was always righted again. The drivers had as much as they could do to support their sledges among these sastrugi, but while supporting the sledges, they had at the same time a support for themselves. It was worse for us who had no sledges, but by keeping in the wake of them we could see where the irregularities lay, and thus get over them. Hanssen deserves a special word of praise for his driving on this surface in such weather. It is a difficult matter to drive Eskimo dogs forward when they cannot see; but Hanssen managed it well, both getting the dogs on and steering his course by compass. One would not think it possible to keep an approximately right course when the uneven ground gives such violent shocks that the needle flies several times round the compass, and is no sooner still again than it recommences the same dance; but when at last we got an observation, it turned out that Hanssen had steered to a hair, for the observations and dead reckoning agreed to a mile. In spite of all hindrances, and of being able to see nothing, the sledge-meters showed nearly twenty-five miles. The hypsometer showed 11,070 feet above the sea; we had therefore reached a greater altitude than the Butcher's.

6 December brought the same weather: thick snow, sky and plain all one, nothing to be seen. Nevertheless we made splendid progress. The sastrugi gradually became levelled out, until the surface was perfectly smooth; it was a relief to have even ground to go upon once more. These irregularities that one was constantly falling over were a nuisance; if we had met with them in our usual surroundings it would not have mattered so much; but up here on the high ground, where we had to stand and gasp for breath every time we rolled over, it was certainly not pleasant.

That day we passed 88° S., and camped in 88° 9′ S. A great surprise awaited us in the tent that evening. I expected to find, as on the previous evening, that the boiling-point had fallen somewhat; in other words, that it would show a continued rise of the ground, but to our astonishment this was not so. The water boiled at exactly the same temperature as on the preceding day. I tried it several times, to convince myself that there was nothing wrong, each time with the same result. There was great rejoicing among us all when I was able to announce that we had arrived on the top of the plateau.

7 December began like the 6th, with absolutely thick weather, but, as they say, you never know what the day is like before sunset. Possibly I might have chosen a better expression than this last – one more in agreement with the natural conditions – but I will let it stand. Though for several weeks now the sun had not set, my readers will not be so critical as to reproach me with inaccuracy. With a light wind from the north-east, we now went southward at a good speed over the perfectly level plain, with excellent going. The uphill work had taken it out of our dogs, though not to any serious extent. They had turned greedy – there is no denying that – and the half kilo of pemmican they got each day was not enough to fill their stomachs. Early and late they were looking for some-thing – no matter what – to devour. To begin with they contented themselves with such loose objects as ski-bindings, whips, boots, and the like; but as we came to know their proclivities, we took such care of everything that they found no extra meals lying about. But that was not the end of the matter. They then went for the fixed lashings of the sledges, and – if we had allowed it – would very quickly have resolved the various sledges into their compo-nent parts. But we found a way of stopping that: every evening, on halting, the sledges were buried in the snow, so as to hide all the lashings. That was successful; curiously enough, they never tried to force the "snow rampart". I may mention as a curious thing that these ravenous animals, that devoured everything they came across, even to the ebonite points of our ski-sticks, never made any attempt to break into the provision cases. They lay there and went about among the sledges with their noses just on a level with the split cases, seeing and scenting the pemmican, without once making a sign of taking any. But if one raised a lid, they were not long in showing themselves. Then they all came in a great hurry and flocked about the sledges in the hope of getting a little extra bit. I am at a loss to explain this behaviour; that bashfulness was not at the root of it, I am tolerably certain.

During the forenoon the thick, grey curtain of cloud began to grow thinner on the horizon, and for the first time for three days we could see a few miles about us. The feeling was something like that one has on waking from a good nap, rubbing one's eyes and looking around. We had become so accustomed to the grey twilight that this positively dazzled us. Meanwhile, the upper layer of air seemed obstinately to remain the same and to be doing its best to prevent the sun from showing itself. We badly wanted to get a meridian altitude, so that we could determine our latitude. Since 86° 47′ S. we had had no observation, and it was not easy to say when we should get one. Hitherto, the weather conditions on the high ground had not been particularly favourable. Although the prospects were not very promising, we halted at 11 a.m. and made ready to catch the sun if it should be kind enough to look out. Hassel and Wisting used one sextant and artificial horizon, Hanssen and I the other set.

I don't know that I have ever stood and absolutely pulled at the sun to get it out as I did that time. If we got an observation here which agreed with our reckoning, then it would be possible, if the worst came to the worst, to go to the Pole on dead reckoning; but if we got none now, it was a question whether our claim to the Pole would be admitted on the dead reckoning we should be able to produce. Whether my pulling helped or not, it is certain that the sun appeared. It was not very brilliant to begin with, but, practised as we now were in availing ourselves of even the poorest chances, it was good enough. Down it came, was checked by all, and the altitude written down. The curtain of cloud was rent more and more, and before we had finished our work – that is to say, caught the sun at its highest, and convinced ourselves that it was descending again – it was shining in all its glory. We had put away our instruments and were sitting on the sledges, engaged in the calculations. I can safely say that we were excited. What would the result be, after marching blindly for so long and over such impossible ground, as we had been doing? We added and subtracted, and at last there was the result. We looked at each other in sheer incredulity: the result was as astonishing as the most consummate conjuring trick – 88° 16′ S., precisely to a minute the same as our reckoning, 88° 16′ S. If we were forced to go to the Pole on dead reckoning, then surely the most exacting

would admit our right to do so. We put away our observation
books, ate one or two biscuits, and went at it again.

We had a great piece of work before us that day nothing less
than carrying our flag farther south than the foot of man had
trod. We had our silk flag ready; it was made fast to two ski-
sticks and laid on Hanssen's sledge. I had given him orders that
as soon as we had covered the distance to 88°S., which was
Shackleton's farthest south, the flag was to be hoisted on his
sledge. It was my turn as forerunner, and I pushed on. There
was no longer any difficulty in holding one's course; I had the
grandest cloud-formations to steer by, and everything now went
like a machine. First came the forerunner for the time being,
then Hanssen, then Wisting, and finally Bjaaland. The forerunner who was not on duty went where he liked; as a rule he
accompanied one or other of the sledges. I had long ago fallen
into a reverie – far removed from the scene in which I was
moving; what I thought about I do not remember now, but I was
so preoccupied that I had entirely forgotten my surroundings.
Then suddenly I was roused from my dreaming by a jubilant
shout, followed by ringing cheers. I turned round quickly to
discover the reason of this unwonted occurrence, and stood
speechless and overcome.

I find it impossible to express the feelings that possessed me at
this moment. All the sledges had stopped, and from the foremost
of them the Norwegian flag was flying. It shook itself out, waved
and flapped so that the silk rustled; it looked wonderfully well in
the pure, clear air and the shining white surroundings. 88° 23′ was
past; we were farther south than any human being had been. No
other moment of the whole trip affected me like this. The tears
forced their way to my eyes; by no effort of will could I keep them
back. It was the flag yonder that conquered me and my will.
Luckily I was some way in advance of the others, so that I had
time to pull myself together and master my feelings before
reaching my comrades. We all shook hands, with mutual congratulations; we had won our way far by holding together, and we
would go farther yet – to the end.

We did not pass that spot without according our highest tribute
of admiration to the man, who – together with his gallant
companions – had planted his country's flag so infinitely nearer

to the goal than any of his precursors. Sir Ernest Shackleton's name will always be written in the annals of Antarctic exploration in letters of fire. Pluck and grit can work wonders, and I know of no better example of this than what that man has accomplished.

The cameras of course had to come out, and we got an excellent photograph of the scene which none of us will ever forget. We went on a couple of miles more, to 88° 25', and then camped. The weather had improved, and kept on improving all the time. It was now almost perfectly calm, radiantly clear, and, under the circumstances, quite summer-like: −0.4° F. Inside the tent it was quite sultry. This was more than we had expected.

After much consideration and discussion we had come to the conclusion that we ought to lay down a depot – the last one – at this spot. The advantages of lightening our sledges were so great that we should have to risk it. Nor would there be any great risk attached to it, after all, since we should adopt a system of marks that would lead even a blind man back to the place. We had determined to mark it not only at right angles to our course – that is, from east to west – but by snow beacons at every two geographical miles to the south.

We stayed here on the following day to arrange this depot. Hanssen's dogs were real marvels, all of them; nothing seemed to have any effect on them. They had grown rather thinner, of course, but they were still as strong as ever. It was therefore decided not to lighten Hanssen's sledge, but only the two others; both Wisting's and Bjaaland's teams had suffered, especially the latter's. The reduction in weight that was effected was considerable – nearly 110 pounds on each of the two sledges; there was thus about 220 pounds in the depot. The snow here was ill-adapted for building, but we put up quite a respectable monument all the same. It was dogs' pemmican and biscuits that were left behind; we carried with us on the sledges provisions for about a month. If, therefore, contrary to expectation, we should be so unlucky as to miss this depot, we should nevertheless be fairly sure of reaching our depot in 86° 21' before supplies ran short. The cross-marking of the depot was done with sixty splinters of black packing-case on each side, with 100 paces between each. Every other one had a shred of black cloth on the top. The splinters on the east side were all marked, so that on seeing them we should know instantly that we were to the east of the depot. Those on the west had no marks.

The warmth of the past few days seemed to have matured our frost-sores, and we presented an awful appearance. It was Wisting, Hanssen, and I who had suffered the worst damage in the last south-east blizzard; the left side of our faces was one mass of sore, bathed in matter and serum. We looked like the worst type of tramps and ruffians, and would probably not have been recognized by our nearest relations. These sores were a great trouble to us during the latter part of the journey. The slightest gust of wind produced a sensation as if one's face were being cut backwards and forwards with a blunt knife. They lasted a long time, too; I can remember Hanssen removing the last scab when we were coming into Hobart – three months later. We were very lucky in the weather during this depot work; the sun came out all at once, and we had an excellent opportunity of taking some good azimuth observations, the last of any use that we got on the journey.

9 December arrived with the same fine weather and sunshine. True, we felt our frost-sores rather sharply that day, with −18.4°F. and a little breeze dead against us, but that could not be helped. We at once began to put up beacons – a work which was continued with great regularity right up to the Pole. These beacons were not so big as those we had built down on the Barrier; we could see that they would be quite large enough with a height of about 3 feet, as it was, very easy to see the slightest irregularity on this perfectly flat surface. While thus engaged we had an opportunity of becoming thoroughly acquainted with the nature of the snow. Often – very often indeed – on this part of the plateau, to the south of 88° 25′, we had difficulty in getting snow good enough – that is, solid enough for cutting blocks. The snow up here seemed to have fallen very quietly, in light breezes or calms. We could thrust the tent-pole, which was 6 feet long, right down without meeting resistance, which showed that there was no hard layer of snow. The surface was also perfectly level; there was not a sign of sastrugi in any direction.

Every step we now took in advance brought us rapidly nearer the goal; we could feel fairly certain of reaching it on the afternoon of the 14th. It was very natural that our conversation should be chiefly concerned with the time of arrival. None of us would admit that he was nervous, but I am inclined to think that we all had a little touch of that malady. What should we see when we got there? A vast, endless plain, that no eye had yet seen and no foot yet trodden; or – No, it was an impossibility; with the speed at which we had travelled, we must reach the goal first, there could be no doubt about that. And yet – and yet – Wherever there is the smallest loophole, doubt creeps in and gnaws and gnaws and never leaves a poor wretch in peace. "What on earth is Uroa scenting?" It was Bjaaland who made this remark, on one of these last days, when I was going by the side of his sledge and talking to him. "And the strange thing is that he's scenting to the south. It can never be –" Mylius, Ring, and Suggen, showed the same interest in the southerly direction; it was quite extraordinary to see how they raised their heads, with every sign of curiosity, put their noses in the air, and sniffed due south. One would really have thought there was something remarkable to be found there.

From 88° 25′ S. the barometer and hypsometer indicated slowly but surely that the plateau was beginning to descend towards the other side. This was a pleasant surprise to us; we had thus not only found the very summit of the plateau, but also the slope down on the far side. This would have a very important bearing for obtaining an idea of the construction of the whole plateau. On 9 December observations and dead reckoning agreed within a mile. The same result again on the 10th: observation 2 kilometres behind reckoning. The weather and going remained about the same as on the preceding days: light south-easterly breeze, temperature –18.4°F. The snow surface was loose, but ski and sledges glided over it well. On the 11th, the same weather conditions. Temperature –13° F. Observation and reckoning again agreed exactly. Our latitude was 89° 15′ S. On the 12th we reached 89° 30′, reckoning 1 kilometre behind observation. Going and surface as good as ever. Weather splendid – calm with sunshine. The noon observation on the 13th gave 89° 37′ S. Reckoning 89° 38.5′ S. We halted in the afternoon, after going eight geographical miles, and camped in 89° 45′, according to reckoning.

The weather during the forenoon had been just as fine as before; in the afternoon we had some snow-showers from the south-east. It was like the eve of some great festival that night in the tent. One could feel that a great event was at hand. Our flag was taken out again and lashed to the same two ski-sticks as before. Then it was rolled up and laid aside, to be ready when the time came. I was awake several times during the night, and had the same feeling that I can remember as a little boy on the night before Christmas Eve – an intense expectation of what was going to happen. Otherwise I think we slept just as well that night as any other.

On the morning of 14 December the weather was of the finest, just as if it had been made for arriving at the Pole. I am not quite sure, but I believe we despatched our breakfast rather more quickly than usual and were out of the tent sooner, though I must admit that we always accomplished this with all reasonable haste. We went in the usual order – the forerunner, Hanssen, Wisting, Bjaaland, and the reserve forerunner. By noon we had reached 89° 53′ by dead reckoning, and made ready to take the rest in one stage. At 10 a.m. a light breeze had sprung up from the south-east, and it had clouded over, so that we got no noon altitude; but the clouds were not thick, and from time to time we had a glimpse of the sun through them. The going on that day was rather different from what it had been; sometimes the ski went over it well, but at others it was pretty bad. We advanced that day in the same mechanical way as before; not much was said, but eyes were used all the more. Hanssen's neck grew twice as long as before in his endeavour to see a few inches farther. I had asked him before we started to spy out ahead for all he was worth, and he did so with a vengeance. But, however keenly he stared, he could not descry anything but the endless flat plain ahead of us. The dogs had dropped their scenting, and appeared to have lost their interest in the regions about the earth's axis.

At three in the afternoon a simultaneous "Halt!" rang out from the drivers. They had carefully examined their sledge-meters, and they all showed the full distance – our Pole by reckoning. The goal was reached, the journey ended. I cannot say – though I know it would sound much more effective – that the object of my life was attained. That would be romancing rather too bare-facedly. I had better be honest and admit straight out that I have never known any man to be placed in such a diametrically opposite position to the goal of his desires as I was at that moment. The regions around the North Pole – well, yes, the North Pole itself – had attracted me from childhood, and here I was at the South Pole. Can anything more topsy-turvy be imagined?

We reckoned now that we were at the Pole. Of course, every one of us knew that we were not standing on the absolute spot; it would be an impossibility with the time and the instruments at our disposal to ascertain that exact spot. But we were so near it that the few miles which possibly separated us from it could not be of the slightest importance. It was our intention to make a circle round this camp, with a radius of twelve and a half miles (20 kilometres), and to be satisfied with that. After we had halted we collected and congratulated each other. We had good grounds for mutual respect in what had been achieved, and I think that was just the feeling that was expressed in the firm and powerful grasps of the fist that were exchanged. After this we proceeded to the greatest and most solemn act of the whole journey – the planting of our flag. Pride and affection shone in the five pairs of eyes that gazed upon the flag, as it unfurled itself with a sharp crack, and waved over the Pole. I had determined that the act of planting it – the historic event – should be equally divided among us all. It was not for one man to do this; it was for all who had staked their lives in the struggle, and held together through thick and thin. This was the only way in which I could show my gratitude to my comrades in this desolate spot. I could see that they understood and accepted it in the spirit in which it was offered. Five weather-beaten, frost-bitten fists they were that grasped the pole, raised the waving flag in the air, and planted it as the first at the geographical South Pole. "Thus we plant thee, beloved flag, at the South Pole, and give to the plain on which it lies the name of King Haakon VII's Plateau." That moment will certainly be remembered by all of us who stood there.

One gets out of the way of protracted ceremonies in those regions – the shorter they are the better. Everyday life began again at once. When we had got the tent up, Hanssen set about slaughtering Helge, and it was hard for him to have to part from his best friend. Helge had been an uncommonly useful and good-natured dog; without making any fuss he had pulled from morning to night, and had been a shining example to the team.

But during the last week he had quite fallen away, and on our
arrival at the Pole there was only a shadow of the old Helge left.
He was only a drag on the others, and did absolutely no work.
One blow on the skull, and Helge had ceased to live. "What is
death to one is food to another" is a saying that can scarcely find a
better application than these dog meals. Helge was portioned out
on the spot, and within a couple of hours there was nothing left of
him but his teeth and the tuft at the end of his tail. This was the
second of our eighteen dogs that we had lost. The Major, one of
Wisting's fine dogs, left us in 88 deg 25′ S., and never returned.
he was fearfully worn out, and must have gone away to die. We
now had sixteen dogs left, and these we intended to divide into
two equal teams, leaving Bjaaland's sledge behind.

Of course, there was a festivity in the tent that evening – not
that champagne corks were popping and wine flowing – no, we
contented ourselves with a little piece of seal meat each, and it
tasted well and did us good. There was no other sign of festival
indoors. Outside we heard the flag flapping in the breeze. Conversation was lively in the tent that evening, and we talked of
many things. Perhaps, too, our thoughts sent messages home of
what we had done.

Everything we had with us had now to be marked with the
words "South Pole" and the date, to serve afterwards as souve-
nirs. Wisting proved to be a first-class engraver, and many were
the articles he had to mark. Tobacco – in the form of smoke – had
hitherto never made its appearance in the tent. From time to time
I had seen one or two of the others take a quid, but now these
things were to be altered. I had brought with me an old briar pipe,
which bore inscriptions from many places in the Arctic regions,
and now I wanted it marked "South Pole". When I produced my
pipe and was about to mark it, I received an unexpected gift:
Wisting offered me tobacco for the rest of the journey. He had
some cakes of plug in his kit-bag, which he would prefer to see me
smoke. Can anyone grasp what such an offer meant at such a spot,
made to a man who, to tell the truth, is very fond of a smoke after
meals? There are not many who can understand it fully. I
accepted the offer, jumping with joy, and on the way home I
had a pipe of fresh, fine-cut plug every evening. Ah! that Wisting,
he spoiled me entirely. Not only did he give me tobacco, but

every evening – and I must confess I yielded to the temptation after a while, and had a morning smoke as well – he undertook the disagreeable work of cutting the plug and filling my pipe in all kinds of weather.

But we did not let our talk make us forget other things. As we had got no noon altitude, we should have to try and take one at midnight. The weather had brightened again, and it looked as if midnight would be a good time for the observation. We therefore crept into our bags to get a little nap in the intervening hours. In good time – soon after 11 p.m. – we were out again, and ready to catch the sun; the weather was of the best, and the opportunity excellent. We four navigators all had a share in it, as usual, and stood watching the course of the sun. This was a labour of patience, as the difference of altitude was now very slight. The result at which we finally arrived was of great interest, as it clearly shows how unreliable and valueless a single observation like this is in these regions. At 12.30 a.m. we put our instruments away, well satisfied with our work, and quite convinced that it was the midnight altitude that we had observed. The calculations which were carried out immediately afterwards gave us 89° 56′S. We were all well pleased with this result.

The arrangement now was that we should encircle this camp with a radius of about twelve and a half miles. By encircling I do not, of course, mean that we should go round in a circle with this radius; that would have taken us days, and was not to be thought of. The encircling was accomplished in this way: Three men went out in three different directions, two at right angles to the course we had been steering, and one in continuation of that course. To carry out this work I had chosen Wisting, Hassel, and Bjaaland. Having concluded our observations, we put the kettle on to give ourselves a drop of chocolate; the pleasure of standing out there in rather light attire had not exactly put warmth into our bodies. As we were engaged in swallowing the scalding drink, Bjaaland suddenly observed: "I'd like to tackle this encircling straight away. We shall have lots of time to sleep when we get back." Hassel and Wisting were quite of the same opinion, and it was agreed that they should start the work immediately. Here we have yet another example of the good spirit that prevailed in our little community. We had only lately come in from our day's work – a march of about eighteen and a half miles – and now they were asking to be allowed to go on another twenty-five miles. It seemed as if these fellows could never be tired. We therefore turned this meal into a little breakfast – that is to say, each man ate what he wanted of his bread ration, and then they began to get ready for the work. First, three small bags of light windproof stuff were made, and in each of these was placed a paper, giving the position of our camp. In addition, each of them carried a large square flag of the same dark brown material, which could be easily seen at a distance. As flag-poles we elected to use our spare sledge-runners, which were both long – 12 feet – and strong, and which we were going to take off here in any case, to lighten the sledges as much as possible for the return journey.

Thus equipped, and with thirty biscuits as an extra ration, the three men started off in the directions laid down. Their march was by no means free from danger, and does great honour to those who undertook it, not merely without raising the smallest objection, but with the greatest keenness. Let us consider for a moment the risk they ran. Our tent on the boundless plain, without marks of any kind, may very well be compared with a needle in a haystack. From this the three men were to steer out for a distance of twelve and a half miles. Compasses would have been good things to take on such a walk, but our sledge-compasses were too heavy and unsuitable for carrying. They therefore had to go without. They had the sun to go by, certainly, when they started, but who could say how long it would last? The weather was then fine enough, but it was impossible to guarantee that no sudden change would take place. If by bad luck the sun should be hidden, then their own tracks might help them. But to trust to tracks in these regions is a dangerous thing. Before you know where you are the whole plain may be one mass of driving snow, obliterating all tracks as soon as they are made. With the rapid changes of weather we had so often experienced, such a thing was not impossible. That these three risked their lives that morning, when they left the tent at 2.30, there can be no doubt at all, and they all three knew it very well. But if anyone thinks that on this account they took a solemn farewell of us who stayed behind, he is much mistaken. Not a bit; they all vanished in their different directions amid laughter and chaff.

The first thing we did – Hanssen and I – was to set about arranging a lot of trifling matters; there was something to be done here, something there, and above all we had to be ready for the series of observations we were to carry out together, so as to get as accurate a determination of our position as possible. The first observation told us at once how necessary this was. For it turned out that this, instead of giving us a greater altitude than the midnight observation, gave us a smaller one, and it was then clear that we had gone out of the meridian we thought we were following. Now the first thing to be done was to get our north and south line and latitude determined, so that we could find our position once more. Luckily for us, the weather looked as if it would hold. We measured the sun's altitude at every hour from 6 a.m. to 7 p.m., and from these observations found, with some degree of certainty, our latitude and the direction of the meridian.

By nine in the morning we began to expect the return of our comrades; according to our calculation they should then have covered the distance – twenty-five miles. It was not till ten o'clock that Hanssen made out the first black dot on the horizon, and not long after the second and third appeared. We both gave a sigh of relief as they came on; almost simultaneously the three arrived at the tent. We told them the result of our observations up to that time; it looked as if our camp was in about 89° 54′ 30″ S., and that with our encircling we had therefore included the actual Pole. With this result we might very well have been content, but as the weather was so good and gave the impression that it would continue so, and our store of provisions proved on examination to be very ample, we decided to go on for the remaining ten kilometres (five and a half geographical miles), and get our position determined as near to the Pole as possible. Meanwhile the three wanderers turned in – not so much because they were tired, as because it was the right thing to do – and Hanssen and I continued the series of observations.

In the afternoon we again went very carefully through our provision supply before discussing the future. The result was that we had food enough for ourselves and the dogs for eighteen days. The surviving sixteen dogs were divided into two teams of eight each, and the contents of Bjaaland's sledge were shared between Hanssen's and Wisting's. The abandoned sledge was set upright in the snow, and proved to be a splendid mark. The sledge-meter was screwed to the sledge, and we left it there; our other two were quite sufficient for the return journey; they had all shown themselves very accurate. A couple of empty provision cases were also left behind. I wrote in pencil on a piece of case the information that our tent – "Polheim" – would be found five and a half geographical miles north-west quarter west by compass from the sledge. Having put all these things in order the same day, we turned in, very well satisfied.

Early next morning, December 16, we were on our feet again. Bjaaland, who had now left the company of the drivers and been received with jubilation into that of the forerunners, was immediately entrusted with the honourable task of leading the expedition forward to the Pole itself. I assigned this duty, which we all regarded as a distinction, to him as a mark of gratitude to the gallant Telemarkers for their pre-eminent work in the advancement of ski spot. The leader that day had to keep as straight as a line, and if possible to follow the direction of our meridian. A little way after Bjaaland came Hassel, then Hanssen, then Wisting, and I followed a good way behind. I could thus check the direction of the march very accurately, and see that no great deviation was made. Bjaaland on this occasion showed himself a matchless forerunner; he went perfectly straight the whole time. Not once did he incline to one side or the other, and when we arrived at the end of the distance, we could still clearly see the sledge we had set up and take its bearing. This showed it to be absolutely in the right direction.

It was 11 a.m. when we reached our destination. While some of us were putting up the tent, others began to get everything ready for the coming observations. A solid snow pedestal was put up, on which the artificial horizon was to be placed, and a smaller one to rest the sextant on when it was not in use. At 11.30 a.m. the first observation was taken. We divided ourselves into two parties – Hanssen and I in one, Hassel and Wisting in the other. While one party slept, the other took the observations, and the watches were of six hours each. The weather was altogether grand, though the sky was not perfectly bright the whole time. A very light, fine, vaporous curtain would spread across the sky from time to time, and then quickly disappear again. This film of cloud was not thick enough to hide the sun, which we could see the whole time, but the atmosphere seemed to be disturbed. The effect of this was that the sun appeared not to change its altitude for several hours, until it suddenly made a jump.

Observations were now taken every hour through the whole twenty-four. It was very strange to turn in at 6 p.m., and then on turning out again at midnight to find the sun apparently still at the same altitude, and then once more at 6 a.m. to see it still no higher. The altitude had changed, of course, but so slightly that it was imperceptible with the naked eye. To us it appeared as though the sun made the circuit of the heavens at exactly the same altitude. The times of day that I have given here are calculated according to the meridian of Framheim; we continued to reckon our time from this. The observations soon told us that we were not on the absolute Pole, but as close to it as we could hope to get with our instruments.

On 17 December at noon we had completed our observations, and it is certain that we had done all that could be done. In order if possible to come a few inches nearer to the actual Pole, Hanssen and Bjaaland went out four geographical miles (seven kilometres) in the direction of the newly found meridian.

Bjaaland astonished me at dinner that day. Speeches had not hitherto been a feature of this journey, but now Bjaaland evidently thought the time had come, and surprised us all with a really fine oration. My amazement reached its culmination when, at the conclusion of his speech, he produced a cigar-case full of cigars and offered it round. A cigar at the Pole! What do you say to that? But it did not end there. When the cigars had gone round, there were still four left. I was quite touched when he handed the case and cigars to me with the words: "Keep this to remind you of the Pole." I have taken good care of the case, and shall preserve it as one of the many happy signs of my comrades' devotion on this journey. The cigars I shared out afterwards, on Christmas Eve, and they gave us a visible mark of that occasion.

When this festival dinner at the Pole was ended, we began our preparations for departure. First we set up the little tent we had brought with us in case we should be compelled to divide into two parties. It had been made by our able sailmaker, Rønne, and was of very thin windproof gabardine. Its drab colour made it easily

visible against the white surface. Another pole was lashed to the
tent-pole, making its total height about 13 feet. On the top of this
a little Norwegian flag was lashed fast, and underneath it a
pennant, on which "Fram" was painted. The tent was well
secured with guy-ropes on all sides. Inside the tent, in a little
bag, I left a letter, addressed to H. M. the King, giving information of what we had accomplished. The way home was a long one,
and so many things might happen to make it impossible for us to
give an account of our expedition. Besides this letter, I wrote a
short epistle to Captain Scott, who, I assumed, would be the first
to find the tent. Other things we left there were a sextant with a
glass horizon, a hypsometer case, three reindeer-skin foot-bags,
some kamiks and mits.

When everything had been laid inside, we went into the tent,
one by one, to write our names on a tablet we had fastened to the
tent-pole. On this occasion we received the congratulations of our
companions on the successful result, for the following messages
were written on a couple of strips of leather, sewed to the tent:
"Good luck," and "Welcome to 90°." These good wishes, which
we suddenly discovered, put us in very good spirits. They were
signed by Beck and Rönne. They had good faith in us. When we
had finished this we came out, and the tent-door was securely
laced together, so that there was no danger of the wind getting a
hold on that side.

And so goodbye to Polheim. It was a solemn moment when we
bared our heads and bade farewell to our home and our flag. And
then the travelling tent was taken down and the sledges packed.
Now the homeward journey was to begin – homeward, step by
step, mile after mile, until the whole distance was accomplished.
We drove at once into our old tracks and followed them. Many
were the times we turned to send a last look to Polheim. The
vaporous, white air set in again, and it was not long before the last
of Polheim, our little flag, disappeared from view.

Forestalled

Robert F. Scott RN

*A torpedo officer in the Royal Navy with no experience of polar travel,
Robert Falcon Scott was chosen to lead the British National Antarctic
Expedition (1901–4). Scott's chief qualification – aside from being an
officer and a gentleman – was that he was an acquaintance of Sir
Clements Markham, president of the Royal Geographical Society.
Scott inspired love and loyalty, but his amateurishness as a polar leader
was exposed in the expedition's failed bid for the South Pole; Scott and
his companions, Edward Wilson and Ernest Shackleton, almost starved
on the return journey because their rations had been too finely judged.
This disaster notwithstanding, in 1910 Scott was dispatched South
again. Once again, the aim was the South Pole. Once again, Scott made
elementary mistakes. On 4 January 1912, with just two hundred miles to
go to the Pole, Scott chose the party for the final onslaught. Dispensing
with his original plan of a four-man effort, he opted for five men:
himself, Captain Laurence "Titus" Oates, Edgar Evans, Edward
Wilson and "Birdie" Bowers. The extra man meant that the Pole
party was pinched for tent-space and rations. The dogs which might
have been used to haul the party's sledges had already been sent back.*

*Bad judgement was followed by bad luck. As Scott and his men neared
the Pole they hit freakishly inclement conditions. Still they plodded on,
man-hauling their sledges. Always in mind was the Norwegian party led
by Roald Amundsen, somewhere out in the great white making its own
bid for farthest south.*

Night, 15 January

[1912] It is wonderful to think that two long marches would land
us at the Pole. We left our depôt to-day with nine days' provisions, so that it ought to be a certain thing now, and the only

appalling possibility the sight of the Norwegian flag forestalling ours. Little Bowers continues his indefatigable efforts to get good sights, and it is wonderful how he works them up in his sleeping-bag in our congested tent. (Minimum for night –27.5°.) Only 27 miles from the Pole. We *ought* to do it now.

Tuesday 16 January

Camp 68. Height 9,760. T. –23.5°. The worst has happened, or nearly the worst. We marched well in the morning and covered 7½ miles. Noon sight showed us in Lat. 89° 42′ S., and we started off in high spirits in the afternoon, feeling that to-morrow would see us at our destination. About the second hour of the march Bowers' sharp eyes detected what he thought was a cairn; he was uneasy about it, but argued that it must be a sastrugus. Half an hour later he detected a black speck ahead. Soon we knew that this could not be a natural snow feature. We marched on, found that it was a black flag tied to a sledge bearer; near by the remains of a camp; sledge tracks and ski tracks going and coming and the clear trace of dogs' paws – many dogs. This told us the whole story. The Norwegians have forestalled us and are first at the Pole. It is a terrible disappointment, and I am very sorry for my loyal companions. Many thoughts come and much discussion have we had. Tomor-row we must march on to the Pole and then hasten home with all the speed we can compass. All the daydreams must go; it will be a wearisome return. Certainly we are descending in altitude – certainly also the Norwegians found an easy way up.

Wednesday 17 January

Camp 69. T. –22° at start. Night –21°. The Pole. Yes, but under very different circumstances from those expected. We have had a horrible day – add to our disappointment a head wind 4 to 5,* with a temperature –22°, and companions labouring on with cold feet and hands.

* Half a gale. The velocity of wind is denoted by numbers (1–10).

We started at 7.30, none of us having slept much after the shock of our discovery. We followed the Norwegian sledge tracks for some way; as far as we make out there are only two men. In about three miles we passed two small cairns. Then the weather overcast, and the tracks being increasingly drifted up and obviously going too far to the west, we decided to make straight for the Pole according to our calculations. At 12.30 Evans had such cold hands we camped for lunch – an excellent "weekend" one. We had marched 7.4 miles. Lat. sight gave 89° 53′ 37″. We started out and did 6½ miles due south. To-night little Bowers is laying himself out to get sights in terrible difficult circumstances; the wind is blowing hard, T. –21°, and there is that curious damp, cold feeling in the air which chills one to the bone in no time. We have been descending again, I think, but there looks to be a rise ahead; otherwise there is very little that is different from the awful monotony of past days. Great God! this is an awful place and terrible enough for us to have laboured to it without the reward of priority. Well, it is something to have got here, and the wind may be our friend to-morrow. We have had a fat Polar hoosh in spite of our chagrin, and feel comfortable inside – added a small stick of chocolate and the queer taste of a cigarette brought by Wilson. Now for the run home and a desperate struggle. I wonder if we can do it.

Thursday morning, 18 January

Decided after summing up all observations that we were 3.5 miles away from the Pole – one mile beyond it and 3 to the right. More or less in this direction Bowers saw a cairn or tent.

We have just arrived at this tent, 2 miles from our camp, therefore about 1½ miles from the Pole. In the tent we find a record of five Norwegians having been here, as follows:

Roald Amundsen
Olav Olavson Bjaaland
Hilmer Hanssen
Sverre H. Hassel
Oscar Wisting.   16 Dec. 1911.

The tent is fine – a small compact affair supported by a single bamboo. A note from Amundsen, which I keep, asks me to forward a letter to King Haakon!

The following articles have been left in the tent: 3 half bags of reindeer containing a miscellaneous assortment of mits and sleeping socks, very various in description, a sextant, a Norwegian artificial horizon and a hypsometer without boiling-point thermometers, a sextant and hypsometer of English make.

Left a note to say I had visited the tent with companions; Bowers photographing and Wilson sketching. Since lunch we have marched 6.2 miles S.S.E. by compass (i.e. northwards). Sights at lunch gave us $\frac{1}{2}$ to $\frac{3}{4}$ of a mile from the Pole, so we call it the Pole Camp. (Temp. Lunch –21°.) We built a cairn, put up our poor slighted Union Jack, and photographed ourselves – mighty cold work all of it – less than $\frac{1}{2}$ a mile south we saw stuck up an old underrunner of a sledge. This we commandeered as a yard for a floorcloth sail. I imagine it was intended to mark the exact spot of the Pole as near as the Norwegians could fix it. (Height 9,500.) A note attached talked of the tent as being 2 miles from the Pole. Wilson keeps the note. There is no doubt that our predecessors have made thoroughly sure of their mark and fully carried out their programme. I think the Pole is about 9,500 feet in height; this is remarkable, considering that in Lat. 88° we were about 10,500.

We carried the Union Jack about $\frac{3}{4}$ of a mile north with us and left it on a piece of stick as near as we could fix it. I fancy the Norwegians arrived at the pole on the 15th Dec. and left on the 17th, ahead of a date quoted by me in London as ideal, viz. 22 Dec. It looks as though the Norwegian party expected colder weather on the summit than they got; it could scarcely be otherwise from Shackleton's account. Well, we have turned our back now on the goal of our ambition and must face our 800 miles of solid dragging – and goodbye to most of the day-dreams!

Friday 19 January

Lunch 8.1, T. –22.6 deg. Early in the march we picked up a Norwegian cairn and our outward tracks. We followed these to the ominous black flag which had first apprised us of our predecessors' success. We have picked this flag up, using the staff for our sail, and are now camped about $1\frac{1}{2}$ miles further back on our tracks. So that is the last of the Norwegians for the present. The surface undulates considerably about this latitude; it was more evident today than when we were outward bound.

Night camp R. 2. Height 9700. T. –18.5 deg., Minimum –25.6 deg. Came along well this afternoon for three hours, then a rather dreary finish for the last $1\frac{1}{2}$. Weather very curious, snow clouds, looking very dense and spoiling the light, pass overhead from the S., dropping very minute crystals; between showers the sun shows and the wind goes to the S.W. The fine crystals absolutely spoil the surface; we had heavy dragging during the last hour in spite of the light load and a full sail. Our old tracks are drifted up, deep in places, and toothed sastrugi have formed over them. It looks as though this sandy snow was drifted about like sand from place to place. How account for the present state of our three day old tracks and the month old ones of the Norwegians?

It is warmer and pleasanter marching with the wind, but I'm not sure we don't feel the cold more when we stop and camp than we did on the outward march. We pick up our cairns easily, and ought to do so right through, I think; but, of course, one will be a bit anxious till the Three Degree Depot is reached. I'm afraid the return journey is going to be dreadfully tiring and monotonous.

Saturday 20 January

Lunch camp, 9810. We have come along very well this morning, although the surface was terrible bad – 9.3 miles in 5 hours 20 m. This has brought us to our Southern Depot, and we pick up 4 days' food. We carry on 7 days from tonight with 55 miles to go to the Half Degree Depot made on January 10. The same sort of weather and a litle more wind, sail drawing well.

Night camp R. 3. 9860. Temp. –18 deg. It was blowing quite hard and drifting when we started our afternoon march. At first with full sail we went along at a great rate; then we got on to an extraordinary surface, the drifting snow lying in heaps; it clung to the ski, which could only be pushed forward with an effort. The pulling was really awful, but we went steadily on and camped a short way beyond our cairn of the 14th. I'm afraid we are in for a bad pull again tomorrow, luckily the wind holds. I shall be very glad when Bowers gets his ski; I'm afraid he must find these long marches very trying with short legs, but he is an undefeated little sportsman. I think Oates is feeling the cold and fatigue more than most of us. It is blowing pretty hard tonight, but with a good march we have earned one good hoosh and are very comfortable in the tent. It is everything now to keep up a good marching pace; I trust we shall be able to do so and catch the ship. Total march, 18½ miles.

Sunday January 21

R. 4. 10,010. Temp, blizzard, –18 deg. to –11 deg., to –14 deg. now. Awoke to a stiff blizzard; air very thick with snow and sun very dim. We decided not to march owing to likelihood of losing track; expected at least a day of lay up, but whilst at lunch there was a sudden clearance and wind dropped to light breeze. We got ready to march, but gear was so iced up we did not get away till 3.45. Marched till 7.40 – a terribly weary four-hour drag; even with helping wind we only did 5½ miles (6¼ statute). The surface bad, horribly bad on new sastrugi, and decidedly rising again in elevation.

We are going to have a pretty hard time this next 100 miles I expect. If it was difficult to drag downhill over this belt, it will probably be a good deal more difficult to drag up. Luckily the cracks are fairly distinct, though we only see our cairns when less than a mile away; 45 miles to the next depot and 6 days' food in hand – then pick up 7 days' food (T. –22 deg.) and 90 miles to go to the "Three Degree" Depot. Once there we ought to be safe, but we ought to have a day or two in hand on arrival and may have difficulty with following the tracks. However, if we can get a rating sight for our watches tomorrow we shall be independent of the tracks at a pinch.

Monday 22 January

10,000. Temp. –21 deg. I think about the most tiring march we have had; solid pulling the whole way, in spite of the light sledge and some little helping wind at first. Then in the last part of the afternoon the sun came out, and almost immediately we had the whole surface covered with soft snow.

We got away sharp at 8 and marched a solid 9 hours, and thus we have covered 14.5 miles (geo.) but, by Jove! it has been a grind. We are just about on the 89th parallel. Tonight Bowers got a rating sight. I'm afraid we have passed out of the wind area. We are within 2½ miles of the 64th camp cairn, 30 miles from our depot, and with 5 days' food in hand. Ski boots are beginning to show signs of wear; I trust we shall have no giving out of ski or boots, since there are yet so many miles to go. I thought we were climbing today, but the barometer gives no change.

Tuesday 23 January

Lowest Minimum last night –30 deg., Temp, at start –28 deg. Lunch height 10,100. Temp, with wind 6 to 7, –19 deg. Little wind and heavy marching at start. Then wind increased and we did 8.7 miles by lunch, when it was practically blowing a blizzard. The old tracks show so remarkably well that we can follow them without much difficulty – a great piece of luck.

In the afternoon we had to reorganise. Could carry a whole sail. Bowers hung on to the sledge, Evans and Oates had to lengthen out. We came along at a great rate and should have got within an easy march of our depot had not Wilson suddenly discovered that Evans' nose was frostbitten – it was white and hard. We thought it best to camp at 6.45. Got the tent up with some difficulty, and now pretty cosy after good hoosh.

There is no doubt Evans is a good deal run down – his fingers are badly blistered and his nose is rather seriously congested with frequent frost bites. He is very much annoyed with himself, which is not a good sign. I think Wilson, Bowers and I are as fit as possible under the circumstances. Oates gets cold feet. One way and another, I shall be glad to get off the summit! We are

only about 13 miles from our "Degree and half" Depot and
should get there tomorrow. The weather seems to be breaking up.
Pray God we have something of a track to follow to the Three
Degree Depot – once we pick that up we ought to be right.

Wednesday 24 January

Lunch Temp. –8 deg. Things beginning to look a little serious. A
strong wind at the start has developed into a full blizzard at lunch,
and we have had to get into our sleeping-bags. It was a bad
march, but we covered 7 miles. At first Evans, and then Wilson
went ahead to scout for tracks. Bowers guided the sledge alone for
the first hour, then both Oates and he remained alongside it; they
had a fearful time trying to make the pace between the soft
patches. At 12.30 the sun coming ahead made it impossible to
see the tracks further, and we had to stop. By this time the gale
was at its height and we had the dickens of a time getting up the
tent, cold fingers all round. We are only 7 miles from our depot,
but I made sure we should be there tonight. This is the second
full gale since we left the Pole. I don't like the look of it. Is the
weather breaking up? If so, God help us, with the tremendous
summit journey and scant food. Wilson and Bowers are my
standby. I don't like the easy way in which Oates and Evans
get frostbitten.

Thursday 25 January

Temp. Lunch –11 deg., Temp. night –16 deg. Thank God we
found our Half Degree Depot. After lying in our bags yesterday
afternoon and all night, we debated breakfast; decided to have it
later and go without lunch. At the time the gale seemed as bad as
ever, but during breakfast the sun showed and there was light
enough to see the old track. It was a long and terribly cold job
digging out our sledge and breaking camp, but we got through
and on the march without sail, all pulling. This was about 11, and
at about 2.30, to our joy, we saw the red depot flag. We had lunch
and left with 9½ days' provisions, still following the track –

marched till 8 and covered over 5 miles, over 12 in the day. Only 89 miles (geogr.) to the next depot, but it's time we cleared off this plateau. We are not without ailments: Oates suffers from a very cold foot; Evans' fingers and nose are in a bad state, and tonight Wilson is suffering tortures from his eyes. Bowers and I are the only members of the party without troubles just at present. The weather still looks unsettled, and I fear a succession of blizzards at this time of year; the wind is strong from the south, and this afternoon has been very helpful with the full sail. Needless to say I shall sleep much better with our provision bag full again. The only real anxiety now is the finding of the Three Degree Depot. The tracks seem as good as ever so far, sometimes for 30 or 40 yards we lose them under drifts, but then they reappear quite clearly raised above the surface. If the light is good there is not the least difficulty in following. Blizzards are our bugbear, not only stopping our marches, but the cold damp air takes it out of us. Bowers got another rating sight tonight – it was wonderful how he managed to observe in such a horribly cold wind. He has been on ski today whilst Wilson walked by the sledge or pulled ahead of it.

Friday 26 January

Temp. –17 deg. Height 9700, must be high barometer. Started late, 8.50 – for no reason, as I called the hands rather early. We must have fewer delays. There was a good stiff breeze and plenty of drift, but the tracks held. To our old blizzard camp of the 7th we got on well, 7 miles. But beyond the camp we found the tracks completely wiped out. We searched for some time, then marched on a short way and lunched, the weather gradually clearing, though the wind holding. Knowing there were two cairns at four mile intervals, we had little anxiety till we picked up the first far on our right, then steering right by a stroke of fortune, and Bowers' sharp eyes caught a glimpse of the second far on the left. Evidently we made a bad course outward at this part. There is not a sign of our tracks between these cairns, but the last, marking our night camp of the 6th, No. 59, is in the belt of hard sastrugi, and I was comforted to see signs of the track reappearing as we camped.

I hope to goodness we can follow it tomorrow. We marched 16 miles (geo.) today, but made good only 15.4.

Saturday 27 January

R. 10. Temp. −16 deg. (lunch), −14.3 deg. (evening). Minimum − 19 deg. Height 9900. Barometer low? Called the hands half an hour late, but we got away in good time. The forenoon march was over the belt of storm-tossed sastrugi; it looked like a rough sea. Wilson and I pulled in front on ski, the remainder on foot. It was very tricky work following the track, which pretty constantly disappeared, and in fact only showed itself by faint signs any-where – a foot or two of raised sledge-track, a dozen yards of the trail of the sledge-meter wheel, or a spatter of hard snow-flicks where feet had trodden. Sometimes none of these were distinct, but one got an impression of lines which guided. The trouble was that on the outward track one had to shape course constantly to avoid the heaviest mounds, and consequently there were many zig-zags. We lost a good deal over a mile by these halts, in which we unharnessed and went on the search for signs. However, by hook or crook, we managed to stick on the old track. Came on the cairn quite suddenly, marched past it, and camped for lunch at 7 miles. In the afternoon the sastrugi gradually diminished in size and now we are on fairly level ground to-day, the obstruction practically at an end, and, to our joy, the tracks showing up much plainer again. For the last two hours we had no difficulty at all in following them. There has been a nice helpful southerly breeze all day, a clear sky and comparatively warm temperature. The air is dry again, so that tents and equipment are gradually losing their icy condition imposed by the blizzard conditions of the past week.

Our sleeping-bags are slowly but surely getting wetter and I'm afraid it will take a lot of this weather to put them right. However, we all sleep well enough in them, the hours allowed being now on the short side. We are slowly getting more hungry, and it would be an advantage to have a little more food, especially for lunch. If we get to the next depot in a few marches (it is now less than 60 miles and we have a full week's food) we ought to be able to open

out a little, but we can't look for a real feed till we get to the pony
food depot. A long way to go, and, by Jove, this is tremendous
labour.

Sunday 28 January

Lunch, –20 deg. Height, night, 10,130. R. 11. Supper Temp. –18
deg.. Little wind and heavy going in forenoon. We just ran out 8
miles in 5 hours and added another 8 in 3 hours 40 mins. in the
afternoon with a good wind and better surface. It is very difficult
to say if we are going up or down hill; the barometer is quite
different from outward readings. We are 43 miles from the depot,
with six days' food in hand. We are camped opposite our lunch
cairn of the 4th, only half a day's march from the point at which
the last supporting party left us.

Three articles were dropped on our outward march – Oates'
pipe, Bowers' fur mits, and Evans' night boots. We picked up the
boots and mits on the track, and tonight we found the pipe lying
placidly in sight on the snow. The sledge tracks were very easy to
follow today; they are becoming more and more raised, giving a
good line shadow often visible half a mile ahead. If this goes on
and the weather holds we shall get our depot without trouble. I
shall indeed be glad to get it on the sledge. We are getting more
hungry, there is no doubt. The lunch meal is beginning to seem
inadequate. We are pretty thin, especially Evans, but none of us
are feeling worked out. I doubt if we could drag heavy loads, but
we can keep going well with our light one. We talk of food a good
deal more, and shall be glad to open out on it.

Monday 29 January

R. 12. Lunch Temp. –23 deg. Supper Temp. –25 deg. Height
10,000. Excellent march of 19 ½ miles, 10.5 before lunch. Wind
helping greatly, considerable drift; tracks for the most part very
plain. Some time before lunch we picked up the return track of
the supporting party, so that there are now three distinct sledge
impressions. We are only 24 miles from our depot – an easy day

and a half. Given a fine day to-morrow we ought to get it without difficulty. The wind and sastrugi are S.S.E. and S.E. If the weather holds we ought to do the rest of the inland ice journey in little over a week. The surface is very much altered since we passed out. The loose snow has been swept into heaps, hard and wind-tossed. The rest has a glazed appearance, the loose drifting snow no doubt acting on it, polishing it like a sand blast. The sledge with our good wind behind runs splendidly on it; it is all soft and sandy beneath the glaze. We are certainly getting hungrier every day. The day after tomorrow we should be able to increase allowances. It is monotonous work, but, thank God, the miles are coming fast at last. We ought not to be delayed much now with the down-grade in front of us.

Tuesday 30 January

R. 13. 9860. Lunch Temp. –25 deg. Supper Temp. –24.5 deg. Thank the Lord, another fine march – 19 miles. We have passed the last cairn before the depot, the track is clear ahead, the weather fair, the wind helpful, the gradient down – with any luck we should pick up our depot in the middle of the morning march. This is the bright side; the reverse of the medal is serious. Wilson has strained a tendon in his leg; it has given pain all day and is swollen tonight. Of course, he is full of pluck over it, but I don't like the idea of such an accident here. To add to the trouble Evans has dislodged two fingernails tonight; his hands are really bad, and to my surprise he shows signs of losing heart over it. He hasn't been cheerful since the accident. The wind shifted from S.E. to S. and back again all day, but luckily it keeps strong. We can get along with bad fingers, but it (will be) a mighty serious thing if Wilson's leg doesn't improve.

Wednesday 31 January

9800. Lunch Temp. –20 deg. Supper Temp. –20 deg. The day opened fine with a fair breeze; we marched on the depot, [39] picked it up, and lunched an hour later. In the afternoon the surface became fearfully bad, the wind dropped to light southerly air. Ill luck that this should happen just when we have only four men to pull. Wilson rested his leg as much as possible by walking quietly beside the sledge; the result has been good, and tonight there is much less inflammation. I hope he will be all right again soon, but it is trying to have an injured limb in the party. I see we had a very heavy surface here on our outward march. There is no doubt we are travelling over undulations, but the inequality of level does not make a great difference to our pace; it is the sandy crystals that hold us up. There has been very great alteration of the surface since we were last here – the sledge tracks stand high. This afternoon we picked up Bowers' ski – the last thing we have to find on the summit, thank Heaven! Now we have only to go north and so shall welcome strong winds.

Thursday 1 February

R. 15. 9778. Lunch Temp. –20 deg. Supper Temp. –19.8 deg. Heavy collar work most of the day. Wind light. Did 8 miles, 4 $\frac{3}{4}$ hours. Started well in the afternoon and came down a steep slope in quick time; then the surface turned real bad – sandy drifts – very heavy pulling. Working on past 8 p.m. we just fetched a lunch cairn of 29 December, when we were only a week out from the depot. It ought to be easy to get in with a margin, having 8 days' food in hand (full feeding). We have opened out on the $\frac{1}{7}$ th increase and it makes a lot of difference. Wilson's leg much better. Evans' fingers now very bad, two nails coming off, blisters burst.

Friday 2 February

9340. R. 16. Temp.: Lunch –19 deg. Supper –17 deg. We started well on a strong southerly wind. Soon got to a steep grade, when the sledge overran and upset us one after another. We got off our ski, and pulling on foot reeled off 9 miles by lunch at 1.30. Started in the afternoon on foot, going very strong. We noticed a curious circumstance towards the end of the forenoon. The tracks were drifted over, but the drifts formed a sort of causeway along which we pulled. In the afternoon we soon came to a steep slope – the same on which we exchanged sledges on 28 December. All went well till, in trying to keep the track at the same time as my feet, on a very slippery surface, I came an awful "purler" on my shoulder. It is horribly sore tonight and another sick person added to our tent – three out of five injured, and the most troublesome surfaces to come. We shall be lucky if we get through without serious injury. Wilson's leg is better, but might easily get bad again, and Evans' fingers.

At the bottom of the slope this afternoon we came on a confused sea of sastrugi. We lost the track. Later, on soft snow, we picked up E. Evans' return track, which we are now following. We have managed to get off 17 miles. The extra food is certainly helping us, but we are getting pretty hungry. The weather is already a trifle warmer and the altitude lower, and only 80 miles or so to Mount Darwin. It is time we were off the summit – Pray God another four days will see us pretty well clear of it. Our bags are getting very wet and we ought to have more sleep.

Saturday 3 February

R. 17. Temp.: Lunch –20 deg.; Supper –20 deg. Height 9040 feet. Started pretty well on foot; came to steep slope with crevasses (few). I went on ski to avoid another fall, and we took the slope gently with our sail, constantly losing the track, but picked up a much weathered cairn on our right. Vexatious delays, searching for tracks, &c., reduced morning march to 8.1 miles. Afternoon, came along a little better, but again lost tracks on hard slope. Tonight we are near camp of 26 December, but cannot see cairn. Have decided it is waste of time looking for tracks and cairn, and shall push on due north as fast as we can.

The surface is greatly changed since we passed outward, in most places polished smooth, but with heaps of new toothed sastrugi which are disagreeable obstacles. Evans' fingers are going on as well as can be expected, but it will be long before he will be able to help properly with the work. Wilson's leg much better, and my shoulder also, though it gives bad twinges. The extra food is doing us all good, but we ought to have more sleep. Very few more days on the plateau I hope.

Sunday 4 February

R. 18. 8620 feet. Temp.: Lunch –22 deg.; Supper –23 deg. Pulled on foot in the morning over good hard surface and covered 9.7 miles. Just before lunch unexpectedly fell into crevasses, Evans and I together – a second fall for Evans, and I camped. After lunch saw disturbance ahead, and what I took for disturbance (land) to the right. We went on ski over hard shiny descending surface. Did very well, especially towards end of march, covering in all 18.1. We have come down some hundreds of feet. Half way in the march the land showed up splendidly, and I decided to make straight for Mt Darwin, which we are rounding. Every sign points to getting away off this plateau. The temperature is 20 deg. lower than when we were here before; the party is not improving in condition, especially Evans, who is becoming rather dull and incapable. Thank the Lord we have good food at each meal, but we get hungrier in spite of it. Bowers is splendid, full of energy and bustle all the time. I hope we are not going to have trouble with ice-falls.

Monday 5 February

R. 19. Lunch, 8320 ft., Temp. –17 deg.; Supper, 8120 ft, Temp – 17.2 deg. A good forenoon, few crevasses; we covered 10.2 miles. In the afternoon we soon got into difficulties. We saw the land very clearly, but the difficulty is to get at it. An hour after starting we came on huge pressures and great street crevasses partly open. We had to steer more and more to the west, so that our course was very erratic. Late in the march we turned more to the north and again encountered open crevasses across our track. It is very difficult manoeuvring amongst these and I should not like to do it without ski.

We are camped in a very disturbed region, but the wind has fallen very light here, and our camp is comfortable for the first time for many weeks. We may be anything from 25 to 30 miles from our depot, but I wish to goodness we could see a way through the disturbances ahead. Our faces are much cut up by all the winds we have had, mine least of all; the others tell me they feel their noses more going with than against the wind. Evans' nose is almost as bad as his fingers. He is a good deal crocked up.

Tuesday 6 February

Lunch 7900; Supper 7210. Temp. −15 deg. We've had a horrid day and not covered good mileage. On turning out found sky overcast; a beastly position amidst crevasses. Luckily it cleared just before we started. We went straight for Mt Darwin, but in half an hour found ourselves amongst huge open chasms, un-bridged, but not very deep, I think. We turned to the north between two, but to our chagrin they converged into chaotic disturbance. We had to retrace our steps for a mile or so, then struck to the west and got on to a confused sea of sastrugi, pulling very hard; we put up the sail, Evans' nose suffered, Wilson very cold, everything horrid. Camped for lunch in the sastrugi; the only comfort, things looked clearer to the west and we were obviously going downhill. In the afternoon we struggled on, got out of sastrugi and turned over on glazed surface, crossing many crevasses – very easy work on ski. Towards the end of the march we realised the certainty of maintaining a more or less straight course to the depot, and estimate distance 10 to 15 miles.

Food is low and weather uncertain, so that many hours of the day were anxious; but this evening, though we are not as far advanced as I expected, the outlook is much more promising. Evans is the chief anxiety now; his cuts and wounds suppurate, his nose looks very bad, and altogether he shows considerable signs of being played out. Things may mend for him on the glacier, and his wounds get some respite under warmer conditions. I am indeed glad to think we shall so soon have done with plateau conditions. It took us 27 days to reach the Pole and 21 days back – in all 48 days – nearly 7 weeks in low temperature with almost incessant wind.

Sunday 11 February

R. 25. Lunch Temp. $+6.5°$; Supper $+3.5°$. The worst day we have had during the trip and greatly owing to our own fault. We started on a wretched surface with light S.W. wind, sail set, and pulling on ski – in a horrible light, which made everything look fantastic. As we went on the light got worse, and suddenly we found ourselves in pressure. Then came the fatal decision to steer east. We went on for 6 hours, hoping to do a good distance, which in fact I suppose we did, but for the last hour or two we pressed on into a regular trap. Getting on to a good surface we did not reduce our lunch meal, and thought all going well, but half an hour after lunch we got into the worst ice mess I have ever been in. For three hours we plunged on on ski, first thinking we were too much to the right, then too much to the left; meanwhile the disturbance got worse and my spirits received a very rude shock. There were times when it seemed almost impossible to find a way out of the awful turmoil in which we found ourselves. At length, arguing that there must be a way on our left, we plunged in that direction. It got worse, harder, more icy and crevassed. We could not manage our ski and pulled on foot, falling into crevasses every minute – most luckily with no bad accident. At length we saw a smoother slope towards the land, pushed for it, but knew it was a woefully long way from us. The turmoil changed in character, irregular crevassed surface giving way to huge chasms, closely packed and most difficult to cross. It was very heavy work, but we had grown desperate. We won through at 10 p.m. and I write after 12 hours on the march. I *think* we are on or about the right track now, but we are still a good number of miles from the depôt, so we reduced rations tonight. We had three pemmican meals left and decided to make them into four. Tomorrow's lunch must serve for two if we do not make big progress. It was a test of our endurance on the march and our fitness with small supper. We have come through well. A good wind has come down the glacier which is clearing the sky and surface. Pray God the wind holds tomorrow.

Wednesday 14 February

There is no getting away from the fact that we are not pulling strong: probably none of us. Wilson's leg still troubles him and he doesn't like to trust himself on ski; but the worst case is Evans, who is giving us serious anxiety. This morning he suddenly disclosed a huge blister on his foot. It delayed us on the march, when he had to have his crampon readjusted. Sometimes I fear he is going from bad to worse, but I trust he will pick up again when we come to steady work on ski like this afternoon. He is hungry and so is Wilson. We can't risk opening out our food again, and as cook at present I am serving something under full allowance. We are inclined to get slack and slow with our camping arrangements, and small delays increase. I have talked of the matter tonight and hope for improvement. We cannot do distance without the hours. The next depôt some 30 miles away and nearly 3 days' food in hand.

Saturday 17 February

A very terrible day. Evans looked a little better after a good sleep, and declared, as he always did, that he was quite well. He started in his place on the traces, but half an hour later worked his ski shoes adrift, and had to leave the sledge. The surface was awful, the soft recently fallen snow clogging the ski and runners at every step, the sledge groaning, the sky overcast, and the land hazy. We stopped after about one hour, and Evans came up again, but very slowly. Half an hour later he dropped out again on the same plea. He asked Bowers to lend him a piece of string. I cautioned him to come on as quickly as he could, and he answered cheerfully as I thought. We had to push on, and the remainder of us were forced to pull very hard, sweating heavily. Abreast the Monument Rock we stopped, and seeing Evans a long way astern, I camped for lunch. There was no alarm at first, and we prepared tea and our own meal, consuming the latter. After lunch, and Evans still not appearing, we looked out, to see him still afar off. By this time we were alarmed, and all four started back on ski. I was first to reach the poor man and shocked at his appearance; he was on his knees with clothing disarranged, hands uncovered and frostbitten, and a wild look in his eyes. Asked what was the matter, he replied with a slow speech that he didn't know, but thought he must have fainted. We got him on his feet, but after two or three steps he sank down again. He showed every sign of complete collapse. Wilson, Bowers, and I went back for the sledge, whilst Oates remained with him. When we returned he was practically unconscious, and when we got him into the tent quite comatose. He died quietly at 12.30 a.m. On discussing the symptoms we think he began to get weaker just before we reached the Pole, and that his downward path was accelerated first by the shock of his frostbitten fingers, and later by falls during rough travelling on the glacier, further by his loss of all confidence in himself. Wilson thinks it certain he must have injured his brain by a fall. It is a terrible thing to lose a companion in this way, but calm reflection shows that there could not have been a better ending to the terrible anxieties of the past week. Discussion of the situation at lunch yesterday shows us what a desperate pass we were in with a sick man on our hands so far from home . . .

Friday 2 March

Lunch. Misfortunes rarely come singly. We marched to the [Middle Barrier] depôt fairly easily yesterday afternoon, and since that have suffered three distinct blows which have placed us in a bad position. First we found a shortage of oil; with most rigid economy it can scarce carry us to the next depôt on this surface [71 miles away]. Second, Titus Oates disclosed his feet, the toes showing very bad indeed, evidently bitten by the late temperatures. The third blow came in the night, when the wind, which we had hailed with some joy, brought dark overcast weather. It fell below −40° in the night, and this morning it took $1\frac{1}{2}$ hours to get our foot-gear on, but we got away before eight. We lost cairn and tracks together and made as steady as we could N. by W., but have seen nothing. Worse was to come – the surface is simply awful. In spite of strong wind and full sail we have only done $5\frac{1}{2}$ miles. We are in a *very* queer street, since there is no doubt we cannot do the extra marches and feel the cold horribly.

Monday 5 March

Lunch. Regret to say going from bad to worse. We got a slant of wind yesterday afternoon, and going on 5 hours we converted our wretched morning run of $3\frac{1}{2}$ miles into something over 9. We went to bed on a cup of cocoa and pemmican solid with the chill off. (R. 47.) The result is telling on all, but mainly on Oates, whose feet are in a wretched condition. One swelled up tremendously last night and he is very lame this morning. We started march on tea and pemmican as last night – we pretend to prefer the pemmican this way. Marched for 5 hours this morning over a slightly better surface covered with high moundy sastrugi. Sledge capsized twice; we pulled on foot, covering about $5\frac{1}{2}$ miles. We are two pony marches and 4 miles about from our depôt. Our fuel dreadfully low and the poor Soldier nearly done. It is pathetic enough because we can do nothing for him; more hot food might do a little, but only a little, I fear. We none of us expected these terribly low temperatures, and of the rest of us Wilson is feeling them most; mainly, I fear, from his self-sacrificing devotion in doctoring Oates' feet. We cannot help each other, each has enough to do to take care of himself. We get cold on the march when the trudging is heavy, and the wind pierces our worn garments. The others, all of them, are unendingly cheerful when in the tent. We mean to see the game through with a proper spirit, but it's tough work to be pulling harder than we ever pulled in our lives for long hours, and to feel that the progress is so slow. One can only say "God help us!" and plod on our weary way, cold and very miserable, though outwardly cheerful. We talk of all sorts of subjects in the tent, not much of food now, since we decided to take the risk of running a full ration. We simply couldn't go hungry at this time.

Saturday 10 March

Things steadily downhill. Oates' foot worse. He has rare pluck and must know that he can never get through. He asked Wilson if he had a chance this morning, and of course Bill had to say he didn't know. In point of fact he has none. Apart from him, if he went under now, I doubt whether we could get through. With great care we might have a dog's chance, but no more. The weather conditions are awful, and our gear gets steadily more icy and difficult to manage. At the same time, of course, poor Titus is the greatest handicap. He keeps us waiting in the morning until we have partly lost the warming effect of our good breakfast, when the only wise policy is to be up and away at once; again at lunch. Poor chap! it is too pathetic to watch him; one cannot but try to cheer him up.

Yesterday we marched up the depôt, Mt Hooper. Cold comfort. Shortage on our allowance all round . . .

Sunday 11 March

Titus Oates is very near the end, one feels. What we or he will do, God only knows. We discussed the matter after breakfast; he is a brave fine fellow and understands the situation, but he practically asked for advice. Nothing could be said but to urge him to march as long as he could. One satisfactory result to the discussion; I practically ordered Wilson to hand over the means of ending our troubles to us, so that any one of us may know how to do so. Wilson had no choice between doing so and our ransacking the medicine case. We have 30 opium tabloids apiece and he is left with a tube of morphine. So far the tragical side of our story.

The sky was completely overcast when we started this morning. We could see nothing, lost the tracks, and doubtless have been swaying a good deal since – 3.1 miles for the forenoon – terribly heavy dragging – expected it. Know that 6 miles is about the limit of our endurance now, if we get no help from wind or surfaces. We have 7 days' food and should be about 55 miles from One Ton Camp to-night, 6 × 7 = 42, leaving us 13 miles short of our distance, even if things get no worse. Meanwhile the season rapidly advances . . .

Wednesday 14 March

No doubt about the going downhill, but everything going wrong for us. Yesterday we woke to a strong northerly wind with temp.

–37°. Couldn't face it, so remained in camp till 2, then did 5¼ miles. Wanted to march later, but party feeling the cold badly as the breeze (N.) never took off entirely, and as the sun sank the temp. fell. Long time getting supper in dark.

This morning started with southerly breeze, set sail and passed another cairn at good speed; halfway, however, the wind shifted to W. by S. or W.S.W., blew through our wind clothes and into our mits. Poor Wilson horribly cold, could [not] get off ski for some time. Bowers and I practically made camp, and when we got into the tent at last we were all deadly cold. Then temp. now midday down –13° and the wind strong. We *must* go on, but now the making of every camp must be more difficult and dangerous. It must be near the end, but a pretty merciful end. Poor Oates got it again in the foot. I shudder to think what it will be like tomorrow. It is only with greatest pains rest of us keep off frostbites. No idea there could be temperatures like this at this time of year with such winds. Truly awful outside the tent. Must fight it out to the last biscuit, but can't reduce rations.

Friday 16 March or Saturday 17

Lost track of dates, but think the last correct. Tragedy all along the line. At lunch, the day before yesterday, poor Titus Oates said he couldn't go on; he proposed we should leave him in his sleeping-bag. That we could not do, and we induced him to come on, on the afternoon march. In spite of its awful nature for him he struggled on and we made a few miles. At night he was worse and we knew the end had come.

Should this be found I want these facts recorded. Oates' last thoughts were of his mother, but immediately before he took pride in thinking that his regiment would be pleased with the bold way in which he met his death. We can testify to his bravery. He has borne intense suffering for weeks without complaint, and to the very last was able and willing to discuss outside subjects. He did not – would not – give up hope till the very end. He was a brave soul. This was the end. He slept through the night before last, hoping not to wake; but he woke in the morning – yesterday. It was blowing a blizzard. He said, "I am just going outside and may be some time." He went out into the blizzard and we have not seen him since.

I take this opportunity of saying that we have stuck to our sick companions to the last. In case of Edgar Evans, when absolutely out of food and he lay insensible, the safety of the remainder seemed to demand his abandonment, but Providence mercifully removed him at this critical moment. He died a natural death, and we did not leave him till two hours after his death. We knew that poor Oates was walking to his death, but though we tried to dissuade him, we knew it was the act of a brave man and an English gentleman. We all hope to meet the end with a similar spirit, and assuredly the end is not far.

I can only write at lunch and then only occasionally. The cold is intense, −40° at midday. My companions are unendingly cheerful, but we are all on the verge of serious frostbites, and though we constantly talk of fetching through, I don't think any one of us believes it in his heart.

We are cold on the march now, and at all times except meals. Yesterday we had to lie up for a blizzard and today we move dreadfully slowly. We are at No. 14 pony camp, only two pony marches from One Ton Depôt. We leave here our theodolite, a camera, and Oates' sleeping-bags. Diaries, etc., and geological specimens carried at Wilson's special request, will be found with us or on our sledge.

Sunday 18 March

Today, lunch, we are 21 miles from the depôt. Ill fortune presses, but better may come. We have had more wind and drift from ahead yesterday; had to stop marching; wind N.W., force 4, temp. −35°. No human being could face it, and we are worn out *nearly*.

My right foot has gone, nearly all the toes – two days ago I was proud possessor of best feet. These are the steps of my downfall. Like an ass I mixed a small spoonful of curry powder with my melted pemmican – it gave me violent indigestion. I lay awake and in pain all night; woke and felt done on the march; foot went and I didn't know it. A very small measure of neglect and I have a foot which is not pleasant to contemplate. Bowers takes first place in condition, but there is not much to choose after all. The others are still confident of getting through – or pretend to be – I don't know! We have the last *half* fill of oil in our primus and a very small quantity of spirit – this alone between us and thirst. The wind is fair for the moment, and that is perhaps a fact to help. The mileage would have seemed ridiculously small on our outward journey.

Monday 19 March

Lunch. We camped with difficulty last night and were dreadfully cold till after our supper of cold pemmican and biscuit and a half a pannikin of cocoa cooked over the spirit. Then, contrary to expectation, we got warm and all slept well. Today we started in the usual dragging manner. Sledge dreadfully heavy. We are 15½ miles from the depôt and ought to get there in three days. What progress! We have two days' food, but barely a day's fuel. All our feet are getting bad – Wilson's best, my right foot worse, left all right. There is no chance to nurse one's feet till we can get hot food into us. Amputation is the least I can hope for now, but will the trouble spread? That is the serious question. The weather doesn't give us a chance – the wind from N. to N.W. and –40° temp to-day.

Wednesday 21 March

Got within 11 miles of depôt Monday night; had to lie up all yesterday in severe blizzard. Today forlorn hope, Wilson and Bowers going to depôt for fuel.

22 and 23 Blizzard bad as ever – Wilson and Bowers unable to start – tomorrow last chance – no fuel and only one or two [rations] of food left – must be near the end. Have decided it shall be natural – we shall march for the depôt with or without our effects and die in our tracks.

[Thursday] 29 March

Since the 21st we have had a continuous gale from W.S.W. and S.W. We had fuel to make two cups of tea apiece and bare food for two days on the 20th. Every day we have been ready to start for our depôt 11 *miles* away, but outside the door of the tent it remains a scene of whirling drift. I do not think we can hope for any better things now. We shall stick it out to the end, but we are getting weaker, of course, and the end cannot be far.

It seems a pity, but I do not think I can write more.

R. SCOTT.

Last entry.
For God's sake look after our people.

The bodies of Scott and his companions were found on 12 November 1912. Among the search party was Lieutenant Atkinson:

Eight months afterwards we found the tent. It was an object partially snowed up and looking like a cairn. Before it were the ski sticks and in front of them a bamboo which probably was the mast of the sledge. The tent was practically on the line of cairns which we had built in the previous season. It was within a quarter of a mile of the remains of the cairn, which showed as a small hummock beneath the snow.

Inside the tent were the bodies of Captain Scott, Doctor Wilson, and Lieutenant Bowers. Wilson and Bowers were found in the attitude of sleep, their sleeping-bags closed over their heads as they would naturally close them.

Scott died later. He had thrown back the flaps of his sleeping-bag and opened his coat. The little wallet containing the three notebooks was under his shoulders, and his arm was flung across Wilson. They had pitched their tent well, and it had withstood all the blizzards of an exceptionally hard winter. Each man of the Expedition recognized the bodies. From Captain Scott's diary*

---

* Atkinson found, as well as Scott's diary, his farewell letters. See Appendix I

I found his reasons for this disaster. When the men had been assembled I read to them these reasons, the place of death of Petty Officer Evans, and the story of Captain Oates' heroic end.

We recovered all their gear and dug out the sledge with their belongings on it. Amongst these were 35 lbs of very important geological specimens which had been collected on the moraines of the Beardmore Glacier; at Doctor Wilson's request they had stuck to these up to the very end, even when disaster stared them in the face and they knew that the specimens were so much weight added to what they had to pull.

When everything had been gathered up, we covered them with the outer tent and read the Burial Service. From this time until well into the next day we started to build a mighty cairn above them. This cairn was finished the next morning, and upon it a rough cross was placed, made from the greater portion of two skis, and on either side were up-ended two sledges, and they were fixed firmly in the snow, to be an added mark. Between the eastern sledge and the cairn a bamboo was placed, containing a metal cylinder, and in this the following record was left: –

12 November 1912, lat. 79 degrees, 50 mins. South. This cross and cairn are erected over the bodies of Captain Scott, C.V.O., R.N., Doctor E.A. Wilson, M.B., B.C. Cantab., and Lieutenant H. R. Bowers, Royal Indian Marine – a slight token to perpetuate their successful and gallant attempt to reach the Pole. This they did on 17 January 1912, after the Norwegian Expedition had already done so. Inclement weather with lack of fuel as the cause of their death. Also to commemorate their two gallant comrades, Captain L. E. G. Oates of the Inniskilling Dragoons, who walked to his death in a blizzard to save his comrades about eighteen miles south of this position; also of Seaman Edgar Evans, who died at the foot of the Beardmore Glacier. "The Lord gave and the Lord taketh away; blessed be the name of the Lord."

This was signed by all the members of the party. I decided then to march twenty miles south with the whole of the Expedition and try to find the body of Captain Oates.

For half that day we proceeded south, as far as possible along the line of the previous season's march. On one of the old pony walls, which was simply marked by a ridge of the surface of the snow, we found Oates' sleeping-bag, which they had brought along with them after he had left.

The next day we proceeded thirteen more miles south, hoping and searching to find his body. When we arrived at the place where he had left them, we saw that there was no chance of doing so. The kindly snow had covered his body, giving him a fitting burial. Here, again, as near to the site of the death as we could judge, we built another cairn to his memory, and placed thereon a small cross and the following record:

Hereabouts died a very gallant gentleman, Captain L. E. G. Oates of the Inniskilling Dragoons. In March 1912, returning from the Pole, he walked willingly to his death in a blizzard, to try and save his comrades, beset by hardships. This note is left by the Relief Expedition of 1912.

It was signed by Cherry-Garrard and myself.

On the second day we came again to the resting-place of the three and bade them a final farewell. There alone in their greatness they will lie without change or bodily decay, with the most fitting tomb in the world above them.

Atkinson, Cherry-Garrard and the search party then turned away, but the gaze of the world has found it hard to leave the tragic scenes of Scott's last journey. Some see the responsible frailties of Scott's leadership, some seek the epitome of human bravery.

Both, perhaps, lie there in the snow and ice, eleven miles from One Ton Depot.

Last Man Walking

Douglas Mawson

A British-Australian geologist, Mawson was introduced to Antarctica by Shackleton's "Farthest South" expedition of 1907–9, during which he co-discovered the South Magnetic Pole. Two years later, Mawson was appointed to the great white road again, this time as leader of the Australasian Antarctic Expedition. Mawson entitled his memoirs of the expedition Home of the Blizzard *on account of the 300-kilometre-an-hour winds which blew in the base camp region. In November 1912 Mawson, accompanied by Dr Xavier Mertz, a Swiss mountaineer, and Lieutenant B.E.S. Ninnis set out to explore George V Land:*

14 December 1912

When next I looked back, it was in response to the anxious gaze of Mertz who had turned round and halted in his tracks. Behind me nothing met the eye except my own sledge tracks running back in the distance. Where were Ninnis and his sledge?

I hastened back along the trail thinking that a rise in the ground obscured the view. There was no such good fortune, however, for I came to a gaping hole in the surface about eleven feet wide. The lid of the crevasse that had caused me so little thought had broken in; two sledge tracks led up to it on the far side – only one continued beyond.

Frantically waving to Mertz to bring up my sledge, upon which there was some alpine rope, I leaned over and shouted into the dark depths below. No sound came back but the moaning of a dog, caught on a shelf just visible 150 feet below. The poor creature appeared to have a broken back, for it was attempting to sit up with the front part of its body, while the hinder portion lay limp. Another dog lay motionless by its side. Close by was what appeared in the gloom to be the remains of the tent and a canvas foodtank containing a fortnight's supply.

We broke back the edge of the hard snow lid and, secured by a rope, took turns leaning over, calling into the darkness in the hope that our companion might be still alive. For three hours we called unceasingly but no answering sound came back. The dog had ceased to moan and lay without a movement. A chill draught rose out of the abyss. We felt that there was no hope.

It was difficult to realize that Ninnis, who was a young giant in build, so jovial and so real but a few minutes before, should thus have vanished without even a sound. It seemed so incredible that we half expected, on turning round, to find him standing there.

Why had the first sledge escaped? It seemed that I had been fortunate, as my sledge had crossed diagonally, with a greater chance of breaking the lid. The sledges were within thirty pounds of the same weight. The explanation appeared to be that Ninnis had walked by the side of his sledge, whereas I had crossed it sitting on the sledge. The whole weight of a man's body bearing on his foot is a formidable load, and no doubt was sufficient to smash the arch of the roof.

By means of a fishing line we ascertained that it was 150 feet sheer to the ledge upon which the remains were seen; on either side the crevasse descended into blackness. It seemed so very far down there and the dogs looked so small that we got out the field-glass to complete the scrutiny of the depths.

All our available rope was tied together but the total length was insufficient to reach the ledge, and any idea of going below to investigate and to secure some of the food had to be abandoned.

Later in the afternoon Mertz and I went on to a higher point in order to obtain a better view of our surroundings and to see if anything helpful lay ahead. In that direction, however, the prospect of reaching the sea, where lay chances of obtaining seal and penguin meat, was hopeless on account of the appalling manner in which the coastal slopes were shattered. At a point 2,400 feet above sea-level and $315\frac{3}{4}$ miles eastward from the Hut, a complete set of observations was taken.

We returned to the crevasse to consider what was to be done and prepare for the future. At regular intervals we called down into those dark depths in case our companion might not have been killed outright, and, in the meantime, have become unconscious. There was no reply.

A weight was lowered on the fishing line as far as the dog which had earlier shown some signs of life, but there was no response. All were dead, swallowed up in an instant . . .

At 9 p.m. we stood by the side of the crevasse and I read the burial service. Then Mertz shook me by the hand with a short "Thank you!" and we turned away to harness up the dogs . . .

The night of 6 January [1913] was long and wearisome as I tossed about sleeplessly, mindful that for both of us our chances of reaching succour were now slipping silently and relentlessly away. I was aching to get on, but there could be no question of abandoning my companion whose condition now set the pace.

The morning of 7 January opened with better weather, for there was little wind and no snow falling; even the sun appeared gleaming through the clouds.

In view of the seriousness of the position it had been agreed overnight that at all costs we would go on in the morning, sledgesailing with Mertz in his bag strapped on the sledge. It was therefore a doubly sad blow that morning to find that my companion was again touched with dysentery and so weak as to be quite helpless. After tucking him into the bag again, I slid into my own in order to kill time and keep warm, for the cold had a new sting about it in those days of want.

At 10 a.m. hearing a rustle from my companion's bag I rose to find him in a fit. Shortly afterwards he became normal and exchanged a few words, but did not appear to realize that anything out of the way had happened.

The information that this incident conveyed fell upon me like a thunderbolt, for it was certain that my companion was in a very serious state with little hope of any alleviation, for he was already unable to assimilate the meagre foods available.

There was no prospect of proceeding so I settled myself to stand by my stricken comrade and ease his sufferings as far as possible. It would require a miracle to bring him round to a fit travelling condition, but I prayed that it might be granted.

After noon he improved and drank some thick cocoa and soup.

Later in the afternoon he had several more fits and then, becoming delirious, talked incoherently until midnight. Most of that time his strength returned and he struggled to climb out of the sleeping-bag, keeping me very busy tucking him in again. About midnight he appeared to doze off to sleep and with a feeling of relief I slid down into my own bag, not to sleep, though weary enough, but to get warm again and to think matters over. After a couple of hours, having felt no movement, I stretched out my arm and found that my comrade was stiff in death. He had been accepted into "the peace that passeth all understanding".

It was unutterably sad that he should have perished thus, after the splendid work he had accomplished not only on that particular sledging journey but throughout the expedition. No one could have done better. Favoured with a generous and lovable character, he had been a general favourite amongst all the members of the expedition. Now all was over, he had done his duty and passed on. All that remained was his mortal frame which, toggled up in his sleeping-bag, still offered some sense of companionship as I threw myself down for the remainder of the night, revolving in my mind all that lay behind and the chances of the future.

Outside the bowl of chaos was brimming with drift-snow and as I lay in the sleeping-bag beside my dead companion I wondered how, in such conditions, I would manage to break and pitch camp single-handed. There appeared to be little hope of reaching the Hut, still 100 miles away. It was easy to sleep in the bag, and the weather was cruel outside. But inaction is hard to bear and I braced myself together determined to put up a good fight.

Failing to reach the Hut it would be something done if I managed to get to some prominent point likely to catch the eye of a search-party, where a cairn might be erected and our diaries cached. So I commenced to modify the sledge and camping gear to meet fresh requirements.

The sky remained clouded, but the wind fell off to a calm which lasted several hours. I took the opportunity to set to work on the sledge, sawing it in halves with a pocket tool and discarding the rear section. A mast was made out of one of the rails no longer required, and a spar was cut from the other. Finally, the load was cut down to a minimum by the elimination of all but the barest necessities, the abandoned articles including, sad to relate, all that remained of the exposed photographic films.

Late that evening, the 8th, I took the body of Mertz, still toggled up in his bag, outside the tent, piled snow blocks around it and raised a rough cross made of the two discarded halves of the sledge runners.

On 9 January the weather was overcast and fairly thick drift was flying in a gale of wind, reaching about fifty miles an hour. As certain matters still required attention and my chances of re-erecting the tent were rather doubtful . . . the start was delayed.

Part of the time that day was occupied with cutting up a waterproof clothes-bag and Mertz's burberry jacket and sewing them together to form a sail. Before retiring to rest in the evening I read through the burial service and put the finishing touches on the grave.

10 January arrived in a turmoil of wind and thick drift. The start was still further delayed. I spent part of the time in reckoning up the food remaining and in cooking the rest of the dog meat, this latter operation serving the good object of lightening the load, in that the kerosene for the purpose was consumed there and then and had not to be dragged forward for subsequent use. Late in the afternoon the wind fell and the sun peered amongst the clouds just as I was in the middle of a long job riveting and lashing the broken shovel.

The next day, 11 January, a beautiful, calm day of sunshine, I set out over a good surface with a slight down grade.

From the start my feet felt curiously lumpy and sore. They had become so painful after a mile of walking that I decided to examine them on the spot, sitting in the lee of the sledge in brilliant sunshine. I had not had my socks off for some days for, while lying in camp, it had not seemed necessary. On taking off the third and inner pair of socks the sight of my feet gave me quite a shock, for the thickened skin of the soles had separated in each case as a complete layer, and abundant watery fluid had escaped, saturating the sock. The new skin beneath was very much abraded and raw. Several of my toes had commenced to blacken and fester near the tips and the nails were puffed and loose.

I began to wonder if there was ever to be a day without some special disappointment. However, there was nothing to be done but make the best of it. I smeared the new skin and the raw surfaces with lanoline, of which there was fortunately a good store, and then with the aid of bandages bound the old skin casts back in place, for these were comfortable and soft in contact with the abraded surface. Over the bandages were slipped six pairs of thick woollen socks, then fur boots and finally crampon over-shoes. The latter, having large stiff soles, spread the weight nicely and saved my feet from the jagged ice encountered shortly afterwards.

So glorious was it to feel the sun on one's skin after being without it for so long that I next removed most of my clothing and bathed my body in the rays until my flesh fairly tingled – a wonderful sensation which spread throughout my whole person, and made me feel stronger and happier . . .

[17 January] A start was made at 8 a.m. and the pulling proved more easy than on the previous day. Some two miles had been negotiated in safety when an event occurred which, but for a miracle, would have terminated the story then and there. Never have I come so near to an end; never has anyone more miracu-lously escaped.

I was hauling the sledge through deep snow up a fairly steep sloop when my feet broke through into a crevasse. Fortunately as I fell I caught my weight with my arms on the edge and did not plunge in further than the thighs. The outline of the crevasse did not show through the blanket of snow on the surface, but an idea of the trend was obtained with a stick. I decided to try a crossing about fifty yards further along, hoping that there it would be better bridged. Alas! it took an unexpected turn catching me unawares. This time I shot through the centre of the bridge in a flash, but the latter part of the fall was decelerated by the friction of the harness ropes which, as the sledge ran up, sawed back into the thick compact snow forming the margin of the lid. Having seen my comrades perish in diverse ways and having lost hope of ever reaching the Hut, I had already many times speculated on what the end would be like. So it happened that as I fell through into the crevasse the thought "so this is the end" blazed up in my mind, for it was to be expected that the next moment the sledge would follow through, crash on my head and all go to the unseen bottom. But the unexpected happened and the sledge held, the deep snow acting as a brake.

In the moment that elapsed before the rope ceased to descend, delaying the issue, a great regret swept through my mind, namely, that after having stinted myself so assiduously in order to save food, I should pass on now to eternity without the satisfaction of what remained – to such an extent does food take possession of one under such circumstances. Realizing that the sledge was holding I began to look around. The crevasse was somewhat over six feet wide and sheer-walled, descending into blue depths below. My clothes, which, with a view to ventilation, had been but loosely secured, were now stuffed with snow broken from the roof, and very chilly it was. Above at the other end of the fourteen-foot rope, was the daylight seen through the hole in the lid.

In my weak condition, the prospect of climbing out seemed very poor indeed, but in a few moments the struggle was begun. A great effort brought a knot in the rope within my grasp, and, after a moment's rest, I was able to draw myself up and reach another, and, at length, hauled my body on to the overhanging snow-lid. Then, when all appeared to be well and before I could get to quite solid ground, a further section of the lid gave way, precipitating me once more to the full length of the rope.

There, exhausted, weak and chilled, hanging freely in space and slowly turning round as the rope twisted one way and the other, I felt that I had done my utmost and failed, that I had no more strength to try again and that all was over except the passing. It was to be a miserable and slow end and I reflected with disappointment that there was in my pocket no antidote to speed matters; but there always remained the alternative of slipping from the harness. There on the brink of the great Beyond I well remember how I looked forward to the peace of the great release – how almost excited I was at the prospect of the unknown to be unveiled. From those flights of mind I came back to earth, and remembering how Providence had miraculously brought me so far, felt that nothing was impossible and determined to act up to Service's lines:

Just have one more try – it's dead easy to die,
    It's the keeping-on-living that's hard.

My strength was fast ebbing; in a few minutes it would be too late. It was the occasion for a supreme attempt. Fired by the passion that burns the blood in the act of strife, new power seemed to come as I applied myself to one last tremendous effort. The struggle occupied some time, but I slowly worked upward to the surface. This time emerging feet first, still clinging to the rope, I pushed myself out extended at full length on the lid and then shuffled safely on to the solid ground at the side. Then came the reaction from the great nerve strain and lying there alongside the sledge my mind faded into a blank.

When consciousness returned it was a full hour or two later, for I was partly covered with newly fallen snow and numb with the cold. I took at least three hours to erect the tent, get things snugly inside and clear the snow from my clothes. Between each movement, almost, I had to rest. Then reclining in luxury in the sleeping-bag I ate a little food and thought matters over. It was a time when the mood of the Persian philosopher appealed to me:

Unborn Tomorrow and dead Yesterday,
Why fret about them if Today be sweet?

I was confronted with this problem: whether it was better to enjoy life for a few days, sleeping and eating my fill until the provisions gave out, or to "plug on" again in hunger with the prospect of plunging at any moment into eternity without the supreme satisfaction and pleasure of the food. While thus cogitating an idea presented itself which greatly improved the prospects and clinched the decision to go ahead. It was to construct a ladder from a length of alpine rope that remained; one end was to be secured to the bow of the sledge and the other carried over my left shoulder and loosely attached to the sledge harness. Thus if I fell into a crevasse again, provided the sledge was not also engulfed, it would be easy for me, even though weakened by starvation, to scramble out by the ladder.

Notwithstanding the possibilities of the rope-ladder, I could not sleep properly, for my nerves had been overtaxed. All night long considerable wind and drift continued.

On the 19th it was overcast and light snow falling; very dispiriting conditions after the experience of the day before, but I resolved to go ahead and leave the rest to Providence . . .

[29 January] I was travelling along on an even down grade and was wondering how long the two pounds of food which remained would last, when something dark loomed through the haze of the drift a short distance away to the right. All sorts of possibilities raced through my mind as I headed the sledge for it. The unexpected had happened – in thick weather I had run fairly into a cairn of snow blocks erected by McLean, Hodgeman and Hurley, who had been out searching for my party. On the top of the mound, outlined in black bunting, was a bag of food, left on the chance that it might be picked up by us. In a tin was a note stating the bearing and distance of the mound from Aladdin's Cave (E. 30° S., distance 23 miles), and mentioning that the ship had arrived at the Hut and was waiting, and had brought the news that Amundsen had reached the Pole, and that Scott was remaining another year in Antarctica.

It certainly was remarkably good fortune that I had come upon the depot of food; a few hundred yards to either side and it would have been lost to sight in the drift. On reading the note carefully I found that I had just missed by six hours what would have been crowning good luck, for it appeared that the search party had left the mound at 8 a.m. that very day . . . It was about 2 p.m. when I reached it. Thus, during the night of the 28th our camps had been only some five miles apart.

Hauling down the bag of food I tore it open in the lee of the cairn and in my greed scattered the contents about on the ground. Having partaken heartily of frozen pemmican, I stuffed my pocket, bundled the rest into a bag on the sledge and started off in high glee, stimulated in body and mind. As I left the depot there appeared to be nothing on earth that could prevent me reaching the Hut within a couple of days, but a fresh obstacle with which I had not reckoned was to arise and cause further delay, leading to far-reaching results.

It happened that after several hours' march the surface changed from snow to polished névé and then to slippery ice. I could scarcely keep on my feet at all, falling every few moments and bruising my emaciated self until I expected to see my bones burst through the clothes. How I regretted having abandoned those crampons after crossing the Mertz Glacier; shod with them, all would be easy.

With nothing but finnesko on the feet, to walk over such a sloping surface would have been difficult enough in the wind without any other hindrance; with the sledge sidling down the slope and tugging at one, it was quite impossible. I found that I had made too far to the east and to reach Aladdin's Cave had unfortunately to strike across the wind.

Before giving up, I even tried crawling on my hands and knees.

However, the day's run, fourteen miles, was by no means a poor one.

Having erected the tent I set to work to improvise crampons. With this object in view the theodolite case was cut up, providing two flat pieces of wood into which were stuck as many screws and nails as could be procured by dismantling the sledgemeter and the theodolite itself. In the repair-bag there were still a few ice-nails which at this time were of great use.

Late the next day, the wind which had risen in the night fell off and a start was made westwards over the ice slopes with the pieces of nail-studded wood lashed to my feet. A glorious expanse of sea lay to the north and several recognizable points on the coast were clearly in view to east and west.

The crampons were not a complete success for they gradually broke up, lasting only a distance of six miles . . .

A blizzard was in full career on 31 January and I spent all day and most of the night on the crampons. On 1 February the wind and drift had subsided late in the afternoon, and I got under way expecting great things from the new crampons. The beacon marking Aladdin's Cave was clearly visible as a black dot on the ice slopes to the west.

At 7 p.m. that haven within the ice was attained. It took but a few moments to dig away the snow and throw back the canvas flap sealing the entrance. A moment later I slid down inside, arriving amidst familiar surroundings. Something unusual in one

corner caught the eye – three oranges and a pineapple – circum-
stantial evidence of the arrival of the *Aurora*.

The improvised crampons had given way and were squeezing
my feet painfully. I rummaged about amongst a pile of food-bags,
hoping to find some crampons or leather boots, but was disappointed, so there was nothing left but to repair the damaged
ones. That done and a drink of hot milk having been prepared, I
packed up to make a start for the Hut. On climbing out of the cave
imagine my disappointment at finding a strong wind and drift
had risen. To have attempted the descent of the five and a half
miles of steep ice slope to the Hut with such inadequate and
fragile crampons, weak as I still was, would have been only as a
last resort. So I camped in the comfortable cave and hoped for
better weather next day.

But the blizzard droned on night and day for over a week with
never a break. Think of my feelings as I sat within the cave, so
near and yet so far from the Hut, impatient and anxious, ready to
spring out and take the trail at a moment's notice. Improvements
to the crampons kept me busy for a time; then, as there was a
couple of old boxes lying about, I set to work and constructed a
second emergency pair in case the others should break up during
the descent. I tried the makeshift crampons on the ice outside,
but was disappointed to find that they had not sufficient grip to
face the wind, so had to abandon the idea of attempting the
descent during the continuance of the blizzard. Nevertheless, by
8 February my anxiety as to what was happening at the Hut
reached such a pitch that I resolved to try the passage in spite of
everything, having worked out a plan whereby I was to sit on the
sledge and sail down as far as possible.

Whilst these preparations were in progress the wind slackened.
At last the longed-for event was to be realized. I snatched a hasty
meal and set off. Before a couple of miles had been covered the
wind had fallen off altogether, and after that it was gloriously
calm and clear.

I had reached within one and a half miles of the Hut and there
was no sign of the *Aurora* lying in the offing. I was comforted
with the thought that she might still be at the anchorage and have
swung inshore so as to be hidden under the ice cliffs. But even as I
gazed about seeking for a clue, a speck on the north-west horizon

caught my eye and my hopes went down. It looked like a distant ship – Was it the *Aurora*? Well, what matter! the long journey was at an end – a terrible chapter of my life was concluded!

Then the rocks around winter quarters began to come into view; part of the basin of the Boat Harbour appeared, and lo! there were human figures! They almost seemed unreal – was it all a dream? No, indeed, for after a brief moment one of them observed me and waved an arm – I replied – there was a commotion and they all ran towards the Hut. Then they were lost, hidden by the crest of the first steep slope. It almost seemed to me that they had run away to hide.

Minutes passed as I slowly descended trailing the sledge. Then a head rose over the brow of the hill and there was Bickerton, breathless after a long run uphill. I expect for a while he wondered which of us it was. Soon we had shaken hands and he knew all in a few brief words, I for my part learning that the ship had left earlier that very day.

On his eventual return home Mawson was given a knighthood. In addition to its discovery of George V Land, Mawson's expedition had found Queen Mary Land and garnered a huge amount of scientific data. Of the "Heroic Age" missions South, the Australasian Antarctic Expedition was to be counted amongst the most successful.

The Loss of the *Endurance*

Ernest Shackleton

*After failing to reach the Pole in 1908, Shackleton returned South in
1914; his intention, now that the Pole had been achieved by both
Amundsen and Scott, was to cross the entire mass of Antarctica.
Things went wrong from the start. The expedition's ship, the*
Endurance, *was frozen firm in the Weddell Sea:*

The pressure-ridges, massive and threatening, testified to the
overwhelming nature of the forces that were at work. Huge blocks
of ice, weighing many tons, were lifted into the air and tossed
aside as other masses rose beneath them. We were helpless
intruders in a strange world, our lives dependent upon the play
of grim elementary forces that made a mock of our puny efforts. I
scarcely dared hope now that the *Endurance* would live, and
throughout that anxious day I reviewed again the plans made
long before for the sledging journey that we must make in the
event of our having to take to the ice. We were ready, as far as
forethought could make us, for every contingency. Stores, dogs,
sledges, and equipment were ready to be moved from the ship at a
moment's notice.

The following day brought bright clear weather, with a blue
sky. The sunshine was inspiriting. The roar of pressure could be
heard all around us. New ridges were rising, and I could see as the
day wore on that the lines of major disturbance were drawing
nearer to the ship. The *Endurance* suffered some strains at
intervals. Listening below, I could hear the creaking and groaning of her timbers, the pistol-like cracks that told of the starting of
a trenail or plank, and the faint, indefinable whispers of our ship's
distress. Overhead the sun shone serenely; occasional fleecy
clouds drifted before the southerly breeze, and the light glinted

and sparkled on the million facets of the new pressure-ridges. The day passed slowly. At 7 p.m. very heavy pressure developed, with twisting strains that racked the ship fore and aft. The butts of planking were opened four and five inches on the starboard side, and at the same time we could see from the bridge that the ship was bending like a bow under titanic pressure. Almost like a living creature, she resisted the forces that would crush her; but it was a one-sided battle. Millions of tons of ice pressed inexorably upon the little ship that had dared the challenge of the Antarctic. The *Endurance* was now leaking badly, and at 9 p.m. I gave the order to lower boats, gear, provisions, and sledges to the floe, and move them to the flat ice a little way from the ship. The working of the ice closed he leaks slightly at midnight, but all hands were pumping all night. A strange occurrence was the sudden appearance of eight emperor penguins from a crack 100 yds away at the moment when the pressure upon the ship was at its climax. They walked a little way towards us, halted, and after a few ordinary calls proceeded to utter weird cries that sounded like a dirge for the ship. None of us had ever before heard the emperors utter any other than the most simple calls or cries, and the effect of this concerted effort was almost startling.

Then came a fateful day – Wednesday, October 27 [1915]. The position was lat. 69° 5′ S., long. 51° 30′ W. The temperature was – 8.5° Fahr., a gentle southerly breeze was blowing and the sun shone in a clear sky.

*After long months of ceaseless anxiety and strain, after times when hope beat high and times when the outlook was black indeed, the end of the *Endurance* has come. But though we have been compelled to abandon the ship, which is crushed beyond all hope of ever being righted, we are alive and well, and we have stores and equipment for the task that lies before us. The task is to reach land with all the members of the Expedition. It is hard to write what I feel. To a sailor his ship is more than a floating home, and in the *Endurance* I had centred ambitions, hopes, and desires. Now, straining and groaning, her timbers cracking and her wounds gaping, she is slowly giving up her sentient life at the very outset of her career. She is crushed and abandoned after

* From the diary.

drifting more than 570 miles in a north-westerly direction during the 281 days since she became locked in the ice. The distance from the point where she became beset to the place where she now rests mortally hurt in the grip of the floes is 573 miles, but the total drift through all observed positions has been 1186 miles, and probably we actually covered more than 1500 miles. We are now 346 miles from Paulet Island, the nearest point where there is any possibility of finding food and shelter. A small hut built there by the Swedish expedition in 1902 is filled with stores left by the Argentine relief ship. I know all about those stores, for I purchased them in London on behalf of the Argentine Government when they asked me to equip the relief expedition. The distance to the nearest barrier west of us is about 180 miles, but a party going there would still be about 360 miles from Paulet Island and there would be no means of sustaining life on the barrier. We could not take from here food enough for the whole journey; the weight would be too great.

This morning, our last on the ship, the weather was clear, with a gentle south-south-easterly to south-south-westerly breeze. From the crow's-nest there was no sign of land of any sort. The pressure was increasing steadily, and the passing hours brought no relief or respite for the ship. The attack of the ice reached its climax at 4 p.m. The ship was hove stern up by the pressure, and the driving floe, moving laterally across the stern, split the rudder and tore out the rudder-post and stern-post. Then, while we watched, the ice loosened and the *Endurance* sank a little. The decks were breaking upwards and the water was pouring in below. Again the pressure began, and at 5 p.m. I ordered all hands on to the ice. The twisting, grinding floes were working their will at last on the ship. It was a sickening sensation to feel the decks breaking up under one's feet, the great beams bending and then snapping with a noise like heavy gun-fire. The water was overmastering the pumps, and to avoid an explosion when it reached the boilers I had to give orders for the fires to be drawn and the steam let down. The plans for abandoning the ship in case of emergency had been made well in advance, and men and dogs descended to the floe and made their way to the comparative safety of an unbroken portion of the floe without a hitch. Just before leaving, I looked down the engine-room skylight as I stood on the quivering deck, and saw the engines dropping sideways as the stays and bed-plates gave way. I cannot describe the impression of relentless destruction that was forced upon me as I looked down and around. The floes, with the force of millions of tons of moving ice behind them, were simply annihilating the ship . . .

Tonight the temperature has dropped to −16°Fahr., and most of the men are cold and uncomfortable. After the tents had been pitched I mustered all hands and explained the position to them briefly and, I hope, clearly. I have told them the distance to the Barrier and the distance to Paulet Island, and have stated that I propose to try to march with equipment across the ice in the direction of Paulet Island. I thanked the men for the steadiness and good *moral* they have shown in these trying circumstances, and told them I had no doubt that, provided they continued to work their utmost and to trust me, we will all reach safety in the end. Then we had supper, which the cook had prepared at the big blubber stove, and after a watch had been set all hands except the watch turned in.

For myself, I could not sleep. The destruction and abandonment of the ship was no sudden shock. The disaster had been looming ahead for many months, and I had studied my plans for all contingencies a hundred times. But the thoughts that came to me as I walked up and down in the darkness were not particularly cheerful. The task now was to secure the safety of the party, and to that I must bend my energies and mental power and apply every bit of knowledge that experience of the Antarctic had given me. The task was likely to be long and strenuous, and an ordered mind and a clear programme were essential if we were to come through without loss of life. A man must shape himself to a new mark directly the old one goes to ground.

At midnight I was pacing the ice, listening to the grinding floe and to the groans and crashes that told of the death-agony of the *Endurance*, when I noticed suddenly a crack running across our floe right through the camp. The alarm-whistle brought all hands tumbling out, and we moved the tents and stores lying on what was now the smaller portion of the floe to the larger portion. Nothing more could be done at that moment, and the men turned in again; but there was little sleep. Each time I came to the end of my beat on the floe I could just see in the darkness the uprearing piles of pressure-ice, which toppled over and narrowed still further the little floating island we occupied. I did not notice at the time that my tent, which had been on the wrong side of the crack, had not been erected again. Hudson and James had managed to squeeze themselves into other tents, and Hurley had wrapped himself in the canvas of No. 1 tent. I discovered this about 5 a.m. All night long the electric light gleamed from the stern of the dying *Endurance*. Hussey had left this light switched on when he took a last observation, and, like a lamp in a cottage window, it braved the night until in the early morning the *Endurance* received a particularly violent squeeze. There was a sound of rending beams and the light disappeared. The connexion had been cut.

Morning came in chill and cheerless. All hands were stiff and weary after their first disturbed night on the floe. Just at daybreak I went over to the *Endurance* with Wild and Hurley, in order to retrieve some tins of petrol that could be used to boil up milk for the rest of the men. The ship presented a painful spectacle of chaos and wreck. The jib-boom and bowsprit had snapped off during the night and now lay at right angles to the ship, with the chains, martingale, and bobstay dragging them as the vessel quivered and moved in the grinding pack. The ice had driven over the forecastle and she was well down by the head. We secured two tins of petrol with some difficulty, and postponed the further examination of the ship until after breakfast. Jumping across cracks with the tins, we soon reached camp, and built a fireplace out of the triangular watertight tanks we had ripped from the lifeboat. This we had done in order to make more room. Then we pierced a petrol-tin in half a dozen places with an ice-axe and set fire to it. The petrol blazed fiercely under the five-gallon drum we used as a cooker, and the hot milk was ready in quick time. Then we three ministering angels went round the tents with the life-giving drink, and were surprised and a trifle chagrined at the matter-of-fact manner in which some of the men accepted this contribution to their comfort. They did not quite understand what work we had done for them in the early dawn, and I heard Wild say, "If any of you gentlemen would like your boots cleaned just put them outside!" This was his gentle way of reminding them that a little thanks will go a long way on such occasions.

The cook prepared breakfast, which consisted of biscuit and hoosh, at 8 a.m., and I then went over to the *Endurance* again and made a fuller examination of the wreck. Only six of the cabins had not been pierced by floes and blocks of ice. Every one of the starboard cabins had been crushed. The whole of the after part of the ship had been crushed concertina fashion. The forecastle and the Ritz were submerged, and the wardroom was three-quarters full of ice. The starboard side of the wardroom had come away. The motor-engine forward had been driven through the galley. Petrol-cases that had been stacked on the fore-deck had been driven by the floe through the wall into the wardroom and had carried before them a large picture. Curiously enough, the glass of this picture had not been cracked, whereas in the immediate neighbourhood I saw heavy iron davits that had been twisted and bent like the ironwork of a wrecked train. The ship was being crushed remorselessly.

Under a dull, overcast sky I returned to camp and examined our situation. The floe occupied by the camp was still subject to pressure, and I thought it wise to move to a larger and apparently stronger floe about 200 yds away, off the starboard bow of the ship. This camp was to become known as Dump Camp, owing to the amount of stuff that was thrown away there. We could not afford to carry unnecessary gear, and a drastic sorting of equipment took place. I decided to issue a complete new set of Burberrys and underclothing to each man, and also a supply of new socks. The camp was transferred to the larger floe quickly, and I began there to direct the preparations for the long journey across the floes to Paulet Island or Snow Hill.

Hurley meanwhile had rigged his kinematograph-camera and was getting pictures of the *Endurance* in her death-throes. While he was engaged thus, the ice, driving against the standing rigging and the fore-, main- and mizzen-masts, snapped the shrouds. The foretop and topgallant-mast came down with a run and hung in wreckage on the fore-mast with the foreyard vertical. The mainmast followed immediately, snapping off about 10 ft above the main deck. The crow's-nest fell within 10 ft of where Hurley stood turning the handle of his camera, but he did not stop the machine, and so secured a unique, though sad, picture.

The issue of clothing was quickly accomplished. Sleeping-bags were required also. We had eighteen fur bags, and it was necessary, therefore, to issue ten of the Jaeger woollen bags in order to provide for the twenty-eight men of the party. The woollen bags were lighter and less warm than the reindeer bags, and so each man who received one of them was allowed also a reindeer-skin to lie upon. It seemed fair to distribute the fur bags by lot, but some of us older hands did not join in the lottery. We thought we could do quite as well with the Jaegers as with the furs. With quick dispatch the clothing was apportioned, and then we turned one of the boats on its side and supported it with two broken oars to make a lee for the galley. The cook got the blubber-stove going, and a little later, when I was sitting round the corner of the stove, I heard one man say, "Cook, I like my tea strong." Another joined in, "Cook, I like mine weak." It was pleasant to know that their minds were untroubled, but I thought the time opportune to mention that the tea would be the same for all hands and that we would be fortunate if two months later we had any tea at all. It occurred to me at the time that the incident had psychological interest. Here were men, their home crushed, the camp pitched on the unstable floes, and their chance of reaching safety apparently remote, calmly attending to the details of existence and giving their attention to such trifles as the strength of a brew of tea.

During the afternoon the work continued. Every now and then we heard a noise like heavy guns or distant thunder, caused by the floes grinding together. The pressure caused by the congestion in this area of the pack is producing a scene of absolute chaos. The floes grind stupendously, throw up great ridges, and shatter one another mercilessly. The ridges, or hedge-rows, marking the pressure-lines that border the fast-diminishing pieces of smooth floe-ice, are enormous. The ice moves majestically, irresistibly. Human effort is not futile, but man fights against the giant forces of Nature in a spirit of humility. One has a sense of dependence on the Higher Power. Today two seals, a Weddell and a crab-eater, came close to the camp and were shot. Four others were chased back into the water, for their presence disturbed the dog teams, and this meant floggings and trouble with the harness. The arrangement of the tents has been completed and their internal management settled. Each tent has a mess orderly, the duty being taken in turn on an alphabetical rota. The orderly takes the hoosh-pots of his tent to the galley, gets all the hoosh he is allowed, and, after the meal, cleans the vessels with snow and stores them in sledge or boat ready for a possible move.

29 October

We passed a quiet night, although the pressure was grinding around us. Our floe is a heavy one and it withstood the blows it received. . . . The ship is still afloat, with the spurs of the pack driven through her and holding her up. The forecastle-head is under water, the decks are burst up by the pressure, the wreckage lies around in dismal confusion, but over all the blue ensign flies still.

The Boat Journey

F. A. Worsley

After the sinking of the Endurance *in October 1915 in the Weddell Sea, Shackleton's expedition camped on the ice, which steadily drifted north, shrinking and cracking all the while, until the floe beneath the men measured only 200 feet by 100 feet. At this, the expedition escaped into three lifeboats on 16 April 1916 and made their way to Elephant Island in the South Shetlands. This was not salvation, however, for Elephant Island was barren and uninhabited. Relief would have to be secured from further across the sea; it was determined that six men – Shackleton himself, Crean, McNeish, Vincent, McCarthy and the* Endurance's *captain – would sail to South Georgia, 800 miles away across the most savage sea in the world, in the 22-feet-long lifeboat, the* James Caird:

After noon the gale and sea increased, with intense cold. We rolled the sails up and stowed them below in the already confined space, to prevent them freezing, holding a mass of ice and capsizing the boat with top weight. The seas breaking on the boat froze and cased her heavily with ice, but we should have been worse off without the sea anchor.

To keep a boat afloat in very heavy weather, two things are almost necessities – oil to mollify the seas, and a sea anchor to ride to. Of oil we had ample for one day's gale – we had ten days' gales on this passage. A sea anchor consists of a canvas cone or bag, three to four feet long, the mouth nearly as wide and a small hole at the other end. Four small lines at the mouth are spliced into a "thimble", to which the rope is attached. When a gale is so heavy that a boat cannot run before it, she takes in sail and heaves to by throwing the sea-anchor over, with one end of the rope passed through the thimble, and the other end fast in the bows. Having no other rope, we used the painter. By dragging in the sea – the water escaping through the small hole – the sea anchor holds the boat head to wind and sea, the best position for riding out a gale.

We saw a few penguins in the afternoon, three hundred miles from any land. They were quite indifferent to the gale or the cold; we felt envious of them. By the bitter cold of the gale we reckoned it blew straight off pack ice not far away.

We drank our seal oil, black and odoriferous, as it was not worth keeping for one day of the gale and its calories were so valuable. A matter of latitude – what would have made us ill in the tropics was nectar here!

The ice increased on the boat till we had to excavate the four oars from a mound of it. They caught so much freezing water that we were forced to throw two overboard, and lash the others one on each side, for a railing from the mainshrouds to the mizen-mast, eighteen inches above the "deck." They held very little ice then, and there was less danger of falling overboard. This was a serious sacrifice, but we could not get the other two oars below.

All night the breaking seas froze over her. This had one advantage; it stopped intermittent bucketsful pouring through the "deck" and down our necks, but pumping and baling had still to be done at frequent intervals.

The eighth day the gale held steadily throughout from south-southwest, with a very heavy, lumpy sea. It was impossible to write – even a few remarks. These would have been illegible – but anyway unprintable – owing to the violent jerky contortions of the *Caird*. She was heavily iced all over outside, and a quantity of ice had formed inside her.

Sir Ernest had the "Primus" going day and night as long as we could stand the fumes, then it would be put out for an hour. This and a generous drink of life-giving hot milk every four hours, at the relief of the watches, kept all hands from any ill effects.

All gear was wet through. The sleeping bags had a nasty sour-bread kind of smell, and were on the point of fermenting. I believe, in fact, that a certain amount of fermentation had started, and so prevented us feeling the cold quite so much in our sleep, as we called it.

We all smelt as well, or rather as ill, as our bags. We used to long for a hot bath or clean, dry clothes.

May Day. The ice on the boat got so thick and heavy that she was riding deep and had a tendency to capsize. Something had to be done, and quickly, so we took it in turns to crawl out with an axe and chop off the ice. What a job! The boat leaped and kicked like a mad mule; she was covered fifteen inches deep in a casing of ice like a turtleback, with slush all over where the last sea was freezing. First you chopped a handhold, then a kneehold, and then chopped off ice hastily but carefully, with an occasional sea washing over you. After four or five minutes – "fed up" or frostbitten – you slid back into shelter, and the next man took up the work. It was a case of "one hand for yourself, and one for the King," for if a man had gone overboard then, it would have been good-bye. Finally, we got the bulk of it off, and were satisfied. All night the gale continued heavily from south-southwest.

The ninth day. In the forenoon a heavy sea struck the *Caird*. Almost immediately her bows fell off till the sea was abeam. The great cake of ice that had formed on the painter at the bows, in such a position that we could not smash it off, had swung to and fro, round and round, till it had sawed and chafed through the painter. So we lost both rope and sea anchor, which seemed a double disaster to us.

We beat the ice off the jib, reefed and set it on the mainmast.

By 11 a.m. the gale had eased enough for us to set the reefed lug and jib and run drunkenly before the wind and sea.

This fierce, cold gale had lasted at its height for forty-eight hours. During that period we had, no fewer than three times – once practically in the dark – to crawl out on top of the boat to chop and scrape the ice off. We all agreed it was the worst job we had ever taken on in our lives.

I estimated that day's drift at thirty-six miles – sixty-six miles to northeast during the time we were hove to. The boat's antics were almost as bad as before. The dead reckoning figures were made one at a time by jabbing with the pencil as occasion offered. By strict economy I confined their numbers to twenty-five. It was impossible to write – perhaps I should say it was impossible to force oneself to try.

The reindeer bags were now so miserable to get into that when we had finished our watch and it was time to turn in, we had serious doubts as to whether it was worth while. The smell of cured skin constantly soaked and slept in was appalling. First you undressed; that is, you took off your boots, and throwing back the flap of the bag thrust your legs in hurriedly. It felt like getting between frozen rawhide – which it was. You kicked your feet violently together for two minutes to warm them and the bag, then slid in to the waist. Again you kicked your feet and knocked your knees together and then like a little hero made a sudden brave plunge right inside. At first, while you knocked your feet together, it felt like an icehouse, and then it began to thaw out and you wished it hadn't – it smelt so, and the moulting hairs got into eyes, mouth, and nose. So, coughing, sneezing, and spluttering, you kicked your feet valiantly together till there was enough warmth in them to allow you to sleep for perhaps an hour. When you awoke you kicked again till you fell asleep, and so on.

After this gale the bags were in such a hopeless, sloppy, slimy mess, and weighed so heavily, that Sir Ernest had the worst two thrown overboard.

All that day and night we held on our erratic course before the gale.

In steering a small boat before a heavy gale don't look back – it may disconcert you. Fix your eye on a cloud or breaking sea right ahead and keep her straight – if you can. When you hear a roaring Bull of Bashan, with a wet nose, galloping up behind you, keep your shoulders hunched up to your ears – till you get it, then yell, "Pump and balers." There's no need to, for they're hard at it already, but it shows you're alive, all right.

A great find – an inch of candle in the socket of the compass lamp. At night I lit it and, dropping a few spots of grease on the compass glass, stuck it three inches to the right of the centre. Then the procedure was to strike a flaming match once a watch at night for a smoke, and to light this piece of candle for a few minutes. Sheltered by our hands, its flickering light enabled the helmsman to correct the course and check it off by the sea, wind, and fluttering pennant. No need to blow it out, the wind did that, then all was darkness again, except for Tom Crean or Macarty's dully glowing pipe. About this time the compass glass got broken. We mended it with strips of sticking plaster from the medicine chest.

After my "trick" at the helm in the middle watch, when extra cold and wet, I got stiffened in the crouching position I had assumed to dodge the seas, and had to be hauled inside, massaged, and opened out like a jackknife before I could get into my sleeping bag.

A few scribbled remarks in my navigating book ran: "Bags and finneskoe moulting at a great rate – 'feathers' everywhere – most objectionable in hoosh. My finneskoe are now quite bald. We are all suffering from superficially frostbitten feet, Macarty is the most irrepressible optimist I've ever met. When I relieved him at the helm, boat iced over and seas pouring down our necks, one came right over us and I felt like swearing, but just kept it back, and he informed me with a cheerful grin 'It's a foine day, sorr.' I had been feeling a bit sour before, but this shamed me. His cheeriness does brighten things up."

As a rule, when a sea wets a sailor through, he swears at it, and comprehensively and impartially curses everything in sight, beginning with the ship and the "old man" – if he's not within hearing; but on this passage we said nothing when a sea hit us in the face. It was grin and bear it; for it was Sir Ernest's theory that by keeping our tempers and general cheeriness we each helped to keep one another up. We all lived up to this to the best of our ability, but Macarty was a marvel.

After the third day our feet and legs had swelled, and began to be superficially frostbitten from the constant soaking in sea water, with the temperature at times nearly down to zero; and the lack of exercise. During the last gale they assumed a dead-white colour and lost surface feeling.

Our footgear consisted of two pairs of Jaeger wool socks, homemade felt shoes, ankle-high (mine were Greenstreet's handiwork), and, over all, finneskoe (reindeer-skin boots), hair out and skin in, when we started – now it was skin inside and out. When your feet got unbearably cold you took off your footgear and, rinsing your socks in the sea, wiped your feet, wrung out your socks, and again wiped your feet before replacing your footgear. This was the wag's opportunity. While busily engaged with your socks he would prick your toe with a "Primus" pricker. Getting no response he would prick higher and higher up foot and leg, till the victim suddenly jumped, yelled, or swore according to temperament. This was not merely horseplay or idle curiosity – it was also an index as to how one's feet and legs were standing the rigours of the passage.

To prevent my feet getting worse, I adopted a system of wriggling them constantly, contracting and relaxing my toes until quite tired, waiting a minute, then wriggling them again, and so on. I think it saved my feet a good deal.

At midnight Shackleton relieved me. The southwest gale had been steadily increasing with snow squalls for eight hours and there was a heavy cross sea running which caused us to ship more seas over the boat even than usual. Just before he crawled out from under the canvas a sea struck me full in the face and the front as I stood aft steering with the lee yoke line to keep her out of the wind. The water was running out of me as he relieved me at the helm and then another sea dashed over the two of us. "Pretty juicy," he said, and we both forced a laugh. I crawled below and into my sodden sleeping bag. In spite of wet and cold I fell asleep instantly, but soon after something awakened me. Then I heard Shackleton shout "It's clearing, boys!" and immediately after, "For God's sake, hold on! It's got us!" The line of white along the southern horizon that he had taken for the sky clearing was, in fact, the foaming crest of an enormous sea. I was crawling out of my bag as the sea struck us. There was a roaring of water around and above us – it was almost as though we had foundered. The boat seemed full of water. We other five men seized any receptacle we could find and pushed, scooped, and baled the water out for dear life. While Shackleton held her up to the wind, we worked like madmen, but for five minutes it was uncertain whether we would succeed or not.

We could not keep that pace up – gradually we eased off as we realized that we had saved our lives. With the aid of the little homemade pump and two dippers it took us nearly an hour to get rid of the water and restore the boat to her normal state of having only a few gallons of water washing about the bilges through the stones and shingle. The wave that had struck us was so sudden and enormous that I have since come to the conclusion that it may have been caused by the capsizing of some great iceberg unseen and unheard by us in the darkness and the heavy gale.

The tenth day. In the morning the southwest gale moderated and backed to west with great white cumulus clouds racing overhead, and clear weather. "Old Jamaica" showed his face through the clouds and I made the position 56° 13′S and 45°38′W. The run was N55°E sixty-two miles, 444 since leaving Elephant Island. We had done more than half the distance, and had a happy feeling of certainty that we should succeed in our adventure.

Crossing South Georgia

Ernest Shackleton

After Shackleton's boat journey to South Georgia (see pp380ff), his rescue mission was still faced with the challenge of traversing the island to reach the whaling station at Stromness:

A fresh west-southwesterly breeze was blowing on the following morning (Wednesday 17 May), with misty squalls, sleet, and rain. I took Worsley with me on a pioneer journey to the west with the object of examining the country to be traversed at the beginning of the overland journey. We went round the seaward end of the snouted glacier, and after tramping about a mile over stony ground and snow-coated debris, we crossed some big ridges of scree and moraines. We found that there was good going for a sledge as far as the northeast corner of the bay, but did not get much information regarding the conditions farther on owing to the view becoming obscured by a snow squall. We waited a quarter of an hour for the weather to clear but were forced to turn back without having seen more of the country. I had satisfied myself, however, that we could reach a good snow slope leading apparently to the inland ice. Worsley reckoned from the chart that the distance from our camp to Husvik, on an east magnetic course, was seventeen geographical miles, but we could not expect to follow a direct line. The carpenter started making a sledge for use on the overland journey. The materials at his disposal were limited in quantity and scarcely suitable in quality.

We overhauled our gear on Thursday 18 May and hauled our sledge to the lower edge of the snouted glacier. The vehicle proved heavy and cumbrous. We had to lift it empty over bare patches of rock along the shore, and I realized that it would be too heavy for three men to manage amid the snow plains, glaciers, and peaks of the interior. Worsley and Crean were coming with me, and after consultation we decided to leave the sleeping bags behind us and make the journey in very light marching order. We would take three days' provisions for each man in the form of sledging ration and biscuit. The food was to be packed in three sacks, so that each member of the party could carry his own supply. Then we were to take the Primus lamp filled with oil, the small cooker, the carpenter's adze (for use as an ice axe), and the alpine rope, which made a total length of fifty feet when knotted. We might have to lower ourselves down steep slopes or cross crevassed glaciers. The filled lamp would provide six hot meals, which would consist of sledging ration boiled up with biscuit. There were two boxes of matches left, one full and the other partially used. We left the full box with the men at the camp and took the second box, which contained forty-eight matches. I was unfortunate as regarded footgear, since I had given away my heavy Burberry boots on the floe, and had now a comparatively light pair in poor condition. The carpenter assisted me by putting several screws in the sole of each boot with the object of providing a grip on the ice. The screws came out of the *James Caird*.

We turned in early that night, but sleep did not come to me. My mind was busy with the task of the following day. The weather was clear and the outlook for an early start in the morning was good. We were going to leave a weak party behind us in the camp. Vincent was still in the same condition, and he could not march. McNeish was pretty well broken up. The two men were not capable of managing for themselves and McCarthy must stay to look after them. He might have a difficult task if we failed to reach the whaling station. The distance to Husvik, according to the chart, was no more than seventeen geographical miles in a direct line, but we had very scanty knowledge of the conditions of the interior. No man had ever penetrated a mile from the coast of South Georgia at any point, and the whalers I knew regarded the country as inaccessible. During that day, while we were walking to the snouted glacier, we had seen three wild duck flying towards the head of the bay from the eastward. I hoped that the presence of these birds indicated tussock land and not snow fields and glaciers in the interior, but the hope was not a very bright one.

We turned out at 2 a.m. on the Friday morning and had our hoosh ready an hour later. The full moon was shining in a practically cloudless sky, its rays reflected gloriously from the pinnacles and crevassed ice of the adjacent glaciers. The huge peaks of the mountains stood in bold relief against the sky and threw dark shadows on the waters of the sound. There was no need for delay, and we made a start as soon as we had eaten our meal. McNeish walked about 200 yds with us; he could do no more. Then we said good-bye and he turned back to the camp. The first task was to get round the edge of the snouted glacier, which had points like fingers projecting towards the sea. The waves were reaching the points of these fingers, and we had to rush from one across to another when the waters receded. We soon reached the east side of the glacier and noticed its great activity at this point. Changes had occurred within the preceding twenty-four hours. Some huge pieces had broken off, and the masses of mud and stone that were being driven before the advancing ice showed movement. The glacier was like a gigantic plough driving irresistibly towards the sea.

Lying on the beach beyond the glacier was wreckage that told of many ill-fated ships. We noticed stanchions of teakwood, liberally carved, that must have come from ships of the older type; ironbound timbers with the iron almost rusted through; battered barrels and all the usual debris of the ocean. We had difficulties and anxieties of our own, but as we passed that graveyard of the sea we thought of the many tragedies written in the wave-worn fragments of lost vessels. We did not pause, and soon we were ascending a snow slope, heading due east on the last lap of our long trail.

The snow surface was disappointing. Two days before we had been able to move rapidly on hard, packed snow; now we sank over our ankles at each step and progress was slow. After two hours' steady climbing we were 2500 ft above sea level. The weather continued fine and calm, and as the ridges drew nearer and the western coast of the island spread out below, the bright moonlight showed us that the interior was broken tremendously. High peaks, impassable cliffs, steep snow slopes, and sharply descending glaciers were prominent features in all directions, with stretches of snow plain overlaying the ice sheet of the interior. The slope we were ascending mounted to a ridge and our course lay direct to the top. The moon, which proved a good friend during this journey, threw a long shadow at one point and told us that the surface was broken in our path. Warned in time, we avoided a huge hole capable of swallowing an army. The bay was now about three miles away, and the continued roaring of a big glacier at the head of the bay came to our ears. This glacier, which we had noticed during the stay at Peggotty Camp, seemed to be calving almost continuously.

I had hoped to get a view of the country ahead of us from the top of the slope, but as the surface became more level beneath our feet, a thick fog drifted down. The moon became obscured and produced a diffused light that was more trying than darkness, since it illuminated the fog without guiding our steps. We roped ourselves together as a precaution against holes, crevasses, and precipices, and I broke trail through the soft snow. With almost the full length of the rope between myself and the last man we were able to steer an approximately straight course, since, if I veered to the right or the left when marching into the blank wall of the fog, the last man on the rope could shout a direction. So, like a ship with its "port", "starboard", "steady", we tramped through the fog for the next two hours.

Then, as daylight came, the fog thinned and lifted, and from an elevation of about 3,000 ft we looked down on what seemed to be a huge frozen lake with its farther shores still obscured by the fog. We halted there to eat a bit of biscuit while we discussed whether we would go down and cross the flat surface of the lake, or keep on the ridge we had already reached. I decided to go down, since the lake lay on our course. After an hour of comparatively easy travel through the snow we noticed the thin beginnings of crevasses. Soon they were increasing in size and showing fractures, indicating that we were traveling on a glacier. As the daylight brightened the fog dissipated; the lake could be seen more clearly, but still we could not discover its east shore. A little later the fog lifted completely, and then we saw that our lake stretched to the horizon, and realized suddenly that we were looking down upon the open sea on the east coast of the island. The slight pulsation at the shore showed that the sea was not even frozen; it was the bad light that had deceived us. Evidently we were at the top of Possession Bay, and the island at that point could not be more than five miles across from the head of King Haakon Bay. Our rough chart was inaccurate. There was nothing for it but to start up the glacier again. That was about seven o'clock in the morning, and by nine o'clock we had more than recovered our lost ground. We regained the ridge and then struck southeast, for the chart showed that two more bays indented the coast before Stromness. It was comforting to realize that we would have the eastern water in sight during our journey, although we could see there was no way around the shoreline owing to steep cliffs and glaciers. Men lived in houses lit by electric light on the east coast. News of the outside world waited us there, and, above all, the east coast meant for us the means of rescuing the twenty-two men we had left on Elephant Island.

The sun rose in the sky with every appearance of a fine day, and we grew warmer as we toiled through the soft snow. Ahead of us lay the ridges and spurs of a range of mountains, the transverse range that we had noticed from the bay. We were traveling over a gently rising plateau, and at the end of an hour we found ourselves growing uncomfortably hot. Years before, on an earlier expedition, I had declared that I would never again growl at the heat of the sun, and my resolution had been strengthened during the boat journey. I called it to mind as the sun beat fiercely on the blinding white snow slope. After passing an area of crevasses we paused for our first meal. We dug a hole in the snow about three feet deep with the adze and put the Primus into it. There was no wind at the moment, but a gust might come suddenly. A hot hoosh was soon eaten and we plodded on towards a sharp ridge between two of the peaks already mentioned. By 11 a.m. we were almost at the crest. The slope had become precipitous and it was necessary to cut steps as we advanced. The adze proved an excellent instrument for this purpose, a blow sufficing to provide a foothold. Anxiously but hopefully I cut the last few steps and stood upon the razorback, while the other men held the rope and waited for my news. The outlook was disappointing. I looked down a sheer precipice to a chaos of crumpled ice 1,500 ft below. There was no way down for us. The country to the east was a great snow upland, sloping upwards for a distance of seven or

eight miles to a height of over 4,000 ft. To the north it fell away
steeply in glaciers into the bays, and to the south it was broken by
huge outfalls from the inland ice sheet. Our path lay between the
glaciers and the outfalls, but first we had to descend from the
ridge on which we stood.

Cutting steps with the adze, we moved in a lateral direction
round the base of a dolomite, which blocked our view to the
north. The same precipice confronted us. Away to the northeast
there appeared to be a snow slope that might give a path to the
lower country, and so we retraced our steps down the long slope
that had taken us three hours to climb. We were at the bottom in
an hour. We were now feeling the strain of the unaccustomed
marching. We had done little walking since January and our
muscles were out of tune. Skirting the base of the mountain above
us, we came to a gigantic bergschrund, a mile and a half long and
1,000 ft deep. This tremendous gully, cut in the snow and ice by
the fierce winds blowing round the mountain, was semicircular in
form, and it ended in a gentle incline. We passed through it,
under the towering precipice of ice, and at the far end we had
another meal and a short rest. This was at 12:30 p.m. Half a pot of
steaming Bovril ration warmed us up, and when we marched
again ice inclines at angles of 45 degrees did not look quite as
formidable as before.

Once more we started for the crest. After another weary climb
we reached the top. The snow lay thinly on blue ice at the ridge,
and we had to cut steps over the last fifty yards. The same
precipice lay below, and my eyes searched vainly for a way down.
The hot sun had loosened the snow, which was now in a
treacherous condition, and we had to pick our way carefully.
Looking back, we could see that a fog was rolling up behind us
and meeting in the valleys a fog that was coming up from the east.
The creeping grey clouds were a plain warning that we must get
down to lower levels before becoming enveloped.

The ridge was studded with peaks, which prevented us getting
a clear view either to the right or to the left. The situation in this
respect seemed no better at other points within our reach, and I
had to decide that our course lay back the way we had come. The
afternoon was wearing on and the fog was rolling up ominously
from the west. It was of the utmost importance for us to get

down into the next valley before dark. We were now up 4,500 ft and the night temperature at that elevation would be very low. We had no tent and no sleeping bags, and our clothes had endured much rough usage and had weathered many storms during the last ten months. In the distance, down the valley below us, we could see tussock grass close to the shore, and if we could get down it might be possible to dig out a hole in one of the lower snowbanks, line it with dry grass, and make ourselves fairly comfortable for the night. Back we went, and after a detour we reached the top of another ridge in the fading light. After a glance over the top I turned to the anxious faces of the two men behind me and said, "Come on, boys." Within a minute they stood beside me on the ice ridge. The surface fell away at a sharp incline in front of us, but it merged into a snow slope. We could not see the bottom clearly owing to mist and bad light, and the possibility of the slope ending in a sheer fall occurred to us; but the fog that was creeping up behind allowed no time for hesitation. We descended slowly at first, cutting steps in the hard snow; then the surface became softer, indicating that the gradient was less severe. There could be no turning back now, so we unroped and slid in the fashion of youthful days. When we stopped on a snow bank at the foot of the slope we found that we had descended at least 900 ft in two or three minutes. We looked back and saw the grey fingers of the fog appearing on the ridge, as though reaching after the intruders into untrodden wilds. But we had escaped.

The country to the east was an ascending snow upland dividing the glaciers of the north coast from the outfalls of the south. We had seen from the top that our course lay between two huge masses of crevasses, and we thought that the road ahead lay clear. This belief and the increasing cold made us abandon the idea of camping. We had another meal at 6 p.m. A little breeze made cooking difficult in spite of the shelter provided for the cooker by a hole. Crean was the cook, and Worsley and I lay on the snow to windward of the lamp so as to break the wind with our bodies. The meal over, we started up the long, gentle ascent. Night was upon us, and for an hour we plodded along in almost complete darkness, watching warily for signs of crevasses. Then about 8 p.m. a glow which we had seen behind the jagged peaks resolved itself into the full moon, which rose ahead of us and made a silver pathway for our feet. Along that pathway in the wake of the moon we advanced in safety, with the shadows cast by the edges of crevasses showing black on either side of us. Onwards and upwards through soft snow we marched, resting now and then on hard patches which had revealed themselves by glittering ahead of us in the white light. By midnight we were again at an elevation of about 4,000 ft. Still we were following the light, for as the moon swung round towards the northeast our path curved in that direction. The friendly moon seemed to pilot our weary feet. We could have had no better guide. If in bright daylight we had made that march we would have followed the course that was traced for us that night.

Midnight found us approaching the edge of a great snow field, pierced by isolated nunataks which cast long shadows like black rivers across the white expanse. A gentle slope to the northeast lured our all-too-willing feet in that direction. We thought that at the base of the slope lay Stromness Bay. After we had descended about 300 ft a thin wind began to attack us. We had now been on the march for over twenty hours, only halting for our occasional meals. Wisps of cloud drove over the high peaks to the southward, warning us that wind and snow were likely to come. After 1 a.m. we cut a pit in the snow, piled up loose snow around it, and started the Primus again. The hot food gave us another renewal of energy. Worsley and Crean sang their old songs when the Primus was going merrily. Laughter was in our hearts, though not on our parched and cracked lips.

We were up and away again within half an hour, still downward to the coast. We felt almost sure now that we were above Stromness Bay. A dark object down at the foot of the slope looked like Mutton Island, which lies off Husvik. I suppose our desires were giving wings to our fancies, for we pointed out joyfully various landmarks revealed by the now vagrant light of the moon, whose friendly face was cloud-swept. Our high hopes were soon shattered. Crevasses warned us that we were on another glacier, and soon we looked down almost to the seaward edge of the great riven ice mass. I knew there was no glacier in Stromness and realized that this must be Fortuna Glacier. The disappointment was severe. Back we turned and tramped up the glacier again, not directly tracing our steps but working at a tangent to the southeast. We were very tired.

At 5 a.m. we were at the foot of the rocky spurs of the range. We were tired, and the wind that blew down from the heights was chilling us. We decided to get down under the lee of a rock for a rest. We put our sticks and the adze on the snow, sat down on them as close to one another as possible, and put our arms round each other. The wind was bringing a little drift with it and the white dust lay on our clothes. I thought that we might be able to keep warm and have half an hour's rest this way. Within a minute my two companions were fast asleep. I realized that it would be disastrous if we all slumbered together, for sleep under such conditions merges into death. After five minutes I shook them into consciousness again, told them that they had slept for half an hour, and gave the word for a fresh start. We were so stiff that for the first two or three hundred yards we marched with our knees bent. A jagged line of peaks with a gap like a broken tooth confronted us. This was the ridge that runs in a southerly direction from Fortuna Bay, and our course eastward to Stromness lay across it. A very steep slope led up to the ridge and an icy wind burst through the gap.

We went through the gap at 6 a.m. with anxious hearts as well as weary bodies. If the farther slope had proved impassable our situation would have been almost desperate; but the worst was turning to the best for us. The twisted, wave-like rock formations of Husvik Harbor appeared right ahead in the opening of dawn. Without a word we shook hands with one another. To our minds the journey was over, though as a matter of fact twelve miles of difficult country had still to be traversed. A gentle snow slope descended at our feet towards a valley that separated our ridge from the hills immediately behind Husvik, and as we stood gazing Worsley said solemnly, "Boss, it looks too good to be true!" Down we went, to be checked presently by the sight of water 2,500 ft below. We could see the little wave ripples on the black beach, penguins strutting to and fro, and dark objects that looked like seals lolling lazily on the sand. This was an eastern arm of Fortuna Bay, separated by the ridge from the arm we had seen below us during the night. The slope we were traversing appeared to end in a precipice above this beach. But our revived spirits were not to be damped by difficulties on the last stage of the journey, and we camped cheerfully for breakfast. While Worsley and Crean were digging a hole for the lamp and starting the cooker I climbed a ridge above us, cutting steps with the adze, in order to secure an extended view of the country below. At 6:30 a.m. I thought I heard the sound of a steam whistle. I dared not be certain, but I knew that the men at the whaling station would be called from their beds about that time. Descending to the camp I told the others, and in intense excitement we watched the chronometer for seven o'clock, when the whalers would be summoned to work. Right to the minute the steam whistle came to us, borne clearly on the wind across the intervening miles of rock and snow. Never had any one of us heard sweeter music. It was the first sound created by outside human agency that had come to our ears since we left Stromness Bay in December 1914. That whistle told us that men were living near, that ships were ready, and that within a few hours we should be on our way back to Elephant Island to the rescue of the men waiting there under the watch and ward of Wild. It was a moment hard to describe. Pain and ache, boat journeys, marches, hunger and fatigue seemed to belong to the limbo of forgotten things, and there remained only the perfect contentment that comes of work accomplished.

My examination of the country from a higher point had not provided definite information, and after descending I put the situation before Worsley and Crean. Our obvious course lay down a snow slope in the direction of Husvik. "Boys," I said, "this snow slope seems to end in a precipice, but perhaps there is no precipice. If we don't go down we shall have to make a detour of at least five miles before we reach level going. What shall it be?" They both replied at once. "Try the slope." So we started away again downwards. We abandoned the Primus lamp, now empty, at the breakfast camp and carried with us one ration and a biscuit each. The deepest snow we had yet encountered clogged our feet, but we plodded downward, and after descending about 500 ft, reducing our altitude to 2,000 ft above sea level, we thought we saw the way clear ahead. A steep gradient of blue ice was the next obstacle. Worsley and Crean got a firm footing in a hole excavated with the adze and then lowered me as I cut steps until the full 50 ft of our alpine rope was out. Then I made a hole big enough for the three of us, and the other two men came down the steps. My end of the rope was anchored to the adze and I had settled myself in the hole braced for a strain in case they slipped. When we all stood in the second hole I went down again to make more steps, and in this laborious fashion we spent two hours descending about 500 ft. Halfway down we had to strike away diagonally to the left, for we noticed that the fragments of ice loosened by the adze were taking a leap into space at the bottom of the slope. Eventually we got off the steep ice, very gratefully, at a point where some rocks protruded, and we could see then that there was a perilous precipice directly below the point where we had started to cut steps. A slide down a slippery slope, with the adze and our cooker going ahead, completed this descent, and incidentally did considerable damage to our much-tried trousers.

When we picked ourselves up at the bottom we were not more than 1,500 ft above the sea. The slope was comparatively easy. Water was running beneath the snow, making "pockets" between the rocks that protruded above the white surface. The shells of snow over these pockets were traps for our feet; but we scrambled down, and presently came to patches of tussock. A few minutes later we reached the sandy beach. The tracks of some animals were to be seen, and we were puzzled until I remembered that reindeer, brought from Norway, had been placed on the island and now ranged along the lower land of the eastern coast. We did not pause to investigate. Our minds were set upon reaching the haunts of man, and at our best speed we went along the beach to another rising ridge of tussock. Here we saw the first evidence of the proximity of man, whose work, as is so often the case, was one of destruction. A recently killed seal was lying there, and presently we saw several other bodies bearing the marks of bullet wounds. I learned that men from the whaling station at Stromness sometimes go round to Fortuna Bay by boat to shoot seals.

Noon found us well up the slope on the other side of the bay working east-southest, and half an hour later we were on a flat plateau, with one more ridge to cross before we descended into Husvik. I was leading the way over this plateau when I suddenly found myself up to my knees in water and quickly sinking deeper through the snow crust. I flung myself down and called to the others to do the same, so as to distribute our weight on the treacherous surface. We were on top of a small lake, snow-covered. After lying still for a few moments, we got to our feet and walked delicately, like Agag, for 200 yds, until a rise in the surface showed us that we were clear of the lake.

At 1:30 p.m. we climbed round a final ridge and saw a little steamer, a whaling boat, entering the bay 2,500 ft below. A few moments later, as we hurried forward, the masts of a sailing ship lying at a wharf came in sight. Minute figures moving to and fro about the boats caught our gaze, and then we saw the sheds and factory of Stromness whaling station. We paused and shook hands, a form of mutual congratulation that had seemed necessary on four other occasions in the course of the expedition. The first time was when we landed on Elephant Island, the second when we reached South Georgia, and the third when we reached the ridge and saw the snow slope stretching below on the first day of the overland journey, then when we saw Husvik rocks.

Cautiously we started down the slope that led to warmth and comfort. The last lap of the journey proved extraordinarily difficult. Vainly we searched for a safe, or a reasonably safe, way down from the steep ice-clad mountainside. The sole possible pathway seemed to be a channel cut by water running from the upland. Down through icy water we followed the course of this stream. We were wet to the waist, shivering, cold, and tired. Presently our ears detected an unwelcome sound that might have been musical under other conditions. It was the splashing of a waterfall, and we were at the wrong end. When we reached the top of this fall we peered over cautiously and discovered that there was a drop of 25 or 30 ft, with impassable ice cliffs on both sides. To go up again was scarcely thinkable in our utterly wearied condition. The way down was through the waterfall itself. We made fast one end of our rope to a boulder with some difficulty, due to the fact that the rocks had been worn smooth by the running water. Then Worsley and I lowered Crean, who was the heaviest man. He disappeared altogether in the falling water and came out gasping at the bottom. I went next, sliding down the rope, and Worsley, who was the lightest and most nimble member of the party, came last. At the bottom of the fall we were able to stand again on dry land. The rope could not be recovered.

We had flung down the adze from the top of the fall and also the logbook and the cooker wrapped in one of our blouses. That was all, except our wet clothes, that we brought out of the Antarctic, which we had entered a year and a half before with well-found ship, full equipment, and high hopes. That was all of tangible things; but in memories we were rich. We had pierced the veneer of outside things. We had "suffered, starved, and triumphed, groveled down yet grasped at glory, grown bigger in the bigness of the whole." We had seen God in his splendors, heard the text that Nature renders. We had reached the naked soul of men.

Shivering with cold, yet with hearts light and happy, we set off towards the whaling station, now not more than a mile and a half distant. The difficulties of the journey lay behind us. We tried to straighten ourselves up a bit for the thought that there might be women at the station made us painfully conscious of our uncivilized appearance. Our beards were long and our hair was matted. We were unwashed and the garments that we had worn for nearly a year without a change were tattered and stained. Three more unpleasant-looking ruffians could hardly have been imagined. Worsley produced several safety pins from some corner of his garments and effected some temporary repairs that really emphasized his general disrepair. Down we hurried, and when quite close to the station we met two small boys ten or twelve years of age. I asked these lads where the manager's house was situated. They did not answer. They gave us one look – a comprehensive look that did not need to be repeated. Then they ran from us as fast as their legs would carry them. We reached the outskirts of the station and passed through the "digesting-house", which was dark inside. Emerging at the other end, we met an old man, who started as if he had seen the Devil himself and gave us no time to ask any question. He hurried away. This greeting was not friendly. Then we came to the wharf, where the man in charge stuck to his station. I asked him if Mr Sorlle (the manager) was in the house.

"Yes," he said as he stared at us.

"We would like to see him," said I.

"Who are you?" he asked.

"We have lost our ship and come over the island," I replied.

"You have come over the island?" he said in a tone of entire disbelief.

The man went towards the manager's house and we followed him. I learned afterwards that he said to Mr Sorlle: "There are three funny-looking men outside, who say they have come over the island and they know you. I have left them outside." A very necessary precaution from his point of view.

Mr Sorlle came out to the door and said, "Well?"

"Don't you know me?" I said.

"I know your voice," he replied doubtfully. "You're the mate of the *Daisy*."

"My name is Shackleton," I said.

Immediately, he put out his hand and said, "Come in. Come in."

"Tell me, when was the war over?" I asked.

"The war is not over," he answered. "Millions are being killed. Europe is mad. The world is mad."

The "Boss", as Shackleton was known, then went back and rescued every man of his party.

Alone

Richard E. Byrd

In 1933–4 the American adventurer Richard E Byrd, possessor of a dubious claim to having flown the North Pole and a definite claim to having first flown over the South Pole, spent five winter months alone in the Bolling Advance Weather Base. Despite its grandiose name, the base, sited at 80° 08′ South, was a rudimentary hut. Outside the temperature dropped to as low as –83°F.

Out of the cold and out of the east came the wind. It came on gradually, as if the sheer weight of the cold were almost too much to be moved. On the night of the 21st the barometer started down. The night was black as a thunderhead when I made my first trip topside; and a tension in the wind, a bulking of shadows in the night indicated that a new storm centre was forming. Next morning, glad of an excuse to stay underground, I worked a long time on the Escape Tunnel by the light of a red candle standing in a snow recess. That day I pushed the emergency exit to a distance of twenty-two feet, the farthest it was ever to go. My stint done, I sat down on a box, thinking how beautiful was the red of the candle, how white the rough-hewn snow. Soon I became aware of an increasing clatter of the anemometer cups. Realizing that the wind was picking up, I went topside to make sure that everything was secured. It is a queer experience to watch a blizzard rise. First there is the wind, rising out of nowhere. Then the Barrier unwrenches itself from quietude; and the surface, which just before had seemed as hard and polished as metal, begins to run like a making sea. Sometimes, if the wind strikes hard, the drift comes across the Barrier like a hurrying white cloud, tossed hundreds of feet in the air. Other times the growth is gradual. You become conscious of a general slithering movement on all sides. The air fills with tiny scraping and sliding and rustling sounds as the first loose crystals stir. In a little while they are moving as solidly as an incoming tide, which creams over the ankles, then surges to the waist, and finally is at the throat. I have walked in drift so thick as not to be able to see a foot ahead of me; yet, when I glanced up, I could see the stars shining through the thin layer just overhead.

Smoking tendrils were creeping up the anemometer pole when I finished my inspection. I hurriedly made the trapdoor fast, as a sailor might batten down a hatch; and knowing that my ship was well secured, I retired to the cabin to ride out the storm. It could not reach me, hidden deep in the Barrier crust; nevertheless the sounds came down. The gale sobbed in the ventilators, shook the stovepipe until I thought it would be jerked out by the roots, pounded the roof with sledge-hammer blows. I could actually feel the suction effect through the pervious snow. A breeze flickered in the room and the tunnels. The candles wavered and went out. My only light was the feeble storm lantern.

Even so, I didn't have any idea how really bad it was until I went aloft for an observation. As I pushed back the trapdoor, the drift met me like a moving wall. It was only a few steps from the ladder to the instrument shelter, but it seemed more like a mile. The air came at me in snowy rushes; I breasted it as I might a heavy surf. No night had ever seemed so dark. The beam from the flashlight was choked in its throat; I could not see my hand before my face.

My windproofs were caked with drift by the time I got below. I had a vague feeling that something had changed while I was gone, but what, I couldn't tell. Presently I noticed that the shack was appreciably colder. Raising the stove lid, I was surprised to find that the fire was out, though the tank was half full. I decided that I must have turned off the valve unconsciously before going aloft; but, when I put a match to the burner, the draught down the pipe blew out the flame. The wind, then, must have killed the fire. I got it going again, and watched it carefully.

The blizzard vaulted to gale force. Above the roar the deep, taut thrumming note of the radio antenna and the anemometer guy wires reminded me of wind in a ship's rigging. The wind direction trace turned scratchy on the sheet; no doubt drift had short-circuited the electric contacts, I decided. Realizing that it was hopeless to attempt to try to keep them clear, I let the instrument be. There were other ways of getting the wind direction. I tied a handkerchief to a bamboo pole and ran it through the outlet ventilator; with a flashlight I could tell which way the cloth was whipped. I did this at hourly intervals, noting any change of direction on the sheet. But by 2 o'clock in the morning I had had enough of this periscope sighting. If I expected to sleep and at the same time maintain the continuity of the records, I had no choice but to clean the contact points.

The wind was blowing hard then. The Barrier shook from the concussions overhead; and the noise was as if the entire physical world were tearing itself to pieces. I could scarcely heave the trapdoor open. The instant it came clear I was plunged into a blinding smother. I came out crawling, clinging to the handle of the door until I made sure of my bearings. Then I let the door fall shut, not wanting the tunnel filled with drift. To see was impossible. Millions of tiny pellets exploded in my eyes, stinging like BB shot. It was even hard to breathe, because snow instantly clogged the mouth and nostrils. I made my way toward the anemometer pole on hands and knees, scared that I might be bowled off my feet if I stood erect; one false step and I should be lost for ever.

I found the pole all right; but not until my head collided with a cleat. I managed to climb it, too, though ten million ghosts were tearing at me, ramming their thumbs into my eyes. But the errand was useless. Drift as thick as this would mess up the contact points as quickly as they were cleared; besides, the wind cups were spinning so fast that I stood a good chance of losing a couple of fingers in the process. Coming down the pole, I had a sense of being whirled violently through the air, with no control over my movements. The trapdoor was completely buried when I found it again, after scraping around for some time with my mittens. I pulled at the handle, first with one hand, then with both. It did not give. It's a tight fit, anyway, I mumbled to myself. The drift has probably wedged the corners. Standing astride the hatch, I braced myself and heaved with all my strength. I might just as well have tried hoisting the Barrier.

Panic took me then, I must confess. Reason fled. I clawed at the

three-foot square of timber like a madman. I beat on it with my
fists, trying to shake the snow loose; and, when that did no good, I
lay flat on my belly and pulled until my hands went weak from
cold and weariness. Then I crooked my elbow, put my face down,
and said over and over again, You damn fool, you damn fool.
Here for weeks I had been defending myself against the danger of
being penned inside the shack; instead, I was now locked out; and
nothing could be worse, especially since I had only a wool parka
and pants under my wind-proofs. Just two feet below was
sanctuary – warmth, food, tools, all the means of survival. All
these things were an arm's length away, but I was powerless to
reach them.

There is something extravagantly insensate about an Antarctic
blizzard at night. Its vindictiveness cannot be measured on an
anemometer sheet. It is more than just wind; it is a solid wall of
snow moving at gale force, pounding like surf.* The whole
malevolent rush is concentrated upon you as upon a personal
enemy. In the senseless explosion of sound you are reduced to a
crawling thing on the margin of a disintegrating world; you can't
see, you can't hear, you can hardly move. The lungs gasp after the
air sucked out of them, and the brain is shaken. Nothing in the
world will so quickly isolate a man.

Half-frozen, I stabbed toward one of the ventilators, a few feet
away. My mittens touched something round and cold. Cupping it
in my hands, I pulled myself up. This was the outlet ventilator.
Just why, I don't know – but instinct made me kneel and press my
face against the opening. Nothing in the room was visible, but a
dim patch of light illuminated the floor, and warmth rose up to
my face. That steadied me.

Still kneeling, I turned my back to the blizzard and considered
what might be done. I thought of breaking in the windows in the
roof, but they lay two feet down in hard crust, and were re-
inforced with wire besides. If I only had something to dig with, I
could break the crust and stamp the windows in with my feet.
The pipe cupped between my hands supplied the first inspiration; maybe I could use that to dig with. It, too, was wedged tight;

* Because of this blinding, suffocating drift, in the Antarctic winds of
only moderate velocity have the punishing force of full-fledged hurri-
canes elsewhere.

I pulled until my arms ached, without budging it; I had lost all track of time, and the despairing thought came to me that I was lost in a task without an end. Then I remembered the shovel. A week before, after levelling drift from the last light blow, I had stabbed a shovel handle up in the crust somewhere to leeward. That shovel would save me. But how to find it in the avalanche of the blizzard?

I lay down and stretched out full length. Still holding the pipe, I thrashed around with my feet, but pummelled only empty air. Then I worked back to the hatch. The hard edges at the opening provided another grip, and again I stretched out and kicked. Again no luck. I dared not let go until I had something else familiar to cling to. My foot came up against the other ventilator pipe. I edged back to that, and from the new anchorage repeated the manœuvre. This time my ankle struck something hard. When I felt it and recognized the handle, I wanted to caress it.

Embracing this thrice-blessed tool, I inched back to the trapdoor. The handle of the shovel was just small enough to pass under the little wooden bridge which served as a grip. I got both hands on the shovel and tried to wrench the door up; my strength was not enough, however. So I lay down flat on my belly and worked my shoulders under the shovel. Then I heaved, the door sprang open, and I rolled down the shaft. When I tumbled into the light and warmth of the room, I kept thinking, How wonderful, how perfectly wonderful.

My wrist watch had stopped; the chronometers showed that I had been gone just under an hour. The stove had blown out again, but I did not bother to light it. Enough warmth remained for me to undress. I was exhausted; it was all I could do to hoist myself into the bunk. But I did not sleep at first. The blizzard scuffled and pounded gigantically overhead; and my mind refused to drop the thought of what I might still be doing if the shovel hadn't been there. Still struggling, probably. Or maybe not. There are harder ways to die than freezing to death. The lush numbness and the peace that lulls the mind when the ears cease listening to the blizzard's ridiculous noise, could make death seem easy.

*The hut, however, was not a complete sanctuary, for Byrd was
frequently forced to inhale fumes, containing high levels of carbon
monoxide, from his stove:*

As I saw the situation, the necessities were these: To survive I
must continue to husband my strength, doing whatever had to
be done in the simplest manner possible and without strain. I
must sleep and eat and build up strength. To avoid further
poisoning from the fumes, I must use the stove sparingly and
the gasoline pressure lantern not at all. Giving up the lantern
meant surrendering its bright light, which was one of my few
luxuries; but I could do without luxuries for a while. As to the
stove, the choice there lay between freezing and inevitable
poisoning. Cold I could feel, but carbon monoxide was invisible
and tasteless. So I chose the cold, knowing that the sleeping bag
provided a retreat. From now on, I decided, I would make a
strict rule of doing without the fire for two or three hours every
afternoon.

So much for the practical procedure. If I depended on this
alone, I should go mad from the hourly reminders of my own
futility. Something more – the will and desire to endure these
hardships – was necessary. They must come from deep inside
me. But how? By taking control of my thought. By extirpating
all lugubrious ideas the instant they appeared and dwelling
only on those conceptions which would make for peace. A
discordant mind, black with confusion and despair, would
finish me off as thoroughly as the cold. Discipline of this
sort is not easy. Even in April's and May's serenity I had
failed to master it entirely.

That evening I made a desperate effort to make these conclu-
sions work for me. Although my stomach was rebellious, I forced
down a big bowl of thin soup, plus some vegetables and milk.
Then I put the fire out; afterwards, propped up in the sleeping
bag, I tried to play Canfield. But the games, I remember, went
against me; and this made me profoundly irritable. I tried to read
Ben Ames Williams' *All the Brothers Were Valiant*; but, after a
page or two, the letters became indistinct; and my eyes ached – in
fact, they had never stopped aching. I cursed inwardly, telling

myself that the way the cards fell and the state of my eyes were typical of my wretched luck. The truth is that the dim light from the lantern was beginning to get on my nerves. In spite of my earlier resolve to dispense with it, I would have lighted the pressure lantern, except that I wasn't able to pump up the pressure. Only when you've been through something like that do you begin to appreciate how utterly precious light is.

Something persuaded me to take down the shaving mirror from its nail near the shelf. The face that looked back at me was that of an old and feeble man. The cheeks were sunken and scabrous from frostbite, and the bloodshot eyes were those of a man who has been on a prolonged debauch. Something broke inside me then. What was to be gained by struggling? No matter what happened, if I survived at all, I should always be a physical wreck, a burden upon my family. It was a dreadful business. All the fine conceptions of the afternoon dissolved in black despair.

The dark side of a man's mind seems to be a sort of antenna turned to catch gloomy thoughts from all directions. I found it so with mine. That was an evil night. It was as if all the world's vindictiveness were concentrated upon me as upon a personal enemy. I sank to depths of disillusionment which I had not believed possible. It would be tedious to discuss them. Misery, after all, is the tritest of emotions. All that need be said is that eventually my faith began to make itself felt; and by concentrating on it and reaffirming the truth about the universe as I saw it, I was able again to fill my mind with the fine and comforting things of the world that had seemed irretrievably lost. I surrounded myself with my family and my friends; I projected myself into the sunlight, into the midst of green, growing things. I thought of all the things I would do when I got home; and a thousand matters which had never been more than casual now became surpassingly attractive and important. But time after time I slipped back into despond. Concentration was difficult, and only by the utmost persistence could I bring myself out of it. But ultimately the disorder left my mind; and, when I blew out the candles and the lantern, I was living in the world of the imagination – a simple, uncomplicated world made up of people who wished each other well, who were peaceful and easy-going and kindly.

The aches and pains had not subsided; and it took me several hours to fall asleep; but that night I slept better than on any night since 31 May [several days earlier]; and in the morning was better in mind and body both.

The First Men in the White Eden

John Rymill

*Rymill was the leader of a 1934 British expedition to Graham Land,
a hitherto unexplored region of Western Antarctica.*

Coming from the dark, heaving ocean into the quiet channels of
north Graham Land was an amazing contrast, for one was
suddenly transported from the dull, dreary expanse of a lea-
den-coloured sea into the full beauties of a polar land. The day
we passed through De Gerlache Strait and Neumayer Channel
on our way to Port Lockroy was clear and sunny with a
cloudless sky, giving us a good opportunity to appreciate the
grandeur of the scenery amongst which we should make our
home for the next two years. These channels, though deep, are
in places less than a mile wide, and are fringed with ice-cliffs
some hundred feet high, with serrated edges following the
shore-line and forming little bays and points. Behind the
ice-cliffs the mountain ranges rise to snowy peaks 4000 or
5000 feet above the water. There is dark rock exposed on
the mountain sides, but the most striking features are the
hanging glaciers and ice-falls, showing every shade of blue
and green as they are caught by the sun's rays, or else darkened
by shadows. The sea itself was oily calm with that strange misty
glow which seems peculiar to the cold water of the polar regions
when there is no wind. On the surface small icebergs and
smaller growlers, newly broken from the cliffs, lay sparkling
in the sun like vast jewels set in the long winding channel. The
only sounds that could be heard were the occasional roar of an
avalanche, or a dull grumbling as an ice-cliff calved, and
perhaps the cry of a Dominican gull going to or from its
breeding-ground near by.

We had a wonderful view this afternoon. When the sky cleared, the clouds over the Graham Land mountains to the east remained dark, but took on lighter shades as they faded into long streamers towards the zenith, where their edges were touched with the reds and orange of the sunset light from the north. Down the western horizon the great mountain ranges of Alexander I Island stood out mysteriously, showing a pale copper colour against a dark grey haze into which they gradually disappeared further south, while the soft winter twilight made the whole scene look coldly beautiful, but rather awe-inspiring. As we sledged along I was impressed by the thought that here was all this strange grandeur round us, and we – people of the 20th century who had left an overcrowded land only a few months before – were the first to see it since the world began.

We were still 130 miles from home, but this first sight of well-known landmarks and the sea – always a thing of life even when frozen – gave us a pleasant sensation of familiarity which was a relief after the austere country through which we had been travelling for the last forty-five days: a country which had known eternal peace until we, two punny little black dots in its vastness, had the impudence to lift the curtain for a few brief days and look upon its beauty. Now that we were leaving it behind I had a feeling of intense pleasure in knowing that we had travelled its glaciers and scaled its mountains and come through safely. But this feeling was tinged with one of loss as though a friend had died, for the curtain had again dropped, and, in dropping, had hidden a scene difficult to put into words. Day after day we had travelled through silence which was absolute, not a depressing silence as of the dead, but a silence that had never known life. Even more impressive had been the sheer immensity of the country, and the atmosphere of mystery which seemed to dwarf us – the great mountains which have stood there untroubled for countless years, and the glaciers slowly forcing their way downwards, occasionally muttering in their depths to remind us that even here time goes on. And to think that when we return to England one of the first questions we shall be asked – probably by a well-fed businessman whose God is his bank-book – will be, "Why did you go there?" How can one reply other than flippantly to such a mentality? But the high plateau of Graham Land is no place to indulge in daydreams, and we hurried on.

Going All the Way

Vivian Fuchs

The sometime director of the Falkland Islands Dependencies Survey, Fuchs was both the mover and leader of the 1955–8 Commonwealth Trans-Antarctic Expedition, the belated British bid to fulfil Shackleton's dream of an overland crossing of the entire southern continent.

Camp Life

Below Fuchs recounts the expedition's second winter holed up doing preparations for the crossing.

We were concerned for our dogs. At Scott Base, where there were sixty, they were able to live outside all through the winter and, again when the moon came up each month, they were harnessed to their sledges and given a run. Racing over the rough sea ice was an exhilarating experience for both dogs and men as it was impossible to pick out obstacles in the moonlight – for the driver the only thing to do was to cling to the sledge and hope for the best.

At Shackleton, as the winds rose and the temperatures fell, they lay curled up on the snow above our buried hut, with only their fur and blubber to protect them. As the wind continually swept the snow from the hard compacted surface, they were even denied the usual protection of accumulating drift to keep them warm. Sometimes when we went to visit them they would rise to greet us, but often their warmth had melted the snow, which had then frozen again and tore the hair from their bodies as they struggled to their feet.

We decided to dig new tunnels for their protection and determined that there must be plenty of headroom as well as space to saw up the seal meat under shelter. Making a tunnel 140 feet long by 8 feet deep and 4 feet wide, we cut alcoves in the walls on alternate sides to prevent the dogs reaching each other at the ends of their chains. Later on, the main power system provided the tunnel with electricity for twelve hours each day, and the dogs lived in considerable comfort and relative warmth – for even with an outdoor temperature of –60°F, the heat from their bodies kept the tunnel just above zero.

One of the least popular chores was cutting up the seal meat. The carcase had first to be dug out from the snow and then cut into pieces by two men using a great cross-cut saw. These were then split up with an axe or sawn into "logs" weighing four to six pounds. One such "log" was fed to each dog every other day . . .

All the bases were carrying out scientific work. At South Ice a Dexion lattice mast was erected which soon became festooned with recording instruments, including anemometers and thermometers every few feet right down to the surface. These provided Hal Lister with wind and temperature records for his glaciological work. At the top of the mast was a small red light which could be switched on from inside the hut to call an absorbed scientist in when lunch was ready.

Jon Stephenson was studying ice crystals, and to obtain the specimens he dug a pit 50 feet deep from inside one of the snow tunnels. From this depth he bored a hole for another 100 feet down, bringing up a core of ice in sections 18 inches long. By studying the snow strata both in the walls of the pit and in the cores, much was learnt about the annual snow fall for centuries past. In fact, the snow recovered from the deepest point fell at the time of the Battle of Agincourt!

At Shackleton Allan Rogers had some complicated instruments called Integrating Motor Pneumotachographs (known as "IMPS" for short), with which he could measure and study the energy expended by a man both at work and at rest – provided, of course, that he could persuade any of us to put up with the discomfort of wearing a mask over his face and a pack on his back while going about his normal work. Soon, members of the party could be seen cooking or sweeping, hauling sledges or building, while wearing IMPS.

Geoffrey Pratt very helpfully undertook to wear the instrument day and night (except at meals) for a whole week. He found it an irksome and uncomfortable experience and even suffered from frostbite on his face through wearing the mask long hours out of doors, in temperatures below $-50°F$. However, in the end it was poor Allan who had the worst of it, because he had to follow Geoffrey about all day to see that the IMP was working, and so had to help his energetic subject with all kinds of tasks which were certainly nothing to do with a doctor. Then at mealtimes Allan had to weigh all the food that Geoffrey ate besides questioning the cook to find out what had gone into making the various dishes. This was necessary so that the energy consumed by Geoffrey in the form of food could be compared with energy he expended. So it was that mealtimes passed with Geoffrey eating heartily and poor Allan still hard at work in the kitchen, with often the prospect of little left for him to eat!

After one sleepless night due to the gurgling noises made by Geoffrey and the IMP while he slept, we banished him from the bunk-room to the attic. Still there was no rest for Allan, for he had to follow him and even remain awake to see that the mask was not displaced by his "guinea-pig" while he slept. At the end of the week it was the doctor who was exhausted!

An outdoor task undertaken by David Pratt was the measurement of friction between different types of sledge-runner materials in varying temperatures and on different types of snow surfaces. He used small manhauled sledges carrying a known load, the amount of effort required to keep the sledge in movement being measured electrically by strain gauges. He was constantly looking for unsuspecting people to act as hauliers. I was lucky to do my stint of forty hauls in good conditions, with the temperature at only $-19°F$, but a few days later Allan Rogers found himself doing the same thing in $-60°F$. Suddenly he realized that he could make use of the same activity for his IMP work and, in no time at all, the unfortunate Taffy Williams found himself torn from his nice warm radio-room, wearing an IMP and manhauling a sledge in the outer darkness. As he stumbled from one invisible snowdrift to another, Allan and David each cried his own directions, until the protesting Taffy was at last discharged from duty (exhausted), and another victim found . . .

The sun left us on 23 April, but inside our huts we were always busy. At Shackleton each man was duty cook for four days at a time, helped by two "gashmen" who were responsible for bringing in the snow to be melted for our water supply, keeping the stoves supplied with fuel, washing up, keeping the hut tidy, and – perhaps the worst chore of all – disposing of the rubbish. This entailed carrying a twelve-gallon bucket of kitchen waste up a flight of snow steps to the surface where, more often than not, the wind would whip the contents over the gashmen as they staggered away into the drift.

After a time we could bear this no longer, so we dug out an extension tunnel from the bottom of the snow steps, and made a deep waste-pit in an unusual manner. First we made a small hole about 18 inches deep in the snow. Into this we poured a pint of petrol which soaked in immediately. Taking care that there were no small pools of petrol on the surface, a match was applied, and the petrol burnt slowly, gradually melting a cavity. Each time the flames went out more petrol was poured into the deepening hole and set alight, and in two hours, with the use of four gallons of petrol, we had a pit 24 four feet deep. This served us excellently as a waste-pit until the base was abandoned in November.

After a few weeks we noticed that when a bucket of water had been tipped into this waste-pit, there was a pause followed by a distant rumbling gurgle. Then we found that cold air was rising from the pit, and we realized that the bottom of the pit had broken through into a crevasse which ran almost under the base hut.

At Scott Base they had a full-time cook, helped by two duty "gashmen" who were on for a week at a time. On Sundays the cook was given a complete rest and the gashmen prepared the meals, which led to keen competition for original menus.

Many firms had given us labour-saving equipment which greatly added to our comfort at base. Both at Scott and at Shackleton the Singer sewing machines were never idle as we made hundreds of trail flags and mended or modified clothing and tents. During the winter, sledges were stripped down and repaired, dog traces spliced and new dog harnesses made. As there were thirteen of us sharing the hut at Shackleton, each man had the bathroom in turn for a day at a time. At the same time he

did his personal laundry with the Hoover washing machine which
we had been given.

Installing our bathroom had presented us with some unexpected problems. When an Antarctic hut is built on rock, as at
Scott Base, it is very unwise to allow the bathwater to run away
through the normal waste-plug as it will freeze on the rock below,
gradually building up ice beneath the floor and very soon preventing any further escape. We had therefore expected to bale out
our bathwater and empty it outside, but finding our hut at
Shackleton built on a great depth of snow, we now thought that
it would accept the bath waste – as indeed it did. Unfortunately
the bath supplied to us had no waste-plug!

David Stratton told us he had discovered that this type of bath
was made specially for sale in Aden, as Arabs apparently did not
require waste-pipes. But why not? We spent a great deal of time
inventing stories of a long camel caravan winding over the hot
sands of Arabia, each camel bearing two white enamelled castiron
baths like panniers on either side of its swaying humps. But what
on earth did the Arabs do with the waste water when the baths
were finally in use?

We never did find out, but our engineers decided to try to make
a hole in the normal place in the bath and to drain the waste water
away beneath the hut. This was not an easy task without chipping
the enamel or cracking the iron, and during their initial experiments in devising a suitable plug for the hole, the bather was
frequently left sitting in the empty bath, high, dry, soapy, and
unamused . . .

One of the busiest places at each base was the garage workshop.
Here the engineers worked long hours preparing and modifying
the vehicles for the testing time ahead of them. At Scott Base the
original plan was for the depots towards the Pole to be established
by dog teams and for the supplies to be flown in by air. But Ed
Hillary had been very impressed with the performance of his
small Ferguson tractors and finally decided to use these also for
the southern journey. It was a large-scale operation preparing
them. Over the driver's seat was welded a powerful crash bar to
give some protection should the vehicle go down a crevasse or roll
over. Around this a cab, or rather a wind-break, was constructed
from canvas to keep out a little of the Antarctic wind. The track

system was strengthened and an enormous amount of work was done on the tracks themselves to try and improve their grip in soft snow. The motors were overhauled, the electrical wiring system simplified, and any unnecessary parts of the body were cut away to save weight. A light, portable garage was constructed out of canvas, with a collapsible framework of three-quarter-inch piping, in case of a major breakdown; a strong towbar was welded to the front of each vehicle, and sixty-foot lengths of Terylene towrope, with an eight-ton breaking strain, were cut and spliced.

At Shackleton David and Roy worked on the vehicles one after the other, stripping down tracks, welding on recovery equipment for use should they fall into crevasses, and overhauling all the engines. The days were not long enough for everything that had to be done.

As a relaxation our engineers had made a large fish trap out of wire netting which they had lowered through a hole cut in the sea ice, although as the water was three thousand feet deep, there was no hope of bottom fishing. One evening George Lowe and I went down with them to visit this trap. Leaving Shackleton in a brisk wind and heavy snow, we found it difficult to find our way along the two-mile route in the dark, but, helped by the marker stakes and stretches of the old track which had not been drifted over, we reached the edge of the sea ice. The hole through which the trap had been let down was frozen over and when we broke through, countless clusters of ice crystals an inch or more in diameter floated to the surface. When at last we obtained a patch of clear water, we could see hundreds of pink, shrimp-like creatures in the light of our torches. These were *euphausea*, or krill, the main food of many species of whale, and this was all that the trap contained. Not intending to return empty-handed, we collected as many of them as we could, thinking they would make a surprise dish for David Stratton's birthday the next day.

Suddenly there was a swirl of water and a seal surfaced to breathe, but he was as startled as we were and disappeared in an instant. As we turned back towards the Shackleton beacon light shining through the driving snow, it occurred to me that people at home might think us slightly mad to go shrimping in a snowstorm at dead of night in the Antarctic winter – but to us it was a relaxation to leave base and do something different from the daily routine.

Our special dish of sea-food was duly prepared in honour of David's birthday and looked most attractive. We all gathered round as manfully he tackled the delicate pink pile, only to find that each multi-legged corpse contained no more than a few drops of pink oil! . . .

On 21 June – Midwinter Day – we rose late for breakfast, and then everybody helped with the normal chores of sweeping, cleaning and bringing in ice and coal, before dressing to go to the Pratt-Homard cocktail party – although it was darkly rumoured by the non-engineers that the "cocktails" would consist mainly of petrol, flavoured with grease and oil! We set out for the workshop fully clothed in windproofs and gloves, expecting to stumble over the intervening snowdrifts, but to our surprise the snow reflected the flickering light of dozens of paraffin flares marking the 200-yard route.

Inside the workshop it was beautifully warm, for the small coal fire in the annexe was roaring and the temperature of the whole building had been raised to $+$ 35°F. We were able to strip off our outdoor clothing and stand about in comfort admiring the new photographs and coloured posters which decorated the walls. The shouts of welcome which greeted each new arrival and the general air of gaiety was enhanced by a background of Irish jigs from the record-player, and soon someone thought of fixing a large meteorological balloon to the exhaust of a Weasel and starting the engine. Slowly at first, but with increasing speed, it grew to gigantic proportions before exploding with a satisfying bang!

This entertainment was followed by the explanation of Gordon Haslop's strange behaviour during the previous few days. The "Haslop Firework Display" began with a series of detonations spelling "T.A.E." in morse and continued with flares and rockets, while the flitting figure of Gordon could be seen silhouetted against the lights, clearly clutching a beer mug in one hand while setting off fireworks with the other. It was a fine show.

South Ice came through on the radio to exchange greetings and tell us about the roast beef lunch they had just finished and how they were already looking forward to chicken for dinner. At 3.30

p.m. we sat down to a splendid meal which included green turtle soup, roast turkey, plum pudding and ice-cream. The table was decorated with crackers and presents and in due course most of us were wearing paper hats and playing musical instruments.

Later that evening, after a suitable pause for digestion and recovery, we enjoyed a buffet supper, which included even mustard and cress sandwiches (grown in boxes in the loft of the hut), the first fresh vegetable we had tasted since the *Magga Dan* left us. Ralph Lenton felt inspired to entertain us with a wonderful version of the Dance of the Seven Veils, while an improvised band – I imagine the first Antarctic Skiffle Group – played vigorously on any available article.

Such was our Midwinter, and after it we settled down to the second half of the long dark night, always looking forward to the return of the sun in August. We went back to our regular routine of tending our instruments, looking after the dogs, working on the vehicles, digging out buried sledges and the thousand other things which made the time of preparation for spring all too short. We worked hard on the camping equipment, mending tents, binding tent poles with tape or balloon cord to strengthen them, checking and repacking ration boxes, overhauling field radio equipment – all laborious jobs which took many hours.

By the end of July the temperature at Shackleton dropped to – 64°F with a 25 knot wind. At South Ice it was –71°F. But by the beginning of August both bases enjoyed the faint glow of the returning sun reflected from below the horizon. Day by day the light on the clouds became more colourful and steadily increased until it was possible for us to move about outside without the aid of lanterns to light our way.

Sno-cats and Crevasses

With a party of ten Fuchs set out by snow tractor from Shackleton Base, Weddell Sea, on 24 November 1957.

In spite of our late start we made 15 miles before pitching camp for the night, and after 14 miles next day we thought that we were

well set for a long run. Then, as if to laugh at such optimism, a
snow bridge fell away beneath Rock 'n Roll, leaving David
Stratton and myself suspended in mid-air over an enormous hole
– it was about 15 feet wide and 60 feet deep to the first step in the
walls of the crevasse below. Peering out of the driving seat was
distinctly alarming, for I did not know how firmly the vehicle was
wedged against the sides, and in any case there was nothing on to
which I could step out – even the pontoons were inaccessible.
However, David found that on his side he could just about reach
the rear pontoon and we were able to crawl to firm snow across
the ladder-like track as it hung in space over the abyss.

At first sight it looked as if we would have to abandon the
vehicle – a real catastrophe at this early stage of our journey – and
we began to remove everything from inside the cab. Then we
determined to "have a go" and thought out a plan to recover it.
David Pratt and Roy moved the two other Sno-Cats side by side
behind Rock 'n Roll and attached them by steel cables to the rear
towing hook. Next, after careful prospecting along the length of
the crevasse, we found a point where George and Allan could take
their Weasels over and bring them round in front of Rock 'n Roll.
There they were joined in tandem and attached by another cable
to the Sno-Cat's front axle. In this way they formed an anchor,
preventing the front of the vehicle from falling vertically into the
crevasse when an attempt was made to pull it out backwards.

On a Sno-Cat each track runs round a pontoon. These pontoons are themselves free to swivel about the axles in a vertical
plane, which made it very difficult for us to move the front ones
into the correct position to rise over the edge of the crevasse. The
Muskeg was hitched to one of the front pontoons so that it could
swing it as the two Sno-Cats hauled slowly backwards. The other
was helped into position by David Stratton, whom we lowered
into the crevasse on a rope so that he could cut out a ledge to
receive it. When everything was ready we had five vehicles to
control simultaneously.

On a given signal the two Sno-Cats brought their total of 400
horse-power to bear, using the emergency low gear known to us
as "Grandma", while the Weasels kept their lines taut to hold up
the front of Rock 'n Roll as she gradually moved backwards, and
the Muskeg (driven in yet a third direction) brought the free

pontoon safely over the edge and into position. It seemed to require a gargantuan effort and we held our breath as the vehicles strained to perform their tasks. When the recovery was at last safely accomplished, it was discovered that we had left Rock 'n Roll in forward gear all the time! The whole incident had delayed us five hours.

Next day we pressed on over many more crevasses. From our previous experience over the route we believed them to be quite small, but then we received another warning when a crevasse lid 15 feet wide collapsed only a few feet in front of Roy's County of Kent, after all the other five vehicles had passed safely over it. When Roy stopped, his tracks were only three feet from the brink. He now had to reverse away from the hole and find another place where the crevasse could be crossed safely – a very difficult and tedious operation as the two sledges behind him could not be pushed backwards and he could therefore only reverse a few feet at a time. After that we went ahead on skis over the route, probing for crevasses every few yards, and finding a great many which had not been there on our first journey to South Ice. Undoubtedly, during the intervening weeks, the sun had weakened the snow bridges, and now, with more vehicles to worry about, we had to be doubly careful, for we began to find monstrous black caverns beneath the seemingly smooth surface.

By the evening of the 29th we had reached the old 50-Mile Depot, but a number of minor mechanical troubles had arisen; David Pratt and Roy were constantly changing radiators, hunting for coolant leaks in the very complicated engine systems, or trying to cure obstinate ignition troubles. We were particularly worried by the appearance of considerable wear on the rollers of Rock 'n Roll's front left track which had not been seen before she fell into the first crevasse. We were unable to find the cause (later it proved to be nothing to do with the crevasse accident), but I decided we must have a new pontoon and rollers sent out by air from Shackleton.

After leaving the depot we cleared the remaining four miles of crevasses in that particular belt and covered 27 miles in the day. On 1 December we moved 41 miles, but that night County of Kent drove into camp misfiring badly, and needing attention; we also began to dismantle the damaged pontoon on Rock 'n Roll to inspect the bearings. Maintenance work held us up until the 3rd when we travelled for thirteen hours and covered sixty-five miles over the broad undulations of the ice shelf; at the time it seemed only a fair distance, but it proved to be the best mileage we were to make until long after we had passed the South Pole.

We were now only seven miles from the eleven-mile wide crevasse belt lying in front of the ice wall, and with confidence we set out to find the chequered flag which we had planted in October to mark the first of the crevasses. As we saw it and just as I was about to say to David Stratton, "I should stop a little way before you get there", we felt again that horrible, prolonged sinking sensation. The bonnet rose up and up in front of us, then there was a jolt and a pause, long enough to make us think we had settled, followed by a further sickening lurch as the back sank still further. Once more we were down a hole. Carefully we crept out and scrambled to the firm snow surface, where we found the front pontoons holding grimly to the other edge of the chasm while the back of the "cat" was nearly level with the surface. When the others came up they reported that we had been breaking a number of small holes through the surface, and that they had been trying unsuccessfully to attract our attention. Here again was an area where the later season was revealing dangers we had not seen on our reconnaissance run.

As we worked to recover the vehicle it was discovered that the cause of our second lurch was the breaking of four bolts holding the towing hook, for this had torn away from the Sno-Cat and allowed the back to drop deeper. When we had Rock 'n Roll on the surface again we found that the large cast aluminium steering platform for the rear pontoons had been snapped on both sides. Fortunately David Pratt had brought a spare and repair work began at once. This went on late into the night and during the next day, while the rest of us began the endless business of probing our way through the eleven miles of crevasses – it was clear that in spite of our knowledge of the route, it was still going to be slow work.

Owing to lack of time the engineers had been unable to make three more of the complicated forward towing attachments which had been devised for Haywire on the reconnaissance journey. Therefore our three Sno-Cats could not be roped together and were in greater danger of falling into crevasses than the other vehicles. For this reason, and because the loss of a Weasel was less important than the loss of a "cat", we now sent the two Weasels and the Muskeg ahead, roped together. In this way the leading Weasel acted as a crevasse detector.

On the 9th, we were moving forward in this new order over a section of the probed route, when David Stratton, who was skiing ahead to guide my leading Weasel over the prepared track, suddenly pointed back. There behind us we could see two loaded sledges but no third Sno-Cat. At first I feared that David Pratt had dropped right down a crevasse, but then I could just make out a part of the vehicle standing up in front of the sledges. Clearly he was in a bad position and figures could be seen moving about and waving, presumably to call us back.

As we returned on skis, Hal Lister met us to say that all the vehicles would be needed for the recovery, so we unhitched from our various sledges, prodded a turning space for each vehicle, and started back over a course like a switch-back, where the numerous smaller crevasse bridges had sunk or broken through. Arriving at the scene we found Able resting in the crevasse with only the very tips of the front pontoons on the surface, the main weight of the vehicle being supported by the back of the body, and the rear pontoons hanging free.

Here was a very different recovery problem. It would be necessary to support the rear pontoons from below when the vehicle was drawn forwards, for there was certainly no possibility of hauling her out backwards. Luckily, directly beneath Able and about 25 feet down, the walls of the crevasse came very close together, so we all set to with shovels to fill in the hole below, until it was possible for men to stand on the snow filling we had made, and to set lengths of aluminium crevasse bridging in place beneath the pontoons. To secure them, ledges were cut into the walls of the crevasse upon which the aluminium spans could rest at a sloping angle beneath the tracks. The spans had been specially constructed in 14-foot lengths, each weighing 125 lbs and strong enough to carry four tons.

It was impossible to put the bridging into position on both sides at exactly the same angle so the whole structure looked even more precarious than it really was. To be on the safe side steel rope slings were placed round the ends of the bridging pieces and fastened to "dead-men", stout timbers buried several feet below the surface to act as anchors. When all was ready, Rock 'n Roll and County of Kent began to pull ahead, while two Weasels, acting as a drag anchor behind Able, gradually gave way at the back. As Able started slowly to move, the cables taut, there was suddenly a loud crunch as the ledges under the bridging gave way and the vehicle lurched sideways to sink deeper – but, to our great relief, the dead-men held. Then, like some monster rising from the deep, she seemed to heave and wallow her way to the surface, and finally came clear.

When reloading was complete, and all the tools, steel cable, shackles, boards, bridging, ropes and other equipment had been returned to the various vehicles, we set off for the third time over the broken and sagging crevasse bridges along the trail we had already made. With a few diversions, and great care in driving, everyone reached the sledges, hooked up and continued safely to the end of the probed route.

Travelling via the Pole and Depot 700, and with the aid of Sir Edmund Hillary, Fuchs reached the far side of Antarctica on 2 March 1958. He had travelled 2,158 miles across the white desert.

Cape Adare

David Lewis

A New Zealander, Lewis became, in 1973–4, the first person to sail single-handedly to Antarctica. Three years later he returned to the Antarctic in the yacht Solo *with an eight-person expedition funded by the Oceanic Research Foundation. Among the landfalls of the* Solo *expedition was Cape Adare, where Carsten Borchgrevink had made the first over wintering on the continent (in 1899) and where Scott's Northern Party had made their base (1911).*

Midnight had passed. It was now 23 January. A flutter of excitement was caused when Pieter Arriens spotted an Emperor penguin, the only one seen on the entire voyage. Emperors share with Adélies the distinction of being truly Antarctic but, unlike the latter, they breed on the fast ice itself, not on the land at all. The eggs are laid and the chicks reared on the Emperors' enormous vascular feet, where they are enfolded by a protective layer of skin. The little creatures need all the protection they can get for the eggs are laid in the fearful cold of the Antarctic mid-winter blizzards.

Beyond Cape Adare was a snow saddle, behind which the land rose gradually to a gentle rounded summit. The slopes were obviously easy going.

"How about that for a good afternoon's stroll?" I suggested to Fritz, "if you and I can get away."

"Glad to, skipper. Only too pleased to get my feet on something solid after this rocking stuff."

My chagrin was complete when I looked more closely at the map. Me, who really should have known the scale of this Antarctic land! The "hill" I had proposed to stroll up in an afternoon was twenty miles from the landing place. It was as high above sea level as Mount Kosciusko, the summit of Australia!

A more serious cause for concern as we closed in was the inshore pack ice that could now be seen to form a possibly impenetrable barrier between us and the land. Some enormous icebergs came into view, several of which were clearly grounded on the "shoals reported to extend from three to four miles westward of Cape Adare". The prospects of a landing which, hours before, had looked so bright, were now doubtful in the extreme. It was with a heavy heart that I came off watch at 2 a.m. and handed over to Lars.

I was all the more delighted, when awakened at 5 a.m., to find that Lars and Pieter between them had managed to weave their way back and forth across the mouth of Robertson Bay, sometimes down the narrowest of leads, and had now brought *Solo* inside the shoals whereon the bergs were grounded and into a polynia five cables off a rock spire in the shelter of the beetling promontory.

Ridley Beach, a triangular spit of gravel cemented by millennia-old deposits of penguin guano, and a dozen hectares in extent, could be made out from the rigging. It was the site of the old huts. But between us and the beach lay seemingly impenetrable pack, which extended as far as the eye could see. Moreover the pack was moving out towards us at around two knots. Since no open water was visible in the depths of Robertson Bay, it was clear that a current must be sweeping the ice into the bay along the southern shore, which seemed a stone's throw away in that clear atmosphere but was actually eighteen miles off. After their long circuit the floes were emerging past the northern cape where *Solo* lay so uneasily.

Looking to seaward, I saw with some misgiving how the line of grounded bergs revealed more graphically than any chart the presence of the shoals the *Pilot Book* had warned against. The risk of being trapped between the drifting pack and immovable bergs was obvious. Nevertheless, our polynia seemed more or less stationary. Although no open passage to the beach was apparent, I resolved to try for a landing in the Beaufort inflatable.

Pieter, Peter, Ted and I pushed off without any very sanguine hopes. When in doubt try for the shore lead, I thought. And sure enough, right in under the beetling cliff, where the swell boomed hollowly and the backwash sucked noisily away from the ledges,

there was a meandering broken passage between the close pack
and the land. Time and again brash ice rafted underneath the
inflatable until she was brought to a standstill, lifted almost out of
the water. We blessed the propellor guard on the Evinrude, for all
that was necessary was to go into reverse and pole with the
paddles to win free – until the next time. I was more than grateful
too for the Beaufort's stout fabric, since a bad puncture that
would set us floundering in the icy water and scrambling for the
dubious refuge of the nearest floe was no cheerful prospect.

Before long the cliffs receded, to be replaced by steep snow
slopes and a shoreline fronted by an impenetrable jumble of
massive floes grounded on the shelving bottom. Judging by the
height – a metre or more – of their flotation lines above the water,
the tide was low. Further out the drifting mass of floes went
spinning by. In and out along the leads we weaved and, before we
knew it, we were off Ridley Beach itself, searching for an opening
between the close-set grounded floes.

'There's a gap!' called Ted, who was in the bow with his movie
camera. He pointed and I swung the tiller and turned down the
lane he had indicated between the undercut green walls of ice. As
the Beaufort surged up to the shingle we tumbled out dry shod
and ran it up out of reach of the waves. To make doubly sure the
painter was looped round a block of ice. A group of Adélie
penguins emerging from the water (this was clearly their access
road too) made grudging way for us. For Peter Donaldson and
Ted this was their first landing on the Antarctic mainland.

Peter wrote:

I was elated as I jumped from the inflatable on to an icy beach.
Antarctica has fascinated me ever since reading about Scott and
Amundsen as a boy and now I thought "Bloody hell, I've
finally got here". Ted seemed quite surprised when I solemnly
shook his hand. On topping a small rise, we saw an almost
surrealistic sight: an enormous penguin rookery of perhaps a
million Adélies and, right in the middle of this teeming life, sat
our goal – three old wooden huts. Walking across the rookery
towards them, most penguins ignored us. Many adults were
away fishing whilst the chicks sheltered in nurseries from
marauding skuas. However, to our great amusement, one adult

took an instant dislike to David: perhaps it was his bright red insulated suit, but everywhere he went, it followed – snapping at a most uncomfortable height. David maintained some semblance of dignity for a while but this dissolved when the penguin's chick joined the fray for a few snaps.

This last was delightful. After intently watching its elder, the chick waddled up to me with a comical air of bravado. Having delivered its token peck against my heavily quilted thigh, it swaggered back to its parent, so obviously preening itself at its daring as to leave us helpless with laughter.

Before setting out for the huts we called up *Solo* on the walkie-talkie: "*Solo, Solo*, this is Rubber Duck calling *Solo*. Come in please, Over." No reply. "*Solo*, this is Rubber Duck. We have landed on Ridley Beach. Are you all right? Come in please. Over."

But there was still no answer. The transmitter, tested only half an hour before, was no longer working. (This was the only radio failure on the entire trip.) There was no way of knowing whether Lars was receiving us (he was, it turned out) but, in any case, I was anxious for the safety of the ship.

"Let us get over to the huts as fast as we can and do some double-quick time filming. Then we must be on our way back. There isn't even time to climb Cape Adare to look for Hansen's grave," I decided.

The enormous Adélie rookery was far more crowded than the one at Sabrina Islet. Overcrowded, judging by the aggressive behaviour of some of the "nursemaids" and parents, to say nothing of the obviously undesirable sites of nests on the edges of melt pools, and the legions more that stretched as far as one could see up the steep 300-metre slopes of the cape itself. Priestley in 1911 had also noted this overcrowding. Dead chicks lay everywhere, though there was no way of telling in that below-zero climate how many years or even centuries some of them had been there. Certain it was that the ever-attendant skuas were well fed, because they showed little interest in potential strays on the fringes of the crèches.

As we neared the huts and observed that the westernmost had but two walls standing, we naturally assumed it to be the oldest.

"No, that must be Scott's," insisted Pieter. "Look at the construction of this intact hut – tongued and grooved at the corners like a log cabin, heavy half-rounded timbers. It is typical Norwegian." He was obviously right. The thinner boarding and more prodigal use of nails in the tumble-down hut was confirmation if any had been needed. It was with considerable respect that we looked at Borchgrevink's 79 year-old hut and store room (the latter unroofed, as it had been in Priestley's day, but otherwise unchanged) and noted the intact shutters and door, the sand and snow-blasted woodwork and the rusted supporting cables. As we fossicked around it became clear that, while iron and steel rusted in the salt sea air – nails and barrel hoops, for instance – woodwork and even the unidentifiable contents of varnished food cans were preserved intact from decay.

Peter Donaldson conjures up the scene:

As we examined the amazing row of old barrels, bottles, cases of briquettes and food tins buried in the penguin guano, the old faded photographs and verbose descriptions of the inhabitants sprang to life. Perhaps the most interesting relic was half of the boat that had been wrecked and dragged across sea ice in a desperate struggle in 1899. Everywhere penguins sheltered, in boxes and even in the toilet pit. What a place to be when the ship and the penguins have departed, when the wind starts blowing pebbles amongst the desiccated carcasses of long-dead birds. Perhaps venturing here in a small boat made us feel akin to those pioneers but the sight of the small wind-buffeted huts in that desolate place with its pervading aura of death, was startling and extremely moving.

One of the most disturbing sights for me was the extraordinary 15-metre-high ridge of pressure ice, floes distorted and packed one on top of the other, that reared up high above the *inner* margin of Ridley Beach. Suppose we *had* succeeded in bringing *Solo* into Robertson Bay and she had been caught in *that* – to become a compressed filling in a deadly sandwich! Suppose we had lingered too long in the Sturge Island anchorage. The same unimaginable forces that had piled up those five-metre-thick floes would have crushed Solo as flat as a tin can under a steam roller!

"Sorry, Ted. We must finish the filming now and get back to *Solo*." The unfortunate cameraman wrote later: "I was perspiring profusely as I literally ran around trying to cram into one hour's shooting what I had hoped to have several days to do."

We hastened to the Beaufort and pushed off. Back in the narrow leads I was not at all cheered to see that fresh pancake ice, like one-metre-wide waterlily leaves with upturned edges, was forming between the old floes. Despite its being high summer, the sea was beginning to freeze. A cold snap here could trap us.

I was not too anxious to fail to be amused at the clumsy attempts to take-off of the giant petrels that wandered about the floes. These huge birds, larger even than the smaller albatross species, were known to the old sailors as stinking nellies. All birds of the petrel family will regurgitate their stomach contents, with considerable force and accuracy, at intruders who disturb them. Considering the size of the nelly and presumably of its stomach, and the fact that it is a scavenger, the reason for its nickname is not far to seek.

Being so heavy, the nelly needs a long take-off run. We watched them careering over the irregular surfaces of the floes, wings waving wildly, slipping and stumbling and scattering the indignant Adélies in their path and, as often as not, ending ignominiously in the sea in a cloud of spray.

It was no small relief to find *Solo* in much the same place as we had left her, though in a much shrunken polynia. There was time for the rest of the crew to go ashore, but they would have to hurry. As Dot put it in her diary: "Pack seemed to be closing in again but on seeing Jack's face, David decided it should be our turn to go ashore. Fritz, Jack, Lars and me." It was true, as Dot recognised, that I was very conscious of the "rewards" (in terms of time ashore in the Antarctic) that everyone had more than earned during the weary, uncomfortable months at sea, but safety was the primary consideration. A spare walkie-talkie accompanied Rubber Duck so that the party could be recalled at will.

Just as we had, the second shore party found the impact of the enormous penguin rookery overwhelming. "We counted forty or fifty chicks with four or five adults on guard at each nursery, of which there were hundreds, going nearly to the top of Cape

Adare," Dot wrote. She noted that drifted snow, seeping in around the doors and shutters, had filled Borchgrevink's hut. She was impressed too with the splayed-out staves of the barrels, whose hoops had rusted away, and with the penguins nesting within them. Indeed, there was never a box nor a cranny innocent of its round-eyed little denizen to greet the towering intruder with a belligerent "Ark, Ark".

Dot found the huge ridge of pressure ice that towered over the inner side of Ridley Beach as ominous as I had and was not too surprised when I radioed that the pack was moving in rapidly. The returning party found a lot more ice on the way back to *Solo*, but on the way they made one observation which was particularly interesting. In Dot's words: "If we followed the Adélies going to sea via the leads, the way was clear all through the bigger pieces."

In the interim we had not been idle aboard *Solo*. As mentioned earlier, when sea water freezes to form pack ice the salt takes no part in the process and subsequently leaches out, leaving fresh "drinkable" ice, usually by the end of the first season. This ice can be "quarried" for drinking water but the snag is that, if left to itself in the Antarctic, it will not melt but remain on deck as useful as so many blocks of granite. Pieter Arriens had designed a most ingenious but simple device to melt the ice without using extra fuel. A copper coil had been constructed that just fitted inside a large plastic container about twice the size of a bucket. The waste engine cooling water was led into one end of the coil. After circulating through the spirals, a rubber tube carried the waste water to a cockpit drain, where it ran away into the sea. Blocks of ice were packed round the coil. If Pieter was right, the warmth of the engine-cooling water would melt the ice. Now was a good time to put the apparatus to test.

Solo's bow was nosed hard into a large floe, upon which the two Peters, armed with ice saws, axes and crowbars, landed. Soon they were cutting out great snow and ice blocks, with which they staggered back to the yacht. Before long the foredeck was piled so high that it looked like a tumble-down igloo and the melting process was commenced. It worked like a charm. The ice chunks melted with unbelievable rapidity and the melted water was poured into plastic containers. Peter's salinometer came into play.

"Almost pure," he announced, and read off the figures.

"Why, that is a good deal purer than the Adelaide water supply!" exclaimed the delighted Pieter.

But by now the pack was closing in with a vengeance and it was time to recall the second shore party if we were not to be beset. Being beset – held immovably in the pack – is one thing in clear water; I had had four peaceful days of it in *Ice Bird*. It is quite another when the pack is likely to come up against an obstruction and become compressed into the terrifying pressure ridges that can destroy the strongest ship. The grounded bergs and shoals off Cape Adare afforded an excellent setting for such a drama.

As soon as the rest of the crew were aboard, and while the Beaufort was still being manhandled onto the coach roof and the Evinrude lashed in place by the rails, *Solo* was got under way. It was 11.30 a.m., just under six hours since the first party had set out for the shore. The next two and a half hours were anxious ones while the yacht was manoeuvred from lead to lead, always at the direction of someone aloft. As Dot says: "It was a long slow trip out to clear water. Ted did a great job with Lars and Pieter Arriens up the ratlines. Intense concentration all the time. Of course I was, as usual when the men were worried, in the way, so I stayed silently in the stern. Made a cuppa and lay down for a while."

Now was the time for decision. Once *Solo* was in open water outside the pack, the dredge was lowered in an effort to obtain a bottom sample, while I retired below to mull over the charts, sailing directions and ice reports and to decide on our future plan of action. I was amused to note that the compass variation, which is 12°E in Sydney, was 100°E here off Cape Adare, which was beyond – to the south of – the South Magnetic Pole. Thus if the compass had been more sensitive and still working, its north-seeking needle would have pointed a little south of east. That would be a sight not many sailors had seen!

The Killer Under the Water

Gareth Wood

Accompanied by Robert Swan and Roger Mear, Wood undertook the "In the Footsteps of Scott" expedition in 1984–5. The expedition was a signal success; it was the aftermath that was a disaster. Wood's support ship was crushed by ice, leaving him stranded for a second winter in Antarctica. Then, hiking over frozen Backdoor Bay with companions Tim Lovejoy and Steve Broni, Wood was attacked from under the ice:

The going was easy and as I moved over the ice I had no idea that I was being stalked from beneath its surface.

Ahead was a working crack which was slightly more than one stride in width – too far to comfortably cross without jumping. It was covered with a very thin layer of unblemished ice. Innocently, I stepped closer. Would it hold my weight, I wondered, or would I have to jump? Stretching one foot down, I probed it with the tip of my crampon, much as I'd done with dozens of other working cracks in similar circumstances. Suddenly, the surface erupted as the massive head and shoulders of a mature leopard seal, mouth gaping in expectation, crashed through the eggshell covering. It closed its powerful jaws about my right leg, and I fell backward, shocked and helpless in its vise-like grip. Feeling myself being dragged toward a watery grave, I locked my left crampon onto the opposing edge. I knew that once I was in the water, it would be all over.

"Help, help, Steve, Tim, help," I screamed repeatedly. It seemed an age before I finally caught sight of their running figures.

"Kick it, kick it, kick it, get the bloody thing off me, hurry, hurry for Christ's sake, you bastard, you bastard," I yelled hysterically, my gloved hands scrabbling fruitlessly for purchase on the smooth ice behind me as I strained against the seal's prodigious weight.

For one tiny fraction of a second our eyes met. These were not the pleading eyes of a Weddell seal nor the shy glance of a crabeater seal – they were cold and evil with intent. What fear the seal must have recognized in my own during this brief moment of communication, I can only imagine.

"Bloody hell, it's a leopard seal," Steve shouted breathlessly as he leapt across the crack to attack the brute from the opposite side.

"Get the bloody thing off me, kick it, for Christ's sake," I screamed again.

"Aim for its eye, its eye," Tim shouted, his voice verging on panic.

"Bastard! Bastard! Bastard!" Steve chanted in rhythm to his swinging boot.

"Get its eye, blind it," Tim shouted again.

I watched, dazed, as the front tines of Steve's cramponed boot made small, fleshy wounds in the side of the beast's head near its eye. Fifteen or 20 times his foot swung with crushing impact. Blood streamed from the wounds and spattered to the ice with each sickening smack of the boot. The impact of the violent attack vibrated through my body. Stubbornly, the beast continued to grip my leg, which appeared tiny in its jaw. I felt as powerless as a mouse caught by a cat.

"It's backing off," Tim shouted triumphantly as the seal suddenly released its hold and slipped slowly back beneath the surface.

Numbed, confused, and mesmerized by the concentric ripples slapping the edge of the bloodstained hole, I stared entranced at the spot where the frightening beast had disappeared.

"Quick, get him back from the edge," Tim gasped.

Arms had just grabbed me when the seal's monstrous form leapt once more from its watery lair. Lunging at me, it crossed the ice with an awkward gait, streams of bloody water cascading to the ice around it. Its large, interlocking teeth crushed down on my plastic boot.

"My God, we've blown it," I gasped. "Kick it, kick it, for

Christ's sake, kick it," I shouted, the fear in my throat threatening to choke me.

"Its eye, get its eye," Steve shouted as he and Tim again booted its head with the lance-like front tines of their crampons.

Irrational thoughts carreered madly about my brain. What would the ice look like from beneath the surface? What would death be like? As if divorced from life already, I pictured the seal swimming down with my limp, red-coated body in its jaws. I could see pale, green sunlight filtering down through the ice as I descended into the gloom of certain oblivion. It all seemed so real, so peaceful – a silent movie with myself as the reluctant hero.

Tim's tugging at my shoulders pulled me swiftly back to reality – finally vanquished, the animal had retreated to its nether world. They skidded me quickly over the ice a safe distance from the crack. I stood up shakily.

"Lie down, let's have a look," Steve implored, motioning me down.

"No, I'm all right. Thank God it's not broken," I gasped, as I tested my wounded leg by stumbling backward, away from the terror I had just experienced. Glancing down at my torn clothing I saw blood on my leg – whether it was mine or the seal's I was not sure. I unzipped my outer Gore-Tex and fiber-pile pant.

"Oh, my God," I trembled, horrified at the blood and puncture wounds on the front and back of my leg just below my knee.

Melting Point

David Helvarg

Helvarg, an American environmental activist and journalist, visited Antarctica on behalf of the Sierra Club to witness the effects of global warming at first hand:

Clouds, snow, rock, and water hard as black marble are all we can see as we approach Antarctica at the end of our four-day, 900-mile voyage from Punta Arenas, Chile. Up on the bridge the first mate, Robert, is playing Led Zeppelin and talking on the radio with Palmer Station. "Never been this far south without seeing ice," he says.

"That's 'cause we cleared it for you," the base's radioman teases. "Went out in our Zodiacs with blowtorches." We round Bonaparte Point and there it is – Palmer Station, one of three US Antarctic bases administered by the National Science Foundation, prefab blue and white metal buildings with fuel tanks and heavy equipment scattered about, and a boathouse flanked by black rubber Zodiac boats. Behind the station's rocky outcropping looms a calving blue and white glacier; on the surrounding boulder field by Hero Inlet on Anvers Island, we find a greeting committee of Adelie penguins, brown skuas, and elephant seals.

Anvers is 38 miles of granite covered by ice up to 2,000 feet thick. It is part of the Antarctic Peninsula, a 700-mile-long tail to the coldest, driest, highest continent on Earth, a landmass bigger than the United States and Mexico combined, containing more than 70 percent of the world's freshwater and 90 per cent of its ice. Marine and polar climates converge on the peninsula, making it Antarctica's richest wildlife habitat. Researchers jokingly refer to it as "the banana belt".

And that was before global warming.

Bill Fraser, a rangy, weathered, 48-year-old ice veteran from Montana State University, is chief scientist at Palmer, one of 35 researchers and support personnel working there during my visit in the austral summer of 1999. "When I was a graduate student, we were told that climate change was occurring, but we'd never see the effects in our lifetime," Fraser says. "But in the last twenty years I've seen tremendous changes. I've seen islands pop out from under glaciers, species changing places, and landscape ecology altered."

He points upslope. "The Marr glacier used to come within a hundred yards of the station. Its meltwater was the source of our freshwater." Today the glacier is a 400-yard hike across granite rocks and boulders; gull-like skuas splash in the old melt pond while the station is forced to desalinate saltwater. Periodically the artillery rumble of moving ice signals continued glacial retreat, as irregular ice faces collapse into Arthur Harbor amid a blue pall of ice crystals and rolling turquoise waves.

Globally, 1998 was the warmest year on record, breaking previous records set in 1997 and 1995; eight of the ten hottest years in history have occurred in the 1990s. The clue that this warming is related to human activity is that there's more carbon dioxide (from burning fossil fuels) in our atmosphere today than at any time in the past 400,000 years. One of the ways we know this is through ice cores taken from Siple Dome, Vostok, and other sites in the Antarctic interior, which contain trapped bubbles of ancient air. We also know that climate is far less stable than we've imagined, and that the past 10,000 years – the period that's seen the rise of civilization – has been a period of atypical climate stability.

For the past 30 years, climatologists have predicted that planetary warming, when it began, would be most prominent in the polar regions. While the world's average temperature has risen by about one degree Fahrenheit in the past century, the Antarctic Peninsula has warmed by more than 5 degrees in only 50 years – including an incredible 10-degree warming during the winter months. In recent years, pieces of the Larsen B Ice Shelf the size of Rhode Island have calved off the peninsula's eastern shore. That's a sideshow if some predictions are borne out: global-warming scenarios positing a 5-degree temperature rise in the next century project a rise in world sea levels of one to three feet from melting ice. Should the great Western Antarctic Ice Sheet melt – as it apparently has in the past – sea levels could rise by up to 20 feet. Most of the experts who believe the ice will melt don't expect it to do so until sometime after the 21st century. By the time they know for sure, it will be too late to do anything about it.

I may be learning a survival skill for the next millennium, then, when the first thing I do upon arrival is learn how to drive a Zodiac, the fast inflatable boat that, along with thick boots and crampons, provides the main means of transport at Palmer. Soon I'm steering a 15-foot Zodiac through the floating fragments known as brash ice. Spotting a leopard seal on an ice floe, I maneuver to photograph the snaky, blunt-headed predator. A moment later a panicked penguin jumps into my boat, tripping over the gas can. We exchange looks of mutual bewilderment before it leaps onto a pontoon and dives back into the icy blue water.

A few days later I'm out with Bill Fraser and his "Schnappers" (the boat-radio moniker for his seabird researchers, named after a Wisconsin polka band). We tie off on the rocky edge of Humble Island, remove our orange "float coats", and walk to a wide pebbly flat past a dozen burbling 800-pound elephant seals. One rises up just enough to show us a broad pink mouth and issue a belching warning to stay back lest it rouse itself from complete stupor. The elephant seal population, once restricted to more northerly climes, is booming along the now-warming peninsula.

The seals' belches and grunts are soon complemented by the hectic squawking and flipper flapping of thousands of Adelie penguins and their downy chicks, who occupy a series of rocky benches stained clay-red by their droppings. Skuas, looking for a weak chick to feed on, glide overhead.

"These penguins are extremely sensitive indicators of climate change," Fraser says. The pebbled area we're standing on, he explains, is an abandoned Adelie colony. He's been studying the colonies over the past 25 years, and has watched at least one go extinct in the Palmer area every year since 1988. In that time, 15,200 breeding pairs of Adelies declined to 9,200, while the population of chinstrap penguins, who share Adelies' taste for tiny shrimp-like krill, has increased from 6 pairs to 360 pairs. "Here you have two krill predators," says Fraser. "The question we asked ourselves was, why the different trends?"

A clue came in 1988 when the National Science Foundation authorized the first winter cruise in the frozen Weddell Sea on the far side of the peninsula. "We saw trails made by thousands of passing penguins," Fraser recalls. "After about a day and a half, we caught up to this huge line of penguins walking single file toward the edge of the sea ice. They were all Adelies, not a chinstrap among them. We got to the edge and there were about 10,000 birds per square mile."

The population shifts, they concluded, might be a result of abruptly altered habitats. The Adelie feed along the sea ice, the chinstraps in open water. Four out of five Antarctic winters are marked by heavy sea ice, according to Robin Ross, a biological oceanographer from the University of California at Santa Barbara, but in the early 1990s "the cycles of high and low ice began to fall apart. This year's winter sea ice was the lowest on record."

Like the Adelie penguins, plankton-eating krill are dependent on sea ice. The most abundant animal on Earth in terms of total biomass and the base of Antarctica's food web, these crustaceans are consumed by penguins, seals, and whales alike. (A blue whale can consume four tons of krill a day.) "The ice is like an upside-down coral reef," says Ross. "There are lots of bumps and crevasses and caves for krill to hide in. The bottom of the ice is where 70 percent of their larvae are found. Without access to the ice, krill shrink, lose weight, and become more vulnerable."

Ross works off the 240-foot research boat *Laurence M. Gould*, which brought us to Palmer. Her recent trawls along the peninsula have brought up more salps than krill. Salps are open-water jelly creatures that look a bit like floating condoms. Unlike krill, salps reproduce in open water – and may soon fill krill's ecological niche if sea ice continues to decline. Since relatively few creatures feed on salps, a long-term decline in krill could be disastrous for the Antarctic ecosystem.

Back on Humble, I'm waving off a dive-bombing skua while Fraser confers with Rick Sanchez of the US Geological Survey, who clutches a global positioning system unit. Sanchez also has a satellite antenna sticking out of his backpack and a magnesium-shelled laptop computer strapped to an elaborate folding-table rig hanging from his waist and shoulders. He's trying to pace the perimeter (he calls it "the polygon") of an extinct colony of Adelies, but a pile of elephant seals is blocking his way. If he tries to move them they might stampede and crush penguin chicks. Such are the quandaries of high-tech research in Antarctica.

Using 3-D aerial and satellite computer mapping, Fraser and Sanchez are trying to document how global warming is changing the ecology of Antarctica. "We see winter sea ice declining, but we also see warming creating more precipitation in the form of snow," Fraser says. "This snow accumulates on the southern, leeward side of islands, which is where the Adelie colonies are all going extinct, and which is what we're now trying to map. These birds need dry ground to lay and hatch their eggs, but the increased snow is altering the available nesting and chick-rearing habitat. Chinstraps breed later in the season after the snow melts, and so they do better. They're a weedy species. They adapt well to disturbed habitat and can also take fish and squid when krill aren't available because they can dive deeper and feed at night. They're the dandelions of the penguin world."

A similar dynamic is at work among other species. Fur and elephant seals coming in from the north threaten to displace more specialized, ice-dependent seals like Weddells, crabeaters (actually krill eaters), and leopard seals (which eat krill, penguins, crabeaters, and the occasional Zodiac bumper). Worldwide, rapid warming could exacerbate the spread of highly adaptable species like pigeons, rats, deer, and elephant seals and hasten the loss of more specialized endemic creatures like tigers, monarch butterflies, river dolphins, and Adelie penguins.

Climate change is not the first warning issued from the icy continent. In 1981, scientists with the British Antarctic Survey sent up research balloons that detected lower-than-expected levels of protective ozone in the stratosphere. After checking their equipment (they assumed at first their readings were in error) the researchers asked NASA to look at its satellite data, which confirmed a springtime thinning of ozone over Antarctica. Most of the depletion was tracked to chlorofluorocarbons (CFCs), synthetic chemicals widely used in air-conditioning and industrial processes. Without stratospheric ozone, more ultraviolet radiation penetrates the atmosphere, causing genetic damage to plants and animals, including eye damage and higher rates of skin cancer among humans. In response, most of the world's nations signed a treaty banning CFCs and other ozone-depleting chemicals in 1987.

Tad Day, a sandy-haired, 39-year-old professor of plant biology at Arizona State University, drives his Zodiac, *Lucille*, like a race car. For the past five years, Day has been studying how hairgrass and pearlwort, Antarctica's only two native flowering plants, react to increased ultraviolet radiation and a warmer atmosphere. The main study site he and his researchers (radio handle: "Sun-devils") use is Stepping Stone Island, a surprisingly green and rocky isle several miles south of Palmer, surrounded by pale blue icebergs and rumbling glacier, and blessed by a lack of the barnyard odor of penguin colonies.

Amid nesting giant petrels the size of eagles and a friendly skua that he calls Yogi, Day maintains two gardens – fenced to keep fur seals out – with over 90 wire plant frames containing banks of hairgrass and mosslike pearlwort. Each frame has various Aclar, Mylar, and press-polish vinyl filters to control the amount of ultraviolet light and warmth it receives.

Day says he has found that ultraviolet B radiation causes genetic damage and reduces growth somewhat in pearlwort and substantially in hairgrass, while warming improves growth in pearlwort but appears to stunt the grass. "Still, both plants are expanding their range, colonizing new areas where the glaciers are retreating. Both are flowering earlier and producing more seeds, but the relationship is changing. Hairgrass, which was the dominant species, is being displaced by pearlwort."

I ask him what this phenomenon might mean in terms of the rest of the world. "Global warming," he says, "has the capacity to shift the competitive balance of species in ways that we don't understand yet, and that could have important consequences on our ability to produce food and fiber."

"So basically with these greenhouse gases we're doing a kind of giant experiment on the planet?" I suggest.

"Hey," he says, grinning. "You want me to start getting calls from Rush Limbaugh's listeners?"

*   *   *

Day is well aware of the political ramifications of his work. Limbaugh's Dittoheads are just some of the more boisterous targets of a $45 million campaign waged over the last decade by the fossil-fuel industry to promote the idea that there is still no conclusive proof of human impact on climate change. This has included personal attacks on leading scientists, which has made other researchers gun-shy about speaking out in nonprofessional forums. "Scientific uncertainty doesn't play well in politics," explains Robin Ross. "Someone with a strong position has more credibility, even if they're wrong."

Bill Fraser has chosen to speak out about what's happening to Antarctica at climate-change conferences and congressional hearings. His testimony, like that of other mainstream scientists, was challenged by Patrick Michaels, one of a handful of climate "skeptics" regularly paraded through Washington hearings and the media by the fossil-fuel industry. Michaels edits World Climate Report for the Western Fuels Association, an organization of coal producers, and is a senior fellow at the conservative Cato Institute.

"He used data pooling on the whole Antarctic to say there was no warming, but that's not how ecosystems work," complains Fraser. "You can't use those techniques the way he did. These lobbyists are really out to discredit science."

Despite the increasingly grim implications of climate research in Antarctica, it's hard to maintain a sense of gloom and doom on the last wild continent for more than a few hours at a time. At Palmer you need at least two people with radios if you want to take out one of the Zodiacs, so on days when I wasn't working with the Schnappers or Sundevils I'd spend my time looking for a boating partner. Doc Labarre, the station physician who used to work in the emergency room in Kodiak, Alaska, was among those always up for an adventure. One day I headed us toward Loudwater Cove on the far side of Norsel Point. The following seas allowed us to surf the 15-foot craft past the rocky spires of Litchfield Island and around the big breaking waves at Norsel. We then motored around a few apartment-size icebergs, crossing over to a landing opposite the glacier wall. We tied off our bowline, watching a leopard seal sleeping on an adjacent ice floe.

We dumped our "float coats" and climbed several hundred feet up and over rocky scree and down a snowfield splotched with red algae to reach the opening of an ice cave. Inside, the cave was like a dripping blue tunnel, with a clear ice floor showing down to the rocky piedmont. Hard blue glacier ice formed the bumpy roof with its stalactite-like icicles and delicate ice rills forming pressure joints along its edges. Outside we hiked the loose granite, feldspar, and glacial sand until we encountered a fur seal hauled up on shore, several hundred yards from the water on the sharp broken rocks. He barked and whined a warning at us. Nearby ponds and 100-year-old moss beds had attracted brown skuas, who were nesting and soon began dive-bombing us. I got whacked from behind by one of the five-pound scavengers; it felt like a hard slap on the back of the head. We quickly moved away from their nests, climbing back over the exposed glacier rock, past middens of limpet shells and down a rock chimney to where our boat was tied up. The leopard seal was awake now, scrutinizing us as we took off.

We next dropped by Christine, a bouldery island where we walked past a large congregation of elephant seals lounging opposite a colony of Adelies. Crossing the heights we found mossy green swales with ponds full of brine shrimp, then lay out on a rocky beach at the end of a narrow blue channel, sharing the space with two elephant seals that looked to weigh about 500 and 900 pounds. The southern ocean was crystal clear; the sun emerged and turned the sky cobalt blue. Our perch felt almost tropical, the sound of the waves rolling and retreating across smooth, fist-size stones. The elephant seals were blowing, and blinking their huge red eyes, their pupils the size of teaspoons for gathering light in deep diving forays after squid. A fur seal came corkscrewing through the channel's water before paddle-walking ashore and scratching itself with a hind flipper, a blissful expression on its wolfy face. There we were, just five lazy mammals enjoying a bit of sun.

Driving the Zodiac back to Palmer Station we were accompanied by a flight of blue-eyed shags and squads of dolphin-diving penguins in the water. Doc steered while I kept an eye out for whales. The sky clouded over again, turning the water the color of hammered tin. Each buck of the boat sent a slap of icy saltwater spray in our faces. But instead of repelling us, the untempered contact with Antarctic reality invigorated us. We felt right with the wild.

Antarctica is vast and awesome in its indifference to the human condition. At the same time it's become a world center for scientific research and provided us warning of two of our greatest follies: destruction of the ozone layer and the human impact on climate. Through international action we're well on the way to solving the first problem but remain in denial about the second. But the message from the ice is as plain as the penguin bones I found scattered around a dying Adelie colony. Our world, and theirs, are more intertwined than we imagine.

Mind Over Matter

Catharine Hartley

A thirtysomething TV stage-manager with no previous polar experience, Hartley joined an extreme tourism expedition to the South Pole, led by the explorer Geoff Somers:

Over the next three days the pattern became painfully apparent. Eight fit and strong members of the expedition skied at a reasonable rate for eight hours a day, covering a distance of around eleven miles, battling against blasting, icy winds and temperatures of down to –48°C, taking account of wind-chill. We pulled everything behind us in sleds weighing around eleven stone. Imagine that you spend your entire day dragging a full-grown man behind you as you walk about. There were no injuries yet, and although tired at the end of the day, the team was comfortable, and made camp quite happily. The next morning, we would pack everything up into the sleds and set off for another eight hours. Surprisingly, Justin, who had known nothing about Antarctica, was completely comfortable. He was exceptionally strong and his cavalier attitude of "training as you go" seemed to be working. I sensed he found my pace irritating. I was especially conscious I was an obstacle to his obsession with reaching the Pole for the Millennium.

The ninth member – that was me – was in quite a different position. I continued to find the conditions absolutely awful. I developed a chest infection and was coughing up a sinister fluid. No doubt this was because I only gave up smoking after Punta. I was completely unable to keep up with the apparently gentle pace, and this meant the team had to wait on average three times an hour for me to catch up. I had pain in every muscle and was completely annihilated by the end of each day. I knew the team was getting cold waiting for me. In addition, we only had limited food, so we had target mileages, and I could not ask for longer breaks, let alone days off. Least of all could I "finish early" if I was too tired. I felt doomed. I also noticed that the tip of each finger had turned white and felt strangely wooden, a middle finger in particular. I decided to ignore the fact that I was probably getting frostbite.

Four days from Patriot Hills we came across a crevasse field. Geoff was aware this existed from a Japanese adventurer's hand-drawn map. He did not, however, know the exact locality. That day was a whiteout, I was miserable, and my mind felt unconnected to my body. In the afternoon, the wind started to pick up and the terrain became very icy. It became impossible to ski without sliding over so we took our skis off and walked. At this point Geoff was leading, and seeing a change in the surface twenty feet in front, he went ahead. With a ski pole, he probed a line of softer snow. The pole went straight through, opening up a small crevasse of about two feet wide. Below there was a yawning hole at least fifty feet deep. Geoff collected us together and told us to step over the crevasse and not be fooled by the soft snow bridge on top.

We found and crossed a number of such crevasses until we came across one almost four feet across, again, thinly covered with snow. This time Geoff spanned the crevasse with his sled to act as a handrail and had each of us make the step. I was utterly oblivious to my surroundings, locked in my own mind, concentrating on putting one foot in front of the other and keeping up with the sled in front of me. I was coughing continually now and my lungs and chest felt as if they would explode.

In this state of mind and because of the loud wind, I did not register what Geoff had said. Instead of stepping right across the crevasse I put one foot right on the snow bridge at the weakest point. As my foot plunged through I felt Geoff's hands just yank me into the air and on to the safe ice the other side. Crevasses narrow into a V shape as they deepen. Once jammed inside, rescue is extremely difficult. But for us to rope together in the way glaciers are normally crossed could have been as dangerous. Standing around and sorting out equipment could have very quickly brought on frostbite and hypothermia in such cold conditions. On the crevasse field, the line between control and disaster was a very fine one.

The next day, Fiona took one of my food boxes. It was an extremely kind gesture even though she was one of the strongest. Now I comprehended the enormous swallowing of pride attached to giving up a part of my load. First, it acknowledged that I was actually as slow as I thought I was. The others must have been discussing how to speed me up. Second, it was hard to accept help. Most of us want to be strong and capable, few enjoy being needy and vulnerable. I was used to helping and supporting others in everyday life. Finding myself helpless was a torment. But I gratefully accepted Fiona's offer.

We were now travelling eight hours every day, with four breaks. The breaks themselves proved to be stressful for me. In ten minutes I might have to go to the loo in front of seven men. Invariably, my hands were so cold I would fumble helplessly with the zips of my four layers of trousers. With my huge mittens I would often fail to tuck in the four layers of thermal underwear properly, so for the next session would have a bitter wind grinding into my skin.

I would have little time left to stuff as much food and drink into my mouth as I could with increasingly frozen hands. It took all my effort to undo the zip of my bum bag, pull out a frozen Nutrigrain, Pepperami or chocolate bar and put it into my mouth. The temptation was to pull off my gloves to make the whole procedure quick and simple, but to expose my hands at this point would have meant possible frostbite. They were already in agony simply because I had stopped moving for a few minutes. The breaks were strictly timed by one of the team members and at ten minutes there would be a shout of "Time!" We would have to put our skis on, and then haul ourselves up for the next two-hour march. My breaks were often shorter – I had used, perhaps, four minutes catching up with everyone while they were eating. At this point I was generally on the verge of tears, because I was so tired. But there was a real disadvantage if I actually cried. I found tears would freeze round my eyes and make it difficult for me to see properly.

I would spend the first ten minutes after each break moving my hands wildly to get the blood back in them and warm them up. I remember my friend Liza, whom I had met on Pen's selection course, and who had already had polar experience, advising me to "play the piano with my fingers" to keep them from freezing. Because I was exerting myself so much, my goggles would fill up with condensation. The condensation would then quickly freeze and ten minutes into the march I would be almost blind, unable to distinguish much through the thick film of ice.

That evening I set up the tent with Steve. I got out my pee bottle and discovered I stupidly had not emptied it from the morning. It was frozen solid. I put it by the stove to thaw; Steve did not bat an eyelid. A little later, we were having our first warm drink of the evening when Geoff poked his head through the tent door. He looked very serious. "Go for a walk for five minutes," he told Steve. "I need to talk to Catharine."

Quite where Steve was going to walk I don't know, but I knew immediately I was in trouble. It was that tap on the shoulder I had been waiting for. Hurriedly and awkwardly Geoff expressed grave concerns about my ability to continue. It was clear he felt I was quite incapable of making the trip and wanted me off the expedition. He left my tent with the words, "The plane is only sixty miles and a radio call away, I suggest you think about taking it." Steve came nervously back in. "Are you all right, Cath?" he asked. No, I was absolutely shattered. As ever, Steve was kind. I should not go, he argued, things would get better. Not wanting to impose myself on him at that moment, when he was so constantly supportive, I reapplied my five layers of clothing, three pairs of gloves, face mask and goggles and finally reached for a Nicorette chewing gum. Then I visited Mike and Fiona for counselling.

Mike and Fiona could have been sympathetic, but in agreement with Geoff. Then I would be off their backs and the team could continue without my holding them up. Instead, they were extremely supportive. Mike said: "Change your mindset, Catharine. You must have determination just to have come this far, so rather than feeling sorry for yourself, wake up tomorrow with a positive attitude. Geoff hasn't chucked you off; he's simply suggested you go. Show him that you won't, show him that what you lack in physical ability you have tenfold in mental determination. Fight him!"

Their encouragement was enough to strengthen my resolve to continue. I was overwhelmed by their support, especially by

Fiona's. Their sponsorship relied on her breaking that record of being the first British woman to the Pole and she had been the only woman on the trip until just a fortnight before we left. Suddenly to have to share the possibility must have been galling and I had always been uncertain how she must feel about me. A lesser person would have wanted me off at the earliest moment. How selfless she must be.

I could hear the entire "zoo" of Zoë Ball's breakfast show. Knowing I was a fan of it, Steve was recreating it for me in the confines of a tent in the middle of the Antarctic wastelands to give me the best possible start to my day. It worked. I got up terrified but with a fighting attitude. I knew it was very likely my last chance. So my plan was to keep up with the sled in front of me, come what might. I would show Geoff.

I lined up between Steve and Fiona. Steve whispered, "Good luck." Fiona told me to stick to the back of her sled like glue and not let it get more than three feet away from me. Mike gave me a squeeze on the arm and reminded me, "Just fight him." It felt like a self-assertiveness class I had attended some years before. I did as they instructed and out of nowhere I found physical strength. I thought about nothing except not allowing Fiona's sled to get away from my skis. My legs were burning and I was absolutely exhausted but I kept up. At the end of the day, Geoff gave me an approving nod before going into his tent. I went to bed so much happier.

Hartley and companion Fiona Thornewill became the first British women to walk to the South Pole. The following year they walked to the North Pole.

Swimming to Antarctica

Lynne Cox

Holder of the record for swimming the English Channel, the first person to swim the Bering Strait from Alaska to Siberia, Lynne Cox also became, in 2002 the first person to swim a mile off the coast of Antarctica. The water temperature was 32 degrees.

When I hit the water, I went all the way under. I hadn't intended to do that; I hadn't wanted to immerse my head, which could over-stimulate my vagus nerve and cause my heart to stop beating. Dog-paddling as quickly as I could, I popped up in the water, gasping for air. I couldn't catch my breath. I was swimming with my head up, hyperventilating. I kept spinning my arms, trying to get warm, but I couldn't get enough air. I felt like I had a corset tightening around my chest. I told myself to relax, take a deep breath, but I couldn't slow my breath. And I couldn't get enough air in. I tried again. My body wanted air, and it wanted it now. I had to override that reaction of hyperventilating. I had to concentrate on my breath, to press my chest out against the cold water and draw the icy air into my lungs.

My body resisted it. The air was too cold. My body didn't want to draw the cold air deep into my lungs and cool myself from the inside. It wanted to take short breaths so the cold air would be warmed in my mouth before it reached my lungs. I was fighting against myself.

I noticed my arms. They were bright red, and I felt like I was swimming through slush. My arms were thirty-two degrees, as cold as the sea. They were going numb, and so were my legs. I pulled my hands right under my chest so that I was swimming on the upper inches of the sea, trying to minimize my contact with the water. I was swimming fast and it was hard to get enough air.

I began to notice that the cold was pressurizing my body like a giant tourniquet. It was squeezing the blood from the exterior part of my body and pushing it into the core. Everything felt tight. *Focus on your breath*, I told myself. *Slow it down. Let it fill your lungs. You're not going to be able to make it if you keep going at this rate.*

It wasn't working. I was laboring for breath harder than on the test swim. I was in oxygen debt, panting, gasping. My breath was inefficient, and the oxygen debt was compounding. In an attempt to create heat, I was spinning my arms wildly, faster than I'd ever turned them over before. Laura later told me that I was swimming at a rate of ninety strokes per minute, thirty strokes per minute quicker than my normal rate. My body was demanding more oxygen, but I couldn't slow down. Not for a nanosecond. Or I would freeze up and the swim would be over.

An icy wave slapped my face: I choked and felt a wave of panic rise within me. My throat tightened. I tried to clear my throat and breathe. My breath didn't come out. I couldn't get enough air in to clear my throat. I glanced at the crew. They couldn't tell I was in trouble. If I stopped, Dan would jump in and pull me out. I still couldn't get a good breath. I thought of rolling on my back to give myself time to breathe, but I couldn't. It was too cold. I closed my mouth, overrode everything my body was telling me to do, held my breath, and gasped, coughed, cleared my windpipe, and relaxed just a little, just enough to let my guard down and catch another wave in the face. I choked again. I put my face down into the water, hoping this time I could slow my heart rate down. I held my face in the water for two strokes and told myself, *Relax, just turn your head and breathe.*

It was easier to breathe in a more horizontal position. I thought it might be helping. I drew in a deep breath and put my face down again. I knew I couldn't do this for long. I was losing too much heat through my face. The intensity of the cold was as sharp as broken glass. I'd thought that swimming across the Bering Strait in 38-degree water had been tough, but there was a world of difference between 38 degrees and 32. In a few seconds, the cold pierced my skin and penetrated into my muscles. It felt like freezer burn, like touching wet fingers to frozen metal.

Finally I was able to gain control of my breath. I was inhaling and exhaling so deeply I could hear the breath moving in and out of my mouth even though I was wearing earplugs. I kept thinking about breathing, working on keeping it deep and even; that way I didn't have time to think about the cold.

My brain wasn't working as it normally did. It wasn't flowing freely from one idea to another – it was moving mechanically, as if my awareness came from somewhere deep inside my brain. Maybe it was because my body was being assaulted with so many sensations, too different and too complex to recognize. Or maybe it was because my blood and oxygen were going out to the working muscles. I didn't know.

For the next five or six minutes, I continued swimming, telling myself that I was doing well, telling myself that this was what I had trained for. Then something clicked, as if my body had gained equilibrium. It had fully closed down the blood flow in my skin and fingers and toes. My arms and legs were as cold as the water, but I could feel the heat radiating deep within my torso and head, and this gave me confidence. I knew that my body was protecting my brain and vital organs. Staring through the clear, silver-blue water, I examined my fingers; they were red and swollen. They were different than when I'd been swimming in the Bering Strait, when they'd looked like the fingers of a dead person. They looked healthy, and I thought their swollenness would give me more surface area, more to pull with.

I smiled and looked up at the crew, who were in the Zodiacs on either side of me. Each of them was leaning forward, willing me ahead. Their faces were filled with tension. Gabriella, Barry, Dan, and Scott were leaning so far over the Zodiac's pontoon I felt as if they were swimming right beside me. I was sprinting faster than I ever had before, moving faster than the Zodiac, and I was getting fatigued quickly. The water was thicker than on the test swim, and it took more force to pull through on each stroke. My arms ached. I didn't feel right; I couldn't seem to get into any kind of a rhythm. Then I sensed that something was wrong.

We were heading to the left, toward some glaciers. This didn't make sense; we couldn't land there. It was too dangerous. The glaciers could calve and kill us.

"Barry, where are we going?" I shouted, using air I needed for breathing.

He pointed out our direction – right toward the glaciers. I didn't understand. I didn't want to go that way. I wanted to aim for the beach. I was confused. I was moving my arms as fast as they would go, and it was taking all I had. From each moment to the next, I had to tell myself to keep going. The water felt so much colder than on the test swim. It had already worked its way deep into my muscles. My arms and legs were stiff. My strokes were short and choppy. But I kept going, telling myself to trust the crew and focus on the glaciers to watch the outcropping of rocks that was growing larger. I couldn't get into any kind of pace.

Abruptly the Zodiacs zagged to the right. I looked up and thought, *Wow, okay; we're heading for the beach now*. For a moment, I started to feel better. I was able to extend my reach farther, and I could see passengers from the *Orlova* walking along the snowbanks. In the distance, their clothes lost their color and they looked black, like giant penguins. I saw smaller black figures, too – real penguins nesting near the edge of the shore. For a few moments, I felt like I was going to be okay, like I was going to make it in to shore, but then the Zodiacs abruptly turned farther to the right, and we were headed past the beach for another range of glaciers.

Finally, it occurred to me that the *Orlova* had anchored too close to shore for me to swim a mile, so Barry was adding distance by altering the course. And the ship's captain was on the bridge monitoring our course on his GPS and radioing our Zodiacs, updating them on the distance we had traveled. One of the passengers, Mrs. Stokie, who was on the bridge with him, told me later, "The captain was watching you and he was shaking his head. He was an older man, and he had experienced everything. And now he was seeing something new. It was good for him. Still, I think he couldn't believe it."

We continued on right past the beach, toward more glaciers.

"How long have I been swimming?" I asked.

"Fifteen minutes," Barry said.

I had swum a little more than half a mile. I looked up at the shore. If I turned left, I could make it in. I could reach the shore. This struggle could be over. But I wouldn't complete the mile. I had swum farther two days before. But I was tired now, and this was so much harder. I just didn't feel right. I couldn't figure out what the problem was. I kept talking to myself, coaching myself to keep going. Then I felt it; it was the water pressure, and it was increasing on my back. It meant there was a strong current behind me. I looked at the glaciers onshore, using the fixed points to gauge how fast the current was flowing. It was flowing at over a knot. I wondered if I would have enough strength to fight it when we turned around and headed back for the beach. It would cut my speed by half and could cause me to lose heat more rapidly.

Barry and the crew in the Zodiacs couldn't feel what was happening. They had no idea we were moving into a risky area. If the current grew any stronger, it could cost us the swim. Barry motioned for me to swim past a peninsula and across a narrow channel. I lifted my head and pulled my hands directly under my chest, to gain more lift, so I could look across the bay and see if we had any other options for landing. There were no alternatives. This made me very uncomfortable. Chances were good that there would be a strong current flowing into or out of the narrow bay. And if we got caught in that current, all would be lost.

We started across the inlet, and within a moment I could feel that second current, slamming into our right side at two knots, pushing us into the inlet. Without any explanation, I spun around, put my head down, dug my arms into the water, and crabbed into the current. I focused on repositioning myself so I could parallel shore again and head toward Neko Harbor. Barry knew I knew what I was doing. But the abrupt course change caught the Zodiac drivers by surprise. They scattered in different directions, trying to avoid ramming into each other and trying to catch up with me. The motor on the lead Zodiac on my left sputtered and stopped. The second Zodiac immediately pulled up beside me. I sprinted against the current.

"How long have I been swimming?"

"Twenty-one minutes," Barry said. He and all the crew were watching me intently, their faces filled with tension and concern.

I put my head down, and something suddenly clicked. Maybe it was because I knew shore was within reach, or maybe because I got a second wind; I don't know. But I was finally swimming strongly, stretching out and moving fluidly. My arms and legs were as cold as the sea, but I felt the heat within my head and contained in my torso and I thrilled to it, knowing my body had carried me to places no one else had been in only a bathing suit. I looked down into the water; it was a bright blue-gray and so clear that it appeared as if I were swimming through air. The viscosity of the water was different, too; it was thicker than any I had ever swum in. It felt like I was swimming through gelato. And I got more push out of each arm stroke than I ever had before. I looked at the crew. They were leaning so far over the pontoons, as if they were right there with me. I needed to let them know I was okay.

I lifted my head, took a big breath, and shouted, "Barry, I'm swimming to Antarctica!"

I saw the smiles, heard the cheers and laughs, and I felt their energy lift me. They were as thrilled as I was. I swam faster, extending my arms, pulling more strongly, reaching for the shores of Antarctica.

Appendix I

The Last Letters of Robert Falcon Scott RN

In addition to his famous journal of the doomed South Pole expedition, discovered in the tent alongside Scott's corpse were a handful of last letters:

To Kathleen Scott [his wife]

The Great God has called me and I feel it will add a fearful blow to the heavy ones that have fallen on you in life. But take comfort in that I die at peace with the world and myself – not afraid.

Indeed it has been most singularly unfortunate, for the risks I have taken never seemed excessive.

. . . I want to tell you that we have missed getting through by a narrow margin which was justifiably within the risk of such a journey . . . After all, we have given our lives for our country – we have actually made the longest journey on record, and we have been the first Englishmen at the South Pole.

You must understand that it is too cold to write much.

. . . It's a pity the luck doesn't come our way, because every detail of equipment is right.

I shall not have suffered any pain, but leave the world fresh from harness and full of good health and vigour.

Since writing the above we got to within 11 miles of our depôt, with one hot meal and two days' cold food. We should have got through but have been held for *four* days by a frightful storm. I think the best chance has gone. We have decided not to kill ourselves, but to fight to the last for that depôt, but in the fighting there is a painless end.

Make the boy interested in* natural history if you can; it is

---

* Kathleen Scott succeeded admirably in the request, their son, Peter, grew up to be a world-famous ornithologist.

better than games; they encourage it at some schools. I know you will keep him in the open air.

Above all, he must guard and you must guard him against indolence. Make him a strenuous man. I had to force myself into being strenuous, as you know – had always an inclination to be idle.

There is a piece of the Union Jack I put up at the South Pole in my private kit bag, together with Amundsen's black flag and other trifles. Send a small piece of the Union Jack to the King and a small piece to Queen Alexandra.

What lots and lots I could tell you of this journey! How much better has it been than lounging in too great comfort at home! What tales you would have for the boy! But what a price to pay!

Tell Sir Clements I thought much of him and never regretted his putting me in command of the *Discovery*.

To Sir James Barrie

We are showing that Englishmen can still die with a bold spirit, fighting it out to the end. It will be known that we have accomplished our object in reaching the Pole, and that we have done everything possible, even to sacrificing ourselves in order to save sick companions. I think this makes an example for Englishmen of the future, and that the country ought to help those who are left behind to mourn us. I leave my poor girl and your godson, Wilson leaves a widow, and Edgar Evans also a widow in humble circumstances. Do what you can to get their claims recognised. Good-bye. I am not at all afraid of the end, but sad to miss many a humble pleasure which I had planned for the future on our long marches. I may not have proved a great explorer, but we have done the greatest march ever made and come very near to great success . . . We are in a desperate state, feet frozen, etc. No fuel and a long way from food, but it would do your heart good to be in our tent, to hear our songs and the cheery conversation as to what we will do when we get to Hut Point.

Later. – We are very near the end, but have not and will not

lose our good cheer. We have had four days of storm in our tent
and nowhere's food or fuel. We did intend to finish ourselves
when things proved like this, but we have decided to die naturally
in the track.

As a dying man, my dear friend, be good to my wife and child.
Give the boy a chance in life if the State won't do it. He ought to
have good stuff in him . . . I never met a man in my life whom I
admired and loved more than you, but I could never show you
how much your friendship meant to me, for you had much to give
and I nothing.

To Mrs E. A. Wilson [wife of Dr Wilson]

If this letter reaches you, Bill and I will have gone out together.
We are very near it now and I should like you to know how
splendid he was at the end – everlastingly cheerful and ready to
sacrifice himself for others, never a word of blame to me for
leading him into this mess. He is not suffering, luckily, at least
only minor discomforts.

His eyes have a comfortable blue look of hope and his mind
is peaceful with the satisfaction of his faith in regarding
himself as part of the great scheme of the Almighty. I can
do no more to comfort you than to tell you that he died as he
lived, a brave, true man – the best of comrades and staunchest
of friends.

My whole heart goes out to you in pity . . .

To Mrs Bowers
[mother of Lieutenant Henry Bowers]

I am afraid this will reach you after one of the heaviest blows of
your life.

I write when we are very near the end of our journey, and I am
finishing it in company with two gallant, noble gentlemen. One of
these is your son. He had come to be one of my closest and
soundest friends, and I appreciate his wonderful upright nature,
his ability and energy. As the troubles have thickened his daunt-

less spirit ever shone brighter and he has remained cheerful, hopeful, and indomitable to the end.

The ways of Providence are inscrutable, but there must be some reason why such a young, vigorous, and promising life is taken.

To the end he has talked of you and his sisters. One sees what a happy home he must have had, and perhaps it is well to look back on nothing but happiness.

He remains unselfish, self-reliant and splendidly hopeful to the end, believing in God's mercy to you . . .

To Vice-Admiral Sir George le Clerc Egerton [Scott's commanding officer]

I fear we have shot our bolt – but we have been to the Pole and done the longest journey on record.

I hope these letters may find their destination some day.

Subsidiary reasons of our failure to return are due to the sickness of different members of the party, but the real thing that has stopped us is the awful weather and unexpected cold towards the end of the journey.

This traverse of the Barrier has been quite three times as severe as any experience we had on the summit.

There is no accounting for it, but the result has thrown out my calculations, and here we are little more than 100 miles from the base and petering out.

To Vice-Admiral Sir Francis Charles Bridgeman, KCVO KCB

My Dear Sir Francis,

I fear we have shipped up; a close shave; I am writing a few letters which I hope will be delivered some day. I want to thank you for the friendship you gave me of late years, and to tell you how extraordinarily pleasant I found it to serve under you. I want to tell you that I was not too old for this job. It was the younger men that went under first . . .

After all we are setting a good example to our countrymen, if not by getting into a tight place, by facing it like men when we were there. We could have come through had we neglected the sick.

Good-bye, and good-bye to dear Lady Bridgeman.

Yours ever,

R. Scott.

Excuse writing – it is –40 deg., and has been for nigh a month.

To Right Honourable Sir Edgar Speyer, Bart.

Dated 16 March, 1912. Lat. 79.5 deg.

My Dear Sir Edgar,

I hope this may reach you. I fear we must go and that it leaves the Expedition in a bad muddle. But we have been to the Pole and we shall die like gentlemen. I regret only for the women we leave behind.

I thank you a thousand times for your help and support and your generous kindness. If this diary is found it will show how we stuck by dying companions and fought the thing out well to the end. I think this will show that the Spirit of pluck and power to endure has not passed out of our race . . .

Wilson, the best fellow that ever stepped, has sacrificed himself again and again to the sick men of the party . . .

I write to many friends hoping the letters will reach them some time after we are found next year.

We very nearly came through, and it's a pity to have missed it, but lately I have felt that we have overshot our mark. No one is to blame and I hope no attempt will be made to suggest that we have lacked support.

Good-bye to you and your dear kind wife.

Yours ever sincerely,

R. SCOTT.

To J. J. Kinsey, Christchurch

24 March 1912.

My Dear Kinsey,

I'm afraid we are pretty well done – four days of blizzard just as we were getting to the last depot. My thoughts have been with you often. You have been a brick. You will pull the expedition through, I'm sure.

My thoughts are for my wife and boy. Will you do what you can for them if the country won't.

I want the boy to have a good chance in the world, but you know the circumstances well enough.

If I knew the wife and boy were in safe keeping I should have little regret in leaving the world, for I feel that the country need not be ashamed of us – our journey has been the biggest on record, and nothing but the most exceptional hard luck at the end would have caused us to fail to return. We have been to the S. Pole as we set out. God bless you and dear Mrs Kinsey. It is good to remember you and your kindness.

Your friend,

R. SCOTT.

Message to the Public

The causes of the disaster are not due to faulty organization but to misfortune in all risks which had to be undertaken.

1. The loss of pony transport in March 1911 obliged me to start later than I had intended, and obliged the limits of stuff transported to be narrowed.

2. The weather throughout the outward journey, and especially the long gale in 83° S., stopped us.

3. The soft snow in lower reaches of glacier again reduced pace.

We fought these untoward events with a will and conquered, but it cut into our provision reserve.

Every detail of our food supplies, clothing and depôts made on the interior ice-sheet and over that long stretch of 700 miles to the Pole and back, worked out to perfection. The advance party would have returned to the glacier in fine form and with surplus of food, but for the astonishing failure of the man whom we had least expected to fail. Edgar Evans was thought the strongest man of the party.

The Beardmore Glacier is not difficult in fine weather, but on our return we did not get a single completely fine day; this with a sick companion enormously increased our anxieties.

As I have said elsewhere, we got into frightfully rough ice and Edgar Evans received a concussion of the brain – he died a natural death, but left us a shaken party with the season unduly advanced.

But all the facts above enumerated were as nothing to the surprise which awaited us on the Barrier. I maintain that our arrangements for returning were quite adequate, and that no one in the world would have expected the temperatures and surfaces which we encountered at this time of the year. On the summit in lat. 85°, 86° we had –20°, –30°. On the Barrier in lat. 82°, 10,000 feet lower, we had –30° in the day, –47° at night pretty regularly, with continuous head wind during our day marches. It is clear that these circumstances came on very suddenly, and our wreck is certainly due to this sudden advent of severe weather, which does not seem to have any satisfactory cause. I do not think human beings ever came through such a month as we have come through, and we should have got through in spite of the weather but for the sickening of a second companion, Captain Oates, and a shortage of fuel in our depôts for which I cannot account, and finally, but for the storm which has fallen on us within 11 miles of the depôt at which we hoped to secure our final supplies. Surely misfortune could scarcely have exceeded this last blow. We arrived within 11 miles of our old One Ton Camp with fuel for one last meal and food for two days. For four days we have been unable to leave the tent – the gale howling about us. We are weak, writing is difficult, but for my own sake I do not regret this journey, which has shown that Englishmen can endure hardships, help one another, and meet death with as great a fortitude as ever in the past. We took risks, we knew we took them; things have come out against us, and therefore we have no cause for complaint, but bow to the will of Providence, determined still to do our best to the last. But if we have been willing to give our lives to this enterprise, which is for the honour of our country, I appeal to our countrymen to see that those who depend on us are properly cared for.

Had we lived, I should have had a tale to tell of the hardihood, endurance, and courage of my companions which would have stirred the heart of every Englishman. These rough notes and our dead bodies must tell the tale, but surely, surely, a great rich country like ours will see that those who are dependent on us are properly provided for.

Appendix II

The Early Life of Robert Falcon Scott

James M. Barrie

Barrie – the author of Peter Pan *– was a friend of Scott's, and wrote the biographical essay below for the abridgement of Scott's journals edited by Charles Turley and published by Smith, Elder in 1914.*

On the night of my original meeting with Scott he was but lately home from his first adventure into the Antarctic, and my chief recollection of the occasion is that having found the entrancing man I was unable to leave him. In vain he escorted me through the streets of London to my home, for when he had said good-night I then escorted him to his, and so it went on I know not for how long through the small hours. Our talk was largely a comparison of the life of action (which he pooh-poohed) with the loathly life of those who sit at home (which I scorned); but I also remember that he assured me he was of Scots extraction. As the subject never seems to have been resumed between us, I afterwards wondered whether I had drawn this from him with a promise that, if his reply was satisfactory, I would let him go to bed. However, the family traditions (they are nothing more) do bring him from across the border. According to them his great-great-grandfather was the Scott of Brownhead whose estates were sequestered after the '45. His dwelling was razed to the ground and he fled with his wife, to whom after some grim privations a son was born in a fisherman's hut on 14 September 1745. This son eventually settled in Devon, where he prospered, for it was in the beautiful house of Outlands that he died. He had four sons, all in the Royal Navy, of whom the eldest had as youngest child John Edward Scott, father of the Captain Scott who was born at

Outlands on 6 June 1868. About the same date, or perhaps a little earlier, it was decided that the boy should go into the Navy like so many of his for-bears.

I have been asked to write a few pages about those early days of Scott at Outlands, so that the boys who read this book may have some slight acquaintance with the boy who became Captain Scott; and they may be relieved to learn (as it holds out some chance for themselves) that the man who did so many heroic things does not make his first appearance as a hero. He enters history aged six, blue-eyed, long-haired, inexpressibly slight and in velveteen, being held out at arm's length by a servant and painted plank, still rode the waters. With many boys this would be the end of the story, but not with Con. He again retired to the making of gunpowder, and did not desist from his endeavours until he had blown that plank sky-high.

His first knife is a great event in the life of a boy: it is probably the first memory of many of them, and they are nearly always given it on condition that they keep it shut. So it was with Con, and a few minutes after he had sworn that he would not open it he was begging for permission to use it on a tempting sapling. "Very well," his father said grimly, "but remember, if you hurt yourself, don't expect any sympathy from me." The knife was opened, and to cut himself rather badly proved as easy as falling into the leat. The father, however, had not noticed, and the boy put his bleeding hand into his pocket and walked on unconcernedly. He was really considerably damaged; and this is a good story of a child of seven who all his life suffered extreme nausea from the sight of blood; even in the *Discovery* days, to get accustomed to "seeing red", he had to force himself to watch Dr Wilson skinning his specimens.

When he was about eight Con passed out of the hands of a governess, and became a school-boy, first at a day school in Stoke Damerel and later at Stubbington House, Fareham. He rode grandly between Outlands and Stoke Damerel on his pony, Beppo, which bucked in vain when he was on it, but had an ingratiating way of depositing other riders on the road. From what one knows of him later this is a characteristic story. One day he dismounted to look over a gate at a view which impressed him (not very boyish this), and when he recovered from a brown study there was no Beppo to be seen. He walked the seven miles home, but what was characteristic was that he called at police-stations on the way to give practical details of his loss and a description of the pony. Few children would have thought of this, but Scott was naturally a strange mixture of the dreamy and the practical, and never more practical than immediately after he had been dreamy. He forgot place and time altogether when thus abstracted. I remember the first time he dined with me, when a number of well-known men had come to meet him, he arrived some two hours late. He had dressed to come out, then fallen into one of his reveries, forgotten all about the engagement, dined by himself and gone early to bed. Just as he was falling asleep he remembered where he should be, arose hastily and joined us as speedily as possible. It was equally characteristic of him to say of the other guests that it was pleasant to a sailor to meet so many interesting people. When I said that to them the sailor was by far the most interesting person in the room he shouted with mirth. It always amused Scott to find that anyone thought him a person of importance.

I suppose everyone takes for granted that in his childhood, as later when he made his great marches, Scott was muscular and strongly built. This was so far from being the case that there were many anxious consultations over him, and the local doctor said he could not become a sailor as he could never hope to obtain the necessary number of inches round the chest. He was delicate and inclined to be pigeon-breasted. Judging from the portrait of him here printed, in his first uniform as a naval cadet, all this had gone by the time he was thirteen, but unfortunately there are no letters of this period extant; and thus little can be said of his years on the *Britannia* where "you never felt hot in your bunk because you could always twist, and sleep with your feet out at a porthole." He became a cadet captain, a post none can reach who is not thought well of by the other boys as well as by their instructors, but none of them foresaw that he was likely to become anybody in particular. He was still "Old Mooney," as his father had dubbed him, owing to his dreamy mind; it was an effort to him to work hard, he cast a wistful eye on "slackers", he was not a good loser, he was untidy to the point of slovenliness, and he had a fierce temper. All this I think has been proved to me up to the hilt, and as I am very sure that the boy of fifteen or so cannot be very different from the man he grows into, it leaves me puzzled. The Scott I knew, or thought I knew, was physically as hard as nails and flung himself into work or play with a vehemence I cannot remember ever to have seen equalled. I have fished with him, played cricket and football with him and other games, those of his own invention being of a particularly arduous kind, for they always had a moment when the other players were privileged to fling a hard ball at your undefended head. "Slackness" was the last quality you would think of when you saw him bearing down on you with that ball, and it was the last he asked of you if you were bearing down on him. He was equally strenuous of work; indeed I have no clearer recollection of him than his way of running from play to work or work to play, so that there should be the least possible time between. It is the "time between" that is the "slacker's" kingdom, and Scott lived less in it than anyone I can recall. Again, I found him the best of losers, with a shout of delight for every good stroke by an opponent: what is called an ideal sportsman. He was very neat and correct in his dress, quite a model for the youth who come after him, but that we take as a matter of course; it is "good form" in the Navy. His temper I should have said was bullet-proof. I have never seen him begin to lose it for a second of time, and I have seen him in circumstances where the loss of it would have been excusable.

However, "the boy makes the man", and Scott was none of those things I saw in him but something better. The faults of his youth must have lived on in him as in all of us, but he got to know they were there and he took an iron grip of them and never let go his hold. It was this self-control more than anything else that made the man of him of whom we have all become so proud. I get many proofs of this in correspondence dealing with his manhood days which are not strictly within the sphere of this introductory note. The horror of slackness was turned into a very passion for keeping himself "fit". Thus we find him at one time taking charge of a dog, a "Big Dane", so that he could race it all the way between work and home, a distance of three miles. Even when he was getting the *Discovery* ready and doing daily the work of several men, he might have been seen running through the streets of London from Savile Row or the Admiralty to his home, not because there was no time for other methods of progression, but because he must be fit, fit, fit. No more "Old Mooney" for him; he kept an eye for ever on that gentleman, and became doggedly the most practical of men. And practical in the cheeriest of ways. In 1894 a disastrous change came over the fortunes of the family, the father's money being lost, and then Scott was practical indeed. A letter he wrote at this time to his mother, tenderly taking everything and everybody on his shoulders, must be one of the best letters ever written by a son, and I hope it may be some day published. His mother was the great person of his early life, more to him even than his brother or his father, whom circumstances had deprived of the glory of following the sailor's profession and whose ambitions were all bound up in this son, determined that Con should do the big things he had not done himself. For the rest of his life Con became the head of the family, devoting his time and his means to them, not in an it-must-be-done manner, but with joy and even gaiety. He never seems to have shown a gayer front than when the troubles fell, and at a farm to which they retired for a time he became famous as a provider of concerts. Not only must there be no "Old Mooney" in him, but it must be driven out of everyone. His concerts, in which he took a leading part, became celebrated in the district, deputations called to beg for another, and once in these words, "Wull 'ee gie we a concert over our way when the comic young gentleman be here along?"

Some servants having had to go at this period, Scott conceived the idea that he must even help domestically in the house, and took his own bedroom under his charge with results that were satisfactory to the casual eye, though not to the eyes of his sisters. It was about this time that he slew the demon of untidiness so far as his own dress was concerned and doggedly became a model for still younger officers. Not that his dress was fine. While there were others to help he would not spend his small means on himself, and he would arrive home in frayed garments that he had grown out of and in very tarnished lace. But neat as a pin. In the days when he returned from his first voyage in the Antarctic and all England was talking of him, one of his most novel adventures was at last to go to a first-class tailor and be provided with a first-class suit. He was as elated by the possession of this as a child.

When going about the country lecturing in those days he travelled third class, though he was sometimes met at the station by mayors and corporations and red carpets.

The hot tempers of his youth must still have lain hidden, but by now the control was complete. Even in the naval cadet days of which unfortunately there is so little to tell, his old friends who remember the tempers remember also the sunny smile that dissipated them. When I knew him the sunny smile was there frequently, and was indeed his greatest personal adornment, but the tempers never reached the surface. He had become master of his fate and captain of his soul.

In 1886 Scott became a middy on the *Boadicea*, and later on various ships, one of them the *Rover*, of which Admiral Fisher was at that time commander. The Admiral has a recollection of a little black pig having been found under his bunk one night. He cannot swear that Scott was the leading culprit, but Scott was certainly one of several who had to finish the night on deck as a punishment. In 1888 Scott passed his examinations for sublieutenant, with four first-class honours and one second, and so left his boyhood behind. I cannot refrain, however, from adding as a conclusion to these notes a letter from Sir Courtauld Thomson that gives a very attractive glimpse of him in this same year:

In the late winter a quarter of a century ago I had to find my way from San Francisco to Alaska. The railway was snowed up and the only transport available at the moment was an ill-found tramp steamer. My fellow passengers were mostly Californians hurrying off to a new mining camp and, with the crew, looked a very unpleasant lot of ruffians. Three singularly unprepossessing Frisco toughs joined me in my cabin, which was none too large for a single person. I was then told that yet another had somehow to be wedged in. While I was wondering if he could be a more ill-favoured or dirtier specimen of humanity than the others the last comer suddenly appeared – the jolliest and breeziest English naval Second Lieutenant. It was Con Scott. I had never seen him before, but we at once became friends and remained so till the end. He was going up to join his ship which, I think, was the *Amphion*, at Esquimault, B.C.

As soon as we got outside the Golden Gates we ran into a full gale which lasted all the way to Victoria, B.C. The ship was so overcrowded that a large number of women and children were allowed to sleep on the floor of the only saloon there was on condition that they got up early, so that the rest of the passengers could come in for breakfast and the other meals.

I need scarcely say that owing to the heavy weather hardly a woman was able to get up, and the saloon was soon in an indescribable condition. Practically no attempt was made to serve meals, and the few so-called stewards were themselves mostly out of action from drink or sea-sickness.

Nearly all the male passengers who were able to be about spent their time drinking and quarrelling. The deck cargo and some of our top hamper were washed away and the cabins got their share of the waves that were washing the deck.

Then it was I first knew that Con Scott was no ordinary human being. Though at that time still only a boy he practically took command of the passengers and was at once accepted by them as their Boss during the rest of the trip. With a small body of volunteers he led an attack on the saloon – dressed the mothers, washed the children, fed the babies, swabbed down the floors and nursed the sick, and performed every imaginable service for all hands. On deck he settled the quarrels and established order either by his personality, or, if necessary, by his fists. Practically by day and night he worked for the common good, never sparing himself, and with his infectious smile gradually made us all feel the whole thing was jolly good fun.

I daresay there are still some of the passengers like myself who, after a quarter of a century, have imprinted on their minds the vision of this fair-haired English sailor boy with the laughing blue eyes, who at that early age knew how to sacrifice himself for the welfare and happiness of others.

Appendix III

The Antarctic Treaty

The Antarctic Treaty was made on 1 December 1959.

Text of the Antarctic Treaty

The Governments of Argentina, Australia, Belgium, Chile, the French Republic, Japan, New Zealand, Norway, the Union of South Africa, the Union of Soviet Socialist Republics, the United Kingdom of Great Britain and Northern Ireland, and the United States of America,

Recognizing that it is in the interest of all mankind that Antarctica shall continue for ever to be used exclusively for peaceful purposes and shall not become the scene or object of international discord;

Acknowledging the substantial contributions to scientific knowledge resulting from international cooperation in scientific investigation in Antarctica;

Convinced that the establishment of a firm foundation for the continuation and development of such cooperation on the basis of freedom of scientific investigation in Antarctica as applied during the International Geophysical Year accords with the interests of science and the progress of all mankind;

Convinced also that a treaty ensuring the use of Antarctica for peaceful purposes only and the continuance of international harmony in Antarctica will further the purposes and principles embodied in the Charter of the United Nations;

Have agreed as follows:

Article I

1. Antarctica shall be used for peaceful purposes only. There shall be prohibited, inter alia, any measure of a military nature, such as the establishment of military bases and fortifications, the carrying out of military manoeuvres, as well as the testing of any type of weapon.

2. The present Treaty shall not prevent the use of military personnel or equipment for scientific research or for any other peaceful purpose.

Article II

Freedom of scientific investigation in Antarctica and cooperation toward that end, as applied during the International Geophysical Year, shall continue, subject to the provisions of the present Treaty.

Article III

1. In order to promote international cooperation in scientific investigation in Antarctica, as provided for in Article II of the present Treaty, the Contracting Parties agree that, to the greatest extent feasible and practicable:

(a) information regarding plans for scientific programs in Antarctica shall be exchanged to permit maximum economy of and efficiency of operations;

(b) scientific personnel shall be exchanged in Antarctica between expeditions and stations;

(c) scientific observations and results from Antarctica shall be exchanged and made freely available.

Article IV

1. Nothing contained in the present Treaty shall be interpreted as:

(a) a renunciation by any Contracting Party of previously asserted rights of or claims to territorial sovereignty in Antarctica;

(b) a renunciation or diminution by any Contracting Party of any basis of claim to territorial sovereignty in Antarctica which it may have whether as a result of its activities or those of its nationals in Antarctica, or otherwise;

(c) prejudicing the position of any Contracting Party as regards its recognition or non-recognition of any other State's rights of or claim or basis of claim to territorial sovereignty in Antarctica.

2. No acts or activities taking place while the present Treaty is in force shall constitute a basis for asserting, supporting or denying a claim to territorial sovereignty in Antarctica or create any rights of sovereignty in Antarctica. No new claim, or enlargement of an existing claim, to territorial sovereignty in Antarctica shall be asserted while the present Treaty is in force.

Article V

1. Any nuclear explosions in Antarctica and the disposal there of radioactive waste material shall be prohibited.

2. In the event of the conclusion of international agreements concerning the use of nuclear energy, including nuclear explosions and the disposal of radioactive waste material, to which all of the Contracting Parties whose representatives are entitled to participate in the meetings provided for under Article IX are parties, the rules established under such agreements shall apply in Antarctica.

Article VI

The provisions of the present Treaty shall apply to the area south of 60 deg. South Latitude, including all ice shelves, but nothing in the present Treaty shall prejudice or in any way affect the rights, or the exercise of the rights, of any State under international law with regard to the high seas within that area.

Article VII

1. In order to promote the objectives and ensure the observance of the provisions of the present Treaty, each Contracting Party whose representatives are entitled to participate in the meetings referred to in Article IX of the Treaty shall have the right to designate observers to carry out any inspection provided for by the present Article. Observers shall be nationals of the Contracting Parties which designate them. The names of observers shall be communicated to every other Contracting Party having the right to designate observers, and like notice shall be given of the termination of their appointment.

2. Each observer designated in accordance with the provisions of paragraph 1 of this Article shall have complete freedom of access at any time to any or all areas of Antarctica.

3. All areas of Antarctica, including all stations, installations and equipment within those areas, and all ships and aircraft at points of discharging or embarking cargoes or personnel in Antarctica, shall be open at all times to inspection by any observers designated in accordance with paragraph I of this Article.

4. Aerial observation may be carried out at any time over any or all areas of Antarctica by any of the Contracting Parties having the right to designate observers.

5. Each Contracting Party shall, at the time when the present Treaty enters into force for it, inform the other Contracting Parties, and thereafter shall give them notice in advance, of

(a) all expeditions to and within Antarctica, on the part of its ships or nationals, and all expeditions to Antarctica organized in or proceeding from its territory;

(b) all stations in Antarctica occupied by its nationals; and

(c) any military personnel or equipment intended to be introduced by it into Antarctica subject to the conditions prescribed in paragraph 2 of Article I of the present Treaty.

Article VIII

1. In order to facilitate the exercise of their functions under the present Treaty, and without prejudice to the respective positions of the Contracting Parties relating to jurisdiction over all other persons in Antarctica, observers designated under paragraph 1 of Article VII and scientific personnel exchanged under sub-paragraph 1(b) of Article III of the Treaty, and members of the staffs accompanying any such persons, shall be subject only to the jurisdiction of the Contracting Party of which they are nationals in respect of all acts or omissions occurring while they are in Antarctica for the purpose of exercising their functions.

2. Without prejudice to the provisions of paragraph 1 of this Article, and pending the adoption of measures in pursuance of subparagraph 1(e) of Article IX, the Contracting Parties concerned in any case of dispute with regard to the exercise of jurisdiction in Antarctica shall immediately consult together with a view to reaching a mutually acceptable solution.

Article IX

1. Representatives of the Contracting Parties named in the preamble to the present Treaty shall meet at the City of Canberra within two months after the date of entry into force of the Treaty, and thereafter at suitable intervals and places, for the purpose of exchanging information, consulting together on matters of common interest pertaining to Antarctica, and formulating and considering, and recommending to their Governments, measures in furtherance of the principles and objectives of the Treaty, including measures regarding:

(a) use of Antarctica for peaceful purposes only;

(b) facilitation of scientific research in Antarctica;

(c) facilitation of international scientific cooperation in Antarctica;

(d) facilitation of the exercise of the rights of inspection provided for in Article VII of the Treaty;

(e) questions relating to the exercise of jurisdiction in Antarctica;

(f) preservation and conservation of living resources in Antarctica.

2. Each Contracting Party which has become a party to the present Treaty by accession under Article XIII shall be entitled to appoint representatives to participate in the meetings referred to in paragraph 1 of the present Article, during such times as that Contracting Party demonstrates its interest in Antarctica by conducting substantial research activity there, such as the establishment of a scientific station or the despatch of a scientific expedition.

3. Reports from the observers referred to in Article VII of the present Treaty shall be transmitted to the representatives of the Contracting Parties participating in the meetings referred to in paragraph 1 of the present Article.

4. The measures referred to in paragraph 1 of this Article shall become effective when approved by all the Contracting Parties whose representatives were entitled to participate in the meetings held to consider those measures.

5. Any or all of the rights established in the present Treaty may be exercised as from the date of entry into force of the Treaty whether or not any measures facilitating the exercise of such rights have been proposed, considered or approved as provided in this Article.

Article X

Each of the Contracting Parties undertakes to exert appropriate efforts, consistent with the Charter of the United Nations, to the end that no one engages in any activity in Antarctica contrary to the principles or purposes of the present Treaty.

Article XI

1. If any dispute arises between two or more of the Contracting Parties concerning the interpretation or application of the present Treaty, those Contracting Parties shall consult among themselves with a view to having the dispute resolved by negotiation, inquiry, mediation, conciliation, arbitration, judicial settlement or other peaceful means of their own choice.

2. Any dispute of this character not so resolved shall, with the consent, in each case, of all parties to the dispute, be referred to the International Court of Justice for settlement; but failure to reach agreement on reference to the International Court shall not absolve parties to the dispute from the responsibility of continuing to seek to resolve it by any of the various peaceful means referred to in paragraph 1 of this Article.

Article XII

1.–(a) The present Treaty may be modified or amended at any time by unanimous agreement of the Contracting Parties whose representatives are entitled to participate in the meetings provided for under Article IX. Any such modification or amendment shall enter into force when the depositary Government has received notice from all such Contracting Parties that they have ratified it.

(b) Such modification or amendment shall thereafter enter into force as to any other Contracting Party when notice of ratification by it has been received by the depositary Government. Any such Contracting Party from which no notice of ratification is received within a period of two years from the date of entry into force of the modification or amendment in accordance with the provision of subparagraph 1(a) of this Article shall be deemed to have withdrawn from the present Treaty on the date of the expiration of such period.

2.–(a) If after the expiration of thirty years from the date of entry into force of the present Treaty, any of the Contracting Parties whose representatives are entitled to participate in the meetings provided for under Article IX so requests by a communication addressed to the depositary Government, a Conference of all the Contracting Parties shall be held as soon as practicable to review the operation of the Treaty.

(b) Any modification or amendment to the present Treaty which is approved at such a Conference by a majority of the Contracting Parties there represented, including a majority of those whose representatives are entitled to participate in the meetings provided for under Article IX, shall be communicated by the depositary Government to all Contracting Parties immediately after the termination of the Conference and shall enter into force in accordance with the provisions of paragraph 1 of the present Article.

(c) If any such modification or amendment has not entered into force in accordance with the provisions of subparagraph 1(a) of this Article within a period of two years after the date of its communication to all the Contracting Parties, any Contracting Party may at any time after the expiration of that period give notice to the depositary Government of its withdrawal from the present Treaty; and such withdrawal shall take effect two years after the receipt of the notice by the depositary Government.

Article XIII

1. The present Treaty shall be subject to ratification by the signatory States. It shall be open for accession by any State which is a Member of the United Nations, or by any other State which may be invited to accede to the Treaty with the consent of all the Contracting Parties whose representatives are entitled to participate in the meetings provided for under Article IX of the Treaty.

2. Ratification of or accession to the present Treaty shall be effected by each State in accordance with its constitutional processes.

3. Instruments of ratification and instruments of accession shall be deposited with the Government of the United States of America, hereby designated as the depositary Government.

4. The depositary Government shall inform all signatory and acceding States of the date of each deposit of an instrument of ratification or accession, and the date of entry into force of the Treaty and of any modification or amendment thereto.

5. Upon the deposit of instruments of ratification by all the signatory States, the present Treaty shall enter into force for those States and for States which have deposited instruments of accession. Thereafter the Treaty shall enter into force for any acceding State upon the deposit of its instruments of accession.

6. The present Treaty shall be registered by the depositary Government pursuant to Article 102 of the Charter of the United Nations.

Article XIV

The present Treaty, done in the English, French, Russian and Spanish languages, each version being equally authentic, shall be deposited in the archives of the Government of the United States of America, which shall transmit duly certified copies thereof to the Governments of the signatory and acceding States.

In witness thereof, the undersigned Plenipotentiaries, duly authorized, have signed the present Treaty.

Done at Washington this first day of December, one thousand nine hundred and fifty-nine.

Antarctic Treaty Parties

Country, Date Ratified or Acceded to Treaty
Argentina, June 23, 1961
Australia, June 23, 1961
Austria, August 25, 1987
Belgium, July 26, 1960
Brazil, May 16, 1975
Bulgaria, September 11, 1978
Canada, May 4, 1988

Chile, June 23, 1961
China, June 8, 1983
Colombia, January 31, 1989
Cuba, August 16, 1984
Czech Republic, June 14, 1962
Dem People's Rep of Korea, January 21, 1987
Denmark, May 20, 1965
Ecuador, September 15, 1987
Finland, May 15, 1984
France, September 16, 1960
Germany, February 5, 1979
Greece, January 8, 1987
Guatemala, July 31, 1991
Hungary, January 27, 1984
India, August 19, 1983
Italy, March 18, 1981
Japan, August 4, 1960
Netherlands, March 30, 1967
New Zealand, November 1, 1960
Norway, August 24, 1960
Papua New Guinea, March 16, 1981
Peru, April 10, 1981
Poland, June 8, 1961
Rep of Korea, November 28, 1986
Romania, September 15, 1971
Russian Federation, November 2, 1960
Slovak Republic, June 14, 1962
South Africa, June 21, 1960
Spain, March 31, 1982
Sweden, April 24, 1984
Switzerland, November 15, 1990
Turkey, January 24, 1995
Ukraine, October 28, 1992
United Kingdom, May 31, 1960
United States, August 18, 1960
Uruguay, January 11, 1980

Bibliography

The literature of polar exploration is vast, but some of the "nunataks" are:

Roald Amundsen, *The Northwest Passage* (London, 1908)
—— *The South Pole* (London, 1912)
—— *My Polar Flight* (London, 1925)
—— *My Life as an Explorer* (London 1927)
Roald Amundsen and Lincoln Ellsworth, *The First Flight Across the Polar Sea* (London, 1927)
Salomon Andrée et al, *The Andrée Diaries* (London, 1931)
John Barrow, *Voyages of Discovery and Research in the Arctic Regions* (London, 1846)
Owen Beattie and John Greiger, *Frozen in Time: The Fate of the Franklin Expedition* (London, 1987)
Pierre Berton, *The Arctic Grail* (London, 1988)
Richard Byrd, *Skyward* (New York, 1928)
—— *Alone* (London, 1955)
Apsley Cherry-Garrard, *The Worst Journey in the World* (London, 1922)
Mick Conefrey and Tim Jordan, *Icemen* (London, 1998)
James Cook, *A Voyage Towards the South Pole and Round the World. Performed in His Majesty's Ships the RESOLUTION and ADVENTURE. In the years 1772, 1773, 1774, and 1775* (London, 1777)
Frederick Cook, *My Attainment of the Pole; Being the Record of the Expedition that First Reached the Boreal Center 1907–9; With the Final Summary of the Polar Controversy* (New York, 1911)
Frank Debenham, *In the Antarctic; Stories of Scott's Last Expedition* (London, 1952)
E. R. G. R. Evans, *South with Scott* (London, 1921)
George Washington De Long, *The Voyage of the Jeanette. The Ship and Ice Journals of George W. De Long . . . 1879–81* (Boston, 1884)
Ranulph Fiennes, *To the Ends of the Earth* (London, 1995)
Fergus Flemming, *Ninety Degrees North* (London, 2001)

John Franklin, *Narrative of a Journey to the Shores of the Polar Sea in the Years 1819–20–21–22* (2 vols, London, 1823, 1824)

Vivian Fuchs, *Of Ice and Men* (London, 1982)

Mikhail Gromov, *Across the North Pole to America* (Moscow, 1939)

Isaac Hayes, *The Open Polar Sea; A Narrative of a Voyage of Discovery towards the North Pole in the Schooner United States* (London, 1867)

Matthew A. Henson, *A Negro Explorer at the North Pole* (New York, 1912)

Wally Herbert, *Across the Top of the World: The British Trans-Arctic Expedition* (London, 1969)

—— *The Noose of Laurels: The Discovery of the North Pole* (London, 1989)

Clive Holland, *Farthest North: A History of Polar Exploration in Eye-Witness Accounts* (London, 1994)

Roland Huntford, *Scott and Amundsen* (London, 1979)

—— *Shackleton* (New York, 1985)

—— *Nansen* (London, 1997)

Frederick Jackson, *A Thousand Days in the* Arctic (New York, 1899)

A. I. P. Kirwan, *The White Road* (London, 1959)

William Lashly, *Under Scott's Command: Lashly's Antarctic Diaries*, ed. A. R. Ellis (London, 1969)

David Lewis, *Ice Bird* (London, 1976)

Sue Limb and Patrick Cordingley, *Captain Oates, Soldier and Explorer* (London, 1982)

William Laird McKinley, *The Last Voyage of the Karluk* (London, 1999)

Barry Lopez, *Arctic Dreams* (London, 1987)

Jean Malaurie, *Ultima Thule* (Paris, 1990)

Douglas Mawson, *The Home of the Blizzard* (London, 1930)

Fridtjof Nansen, *The First Crossing of Greenland*, trans. H. M. Gepp (London, 1890)

—— *Farthest North; Being a Record of a Voyage of Exploration of the Ship* Fram *1893–6* (London, 1897)

Umberto Nobile, *My Polar Flights: An Account of the Voyages of the Airships* Italia *and* Norge (London, 1961)

W. E. Parry, *Journal of a Voyage for the Discovery of a North-West Passage from the Atlantic to the Pacific* (1821)

—— *Journal of a Second Voyage for the Discovery of a North-West Passage from the Atlantic to the Pacific, in Her Majesty's ships* Fury *and* Hecla (1824)

—— *Third Voyage for the Discovery of a North-West Passage from the Atlantic to the Pacific, in His Majesty's ships* Fury *and* Hecla (1826)

Robert E. Peary, *The North Pole: Its Discovery in 1909 Under the Auspices of the Peary Arctic Club* (New York, 1910)

Herbert G. Ponting, *The Great White South, or With Scott in the Antarctic* (London, 1921)

John Rae, *Narrative of an Expedition to the Shores of the Arctic Sea in 1846–7* (1850)

Knud Rasmussen, *The People of the Polar North: A Record* (London, 1908)

—— *Greenland by the Polar Sea* (London 1921)

James Clark Ross, *A Voyage of Discovery and Research in the Southern and Antarctic Regions* (London, 1847)

John Ross, *A Voyage of Discovery in His Majesty's ships Isabella and Alexander for the purpose of exploring Baffin's bay, and inquiring into the probability of a North-West Passage* (1819)

Robert F. Scott, *The Voyage of the "Discovery"* (London, 1905)

—— *Scott's Last Expedition*, ed. Leonard Huxley (1913)

Ernest Shackleton, South (London, 1919)

—— *The Heart of the Antarctic* (London, 1909)

—— *Aurora Australis* (Antarctica 1908–9; Kensington, Australia, 1988)

—— *Shackleton: His Antarctic Writings*, ed. Christopher Railing (London, 1983)

Francis Spufford, *I May Be Some Time* (London, 1996)

Peter Stark (ed), *Ring of Ice: True Tales of Adventure, Exploration and Arctic Life* (New York, 2000)

Vilhjalmur Stefansson, *My Life with the Eskimo* (1913)

—— *The Friendly Arctic: The Story of Five Years in Polar* Regions (London, 1921)

John Stewart, *Antarctica: An Encyclopedia* (2 vols, Jefferson, NC., 1990)

David Thomson, *Scott's Men* (London, 1977)

Mikhail Vodopyanov, *Moscow–North Pole–Vancouver–Washington* (Moscow, 1939)

Sara Wheeler, *Terra Incognita: Travels in Antarctica* (London, 1997)

Hubert Wilkins, *Under the North Pole: the Wilkins-Ellsworth Submarine Expedition* (New York, 1931)

Edward Wilson, *Diary of the 'Terra Nova' Expedition to the Antarctic, 1910–12*, ed.

H. G. R. King (London, 1972)

F. A. Worsley, *Shackleton's Boat Journey* (London, 1999)

H. Wright, *The Great White North* (New York, 1910)

Glossary

Ablation The loss of snow or ice by melting or evaporation

Anchor ice Submerged ice attached to the sea bed

Brash Wrecked ice from a larger formation

Cairn Marker made from ice, snow or stones

Calve The breaking off of an iceberg from a glacier or ice sheet

Crevasse Crack or gap

Fast ice Sea ice attached to the shore

FID British Antarctic worker (named from the Falkland Islands Dependency Survey)

Finnesko Boots made entirely of fur; worn by early explorers

Frazil ice Slush of pointed ice crystals in the water

Frost smoke Condensed water vapour which forms mist over open sea in cold weather

Hoosh Stew eaten on expedition; usually made from pemmican (q.v.), dry sledging biscuits and water

Ice blink Reflection of light off the ice and onto the underside of clouds

Ice window The breaking up of fast ice in the summer, which allows shipping to reach the Antarctic coast

Lead Open water in pack ice

Moraine Loose rock moved and deposited by a glacier

Mukluks Boots made of sealskin or moose hide (North America)

Névé Bed of frozen snow that has not turned to ice; literally "last year's snow"

Nunatak Rock or mountain standing up through an ice-field

Old ice Ice more than 10 years old

Pancake ice Disks of young ice, formed by wave action

Pemmican Ground dried meat mixed with lard

Sastrugi Furrows or irregularities formed on the ice or snow by the wind

Snow blindness Temporary (usually) loss of sight caused by glare of sunlight off snow or ice

Snow bridge Windblown crust of snow over a crevasse

Tabular berg Recently calved iceberg with straight sides and flat top

Tide crack A crack separating land ice and sea ice

Whiteout The blurring between ground and sky, in which perspective becomes lost, caused by overcast sky descending to the horizon

The Polar Who's Who

Amundsen, Roald (1872–1928). Norwegian explorer. A some-time medical student, between 1902–6 Amundsen sailed the Northwest Passage east to west (the first person to do so) in the smack *Gjoa* and located the Magnetic North Pole. In 1910 he set off in the *Fram* in an attempt to reach the North Pole, but on hearing that Peary (q.v.) had beaten him switched to Antarctica; using dogs for locomotion, Amundsen reached the South Pole in December 1911, a month ahead of Scott (q.v.). In 1918 Amundsen sailed the *Maud* through the Northeast Passage. In 1926 he flew across the North Pole in the airship *Norge* with Lincoln Ellsworth (q.v.) and Umberto Nobile (q.v.). In 1928 he disappeared searching by plane for Nobile's downed airship, *Italia*.

Andrée, Salomon (1854–97). Swedish engineer. An official at the Swedish Patent Office, persuaded several influential backers – including King Oscar II of Sweden and Alfred Nobel, inventor of dynamite – to finance his plan to travel to the North Pole by hydrogen-filled balloon. The *Eagle* accordingly lifted from Danes's Island on 11 July 1897 – and crashed on 14 July at 82° 56′N, 29° 52′E. As Andrée's critics had suggested, the balloon had leaked incessantly. Andrée and his two companions then trudged over the ice to White Island, where they died of hypothermia or disease. Their bodies were not discovered until 1930.

Barrow, John (1764–1848). English naval official. Of humble beginnings, Barrow worked, inter alia, in an iron foundary and on a Greenland whaler before becoming the private secretary to the statesman Lord Macartney. In 1804 Barrow was appointed to the highly influential post of second secretary to the Admiralty, where he sponsored the Arctic explorations of John Ross (q.v.), James Clark Ross (q.v.) and John Franklin (q.v.). The great "back room boy" of British Arctic endeavour, Point Barrow and Barrow Strait in the Arctic were named for him, as was Cape Barrow in Antarctica.

Bellinghausen, Fabian von (1778–1852). Russian navigator. A captain in the Imperial Navy, Bellinghausen was commissioned by Czar Alexander I to explore the Southern Ocean. Bellinghausen crossed the Antarctic Circle on 26 January, 1820, and the next day became the first person to sight the Antarctic Continent; eventually, Bellinghausen probed as far south as 69° 53'S, where he discovered Peter Oy, the southernmost land then recorded.

Byrd, Richard Evelyn (1888–1957). American aviator. A graduate of the US Naval Academy, Evelyn, together with Floyd Bennett, claimed the first aeroplane flight over the North Pole (1926). In 1929 he established "Little America" on the Ross Ice Shelf, Antarctica, his base for the first flight over the South Pole (28 November). He made four more expeditions to Antarctica, including the USAE of 1933–35 and the massive 1946 US Antarctic Developments project.

Cook, Frederick (1865–1940). American explorer. Cook joined Peary's (q.v.) 1891 expedition to Greenland as surgeon, returning in 1893 and 1894. Three years later, he served with de Gerlache's Belgian expedition to the Antarctic. In 1908 he claimed to be the first man to reach the North Pole, but this was questioned by Peary. A committee set up by Copenhagen University found against Cook, his case undermined by his obviously fallacious account of another "first", the ascent of Mount McKinley. His imprisonment for fraud further undermined his reputation.

Cook, James (1728–1779) English explorer. The widest-ranging sea-farer of all time, Cook circumnavigated Antarctica and in 1773 reached a record 71° 10'S. His discovery of South Georgia and its vast seal colonies caused the great rush of seal-hunters south; nearly a third of the sub-Antarctic islands would be discovered by these sealers. On Cook's third great voyage, from 1776–9, he explored the Arctic coasts of North America and

Siberia. His success as a naval explorer owed much to his virtual defeat of scurvy by rations of sauerkraut and "mermalade of carrots".

De Long, George Washington (1844–81). American explorer. In 1879 in the *Jeanette* he attempted to reach the North Pole via the Bering Strait, but was forced to abandon the ship in pack ice. Only two of his crew made the 300-mile sledge and boat journey to the safety of the Siberian coast.

Ellsworth, Lincoln (1880–1951). American aviator. Scion of a coal-mining family, Ellsworth's first brush with polar fame came when he joined Roald Amundsen (q.v.) and Umberto Nobile (q.v.) for the 1926 flight of the *Norge* to the North Pole. Ellsworth's goal thereafter was to fly across Antarctica; he was third time lucky, doing so in 1935. During his 3,400-km flight with pilot Herbert Hollick-Kenyon Ellsworth sighted and named the Eternity and Sentinel ranges. A valedictory visit to Antarctica in 1939 upped the total land claimed by Ellsworth for the USA to over a million square kilometres (Ellsworth Land).

Franklin, John (1786–1847). English naval officer. A veteran of the Napoleonic wars, Franklin turned to Arctic exploration in 1818 with an expedition to Spitsbergen. He surveyed the Canadian Arctic coast 1819–22 and 1825–9 before being appointed governor of Tasmania. In 1845 he returned to the Arctic with *Erebus* and *Terror* in an attempt to find the Northwest Passage. Beleaguered by thick ice in the Victoria Strait, the expedition floundered. Frankin died on 11 June 1847. A hundred or so survivors attempted to walk 900 miles to the Hudson's Bay Company outpost on Back's River but perished en route of malnutrition and scurvy. "Franklin's Lost Expedition" became a *cause célèbre* and more than 50 fruitless searches were organized.

Fuchs, Vivian (1908–99). British Antarctic explorer and scientist. Director of the Falkland Islands Dependencies Survey, he led the 1955–8 Commonwealth Trans-Antarctic Expedition, which included in its ranks the NZ climber Edmund Hillary.

Herbert, Walter "Wally" (1934–) British explorer, brought up in South Africa. In the 1950s he mapped vast tracts of Antarctica for the Falkland Islands Dependencies Survey and came within 200 miles of reaching the South Pole by sledge. In 1968–9 he led the British expedition which made the first surface crossing of the Arctic Ocean. A mountain in the Arctic and a mountain range in Antarctica is named for him. He was knighted in 1999. His books include *Noose of Laurels*, 1989, on the Cook-Peary controversy.

Mawson, Douglas (1882–1958). English-born Australian geologist. Appointed to the scientific staff of Shackleton's *Nimrod* expedition, he was a discoverer – with Alistair Mackay and Professor David – of the South Magnetic Pole (16 January 1909). Two years later Mawson headed the Australasian Antarctic Expedition which explored and claimed King George V Land; it was during this expedition that Mawson endured the harrowing dog-sledge journey that saw the deaths of his companions Ninnis and Mertz. In 1929–31 Mawson headed the British, Australian and New Zealand Antarctic research expedition (BANZARE) which discovered MacRobertson Land.

Nansen, Fridtjof (1861–1930). Norwegian explorer. Nansen's earliest Arctic explorations were a trip in the sealer *Viking* and a crossing of Greenland from east to west. In August 1893 he started his great experiment – intentionally let his boat *Fram* become stuck in the Arctic ice and letting the drift take him North. Which it did, to 84° 04'. There Nansen left the *Fram* and pushing on across the ice reached the highest attitude then attained, 86 14'. Later professor of zoology and oceanography, he was a stalwart supporter of Norwegian independence from Sweden and became Norway's first ambassador to the UK. In 1922 he received the Nobel peace prize for his Russian relief work.

Nobile, Umberto (1885–1978). Italian aviator. An aeronautical engineer by training, Nobile built the airship *Norge* which flew across the North Pole with Amundsen and Ellsworth in 1926. Two years later, Nobile's airship the *Italia* was wrecked returning from the North Pole and an embarrassed Italian fascist regime scapegoated Nobile. Self-exiled in America and Spain, he eventually returned to Italy to be reinstated in the Italian air service.

Parry, William Edward (1790–1855). English naval officer. First dispatched to the Arctic to protect the British whale fisheries there, he then took part in no less than five Arctic expeditions, the last of which – 1827 – included an attempt to reach the North Pole by sledge, which despite its failure set a Northing record of 82°45'.

Peary, Robert Edwin (1856–1920). American sailor. Peary led his first expedition to Greenland at the age of 30, and went on to cross the Greenland ice cap twice and chart the north-east coast. Obsessive in the pursuit of fame, Peary claimed success on third attempt at reaching the North Pole, on 6 April 1919. He then became involved in a long dispute with rival claimant Frederick Cook (q.v.) but recently Peary's claim to the North Pole, like Cook's, has been largely discredited.

Rasmussen, Knud (1879–1933). Part Danish, part Inuit ethnologist and explorer. Led several expeditions to Greenland in support of his theory that the Inuit and Amerindians were descended from tribes of Asia. Established the settlement of Thule on Cape York.

Ross, James Clark (1800–1862). Scottish navigator. Ross joined the Royal Navy at the age of 11, and his exploring was done under its aegis. At 27 he was part of William Edward Parry's (qv) attempt on the North Pole. In 1831 he located the North Magnetic Pole, a success which led the British government to appoint him head of an expedition to locate its Southern equivalent. Setting sail in September 1839 in *Erebus* and *Terror*, shallow-drafted barques of the type promoted by Cook (q.v.), Ross failed in his goal but in the trying discovered the formidable Ross Ice Shelf and set a new Southing record.

Ross, John (1777–1856). Scottish naval officer and explorer, leader of expeditions in 1818 and 1829 in search of the Northwest

Passage, which he believed barred by the "Croker Mountains" (in fact, clouds). Uncle of James Clark Ross (q.v.).

Scott, Robert Falcon (1868–1912). English naval officer. Commanded the National Antarctic Expedition (1900–04) which discovered King Edward VII Land. Promoted captain, in 1910 he embarked in the *Terra Nova* for his second Antarctic expedition and with a sledge party consisting of Edward Wilson, Captain Laurence "Titus" Oates, Bowers and Evans reached the South Pole on 17 January 1912, only to find that Roald Amundsen (q.v.) had beaten them by a month. On the return journey, Scott and the entire party perished. Scott was posthumously knighted, and the Scott Polar Research Institute founded in his memory. He was the father of the ornithologist Sir Peter Scott.

Shackleton, Ernest (1874–1922). Irish explorer. Apprenticed in the merchant navy, Shackleton's Antarctic baptism came as a junior officer under Scott in the *Discovery* expedition (1901–3). Leading his own expedition 1908–9, Shackleton reached to within 97 miles of the South Pole. During his third expedition, his ship *Endeavour* was crushed in the ice and the crew reached Elephant Island, before Shackleton and five others made in 1916 the hazardous 800-mile boat journey to South Georgia. Shackleton died on South Georgia four years later, leading his fourth Antarctic expedition.

Stefansson, Vilhjamur (1879–1962). Canadian Arctic explorer and ethnologist, born of Icelandic parents. Lived and worked among the Inuit from 1908–12, later described in his best-selling *My Life with the Eskimo*, and then led the five-year-long Canadian Arctic Expedition to the Beaufort Sea.

Weddell, James (1787–1834). Scottish sealer. On February 29, 1823, he set a southing record of 74° 15′S in the sea which bears his name. A species of South Orkney seal, discovered by Weddell on the same voyage, is also named for him.

Sources & Acknowledgments

The editor has made every effort to secure the requisite permission to reprint copyrighted material in this volume. In the case of any omissions or errors, please contact the editor c/o the Publishers.

Roald Amundsen, *The South Pole: An Account of the Norwegian Antarctic Expedition in the* Fram, *1910–12*. Trans. A. G. Chater. London, John Murray, 1912

Salamon Andrée, *The Andrée Diaries*. London, John Lane, 1931

Richard E. Byrd, *Alone*. London, Macdonald & Co., 1987

—— *Skyward*. New York, G. P. Putnam's Sons, 1928. Copyright © 1928 The Estate of Richard E. Byrd

Apsley Cherry-Garrard, *The Worst Journey in the World*. *London*, Picador, 1994. Copyright © Angela Mathias 1922, 1965

Frederick A. Cook, *My Attainment of the Pole*. New York, Polar Publications, 1911

George Washington De Long, *The voyage of the* Jeannette. *The ship and ice journals of George W. De Long . . . 1871–81*. Boston, Houghton Mifflin, 1884

T. W. Edgeworth David, *Aurora Australis*. Auckland, SeTo Publishing, 1988. Copyright © SeTo Publishing 1988

Ranulph Fiennes, *To the Ends of the Earth*. London, Mandarin, 1995. Copyright © 1983 Ranulph Fiennes. Reprinted by permission of Curtis Brown

John Franklin, *Narrative of a Journey to the Shores of the Polar Sea*. London, John Murray, 1823

Vivian Fuchs, *Antarctic Adventure*. London, Cassell, 1959. Copyright © The Trans-Antarctic Expedition 1959

D. Haig-Thomas, *Tracks in the Snow*. London, Hodder & Stoughton, 1939

Catharine Hartley, *To the Poles (Without a Beard)*. London, Simon & Schuster, 2002 Copyright © Catharine Hartley 2002

David Helvarg, "On Thin Ice: Antartica Voyage", *Sierra*, November 1999, Sierra Club, 1999. Copyright © Sierra Magazine 1999

David Hempleman-Adams, *Toughing it Out*. London, Orion, 1997. Copyright © 1997 David Hempleman-Adams

Wally Herbert, *Across the Top of the World*. London, Longmans, 1969. Copyright © Wally Herbert 1969

Hjalmar Johansen, *With Nansen in the North; a record of the* Fram *expedition in 1893–6*. London, Ward, Lock & Co., 1899

William Laird McKinlay, *Karluk*. London, Phoenix, 2000. Copyright © William Laird McKinlay 1976

David Lewis, *Voyage to the Ice: The Antarctic expedition of* Solo. Sydney, Australian Broadcasting Commission & William Collins Sons & Co., Ltd, 1979. Copyright © Australian Broadcasting Commission

Barry Lopez, *Arctic Dreams*. London, Picador, 1987. Copyright © 1986 Barry Lopez

D. Mawson, *The Home of the Blizzard*. London, Hodder & Stoughton, 1930

Ejnar Mikkelsen, *Two Against the Ice*. London, The Travel Book Club, n.d.

Fridtjof Nansen, *Farthest North; being the record of a voyage of exploration of the ship* Fram *1893–6*. London, Constable, 1897

Umberto Nobile, *My Polar Flights*. London, Muller, 1961

William Edward Parry, *Narrative of an attempt to reach the North Pole in boats fitted for the purpose, and attached to HM Ship* Hecla *in 1827*. London, John Murray, 1828

Robert Peary, *The North Pole*. London, Hodder & Stoughton, 1910

Knud Rasmussen, *The People of the Polar North*. London, Kegan, Paul, Trench, Trubner, 1908

John Rymill, *Southern Lights*. London, Chatto & Windus, 1938. (This selection of extracts originally appeared in *From the Ends of the Earth*, ed. Augustine Courtauld, Oxford University Press, 1958)

Alastair Scott, *Tracks Across Alaska*. London, John Murray, 1990. Copyright © Alistair Scott 1990

Robert F. Scott, *Scott's Last Expedition*, ed. L Huxley. London, Smith, Elder & Co., 1913

Ernest Shackleton, *The Heart of the Antarctic*. London, Heinemann, 1911

—— *South: The Endurance Expedition*. London, Penguin, 2002

Vilhjalmur Stefansson, *My Life with the Eskimo*. London, Macmillan, 1913

—— *The Friendly Arctic*. London, Macmillan, 1921

George E. Tyson, *Arctic Experiences: containing capt. George E. Tyson's wonderful drift on the ice-floe*, ed. E. Blake. London, Sampson Low, Marston, Low & Searle, 1874

Doug Wilkinson, *Land of the Long Day*. Toronto, Clarke, Irwin & Co., 1955. Copyright © Clarke, Irwin & Company Limited 1955

Gareth Wood & Eric Jamieson, *South Pole: 900 Miles on Foot*. Victoria, B.C. Horsdal & Schubert, 1996

F. A. Worsley, *Shackleton's Boat Journey*. London, Pimlico, 1999. Copyright © The estate of F. A. Worsley

Other titles available from Robinson Publishing

The Mammoth Book of How It Happened Everest
With a foreword by Doug Scott   Ed. Jon E. Lewis **£7.99 [   ]**
Celebrating the 50th anniversary of the first ascent of Everest in 1953, this collection explores the unique experience of climbing to the top of the world.
From the 1921 expedition through to the disasters of the 90s, here are personal
accounts of the tragedy and triumph by those who know the "Death Zone" and
the cruelty and beauty of "Chomolungma" best.

The Mammoth Book of the Edge   Ed. Jon E. Lewis **£7.99 [   ]**
Eyewitness accounts of triumph and tragedy on the world's greatest
mountains. Presenting 25 first-hand accounts on the peaks and "big walls"
of four continents, spanning an arc in time from the golden Victorian age to
the present, this is truly an exploration of the furthest reaches of human daring and endurance.

The Mammoth Book of Endurance & Adventure
                             Ed. Jon E. Lewis **£7.99 [   ]**
Eyewitness recollections from the world's most intrepid adventurers. It recounts over 50 true-life adventures taken from contemporary memoirs, letters
and journals of ordinary mortals who achieved extraordinary things.

Robinson books are available from all good bookshops or direct from the publisher.
Just tick the titles you want and fill in the form below.

TBS Direct
Colchester Road, Frating Green, Colchester, Essex CO7 7DW
Tel: +44 (0) 1206 255777
Fax: +44 (0) 1206 255914
Email: sales@tbs-ltd.co.uk

UK/BFPO customers please allow £1.00 for p&p for the first book, plus 50p
for the second, plus 30p for each additional book up to a maximum charge of
È3.00. Overseas customers (inc. Ireland), please allow £2.00 for the first book,
plus £1.00 for the second, plus 50p for each additional book.

Please send me the titles ticked above.

NAME (Block letters) . . . .

ADDRESS . . . .

. . . .

POSTCODE . . . .

I enclose a cheque/PO (payable to TBS Direct) for . . . .

I wish to pay by Switch/Credit card

Number . . . .

Card Expiry Date . . . .

Switch Issue Number . . . .

Other titles available from Robinson Publishing

Other titles available from Robinson Publishing

The Mammoth Book of Special Forces   Ed. Jon E. Lewis **£7.99 [ ]**
Thirty true and graphic accounts of the most heroic SAS and Special-forces missions ever undertaken into the most dangerous place of all – behind enemy lines. Up-to-date this unputdownable collection includes recent operations into Iraq in 2003, Afghanistan and Bosnia and features the entire range of special forces from SAS, Commandos and Rangers to Navy SEALS and paratroopers.

The Mammoth Book of Fighter Pilots   Ed. Jon E. Lewis **£7.99 [ ]**
Relive the exploits of Manfred von Richthofen, Eddie Rickenbacker, Richard Hillary, Johnnie Johnson, Luftwaffe WWII aces Heinz Knoke and Johannes Steinhoff, and over 20 others. This is a comprehensive and fascinating book about a form of combat that has changed beyond recognition over the last hundred years. It gives vivid insights into both the daily round and the dangers, such as bailing out over enemy territory, surviving in an Iraqi POW camp, or getting shot down in a blazing Spitfire.

The Mammoth Book of Heroes   Ed. Jon E. Lewis **£7.99 [ ]**
True courage is one of the most highly valued attributes of humanity. Gathered together in this volume are over 70 accounts, many of them in the words of those who were there, about men and women who showed real courage, often with their lives on the line. No fictional hero can match the true courage of Ernest Shackleton, the bravery of British soldiers at Rorke's Drift, or the spirit of Annie Sullivan teaching the deaf and blind Helen Keller to speak and read. This is an inspiring collection that celebrates the brave of heart through the ages.

Robinson books are available from all good bookshops or direct from the publisher. Just tick the titles you want and fill in the form below.

TBS Direct
Colchester Road, Frating Green, Colchester, Essex CO7 7DW
Tel: +44 (0) 1206 255777
Fax: +44 (0) 1206 255914
Email: sales@tbs-ltd.co.uk

UK/BFPO customers please allow £1.00 for p&p for the first book, plus 50p for the second, plus 30p for each additional book up to a maximum charge of £3.00. Overseas customers (inc. Ireland), please allow £2.00 for the first book, plus £1.00 for the second, plus 50p for each additional book.

Please send me the titles ticked above.

NAME (Block letters) . . . .

ADDRESS . . . .

. . . .

POSTCODE . . . .

I enclose a cheque/PO (payable to TBS Direct) for . . . .

I wish to pay by Switch/Credit card

Number . . . .

Card Expiry Date . . . .

Switch Issue Number . . . .